The Bowser Family History

THE

BOWSER FAMILY HISTORY

BY

ADDISON BARTHOLOMEW BOWSER, A. M.

AUTHORIZED AND PUBLISHED BY THE EXECUTIVE COMMITTEE OF THE BOWSER REUNION WHICH MEETS ANNUALLY AT KITTANNING, ARMSTRONG COUNTY, PENNSYLVANIA, ON THE LAST TUESDAY OF AUGUST

EXCELSIOR PRINTING COMPANY
CHICAGO, ILLINOIS
MCMXXII

PREFACE 1217090

The following pages present what we believe to be the first attempt to write a history of the "Bausser," now, Bowser family. When our ancestors came to this country they spelled their name "Bausser," and "Bousser." In many instances there was but one "s" used. The change from the former spelling to "Bowser" was gradual and, we believe, now complete. The last on our record to use "Bouser" was Adam Bouser in his will recorded in Armstrong County, Pa.

The reader will get clearly in his mind that we are of Teutonic blood. The chief source of our German ancestry was in the Alemanni tribe occupying upper Switzerland and adjacent provinces. The French still speak of the German as Alemagne. This territory was subsequently called the "Palatine." An overflow reached the Rhine and was called the "Lower Palatine." From this land then, came the scores of "Pennsylvania Dutch," to the virgin forests of Pennsylvania. Among them was Mathias Bausser, Sr., who landed at Philadelphia, September 28, 1733. He and his family made the long voyage from Rotterdam, Holland, on the brigantine "Richard and Elizabeth." The same year Daniel Bousser and two brothers came via Baltimore, Md. The story of the settlement of this small family, chiefly in Pennsylvania, and their development down to the present, the reader will find in the following pages. We wish to express our grateful acknowledgment of the aid given us in finding the descendants of Daniel Bousser, by Jacob C. Bowser, of Erie, Pa., the Kittanning Daily Leader-Times for use of several cuts. Also the invaluable help rendered by Chas. A. Bowser, of California, who is himself preparing a genealogy and history of the Bowser people. Also to the Executive Committee for their sympathetic interest and manifold kindnesses during the protracted years this history has been in process of preparation, and also for the promptness with which they provided for its publication when it was ready.

Sincerely your cousin,

Ford City Pa. A. B. Bowser.
May 1, 1922

CHAPTER I

THE HOMELAND

History has its sources, like the ancient Nile, hidden in the mysterious and impenetrable reaches of the unexplored and unknown. The painter trails his art backward to the crude sketches left on the rocks by the aborigines. Back of that the unknown. The writer of human history begins at the boundary of Mythology. On this side we have tangibilities, features, forms, facts though scanty, countries, names and periods of time.

In preparing a family history such as is undertaken in this work, the writer's first task is to know from what race his forebears sprang. What native land reared them? What valleys grew golden with their annual harvests? What cities educated their children? What rivers bore upon their bosom their rugged crafts of commerce? What sort of government ruled them? What ideals inspired them with heroic manhood, and lastly, what religious impulses moulded their characters and awakened the innate love of justice and liberty and hatred toward despotism whether of government or religion? We have a deeper regard for Christian denominations, when we are acquainted with the tyranny and persecution against which they revolted. In peaceful America where all creeds and names alike are under the same kindly protection of the state we would little suspect how dearly the pioneers of these Christian bodies paid for the right to breathe and think and worship God according to their consciences. And there is a soul stirring history back of these European emigrations to the new world. We think with pride of our heroic ancestors who braved the perils of the sea, and the uncertainties of a life in a wilderness, in a strange land, rather than submit to oppression. We regret that space will not permit us to yield to the inclination to marshal a greater array of the terrific iniquities our brave people suffered across the seas.

When the writer began the task of collecting data for this history there was no one of our people so far as he could discover who knew from what land the Bowsers emigrated. There was a tradition that we came from Germany; others said from Holland, yet others, from France. Following the clue of the first we were happy to discover the truth. It seemed most reasonable to begin with the language. A people's language would, it would seem obvious, be a direct index to their nationality. If, for example, an emigrant came to America speaking the Welsh language we would rightly conclude he came from Wales. That our people were not Hollanders was evident because they did not speak Dutch. They were not French for the same reason; and if from Germany, certainly not from the North German states. The people of Europe, though dwelling in comparatively small areas, have distinctive languages. And their languages have been fixed in literature, books of history, science, poetry, and especially in the Bible. Our Bowser forefathers therefore left a homeland in which the same language was spoken which they spoke in this country, which, as all know, has been called "Pennsylvania Dutch." The term "Pennsylvania Dutch" is a misnomer. There is no such a language. It has been supposed by many as we ourselves once thought, that "Pennsylvania Dutch" was a corrupted German, the result of natural variations due to ignorance and long separation from its pure springs. We now know it is not a corrupted tongue but native to a part of Switzerland and the Rheinish Palatinate, a principality in the Southern part of Germany. From the Palatine, then, came the "Pennsylvania Dutch." Let us henceforth give them their right name "Palatine German."

"We speak of the German language or 'Deutsche Sprache' as embracing, generally, the different languages spoken in all their stages from the earliest history to the present, the languages spoken by the related Teutonic tribes, as the Austrians, Swiss, Alsatians, Bavarians and the like. What Dr. J. A. H. Murray has pointed out about the origin of the principal English dialects may equally well be true of these Germanic idioms. Having no specimens of the languages of the Germans for nearly three centuries after their final settlement, we cannot tell to what extent they originally agreed with or differed from each other, although there must have been some dialectal differences to begin with, which were afterwards increased and multiplied. But, however scanty our means of illustrating the earliest history of these idioms may be, there is no doubt that they were not all related to each other in the same degree. Three main groups are easily distinguishable.

"(1) The Frisian and Saxon, whose nearest relation is English.

"(2) Frankish, Hessian and Thuringian, and

"(3) Alemanni and Bavarian.

"The Frisian is generally regarded as a separate language." (Brittannica.) These represent the Low, Middle and High German.

"The Alemanni is divided into the three main groups, Swabian, Alsatian and Swiss, while Bavaria is constituted by several dialects spoken in Bavaria and Austria. The members of the third group, Upper German, combined with the midland dialects, Hessian and Thuringian, and part of the Frankish dialects, are sources of the High German. The greatest difference prevails between the first (1) group and the third (3). The southern Frankish dialects are very closely akin to the adjacent Upper German idioms. Where German words are incorporated many have changes as the German Schlaf becomes Schlof; fragen, froge, waagen, woge." (Brittannica.) The influence of Luther upon the German language has been tremendous, as his writings, especially his translation of the Bible, were accepted as the best pattern of High German and imitated. Switzerland and Lower German clung for a long time to their native dialects, but the different German states were gradually brought nearer to a common language.

The Palatinate was inhabited by descendants of the group of German tribes called the Rheinfranken with an admixture of the Alemanni, the latter of whom had occupied the land until 496 A. D., when Chlodwig, King of the Franks, defeated them in a battle fought somewhere on the Upper Rhine. Wurtemburg and Switzerland were practically pure Alemanni while the Palatinate is Frankish with a strong infusion of Alemanni blood in certain parts. Hence it follows that "Pennsylvania Dutch," is a dialect—an admixture of Frankish and Alemanni. There are subdivisions in these dialects, the Swabian of Wurtemburg being different from Switzerland, and the mixed speech of the Palatine different from both. The "Pennsylvania Dutch" then has as a basis certain characteristics derived from all of these dialects, modified and harmonized. In brief, the language of our forefathers was a mixture of the original Alemanni, French and German words. The Palatinate, Frankish, Wurtemburg and Switzerland Alemanni—from these stems grew the people who later came to Pennsylvania speaking the Palatine German." (Swiss and German Settlements in Pennsylvania.)

CHAPTER II

THE HOMELAND CONTINUED

CONFEDERATED STATES AND THE THIRTY YEARS WAR

The German people belong to the great Aryan family. At a period before history noticed them, they moved westward into the forests of present Germany and neighboring states. These heathen tribes eventually had to contend with the armies of Caesar. After bitter experiences on account of their unorganized state they began forming federations of states for the purpose of better defense. The Goths were the most important of these groups and the Alemanni came next. The Alemanni held both banks of the Rhine where it is joined by the Moselle and the Main. In the course of centuries there grew up in the varying struggles of the Empire a confederation of provinces or states loosely joined. This confederation embraced at various times parts of France, Austria, Bohemia and the Netherlands. "Under Henry I [918-936] there was greater unity than ever before. At the death of this wise and good king all the land of the German peoples was a part of his kingdom." But Germany never until our own day really became an empire. It is true that at last the "Holy Roman Empire" was as a matter of fact confined to Germany, for the day came, as in the time of Frederick Barbarosa, when the King of Germany was also King of Italy. Thus as we approach the middle centuries Germany was the most powerful kingdom in the world. As the centuries passed, the states, while nominally recognizing the king, were sometimes in alliance with him and again, opposing him, or asserting their independence. It is a long story of war, revolt, conquest, the clash of unscrupulous rulers, with all the varying fortunes of warfare through the early centuries and the Middle Ages until we reach the period with which we are more intimately concerned.

In 1519 began the Reformation under Martin Luther which kept the country in a state of turmoil—a convulsion of animosities and horrors, of human atrocities unspeakable for two centuries. There was continual strife between the Catholics and the followers of Martin Luther until Reformed Calvinism interposed a third element of conflict. The crimes that now one ecclesiastical party then the other according to which at the time had superior strength inflicted, are too gruesome to be narrated, and had better remain buried in the darkness of the past. But it is a matter of history that the reason many of us were born within the fair state of Pennsylvania instead of on the banks of the Rhine is because the incredible, wanton and savage quarrels among people of the same race became intolerable, and our forefathers discerned their only hope of tranquility and safety was to leave their country entirely. This will be better understood when we remember that war raged for 30 years. Thirty years when the country rocked and groaned and panted and burned in the most senseless war of history next to the late World War. Cities were devoured in flames, farm buildings destroyed, horses and cattle appropriated by contending armies, and the people slaughtered with a fiendish glee that would have made a Comanche blush. Thirty thousand fled from little Bohemia alone under the cruel hand of Ferdinand II [1619-37]. This cruel, shortsighted king set for himself the task of the coercion of all his subjects to his (the Roman Catholic) faith. The war began in Bohemia and the country was placed under such a system of government that it lost two-thirds of its population. The Palatinate was next invaded and finally brought to submission; and there also the process of "conversion" was carried on with such a ruthlessness that multitudes died at the hands of their inquisitors or fled, exiles from their homes. The fall of Madgeburg may furnish us an example of the relentless horrors of this dreadful war.

Madgeburg was besieged by the Emperor's General, Tilly, and his horde of butchers and fell in 1631. "The most cruel butchery followed, a scene of horrors for which history has no language, when neither innocent childhood nor hopeless old age, when neither sex, rank, youth, nor beauty could disarm the fury of the conquerors. Wives were abused in the arms of their husbands, daughters at the feet of their parents; and the defenseless sex was exposed to the double sacrifice of virtue and life. In a single church 53 women were found beheaded. The Croats amused themselves by throwing children into the flames. Pappenheim's Walloons, with stabbing infants at their mother's breasts. Some officers touched at the dreadful scene ventured to remind Tilly he could stop the carnage. He answered: 'The soldieir must have some reward for his dangers and his toils.' Fearful indeed was the tumult, amid clouds of smoke, heaps of dead bodies, the clash of swords, the crash of falling ruins, the streams of blood. The fearful heat forced the murderers to take refuge for a while in their camp. Scarcely had the fury of the flames abated, than they returned to renew the pillage amid the ruins and ashes of the town. Horrible and revolting to humanity was the scene that presented itself; the living crawling from under the dead, children wandering about with heartrending cries, calling for their parents; more than 6000 bodies were thrown into the Elbe to clear the streets; a much greater number had been consumed by the flames. The whole number of the slain was reckoned at not less than 30,000." (Schiller.)

In 1634 the Palatine was again overrun and laid waste, the inhabitants killed in such numbers only 200 peasants remained in the lower country. "The Thirty Years War, one of the most destructive in all history, fell with especial severity upon the southern part of Germany, as the Palatinate. Not only were cities, towns, and villages devastated in turn by the armies of friends and foes alike; not only did poverty, hardship, murder and rapine follow in the wake of these strange armies, with their multitude of camp followers, but the intellectual, moral and religious character of the German people received a shock that almost threatened them with annihilation." No class of people suffered more than the farmers from whom our people are mostly descended. During this long and bloody conflict their horses and cattle, sheep and goats were carried off by contending armies; their barns and houses reduced to ashes. At the invasion of an army the people fled to hiding places in the marshes or among the rocks of the mountains or in the fastnesses of the forest. Frytog says, "in Heimsburg, in the course of the war, 75 per cent of the inhabitants were destroyed. 66 per cent of the houses, 75 per cent of the horses, 85 per cent of the goats, 82 per cent of the cattle." These things were equally true of the Palatine on account of its exposed position to the ravages of armies. During the Middle Ages it had been one of the most prosperous, influential and enlightened of the German States, and had been favored by enlightened and wise rulers like Hohenstaufen, Frederick the Wise, who recognized the Reformation, and the tolerant Karl Ludwig who protected the Mennonites. The country along the Rhine and Neckar was known as the garden spot of Germany. Elector Frederick V who yielded to the persuasion of Bohemia to become their king aroused the hostility of Emperor Ferdinand II and thus, however well meaning and benevolent his purpose, provoked this long and disastrous war in which, as we have seen, his own state, the Palatine, suffered most. Heidelburg, with its great university was taken by Tilly, 1622. In 1638-9 pestilence added to the sufferings already endured. The people tried to satisfy their hunger with roots and grasses and leaves, even ate the bodies of their dead. The gallows and graveyards had to be guarded, the bodies of children were not safe from their mothers. The scenes in Jerusalem during the siege by Titus were not infrequent in Germany in those terrible days. Under Karl Ludwig the land began to blossom once more. There was a short period of calm. Many who had fled to Switzerland and Holland returned to their devastated homes and began to rebuild. Taxes were low and land abundant; immigrants came from other countries, as England and France. Happy days returned to the banks of the Rhine. The farmer went joyously to his plow and the weaver to his loom and the smith to his forge. Soon the land waved with yellow harvests and instead of the sounds of marching armies, the lowing of cattle and the songs of the birds. But the red devil of war had not finished with our fathers' homeland. In 1674-75 war broke out between France and Holland and again the Palatine was brought to ruin.

CHAPTER III

THE HOMELAND CONTINUED

EDICT OF NANTES AND ITS REVOCATION

The border states of Germany on the south were so intimately associated witih Switzerland and France and related to them by the strong ties of blood, the policies of the kings of France, beneficent or autocratic, affected our fatherland powerfully. There were seasons when the vengeful, fanatical religious and political policies of kings like Chales IX and Louis XIV prevailed. The Palatine became a place of refuge for thousands of French Huguenots and again, when the aggressive and bitter persecution swept like a wave of terror across the borders, our people suffered almost as much as the unfortunate Protestants in France itself. It is worth while then, to recall one great event in this time of the history of France, because it reflects the opinions and policies and tyrannous acts of kings which had much to do with the people of the Palatine and the subsequent emigration of vast numbers to Pennsylvania—we refer to the Edict of Nantes. Henry the IV was one of the greatest and best of the French kings. He joined the Catholic Church because, he reasoned, the majority of his subjects were Catholics, he should identify himself with their system. But he was wise, liberal in his views and tolerant. Henry the III had granted Protestants free exercise of their worship in castles of the Calvinistic lords to the number of 3500 and to one town or borough in each county except in Paris. They were permitted to own property, marry with Catholics and hold public office. These written edicts were often violated by different authorities. But Henry IV maintained them, even extended them and brought the various parliaments to enregister them. At length, on the 15th of April, 1598, he signed and published the famous Edict of Nantes at Paris, his treaty of peace with the Protestants. This treaty, drawn up in 92 open and 56 secret articles, proclaimed the religious position of Protestants in France, the conditions and guarantees of their worship and their relation to the crown and their Catholic fellow-countrymen. The state provided for the salaries of Protestant ministers in their schools and colleges; the children of Protestants were allowed the privileges of the schools and colleges the same as Catholics; that complete justice might be secured to them, courts were instituted where their cases were,—tried before Protestant judges. Many Catholics opposed violently the new edict but the king stood by his agreement. "What I have done," he said, "is for the good of peace. I will cut the roots of all these factions; I will make short work of those who foment them. You must know what I have done has been for a good purpose and let my past behavior go bail for it." The malcontents and intolerant saw they had a strong willed king, a judicious and clear sighted, true patriot, who was sincerely concerned for the public welfare among all his subjects alike. This timely and beneficial act of this good king was a great event in history and of inestimable blessing to the Protestants of the country. Louis XIV is known in history as a bold warrior and unscrupulous king. His long reign was marked by cruel wars, but we remember him chiefly for his antagonism to modern progress in religious liberty. He revoked the Edict of Nantes October 13, 1685, and dealt his own country and the world a blow more fatal than all his wars. "Intoxicated by so much success and so many victories, he fancied that consciences were to be bent like states, and he set about to bring back all his subjects to the Catholic faith. In revoking the Edict of Henry IV he undid the beneficent work of that wise ruler and turned back the civilization of his country many centuries. He set at nought all the rights consecrated by edicts and the long patience of those Protestants whom Mazarin called the 'faithful flock.' Some years later, these reformers left France and carried their skill, labor and manhood into other countries. Hundreds of thousands fled who refused to live under the despotic government that enslaved human consciences. All the princes felt themselves insulted. Protestant Europe, indignant, opened her doors to this choice class of French people." (Guizot History of France, Vol. 4.)

The sixteenth century was marked by these religious disorders. In the midst of religious zeal we find wars, murders, and brutal intolerance. The Huguenots of France, like the Anabaptists of Germany and the Mennonites of Switzerland, were the pioneers in religious liberty and real reform. The world never produced nobler heroes than these brave men who suffered and died for their faith. The Huguenots found the Pope, the king and the chiefs of political positions, determined to destroy them. They were persecuted and calumniated. No crime was too horrible to impute to them, even that of sacrificing little children. Charles IX ordered the great massacre on St. Bartholomew's day, August 24, 1572, when 60,000 Protestants perished.

Eight hundred thousand of them perished in prisons and galleys and on scaffolds. ("Beacon Lights of History," by John Lord.) Louis was not content to subdue or destroy Protestantism in France but advanced against Holland and overran the Palatine, sending an army of 50,000 men, in 1688. Many of the largest and best cities were destroyed. The German Empire at that time had seven electors whose privilege it was to choose the king, of whom one was the Elector Palatine, hence the name frequently occurring in history of the "Elector Palatine." In 1689 Leopold bestowed the eighth electoral privilege upon Earnest Augustus Brunswick Hanover;

ius making the Catholic and Protestant electors equal in number—our each. In 1699, Philip of the Palatine emulated Louis XIV ı his persecution of the Protestants throughout his new possesions. Again a tide of emigration began to flow. The Mennonites, Valloons and the French Huguenots who had found a refuge in ıe Palatine were now driven from the land; many went to Holland, 'russia and America. To the above conditions, religious and politial, we must add the corruption, tyranny, extravagance and heartessness of the rulers of the Palatinate; many attempted to imitate ıe splendor and display of the French Court while the country 'as bleeding to death. What would history say of Abraham Linoln if he had had Congress vote him a billion dollars a year to pend on balls and parties while his soldier boys were bleeding and ying out on the battlefields? So did the harrassed and exploited eople of the Palatine suffer and pray and wait, but light was kinling. A little beacon began to flame on the distant hills. A new oice was heard, in low whispers it is true, but it was a voice of ope; a voice that grew stronger and more insistent—a voice that old of home and peace and fireside and children once more at play nalarmed by the image of a warrior with lance and gun. It told f a new land—a land of great forests and rivers and pine clad hills nd freedom, the land of the Quaker preacher who instituted a Holy Experiment.

We have looked at the background. We have seen that Europe 'as in the throes of a three-headed religious conflict, Lutherism, Catholicism and Reformed Calvinism, in days when passions were ıflammable as powder, when refinements were superficial, where ivilization was built on force and maintained by might, when perseution was savage and the atrocities conceived in human ingenuity 'ere unspeakably horrible. In the heart of this restless, surging, 'arring mass were a few better souls who saw visions and dreamed reams and prayed for the kindly spirit of the Master to come into he hearts of men. And when human bodies could endure no more hey sailed away forever from a land of endless strife to a land f perpetual peace.

CHAPTER IV

PREPARATIONS FOR THE GREAT ADVENTURE

We now reach an interesting chapter in our State History, the history of the tides of emigration that flowed into this new territory and the shores from whence they came, and the background of political, social and religious conditions already hinted at. We are aware that the English who came with Penn and those who followed settled at Philadelphia, and that other nationalities sought homes here where there were hopes of a peaceful home life and such comforts as honest toil should naturally provide. Among them were our Bowser ancestors.

William Penn, a Quaker minister, was given an extensive grant of land in America, now known as Pennsylvania, by Charles II of England in 1681. He published in England and Germany his plan for a self-governing state which he called his "Holy Experiment," a free colony for all mankind, and a liberal scheme by which the land could be purchased. This grant formed a tract 300 by 150 miles in extent, afterwards enlarged by purchase. He proposed his new possessions should be designated by "Sylvania," woods; but the king prefixed the family name, Penn, and thus the Keystone State, the brightest among the galaxy of sisters in our free union, received its title, Pennsylvania.

The great proprietor was far ahead of his age as we learn by his writings on religious and political subjects. One of his treatises is entitled, "The Great Case of Liberty of Conscience," in which he nobly proclaimed what the constitution of the United States secures.

Speaking of the religious intolerance of England in his day, he said: "I abhor two principles in religion, and pity them that own them; the first is obedience upon authority without conviction; and the other, destroying them that differ from me for God's sake. Such a religion is without judgment, though not without teeth."

Penn came to take possession of his land in America in 1682, sailing from England, September 1, and landing at New Castle, Delaware, October 27, one-third of his one hundred comrades having died of smallpox on the voyage. He ascended the Delaware River to Upland, to which he gave the name Chester. Here he convened the Assembly and promulgated his Great Law, namely, that Pennsylvania was to be a Christian State, and that no one could be a citizen or eligible for office who was not a Christian. In the same year he founded Philadelphia and within two years it had a population of 2,500. He found already settled on the west bank of the Delaware, about 6,000 Swedes, Dutch and English, the Swedes had begun a settlement as early as 1638. He gave equal rights to these and to all subsequent settlers from every land. It is not strange, then, that emigrants, desiring to escape the religious and political tyranny of the mother countries, and having the lure of fertile lands at a moderate price, and a government that was committed to the hands of the people themselves, came in ever increasing numbers, English, Quakers, Scottish and Irish Presbyterians, Swiss Mennonites and Dunkards, French Huguenots and Reformed Palatines. The population increased at first at the rate of 1,000 a year and later more rapidly. In 75 years the population exceeded 200,000.

The emigration of the Pilgrims who came on the Mayflower and settled in Massachusetts represented a revolt from the political and religious conditions already noted. They believed their mission in the New World was to establish and enjoy religious freedom. They were set apart a peculiar people by the same Jehovah who called Abraham from Ur of the Chaldees. Before leaving their homeland they went to the church and read the scriptures that told of God's command to Abraham. "Now the Lord said unto Abram, Get thee out of thy country, and from thy Kindred and from thy father's house, unto the land that I will show thee; and I will make thee a great nation, and I will bless thee, and make thy name great: and be thou a blessing: and I will bless them that bless thee, and him that curseth thee will I curse: and in thee shall all the families of the earth be blessed. So Abram went as the Lord had spoken unto him." They marched to the ship singing hymns of praise and sailed away, committing their lives, their future, into the hands of Him who kept and blessed Abraham. They ventured forth to the new land under a tacit covenant, with one another and with God, that they would be obedient to His commands. In the cabin of the vessel they drew up a written compact in which they bound themselves, men, servants and all, to be obedient to its stipulations. This compact or constitution began with, "In the name of God, amen: we whose names are underwritten, have undertaken for the glory of God and the advancement of Christian faith, a voyage to plant the first colony in northern parts of Virginia and do solemnly and mutually in the presence of God, and of one another, covenant," and so forth. This shows the Christian spirit and high purpose of these heroes who landed on the inhospitable shores of New England just sixty-two years before Penn came to Pennsylvania. The principles of liberty were clearly visioned in their attempt to enact laws and constitutions for the sake of all the people and opposed to the iniquitous policy of the old world countries to favor the strong and despise the weak. In the subsequent years, their religious zeal and uncompromising aggression toward all "heterodox" teaching and divergence of opinion from the adopted standards, show their unequivocal devotion to the principles of religious obligation. Their rigorous and relentless prosecution of violators of the laws governing the religious practice of the colony, though it not infrequently resembled the bigoted intolerance they themselves sought to escape in the mother countries; the profound piety of the people; the reverence in which they held the church and the Holy Word of God, exercised a permanent influence upon succeeding generations. The future republic, therefore, laid its first foundation stone in religion, a religion that recognized the great God of Israel as father, defender and hope of the nation. Let us remember that while these New England settlers had made a step in the direction of political liberty, their influence that affected the character of the future national life was chiefly *religious*. Now, if we revert to the history of Pennsylvania we will find the next great influence in moulding and shaping America was *political*. It found its greatest impulse in the doctrines and practical experiments of the far-visioned Quaker preacher, William Penn. His first Assembly and the democratic administration he proposed, coming from an Englishman of the more privileged class, are remarkable. It was in the same year, too, that he made the memorable treaty with the Indians. There is a picture hanging in Independence Hall, Philadelphia, by Benjamin West, which immortalized the event. Under the spreading branches of the elm tree are gathered a company of red men; rings glisten in their ears; skins half conceal their stalwart bodies; women with their babies sit about, the braves leaning on their bows or spears are attentive to the gracious words of the Christian statesman who stands tall and picturesque in the midst of them, behind the group flows placidly the Delaware, the November solemn mood is on the land and the yellow leaves carpet the ground. The treaty made that day was in accord with the broad sympathies of the man who dreamed of a state of freemen in the full exercise of their inalienable rights.

What a contrast between William Penn's treatment of his red-skinned subjects and most of the history that disgraced our relations with these primitive men of the forests! His rules for the Assembly, his treaty with the Indians and his faithful efforts to carry out his pledges mark him as one of the greatest champions of liberty the world has produced,—certainly, when we remember the effect of his Holy Experiment upon the future nation and the European countries as well.

While Roger Williams was preaching the doctrines of soul liberty in New England, Penn was making practical application of that doctrine in political government. No man can be religiously free while under the tyranny of a despotic government.

The Holy Experiment was the dawning of a new era in the new world and the lighting of a beacon that has sent a gleam of hope to the despairing nations of the world. A century or two and the whole world is shaken with this doctrine of Penn. We see today South American countries, Switzerland, France, Portugal, China,—

old, shambling China, republics. Who would have believed it of China, embedded in Oriental torpidity, slumbering down the centuries in benighted exclusiveness, now struggling for a birth of liberty. Thus we see how the principles of our new state, of liberty in religion and freedom in government, have spread to the ends of the earth. And we recognize the hand of God evolving, patiently, but irresistibly, in the history of mankind, the ultimate form and type of government suited to enlightened civilization and which will eventually lie like Elijah's mantel upon the shoulders of all men of every race and color.

CHAPTER V

FIRST SETTLEMENTS IN PENNSYLVANIA

We remember William Penn went through Germany just prior to his first voyage across the sea in 1682 and there preached his Holy Experiment, i. e., his efforts to make Pennsylvania a free colony. In 1683, October 6, in response to Penn's visit to Germany, the good ship Concord arrived at Philadelphia from Crefield and Kreigsheim, Germany, with a small colony of German and Dutch Mennonites. (The Mennonites, it will be remembered, is a name borne by certain Christian communities in Europe and America, disciples of Menno Simons in Switzerland. From this teacher sprang the Regular Baptists [for Menno was a Baptist] of England and thence brought to America; also the Dunkards or German Baptists. When Mack emigrated from Switzerland to America he brought with him his two Dunkard churches entire, all the believers of that faith in the world then. In the free and friendly soil of Pennsylvania, Mack's two little congregations have grown and become a strong and influential church in America.) When these Mennonites landed at Philadelphia, however hearty the welcome accorded them by Penn's English settlers, they resolved to begin a new home back in the woods, so they followed a bridle path for 12 miles and there settled.

They called the place Germantown, now an integral part of the great city of Brotherly Love. Here then began that emigration of German people, chiefly for religious liberty, which was to play the greatest part in this great state's history. These German settlers wrote their kinsmen across the sea of their free community; rich land, new houses in a wonderful country. Others, attracted by the news, came. The word was somehow carried to our distressed people down in the Palatine on the Rhine and in Switzerland, where our people also lived, and there was an awakening such as we can scarcely find a parallel in history. The people who sat in darkness saw a great light.

We can imagine one of our ancestors in the homeland as the twilight falls, after a hard day's toil, sitting at the doorway of his humble home on the Rhine, watching the swallows in their homeward flight and musing on the innocent and joyous life of the creatures of the air. "Why should not human beings live innocently and happily? Why is life for man made perilous and bitter because of the intolerant and savage instincts of man to man?" As the twilight deepens into night and the moonlight bathes the landscape and splashes the river with silver, he lifts his eyes to the distant hills and the familiar scenes are transformed in a wondrous vision into new scenes, a new land, a new home; another river flows peacefully, sparkling in the sun, other hills rise in their majesty, clothed with foliage subdued by the purple haze of summer, a new homeland, as the father of Moses sat at his door and gazed toward the north and saw the land of Canaan, with its Jordan, and valley of Eschol—the land that flowed with milk and honey, and liberty and rest.

"Penn's Woods," the land of smiling rivers and pine-clad hills, of fertile soil and frontier villages where common industry, virtue and mutual struggles leveled all classes, and human sympathy, forbearance and Christian love bound all in a co-operative brotherhood; the land where the three sisters, Hope, Faith and Love, walked forth unhindered; the land where man might lie down to repose and pleasant dreams without the dread of the incendiary's torch or the army's devastating march; the land where little children played together unmolested, sailing their miniature ships or chasing the yellow butterflies, unterrified by cruel men with axes and spears. And thus the vision glowed. But the fancy became a reality by-and-by.

We see these awakened peasants gathering in groups, men clad in homespun, their hands hardened by incessant labor at the plow or in the shop; their shoulders broad, their chests deep, their eyes like the stars. In the center of the group one stands and reads a letter; faces incline toward the reader eagerly. The news! A letter from Pennsylvania! Free land! Liberty and peace! No tyrant kings! How rapidly the Palatine German flowed then! No. armies leaving in their wake a trail of smoke, burnt crops and buildings and murdered women and children Oh, for Pennsylvania! How animated the firesides that night as Hans and Jacob and Ludwig and Mathias rehearse to Mary and Matilina and Katharine and Elizabeth the latest tidings! Now follow community meetings. Emigration is the supreme theme of discussion. But between the homeland on the Rhine and that new Arcadia is the sea. No matter. Plans are matured. Property disposed of except such necessaries as they will require on the voyage. Flat boats are constructed and their families and meagre possessions placed aboard and they drift down the mighty Rhine to the sea. What heroic souls! They leave behind them forever the scenes of their youth, the beloved homeland torn and desolated by incessant warfare.

It is difficult for us in these days of swift ocean steamers to realize the hardships borne by our people, who crossed the Atlantic more than 150 years ago in slow sailing, disreputable, disease infected vessels that required many weeks to make the voyage. The uncertain adventure of individuals who emigrated in that period of our history stirs our admiration. But our people came not as individuals only, but households; in groups of neighbors, forsaking all behind them no matter at what risks; they came as families, parents with their children, who left their unhappy homeland forever,—fathers and mothers, sons and daughters, little children and babies, and committed themselves to the unscrupulous and mercenary shipowners who robbed them of their possessions, huddled them like sheep in the holds of their pestilential ships. It has been estimated that about one-half that sailed away died on that terrible voyage.

Many diaries and letters describing the voyage down the Rhine and across the sea have been preserved. One writer (Muller) describes the journey made by the Bernese Mennonites, 1711. "They were shipped on boats at Berne and at Neuchatel, July 13; meeting at Waugen, they descended the Aar to Laufenburg on the Rhine and thence floated down stream to Basel, which they reached on the 16th. Here they were placed in three ships in which they made the rest of the trip to Holland, whence many reached Pennsylvania. Our friends from Emmenthal and the Oberland found no sympathy among their fellow Swiss, as the towns of Basel and the wooded heights of Jura faded in the distance. Sitting on boxes, bundles, which were piled high in the middle of the boat, could be seen gray haired men and women, old and feeble; yonder stood the young gazing in wonder at the shores as they slipped by. At times they were hopeful and at others sad. From time to time some one would start to sing:

Ein Herzens Weh mir uberkam
Im scheiden uber d'Massen.
Als ich von euch mein Abschied nam
Und dessmals must Verlassen,
Mein Herz war bang
Beharrlich lang:
Es bleibt noch unvergessen
Ob scheid ich gleich,
Bleibt's Herz bei euch,
Wie solt ich euch Vergessen?

Most of our people sailed from Rotterdam. The amount and value of their goods depended upon their previous circumstances. George I published the requirements for the voyage. The emigrant was instructed to present himself to a merchant of Frankfort and pay $15 for each passenger (children one-half); $5 for 70 pounds peas, a measure of oatmeal and the necessary beer, thence shipped via Holland to Virginia. In Holland one-half of the fare must be paid and additional provisions secured: Twenty-four pounds dried beef, 15 pounds cheese, 8½ pounds butter. They were advised also to provide themselves with seeds, implements, linen, stoves, powder and lead and furniture. This meant a full outfit for a settler. It is doubtful if the majority ever had such ample provisions.

The voyage across the water varied with the weather and the sailing capacity of the ship. The letters indicate some ships reached port after a few weeks while others required several months. The great Muhlenburg came over on a vessel that was 102 days making the voyage. Casper Wistar in 1732, the year before our first Bowser came, says: "In the past year one ship sailed about the seas 24 weeks, and of the 150 persons on board, more than 100 miserably died of hunger; on account of the lack of food they caught rats and mice on board, and a mouse sold for 30 Kreutzer." (Dotterer, Perkiomen Region. Volume 2, page 120). Another vessel was 17 weeks on the voyage during which 60 persons died.

The Schwenkfelders came on a boat of 150 tons burden with over 300 persons on board, and one boat was held up with its passengers aboard from September 24 to January 14, waiting favorable weather and landed at Philadelphia April 5, 1748. Hunger was not their only peril. Fevers and smallpox were common scourges. The vessel on which William Penn sailed in 1682 had a number of smallpox victims and 36 died. We have already stated that the occasion of the emigration of these unfortunate people offered the opportunity and temptation to the unscrupulous to take advantage of their ignorance and helpless condition. A class of solicitors called Newlanders traversed the length of the country, picturing in glowing phrases the charms of the New land across the waters and offering inducements to emigrate. Their only interest in these unsuspecting farmers was an opportunity to plunder them. And this they did. The nefarious business of these shipping companies flourished for many years. Boats of every conceivable size and shape were chartered. When these unwary peasants arrived at Holland their goods were taken in exchange or held. "They filled the vessels with passengers and as much of their goods as they saw fit and left the passengers' chests and boxes behind. But the poor people depended upon their chests, etc., as in them were many provisions they had made for the journey, as dried apples, pears, plums, medicines, mustard, vinegar, brandy, better clothing and money; and when these chests were left behind or sent on other vessels they had lack of nourishment."

Saur to Governor Denny, 1755

All suffered alike in this, the rich with the poor; one family of such were sold into service for seven years to pay the cost of transportation after they had been robbed. If parents died on the voyage the children were sold into service to pay the cost of passage. Saur says: "This murdering trade makes my heart ache, especially when I heard that there is more profit by their death than by carrying them alive. The long voyage with its many sorrowful and trying experiences was not entirely devoid of diversions. Many of the young men, undaunted by the ever present misfortune or the storms that threatened them found recreation in wrestling, boxing, debating; others in singing; many others had little inclination to any sort of enjoyment. If they sang it was the songs of the church that breathed their prayers to the great Jehovah. If their life had made them thoughtful and serious in their faith in Him who drew the baby out from among the bulrushes of the Nile was their support; they put their trust in God. Their religious convictions were deep and sincere. They were reconciled to their losses because they believed He made all things work together for good to them that love Him. John Wesley was in a great storm on one of his voyages to Georgia. While they were engaged in a religious service a massive wave struck the ship with great force, splitting the mainsail and "covering the vessel as if a great deep had already swallowed us up." The English passengers were thrown into great confusion and a terrible screaming began. But the Palatines calmly continued the hymn they were singing. Wesley afterward asked one of them, "Was you not afraid?" "I thank God, no," he answered. He asked, "But were not your women and children afraid?" He replied, "No, our women and children are not afraid to die."

But though the adventure meant losses and sickness and death to many, the intrepid voyagers bore their trials manfully and others followed. This flood of emigration began and continued to flow to the land of Penn for 60 years, until interrupted by the Revolutionary War.

With 1710 we begin the adventures of our kinsmen when the Swiss Mennonites came. In 1711 the Mennonites of Switzerland were offered free transportation down the Rhine on condition that they would never return. About this time began the settlement of Lancaster County by Swiss Mennonites where their descendants are to this day. On October 23, 1710, we find a patent for 10,000 acres of land on Pequea Creek, Conestogoe (later a part of Lancaster County) made out in the name of Hans Herr and Martin Kundig, who acted as agents for their countrymen, some of whom had already arrived, others were to come. No sooner had these first settlers been established than they sent Martin Kundig back to the Palatine and Switzerland to bring over those who wished to share their fortunes in what was then an impenetrable forest. And they had an eye to business, these far sighted emigrants, for they settled upon land now known as the garden spot of the United States—Lancaster County. From 1710 the names of Herr and Kundig frequently appear in public records of Pennsylvania, as taking up choice bits of farming land and having them turned over to their countrymen. (Swiss and German Settlements in Pennsylvania.) Among the names of these early settlers in Lancaster we find the names of Hans Herr, a minister of a church established there, Frick, Fluckiger, Bucher and many more; these are of Bernese origin. By 1717 great numbers had come from the Palatine and Switzerland, probably 15,000. The names and settlements of these people are found scattered among the Pennsylvania archives and early histories. To follow them in their new homes is a matter of much labor and research. But in 1727 a law was passed by the Pennsylvania Assembly at Philadelphia requiring all emigrants henceforth on landing to appear before the court and register their names ,the countries from which they came, and the names of the vessels upon which they sailed, and take the oath of allegiance to the King of England. From this period on we have a record. (See Rupp's Thirty Thousand Names) also (Pennsylvania's Archives, Second Series, Vol. XVII.) From 1749 to 1754 lists give names, dates of arrival, name of fatherland, as Wurtemburg, Ebach, Alsace, etc. By 1775, the beginning of the American Revolution, it has been computed the German element in Pennsylvania was about 110,000 or one-third of the population, 300,000.

The mercenary "Newlanders" who went up and down the Palatine persuading the people that America was a land of unparallel richness and beauty, did better than they had intended, for the Palatine pioneers in Pennsylvania found that the half had not been told. By a favoring Providence they left the English city of Philadelphia and penetrated the wilderness westward until they beheld that Paradise of North America now known as Lancaster County. They were not slow to discern the natural attractions of the broad and fertile valley. Having left behind them fields, plowed and torn by war, houses, barns burned, orchards destroyed, one day halted their caravan on the Pequea Creek, of Lancaster County, placed their chests and bundles on the ground, looked out at the scene that was the answer to their dreams, the fact of their visions and said, "Here, let us build our home in this new land. Here God will prosper us!" Far beyond their most ardent hopes has that virgin soil responded for Lancaster County is the richest agricultural county in the United States. It was not long before these thousands of acres of marvellously rich soil, hitherto untouched by the hand of man except spots here and there planted in maize by the Indians, were made to blossom like the rose.

Nowhere can we find a better or truer conception of our Palatine ancestors, their habits of industry, intelligent methods of agriculture, sterling religious principles, and also the prominent aesthetic sense which reveals the love of art, than in the visible characteristics of their surroundings. The orderly arrangement of barns and fences; the mansion, commodious and bright with paint and embowered in trees; the fields laid out in squares enclosed by fences immaculately clean; cattle grazing in luxuriant pasture; teams in plow and reaper whose dotted skins and high spirit indicating good care and kind masters; orchards that glow in the genial springtime with myriads of apple blossoms—all tell the story of character—honesty, industry, piety; clean hands and untarnished name; love of God and the beautiful things He had made. They believed His Word that if they sought first these pure and intrinsic things of the Kingdom,

God would grant whatsoever else were desirable. And He did! They fulfilled their part of the covenant and God kept His part.

Religious Affiliations

We have reason to be proud, therefore, of our lineage. Not only because our ancestors were thrifty and industrious and honest but because of their deeply religious nature. The Bible was the first text book of their schools. The commandments of God they sought to obey implicitly. They accepted the obligations of the church as prior to home and self interests. Six days they devoted to unremitting toil, but the seventh was a Holy day in which they assembled in their churches to worship Him in whom they put their trust. They clung to superstitions handed down from the remote beginnings of Palatine history. "They believed in unlucky days; they planted in the signs of the moon; shingled their houses when the horns of the moon pointed down; a crowing hen or howling dog meant somebody would die; it was bad luck to begin a journey on Friday; a horse shoe nailed on the door would guard against witches and pow-wowing would cure burns and nose bleeding." Many of these primitive vagaries are still believed and observed by their credulous descendants. They hungered for the Word of God. When men like Muhlenberg, Bauman and Mack went among them preaching, they gathered in throngs and were attentive and responsive hearers.

Whitfield, in a letter written April 10, 1740, speaks of "the religious Germans."

The Waldenses, Martin Luther and John Calvin, had prepared the soil in earlier history. Thence sprang the Mennonites and Ana-baptists and Lutherans. The articles of faith of the former two were much the same,—refusal to take oaths; rejection of a paid ministry and infant baptism; simplicity of dress and religious worship; separation of church and state and the right of individual belief and worship. "If any one could persuade out of the Bible they were willing to hear; but neither persecution, fire or sword, prison or exile could bend their wills or make them recant what they believed was the truth."

"One of the divisions of the Mennonite Church, was formed in the Berne Canton of Switzerland, transferred to the Palatine and thence to Pennsylvania. It was founded by Jacob Ammen and known as the Amish denomination. Ammen's purpose was, particularly to preserve the simplicity of dress." There are considerable Amish settlements in Pennsylvania. The men do not shave. Buttons are not allowed but hooks and eyes are used instead. It is a customary sight on the streets of Lewisburg, Pa., to see youths of 18 or 20 years with beards sprouting on ruddy faces, and comely maidens in shaker bonnets, whose bright eyes and glowing cheeks contrast beautifully with the simple dress that scorns the fashions of worldly mortals.

The "River Brethren" is another branch, founded by Jacob Engel, who came from Switzerland in childhood and lived in Conestoga Township. He was a Mennonite but became convinced the church needed a spiritual awakening.

The Dunkards or German Baptists, were founded by Alexander Mack of Schwarzenau, Westphalia, in 1708, though their real origin dates from 1719, when about 20 families came to Pennsylvania and settled at Germantown, Philadelphia, Montgomery, Berks and Lancaster counties. Mack, himself, came to Pennsylvania in 1729. Their doctrines are similar to the Mennonites; like them they disbelieve in infant baptism, refuse to bear arms or take oath. They perform baptism by emersion—"tunker," dipping, hence the name Tunker or Dunkard. But when the nation was in need they did bear arms. Many were enrolled as soldiers of the Revolutionary and Civil wars, and in expeditions against the Indians. [See Pennsylvania Archives, 1st series, Volumes 5, 6, 7, page 378. 2nd series, Volume 10, page 5; Volume 3, and Pennsylvania Mag., Volume 16, page 343.]

The first Bousser to emigrate to America of whom there is a definite record was Mathias Bousser, Sr., with his wife and family. The following records were made in Philadelphia, Sept. 28, 1733: "Palatines,—brigantine Richard and Elizabeth. Christopher Clymer, master, from Rotterdam, and last from Plymouth,—forty-four males above sixteen and thirty-four females; twenty-four males under sixteen and thirty-four females—in all 137.

"Among the names recorded as above sixteen are Mattheus Bausser, Mathies Bausser, Jr., and Christian Bausser. That Mathias Bausser, Sr., was a man of intelligence and capable of writing his own name are indicated by his well written signature—in German. The first Palatines to settle in Lancaster County purchased a large tract of land in 1710, on Pequea Creek. Here this small colony erected some huts and cabins, to serve temporarily as shelters. Here the time and again persecuted and oppressed Swiss, separated from friends and much that makes life agreeable, hoped unmolested to begin anew. Here surrounded on all sides by several clans of Indians, they located in the gloomy, silent shades of a virgin forest, whose undisturbed solitude was yet uncheered by the murmurs of the honey bee or the twitterings of the swallow, these never-failing attendants upon the woodman's ax. For the hum and warblings of those, they had not only the shout and song of the tawny sons of the forest, but also the nocturnal howlings of the ever watchful dog, baying at the sheeny queen of night. By way of variety, their ears were nightly greeted by the shrill, startling whoop of the owl, or by the sinister croakings of some night songsters in the contiguous thickets. This Swiss settlement formed the nucleus, or center of a rapidly increasing Swiss, French and German population, in the Eden of Pennsylvania." [Thirty Thousand names, by Prof. I. Daniel Rupp.]

We find no record of Mathias Bausser, Sr., after his entrance into Pennsylvania, but that he and his family went to their countrymen at Lancaster, is more than probable by the fact that we find his son, Mathias, Jr., there in 1739. [See introduction to names.]

CHAPTER VI

MATHIAS BAUSSER, JR., IN YORK COUNTY

Mathias, Jr., lived at Lancaster until after 1739. He made a permanent settlement in Paradise Township, York County, about one mile north of Abbottstown, which is now in Adams County. He also owned land in Berwick Township which adjoins Paradise. Since 1800 when Adams County was formed out of York County, Berwick Township has been in Adams County. The original grant at Abbottstown contained 235 acres. This tract is now the Paradise Church property, at first called Brandt's Chapel. The Catholic Church which is also on land owned by Mathias Bowser, lies just across the line in Paradise Township, York County. Near this land is the old "Beaver Creek Mill," a three story stone grist mill. On a corner stone is the inscription, John Nawgel Mason,—built by Abraham Swigart, 1794. John Nawgel was probably a son of John Nawgel, Sr., who appointed in his will Mathias Bowser and Wm. Mummert as executors Jan. 15, 1770.

In the York County records, book 2 B., page 13, is recorded the sale by sheriff of "Goods and Chattels, Lands and Tenements of Mathias Bowser, late of said County, Yeoman in his Bailiwick, he should be caused to make as well a debt of 64 pounds 9 shilling and seven pence, etc., which Francis Jacob may for the use of Nicholas Bittinger, etc.—one plantation and mill in Berwick Township containing about 100 acres and *one* plantation and mill in Paradise Township contaiining 200 acres—taken on the 22nd of Sept., 1775, at Yorktown—estate sold publicly to William Baily at Yorktown for 555 pounds, May 1, 1779." This shows Mathias Bowser had been an enterprising and wealthy citizen until about the time of his death; that he had the mental acumen to locate on one of the fairest spots on Pennsylvania soil. The record shows his death at about 1775.

The tax lists of 1769 show the original settlers of Paradise and Jackson townships. The names of Mathias Bowser, with 150 acres of land, and Samuel and Jacob Bowser, single men evidently sons of Mathias. In 1779-82 Samuel was in Paradise Township. In 1782 Jacob was in Dover Township which adjoins Paradise. Jacob owned land in Bedford County in 1783, and there is no record of his being in York County after that year.

In the muster roll of the 6th Company of York County Militia for 1785 among the privates is Samuel Bowser. This company was from Paradise Township. Samuel is again mentioned in the assessment roll of 1799 for Berwick Township, having an assessed value of $528, and Samuel, Jr., $52. In 1811 Samuel, Sr.'s, property was assessed at $2,294. In the York County muster roll, 1777, and 1778,

Captain Peter Zollinger's Company belonged to the 7th Battalion of York County Militia and contained the names of Abram Bowser, Daniel Bowser, Noah Bowser and Jacob Bowser; also the names of John Nagle, Mr. Mummert, and these are residents of Paradise Township. Evidently Noah and Jacob were brothers. Noah is recorded in the tax lists of Berwick Township, 1779, 1780 1781, identically with Samuel, which together with the fact that Mathias owned propery there prior to his death in 1775 indicates they were sons of Mathias. Noah owned 100 acres there in 1779 and 1780, no doubt being the 100 acres mentioned in the sheriff's sale after Mathias' death. In 1781 he had no land, and that year was the last record of Noah in York County. But in 1785 Noah bought land in Frederick County, Md., and was there in 1790, when the first census was taken. In 1796, he was in Bedford County, and moved to Armstrong County in 1802. This Noah was the father of "Steam John," Joseph and other children. His descendants are numbered in many hundreds. Many are still living in Armstrong County, Pa., but others are located in western and other states.

John Bowser and Jacob Bowser were in the same company, the Fifth Battalion, from Paradise Township. Valentine Bowser was another son of Matthias, Jr., born about 1745. He moved to Armstrong County, locating in Sugar Creek, now Washington Township, midway between Montgomeryville and Sherrett, taking up 400 acres of land. He died there in 1836. Mathias Bowser, Jr., and his wife, were members of the Reformed Church when they came to America, but they were members of the German Baptist Brethren (Dunker) Church in 1770. Brumbaugh, speaking of the Little Coneways Congregation near Hanover, says that in 1770 there were 70 members in communion in this congregation among whom were Mathias Bowser, wife and daughter. Jacob Sweigard (Swigart) was one of the first members. Bowsers still cling to this locality, of so great interest to the history of our family. Andrew Bowser lives here. He is a son of Joseph E., who is a grandson of Daniel. These facts gleaned from court records, tax lists and census records, the testimony of many of the aged of our family, and a tradition, that "our ancestors, came from Germany and settled at Little York," corroborate the writer's early belief that Mathias Bowser, Sr., and Esther, his wife, with their children, were the first of our family to come to America. We have given considerable space to Mathias Bowser, Jr., and his family, because he is the connecting link between the vast and thrilling history of the home land beyond the sea and the great Bowser family now numbering thousands and living in many parts of the United States. He was a young man just past his majority with his young wife by his side when the good ship Richard and Elizabeth brought them up the Delaware to Philadelphia in September, 1723, with his father, Mathias, and mother, Esther, and brothers, Christian and Daniel, and other members of that, to us, historic family. After a brief sojourn among friends and neighbors from the homeland now preparing a new home at Lancaster, he followed the trail of the frontiersman to the newly found Paradise of York County. And somewhere within the limits of Paradise Township lies the dust of the indomitable pair, Mathias Bowser, Jr., and his wife, Ann Elizabeth, in graves unmarked and now unknown, who braved the horrors of a voyage across the Atlantic for Liberty and a home.

The descendants of Daniel Bowser of York County affirm that Daniel with two brothers, John and Henry emigrated to this country in 1733, landing at Baltimore. Daniel settled in Manheim Township, York County, Pa. In June, 1774, he bough a tract of 263 acres, about 10 miles south of the land owned by Mathias Bowser. Daniel became a wealthy land owner and reared a large family. The connection between Daniel and Mathias, Jr., we have been unable to ascertain. But it is safe to presume they were closely related. They came to America from the same place, in the same year, 1733. But we can readily understand owing to the urgency of the large numbers of the Palatines at that time seeking passage across the sea and the inadequate sailing accommodations, where a considerable family arrived at Rotterdam they were compelled to separate and one part sail on one ship, while the others came on the next. Mathias, Sr., brought with him several children who must have been children of a close relation. That Daniel moved into York County and settled in the same neighborhood with Mathias, Jr., and several of his children came to Armstrong County and settled in the same locality as the descendants of Mathias, would seem to prove our assumption correct. The other large branch of the Bowser family reared chiefly in Bedford County, whose connection with Mathias, Sr., is a presumption equally obvious,—viz., the family of John Bowser, b. about 1730; d., 1809, and Eve Maria of Lancaster. Their children were Eve, Magdelina, Michael, Elizabeth (married John Mock), and George. George was born about 1755; was a taxable in Lancaster County, 1776. According to the 1790 census he was in Bedford County. In the 1800 census he was in St. Clair Township with a family of nine.

George married Margaret Swartz. One of the sons of George Bowser, Isaac, married Sarah Berkheimer, whose mother was Catharine Bowser, sister of "Commissioner" John, and daughter of David, son of Mathias. Thus establishing a connecting link between the children of George and Mathias Bowser though we do not know certainly what relation the parents were.

CHAPTER VII

BOWSERS IN BEDFORD COUNTY

Those of our family who landed at Philadelphia proceeded to the earlier settlement of their kinsmen at Lancaster, as we have seen, but as the land became fully occupied by the ever increasing tide of emigrants, they found an attractive location in what is now Berks, Adams, York and other counties. Those who landed at Baltimore tarried for a while in Virginia and Maryland, but most of them later joined their relatives in Pennsylvania. During periods of freedom from Indian atrocities, the pioneer settlers, ever in quest of new and better land, moved westward, halted for a while at some fresh outbreak, then moved slowly, steadily westward again. Moving with this tide our fathers found a temporary resting place within the limits of York County and the newly formed county of Bedford. There are many Bowser families, descendants of these early settlers, living in the town of York and throughout the county. The westward fever carried the majority of the York County Bowsers, however, into the next place of temporary sojourn, Bedford County. Because of the importance of this county in our family history we will pause with them here for a moment. This county has an interesting history on account of its association with the names of the famous leaders in our pioneer annals. There is a peculiar charm in its beautiful "coves" and fertile valleys that offered a lure to the early settler who was willing to risk his scalp for a choice tract of virgin soil. Bedfordtown was first known as Raystown. Several cabins were built here in 1850 by a trader named Ray. White explorers had traversed the Bedford County territory as early as 1732. Stephen Franks, a German trader, had a settlement at what is now Frankstown, and John Hart was at Hart's Log, or Hart's Sleeping Place. The "Six Nations" granted the Penns in 1754, a vast body of land now forming the counties of Bedford, Fulton, Perry, Huntingdon, Blair, Mifflin, Snyder, Union and Centre. Prior to that treaty, the Six Nations gave leave to Garrett Prendergrass to occupy and improve 300 acres embracing the present town of Bedford. This was placed on record by the first Prothonotary of the county, Sir Arthur St. Clair. Prendergrass, like Ray, did not long remain in this remote and wild region. The sites of Carlisle and Bedford lay on the road of General Forbes in his march to subdue the French and Indians at Pittsburgh in 1758. Stockade forts were erected here and at the "Juniata Crossings" by Forbes soldiers. A few of these subsequently became settlers of Bedford County by establishing "Tomahawk claims." Land in Bedford County in 1762-63 sold for 9 pounds per 100 acres; rfom 1763 to 1765, 15 pounds, 10 shillings; 1765-84, 5 pounds;

1784 to 1814, 10 pounds. This pound was a "pound currency," which was about one-half the value of an English pound sterling ($5). One of the best known Indian trails passed through Bedford County. Beginning at Harris' Landing (Harrisburg) it passed through Dauphin, Perry, Sherman's Valley in Franklin County, to Black Log, a distance of 72 miles. From Black Log, the Raystown branch, it led through Augwick Valley, Well's Valley in Fulton County, Ray's Cove, Woodcock Valley, Snake Spring, Raystown; thence along the Juniata to Shawnee Cabin Creek, near Schellsburgh in Bedford County, across the Allegheny Mountains, through Brothers' Valley, along Stony Creek in Somerset County, across Laurel Hill, Ligonier Valley, Chestnut Ridge and by Loyalhanna Creek in Westmoreland County to Shannopin Town (Indian) on the Allegheny River at Pittsburgh, making a total of 246 miles. "Many of the first settlers of Bedford County were teamsters, and long lines of their Conestoga wagons trailed the principal highways. The history of the Pittsburgh and Philadelphia Pike forms an interesting chapter of the days when the pioneers were preparing the way for the farms and cities of today. Many a night scene where the hardy teamsters rested in the taven for the night and danced and reveled, would have afforded the great novelist, Walter Scott, a capital theme. Casper Stetler's old tavern on the state road on top of the Allegheny Mountains had a fireplace 12 feet wide and a horse was used to haul logs into the room, coming in a large door on one side and passing through a door on the other. Before this huge fireplace as many as 30 or 40 men would sleep. I have frequently seen 10 of these line teams line up in front of these old-time taverns."—Hon. William Schell in Annals of Bedford County.

After the Revolutionary War the county was rapidly settled. The county was organized in 1771. In 1772 there was a population of only 1,600 in the whole of Somerset and Bedford counties. Some of them had been located less than a year and not many for more than five years. There were but two grist mills and two sawmills in these counties at this date. In 1771 three townships, Bedford, Cumberland and Colerain, embraced all of Bedford County and considerable more, taking in Blair with Tusseys mountain as an eastern boundary. In the preparation of this history the writer visited the county seats of Blair, Bedford and York counties and examined the wills and deeds preserved in the courts. We also went to Reynoldsdale, Alum Bank, Everett, Duncansville, Newry, St. Clairsville, Osterburg, Lutzville, Hopewell, Loysburg, Blue Knob and other places where our ancestors once lived and some of their descendants are still living. We cannot describe our emotions as we stood in the very footprints of our fathers long since deceased, at such well remembered places as Hopewell, St. Clairsville, Loysburg, and Newry, and contemplated the fact that only a century since the sturdy fathers were clearing the forests, with their great ox teams and horses hauling the logs. We imagined we heard the echo of the axes as the fathers and their brawny sons felled the trees. Nor did we forget the scenes of the mothers with their spinning wheels and the girls learning the arts of those primitive homes or helping the men in the fields. The Blue Knob created a picture that will never fade. In its majestic solitude it appeared the end of creation. It is the silent, awe-inspiring Switzerland of Pennsylvania. The inhabitants of its meagre vales call it the "Swyts." It is a group of three mountains, an austere and challenging prospect. In its valleys and nooks, on the banks of its murmuring brooks, settlers founded happy and contented homes. Hopewell was a point of special interest. Here our great grandfather, Valentine Bowser, and Elizabeth Fluke were married. We stood on the farm of our great-great grandfather, John Bowser, of Hopewell Township, three miles from Hopewell Borough on the road to Loysburg, and made pictures of the site of his log house and barn, and where he died in September, 1813. This farm contained 1,100 acres of rolling land buttressed by the Tusseys mountains on the west and intersected by Yellow Creek and the Loysburg road. Most of these superb acres were in wheat at the time of our visit and rapidly yellowing for harvest. On a knoll of this farm was a small burying ground entirely unmarked except that a circle 100 feet in diameter was left inviolate by the plow; around that circle was standing wheat. It is the resting place of John Bowser and his wife Mary, and Nicholas, his son, and wife, and other descendants. Nicholas died about 1862, an old, decrepit man.

The deed to this land is recorded in Volume I, Page 479 (Bedford.) "Know that I, Joseph Haines, of Hopewell Township, made an improvement on a tract of land in March, 1796. Joining lands with Melor and Joseph Snyder, and the Sussies Mountain in Hopewell Township, and on April 5, 1797, for the sum of 26 pounds ten shillings to me in hand by John Bowser, did sell, bargain, quit, etc., claim and interest to said improvement and warrant and defend it from me and my heirs forever unto the said John Bowser of Woodbury Township, of Bedford County, Pa."

Signed in German, April 5, 1797.

His
John (X) Bowser.
Mark

Henry P. Bowser, son of James, son of Nicholas, son of John Bowser, who resides near Hopewell, relates that his father told him his (James) great grandfather came from Germany and he believed his name was Mathias, thus strengthening the link in the evidence that Mathias Bowser, Sr., was the founder of the chief branch of the Bowser family in American. Mathias is said to have brought with him from the old country wagon parts and other farm implements to begin with in the new world, and seems to have been possessed of considerable means. Mr. G. W. Bowser, son of John

H,. son of John (Commissioner), son of David, resides at Osterburg. He writes: "I have been told by my father that David Bowser settled in the woods when a young man, on the farm I own, one and a half miles west of Osterburg, and commenced to clear a small burial place on the same farm, shows that he was 75 years old when he died in 1813; and that he had come from some place in the east toward Philadelphia. He had two sons and several daughters." The will of David Bowser is of special interest as it enables us to link up a large family with the founder, Mathias, Sr. David mentions seven children, Catrout (a female), Elizabeth, Mary, Catherine (who married John Berkheimer), Valentine, John and Esther, and in his will he names a grandson John Mock. David was baptized in the Reformed Church at Lancaster, Pa., May 12, 1739, with Anna Margaret, his sister, children of Mathias Bowser, Jr., and Anna Catherine. David's will is dated October 19, 1810. In Bedford is recorded the will of George Mock dated January 8, 1810, in which he mentions his wife, Eva, and among his children one named John. We conclude that Eva was a sister of Commissioner John and married George Mock. David was in Bedford County in 1798 because he sold land that year in Maryland, in the deed of which is said: "David of Bedford County." We find Noah and David Bowser (sons of Mathias, Jr.) both in Maryland at the same time, and at another time both back in Bedford County; both gave deeds in Maryland while they were living in Bedford County. A deed shows Noah bought land in Bedford County, in 1785, and was in the tax lists in York County, 1781. We conclude David and Noah were brothers and sons of Mathias, Jr.

At Alum Bank, we met Mr. Isaac S. Wright, a man in his 89th year but of good health and remarkable memory. Mr. Wright knew Commissioner John (son of David) whose grandson Polk Bowser was living in the village. Mr. Wright frequently gave the appellation "Davie" John to the Commissioner. We inquired whether he did not so designate him because his father's name was "David." He said that was true. This gave us the first clue to Commissioner John's ancestry and confirmed our belief that David was the son of Mathias, Jr. "David Bowser, great grandfather of Dr. Alex J. Bowser was a descendant of one of the three brothers who emigrated from Switzerland and settled in Pennsylvania. David married Catherine. Among his children was a son John. John, the son of David and Catherine, was born in East St. Clair Township on the farm later possessed by his son. He married Mary Helm and among his children was a son named David H. David H. Bowser, son of John and Mary Helm, was born December 21, 1810, in East St. Clair Township. He moved with his parents to Napier Township. He removed with his parents to Schellsburg in 1874 and later returned to the old Bowser Homestead in East St. Clair Township and died there, 1888. He married Charlotte Potts. Their only child was Dr. Alexander J. Bowser, who died April 11, 1906.

CHAPTER VIII

PERMANENT HOMES IN ARMSTRONG COUNTY

The Bowsers of Armstrong County, Pa., have the distinction of outnumbering the clan in any other county in the world. Individual families may be found throughout the nation, and smaller or larger settlements in several states, but in this county lying on the Allegheny River, they are the most numerous. This county with its capital, Kittanning, has a history of thrilling interest surpassed by few counties in the country. This is due to the fact of its proximity to Fort Duquesne, the junction of the two rivers, Allegheny and Monongahela, forming the Ohio at Pittsburgh, and its intersection by the natural route of travel and commerce between Canada and Fort Duquesne. Here for unknown generations the Indians plied their canoes, pursued the game which once abounded, or led to battle their ever turbulent warriors; and later became the rendezvous of French and Indian marauders. Kittanning was an Indian town and the last native stronghold in Western Pennsylvania to be destroyed. Col. John Armstrong with 307 soldiers besieged the place September 9, 1756, killing many of the Indians, including their half-breed captain, Jacobs, and burning their log huts, thus destroying the last refuge of the red men in Pennsylvania. Armstrong County was formed in March 12, 1800. The southeastern portion was settled early. The proprietary of Pennsylvania by purchase, 1768, added to his territory this part of the county as far west as the Allegheny and the Ohio rivers. Immediately (1769) a land office for the sale of the lately purchased land was opened. Thousands applied for land. There must have been a few settlers in Armstrong County before the Revolutionary War.

"The inhabitants of Hannastown wrote Governor Denny, 1774, for troops as they were imperiled by the removal of troops to Kittanning, a place 25 miles from any settlement."

Captain Andrew Sharp had a settlement at Shelocta as early as 1784. Warrants for land were issued and actual settlements made in the various townships as follows: Bethel, Parks and Gilpin tract, 1792; Kittanning Township, 1773; Red Bank, 1785; Plum Creek, 1766; Wayne, named after General Anthony Wayne, 1794; Kiskiminitas, 1778; Pine and Boggs, 1785; Madison, 1795; Cowanshonnock, 1774; Manor, 1789. (The Penns had 44 Manors surveyed, 1769, in different parts of the state, as reserve tracts. Each manor contained 4887 acres. These manors and all reserve tracts, were deeded by the Penns to Thomas W. Morris, November 27, 1820, for $1.00. This township was one of the 44 manors, hence its name.) Mahoning, 1785; Burrell, 1778; Valley, 1785; South Bend, 1773; Freeport, 1786; South Buffalo, 1786. (Three-fourths of the country west of the river, up to Mahoning, thence west to the Ohio line, south to the boundary, thence north to the Mahoning, were Depreciation Lands, i. e., lands voted by the State Assembly, 1783, for the redemption of depreciation certificates. Immediately north of these lands was a tract set aside by the State Assembly called Donation Lands, which was allotted to Pennsylvania soldiers for their services in the Revolutionary War. This tract embraced all the remaining land of the state west of the Allegheny River from the Depreciation Lands north.) North Buffalo, 1786; West Franklin, 1785; East Franklin, 1786; Sugar Creek, 1793; Washington, 1793; Brady Bend, 1794; Perry, 1796, and Hovey, 1797.

The famous Purchase Line, established between the Northern Colonies and the Indians at the treaty of Fort Stanwix (Rome, N. Y.), November, 1768, was run from Cherry Tree or Canoe Place (the Indians' designation of the head of navigation on the Susquehanna), due west to the Allegheny River at Kittanning. The English Government paid 10,460 pounds for this tremendous steal.

A few adventurous traders and settlers had penetrated the lands on the Allegheny River prior to and immediately following the Revolutionary War. Robt. Brown, one of the first to come to Kittanning in 1798, and not long after settled here with some hunters. At the same time Wm. Watson, John, James and Robt. Watson made a tour along the Cowanshannock Creek, traversed a part of Crooked Creek and the Allegheny River. They saw the evidences of the Indian corn fields at the site of Kittanning. A great aunt, Mrs. Catharine John, told the writer when he was a child, she remembered the slight excavations made by the Indians for their log cabins, on either side of present Market Street, Kittanning. The Indian town was made up of three parts—the first laid on the bench along Market Street—between McKean and Grant Avenue; two others on either side of Market Street, not far from the first. Between that and the river and stretching down the flat ground to the iron mill was an extensive corn field.

The old Hague Hotel, built by Mathias Bowser (see pictures), still standing, is located 200 feet west of the Pennsylvania Railroad crossing on Market Street. The site of this old town landmark is precisely that of the Indian town. Mrs. Margaret Bowser, wife of Jonas Bowser, when a child, visited her Uncle Mathias, when he lived in this house and saw Indian beads his children had found in the yard.

In the Summer of 1791, James Claypoole, with his wife and six children, settled on the site of the county seat, Kittanning, at Truby Run, and built a cabin on what is now lot 75, northwest corner of Arch and Water Streets. but on account of the danger of Indian attacks, left one year later, moving to Pittsburgh. Patrick Dougherty and Andrew Hunter were the next settlers (no date).

Claypoole returned in about a year to the location of his former daring adventure and settled on land he purchased on the river bank, just south of Fort Run, two miles south of Kittanning, where he built a block house. In 1798 he purchased 400 acres from Stone in North Buffalo Township, where the Union Baptist Church now stands. He was the progenitor of the Claypooles and the first Baptist to settle in the County. He died at an advanced age on this farm.

Warrants for land within the limits of the present Manor Township were made to James Claypoole in 1791. Mahoning in 1785; Burrell, 1778; Valley, 1785. (David Loy and Mathias erected a grist mill and saw mill on the Cowanshannock; Mathias purchased seven acres in Kittanning Borough, 1817, and sold the same to David Reynolds six years later for $150.) South Bend, 1773; Freeport, 1786.

The first settlers found these templed hills and broad valleys covered with the most prolific pine and oak timber. They little surmised, however, as they cleared the forests and prepared the primitive soil for cultivation that beneath their feet were hidden unmeasured stores for the advantage of their children and the blessing of mankind. There are within the bounds of this county great ledges of limestone so essential in modern farming; the hills are traversed by several veins of bituminous coal; oil has been produced in the northern part of the county in vast quantity and many fields are still producing oil. Near Kaylor there are two wells that produce from the earth a grade of oil so nearly pure that it is used immediately without any further refining. Natural gas is found in most parts of the county. The towns and villages and many of the country homes are supplied with this cheap and convenient fuel. The manufacture of fire brick has become a great industry, employing many thousands of men, since the discovery of vast beds of the purest fire clay. Add to lime, oil, coal, natural gas, timber and fire clay, a soil that responds promptly to a scientific and proper method of agriculture, growing everything produced in the north temperate zone.

The magnitude of its varied products is seen in the number of railroads that intersect it. Nor should we fail to note the charm of natural scenery which here delights the heart of the student of nature. It has not the sublimity of the Alps nor does it awe the beholder with the stupendous cliffs of our Rockies, but it has a calm, reposeful, romantic beauty of its own; a charm of scene that would have inspired the genius of a Cooper or an Oliver Goldsmith. The Allegheny River flows through the length of the county, bisecting it about midway between east and west. There are stretches where it flows miles without changing its course, then it gracefully yields to the phenomenal winding of the hills. At two points within this county this Belle (Beautiful) River, as the romantic French called it, does it make almost the circumference of a circle, one at Brady's

Bend, and the other just above Mahoning. There are scenes here, many of them, that would enchant any artist; the pastures where the cattle graze, the meadows with tree and brook; the river hills billowed with the pink and white of the laurel blossoms, and the river itself lying far down in the bed wrought out by the ages, where the oars of the lone boatman dip and flash the gold of the afternoon sun and the steel rails that wind along the bank shining like threads of silver—The Belle River! So it is! Kittanning itself is a gem, lying on the bank of this beautiful river.

As the county was rapidly being occupied by settlers it became apparent that Kittanning was the proper site for the county seat. It was laid out and lots sold in 1803 and in one year there were resident one lawyer, three merchants, one hatter, one tailor, one tanner, one mason, three shoemakers, one wheelwright, four joiners and one "rough" carpenter. The first physician settled here in 1810; a harness maker in 1815; weaver in 1811; gunsmith in 1821; tinner in 1823; druggist in 1831; photographer in 1863; plow maker in 1834, and a registered undertaker in 1873. In 1830 there were 90 houses, 10 stores and a courthouse. A ferry was used to carry passengers across the river until 1856, when the first bridge was built. The writer has given a brief chapter on a few salient facts of the history of the county, which, in the Providence of God, was to become the permanent home of the Bowser family.

Into this newly created county came our Bowser people, when the surrounding county was a primeval wilderness. There were no roads and but few ancient Indian trails and bridle paths; the endless forests everywhere. Here and there were a few cleared acres where the daring squatter or pioneer had started an improvement, but otherwise it was the Indian hunting ground without the Indian. Game abounded. Bear, wild turkey and deer provided the settlers' boys ample diversion. It was a day before railroads were dreamed of. To subdue the mighty forests and transform this wilderness into a land of homes and highways, wheat fields and orchards, and communities with the village church and the red schoolhouse was their worthy adventure. The time of their settlement is yet so near to us we have but to take one step backward and we are in the midst of the days, unfortunately forever past, the days of the log house and the loom and spinning wheel, and the candle and scutching block.

They had their own recreations and their life was not without its fun and frolic. Their common hardships brought them into a closer fellowship. They shared more intimately than their ambition's money-making children, the joys of success and the sorrows of misfortunes. In addition to the primitive utensils and tools, they brought with them horses and cattle and in an incredibly short period we find them thrifty farmers, coming to the growing county seat with their produce, of wheat, butter, meat, eggs and whiskey. Many who found no market for their wheat and rye converted them into the commodity of smaller compass. We have an insight into the market conditions of those early days in the account book recently discovered and loaned the writer, of Samuel Houston, beginning May, 1824. Samuel Houston kept store in Kittanning from the founding of the town for many years. His store was on the alley on the north side of Market Street, a half square or less from Water Street. It may be of interest to note some of the entries:

One quart turpentine, 44c; 2/3 yds. sarsnet, 25c.

John Mosgrove ret'd a lot of sanders that was wet.

Judge Orr, ½ lb. Imperial tea, $1.00.

Five lbs. of nails, $6.25. Six bags, $3.00.

One pair coarse shoes, $1.50. One straw bonnet, $3.00.

12 Wilmington stripe, $4.50; 2 lbs. copperas, 25c.

To be paid by William Templeton in whiskey at 25c per gal.

One Leghorn bonnet, $6.25.

5 lb. blistered steel, at 25c.

1 lb. brimstone, 18½c; 2 yds. blue cloth, $5.00.

Sold to ————, 1 qt. whiskey, 12½c.

Butter, 6c per lb. Veal, 4c per lb.

Matthias Bowser, 1 pr. Morocco shoes, 75c.

Rev. John Dickey, 1 empty bottle (here the storekeeper adds "to put oil in").

18 lbs. veal at 4c, 72c; 200 lbs. of flour, $4.00.

18 segars, 16 cents.

Among the patrons of this store of 100 years ago were many whose names are well remembered. Among them were Archibald Dickey, David Reynolds, Matthias Bowser (grandfather of M. L. Bowser of Kittanning), John Mosgrove, Judge Orr, J. P. Shaffer, Rev. John Dickey, John B. Brown, Wm. Templeton, David McKelvey, Michael Truby, Richard Cravenor, David Gilespie, Robt. Brown, John McMullen, Samuel Bowser, Joseph Boney, Josiah Copley, Kia Claypoole, Peggy Sipes. We are grateful for the naive statement about Rev. Dickey's pure intention to fill the "empty bottle" with harmless oil, when it was possible to indulge in a hilarity with whiskey at the grocery store at 25c a gallon, and segars 18 per 16c.

The first Bowser to settle in Armstrong County was Matthias Bowser, who came here from Hopewell Township, Bedford County, in 1798. There were thirteen brothers and sisters, he came first, with his brother Samuel, who went back after five months. The latter returned, accompanied by his widowed sister, Catharine Kline, in 1805, and settled on land he purchased at Walk Chalk, three miles west of Kittanning in East Franklin Township. In 1807 he sold his claim to David Flenner and John Burnheimer, and moved to North Buffalo Township.

Abraham Swigart, who married Elizabeth Bowser, daughter of John of Hopewell, came out in 1805. Valentine Bowser, brother of

Elizabeth Swigart, came to Armstrong County in 1815, and bought a small farm on Glade Run, now known as the Dougherty farm ,and there raised his family of eleven children. Noah Bowser, brother of John of Hopewell, came to Glade Run from Bedford County in 1807, and settled on a 400-acre farm which he later sold to his son Joseph Bowser. Noah had another son, John, called "Steam" John, because he was believed to have been the first miller to apply steam as a motive power in grist mills. Several of his sons were millers, at least George and Samuel. Valentine, mentioned prior to Noah, the writer's great-grandfather, and his wife, Elizabeth (Fluke) never spoke English, but Palatine German ("Pennsylvania Dutch"). This indicates that John Bowser of Hopewell spoke Palatine German, and his children knew no other language. The deeds and wills of the old Bowsers in Bedford and York County, so far as we recall, were signed either in Palatine German or by making a mark. None were signed in English. David Flenner sent his son to Philip Mechling's store for a number of articles. The proprietor was not in, and the clerk did not know young Flenner. The lad had money for the articles he bought except tobacco. He informed the clerk in broken English his dad said they should borax him for the tobacco. The clerk took the tobacco away from the boy. When he reached home and there was no tobacco, Flenner demanded an explanation. The boy answered, "I told the man you said they should borax you for the tobacco, and he took it away from me." It is said the irate father punished the boy for his poor English.

Valentine Bowser, brother of Noah and Hopewell John, located on a farm of 400 acres in Sugar Creek Township, now Washington Township, 2½ miles northeast of Montgomeryville, on land now belonging to Geo. Rickel, Sadler heirs, et al. He came from Bedford County in 1798 and brought a number of young apple trees which he planted on the site of his home, afterward given to his daughter Peggie (Bowser). Sites now owned by Sadler heirs. Three of the trees he planted grew, two are standing now and the third, a massive, wide-spreading tree, has split and both halves fallen, though still living.

Martin John, who married Esther Bowser, sister of Hopewell John and Valentine, came here in 1798 and bought 400 acres beside Valentine. He built a log house on his land which was finally owned by Jonas Bowser and torn down in 1917. This Martin John came from the Palatine, and became the progenitor of the large family of John's, many of whom still reside in the vicinity of the old homestead. The remains of Martin and Esther lie, with several of their children, in a private and neglected spot on land now owned by William Hays in Washington Township.

Adam Bowser, born 1778, and wife, Catharine, born 1780, came to Armstrong County in 1808 and took up 400 acres of land near Centre Hill. Jonas, his brother, came at the same date and took up 200 acres.

Peter Bowser, son of Hopewell John, came in 1825. His sister, Catharine Kline, a widow, came at the same time. John and Nicholas, sons of John of Hopewell, remained at Hopewell; the descendants of Nicholas are still in Hopewell. The daughters of John all came to Armstrong County as follows: Mary, wife of John Burnheimer, in 1807; Julia Ann, wife of David Flenner, in 1807; Elizabeth, wife of Abraham Swigart, 1807; Barbary, wife of Joseph Bowser (son of Jacob, brother of Hopewell John), 1808; Catharine Kline, 1825.

CHAPTER IX

THE BOWSER REUNION

In the year 1900 the first Bowser Reunion was held at the home of Jacob and Sarah Ann (Bowser) Bucher, near Kittanning, Armstrong County, Pa. The Reunion has been held annually ever since, on the last Tuesday of August, with an attendance of 2,000 to 4,000. The forenoon is given over to reunions of families and the reviving of old friendships. For a number of years the aged family with whom the Reunion had its genesis occupied the seats of honor on the platform. They were Benjamin S. Bowser, Elizabeth Bowser, Sophia (Bowser) Wyant, Sarah Ann (Bowser) Bucher, Dr. M. S. Bowser, Joshua Crawford Bowser and James H. Bowser. At the time of this writing but four remain, Sophia (Bowser) Wyant, aged 94; Dr. M. S. Bowser, aged 84; Joshua C. Bowser, and James H. Bowser. Benjamin S. died, aged 92; Elizabeth, aged 82, and Sarah Ann (Bowser) Bucher, 86. Jacob Bucher, husband of Sarah Ann, is still living and hale at the age of 90. After the midday feast there has always been an appropriate program, consisting of music, solos, quartettes, an orchestra by the Bowser boys, songs from the Bowser Song Book prepared by Rev. A. B. Bowser; an obituary report, business, addresses and games. At present these reunions are held in the Armstrong Grove, near Kittanning. An account of these gatherings may be gained from a report taken from the Kittanning Daily Leader, which was accompanied by a number of pictures.

"The Great Bowser Reunion" (1906)

The Bowser Clan enjoy another reunion. Every section of Armstrong County represented and hundreds came from many other states.

There are reunions and reunions held in Armstrong County every year, but none of them have yet equaled, either in point of attendance or the general manifestation of friendliness, the prominence attained by the annual gathering of the great Bowser family, and the assembling of that clan with hundreds of their friends at the old homestead, near Walk Chalk, on Tuesday, was another demonstration of how popular these outings have become.

The weather was ideal. The sun shone forth in all its glory, but the warm rays were comfortably cooled by breezes, which seemed to bear both a tinge of the passing summer and the approaching fall, that swept over the beautiful old farm, and had man himself had the making of the day he could not have planned better.

The attendance was, as usual, large, and although there was no accurate way in which the exact size of the crowd could have been ascertained, it is estimated that the number present was close to two thousand, if that figure was not really surpassed. The throngs came from every direction and as early as 5 o'clock in the morning the procession to the grounds was under way and by noon the fields about the house were fairly black with people and vehicles of every description. Nearly every walk of life was represented in that immense assemblage, too. The minister, the lawyer, the doctor, the mechanic, the farmer, the musician, the educator, the manufacturer and the politician were all there and joined with the young and old, rich and poor, in making the day one of genuine delight.

Most of the morning was devoted to greeting old-time friends and preparing for the events that were programmed for the occasion. At 11 o'clock a short season of music and eloquence was opened on the platform which had been erected in the orchard. Everybody joined heartily in singing "When the Roll Is Called Up Yonder I'll Be There," and following this Rev. I. H. Hankins, of DuBois, sang a touching solo, after which the favorite hymn, "Jesus, Lover of My Soul," was sung by the crowd. An interesting talk on "The History of the Bowsers" was delivered by Rev. A. B. Bowser, of Crafton, in which he explained that the history of the Bowser family, which is now being carefully compiled, was not yet ready to be issued. "Honor Your Friends That Are Gone Before That They May Honor You," was the subject of an address filled with fine thoughts, beautifully expressed by Rev. I. H. Hankins, of DuBois.

At 12 o'clock the audience dispersed for dinner.

Prof. J. C. Tinsman, of Kittanning, made the principal address in the afternoon and his remarks held his hearers' closest attention and won their hearty applause. Rev. Hankins sang "The Laughing Song" so well that the audience demanded an encore, and Rev. Hankins, with Rev. A. B. Bowser, responded with a duet, "Box and Cox."

Business matters were taken up and it was decided to continue all the old officers for another year.

On account of death, however, there was a vacancy in the vice presidency, and Chambers Frick, of Adrain, was elected to that office. The officers of the reunion for the ensuing twelve months are therefore as follows:

Permanent President—Benj. S. Bowser, of Washington Township.

President—Rev. A. B. Bowser, of Crafton.

Vice President—Chambers Frick, of Adrian.

Secretary—J. H. Bowser, of Wickboro.

It was unanimously decided to hold the 1907 reunion at the old homestead again and the probabilities are that the gathering will continue to be held there for several years yet anyways, as the farm is in the heart of the Bowser settlement.

"God Be With You Till We Meet Again" was the concluding song, and Rev. Robert R. Bowser, of the Church of God, Bolivar, led in prayer, closing with the benediction.

The remainder of the afternoon was devoted to social intercourse and indulging in various amusements.

"Uncle Benny" Bowser was prominent everywhere. The homeward journey commenced about the middle of the afternoon, and by 6 o'clock very few persons were left on the grounds.

The best of order prevailed throughout the entire day and not a single unpleasant incident was reported. Many visitors from a distance were in the throngs, among whom were: R. M. Bowser, F. T. and Ella Bowser, of Olean, N. Y.; M. G. Bowser, of Chicora; Mrs. Adaline Schweeter, of New Kensington; Mrs. Kate Kramer, of Irwin; Rev. R. B. Bowser, of Bolivar; William Ekis, of Parkersburg, W. Va.; Levi Ekis, of Parkersburg, W. Va.; Levi Ekis, of Marietta, O.; Mrs. Fred Borling, Mrs. Lebius Russell, of New Kensington; Dr. A. H. Bowser, wife and daughter, of Reynoldsville; C. T. Bowser and wife, of Apollo; the Misses Hazel and Mabel Bowser, of Butler; Mrs. Grace Allbright, of Gibson City, Ill.; C. M. Fair and wife, of Verona; Charles Simpson, of Verona; Mrs. Libbie Hazlett, of McKeesport; Mrs. Samuel Cooper, of Pittsburgh; Mrs. Fred Whaling, of Pittsburgh; Prof. A. J. Bowser and wife, of Butler.

1917 Reunion

Tuesday, August 21, 1917, was the sixteenth annual anniversary of the Bowsers and it was held in the Armstrong Grove, about two and one-half miles from Kittanning, on the west side of the river, and from as early as 7 o'clock in the morning until the sun was kissing the hilltops in the western horizon the grove was a busy hum of voices.

The weather was fine, although a little threatening; what appeared to be a heavy rain went around to the south, about the time announcement for dinner was on, but the Bowsers and their friends were there to spend the day with each other and showed their devotion to Bowser day by staying right there and only a stray drop of rain fell within the confines of our beautiful grove. In a short time all were happy and greetings, so characteristic of Bowser day, continued merrily, for everybody is Bowser for the day. Visiting, meeting friends of others years, renewing acquaintances and forming new ones continued until dinner hour.

After the dinner was over and the faces were shaping up for the Bowser smile the program was called on.

After some introductory remarks by the President, Rev. A. B. Bowser, of Ford City, the assembly sang "My Country, 'Tis of Thee, Sweet Land of Liberty," etc., with Mrs. Bowser at the piano. Everybody sang; the large flag hanging over the platform waved in the breeze and the leaves rustled with joy. Rev. C. T. (Bowser) Jack offered prayer, then all joined in singing "Blest Be the Tie That Binds." A solo was sung by Harold (Bowser) Spang, of Leechburg, and the Treasurer, B. W. Wyant, gave his annual report, followed by an inspiring address.

Frank Bowser played a violin solo, "Poet and Peasant," accompanied by Mrs. W. A. Barry on the piano. J. H. Bowser gave the Secretary's report and in his pleasing manner said some very nice things about the Bowser reunions for the last sixteen years.

Miss Isabelle Bowser, a teacher in the Wilmerding schools, entertained with a beautiful solo, accompanied by her mother, Mrs. A. B. Bowser.

Several vocal selections were rendered by Corbin (Bowser) Wyant, Hyatt (Bowser) Hawk, Charles (Bowser) Smith, Harold (Bowser) Spang, Frank, Wayland and Arda Bowser, with Mrs. Barry at the piano. Then the Bowser Band played.

One thing noticeable at these annual gatherings is the dropping out one by one of the older people. A few years ago we could count about a dozen of the dear old ones, but there were only two of them there today—Jacob Booher, 89, and Sophia Bowser Wyant, in her 90th year.

The nominating committee reported as follows: President, J. H. Bowser, one of the founders of the Bowser Reunion and baby of the family, who has served as its secretary for sixteen years; Rev. A. B. Bowser—he is the historian and hopes to have the history of the family completed by the next anniversary; Treasurer, Chambers (Bowser) Frick; Secretary, Dr. J. B. (Bowser) Wyant, and they were duly elected.

The following are members of the executive committee: H. J. Bowser, M. L. Bowser, Emanuel Bowser, Chambers Frick, B. W. Wyant, William Bowser, A. B. Bowser, S. F. Bucher, C. G. Bowser, Roy Bowser, Jacob L. Bowser, A. J. Bowser and Dr. J. B. F. Wyant.

We Are Boys Again Today

By A. B. Bowser

(Tune—"Maryland, My Maryland.")

Behold! across the grassy plain,
With stately tread and princely train,
From fields afar and foreign shore
The Bowser boys come home once more.

Where Allegheny's waters flow
And noble elms their shadows throw,
We gather on the verdant strand
And clasp again a brother's hand.

'Neath alien skies we oft may roam,
And long for thee, our native home,
Dispersed abroad from east to west,
'Tis here the spot we love the best.

Although the years, on pinion light,
Have borne us swiftly in their flight,
We sing the old songs bright and gay,
For we are boys again today.

CHORUS

Oh! Armstrong County, ever dear!
We love thee through each passing year;
And fondly now our friendship true
Within thy bounds we pledge anew.

CHAPTER X

Wills

I. Joseph D. Bowser, of Franklin Township, March 5, 1845. Probated April 18, 1845. Children: John, Joseph, Sarah M. Swigart, Eunice M. Morrison, Noah, Samuel, Jonas, Peter, Elizabeth.
Witnesses:

Wm. Noble,
Geo. Rarach.

Valentine Bowser

II. Valentine Bowser, of Franklin Township, Armstrong County, Pennsylvania, do make and publish this my last will and testament, hereby revoking and making void all former wills by me heretofore made, as follows:

First: I direct that all my just debts be paid as soon after my decease as possible.

Second: I will and devise all my estate, real and personal, to my beloved wife, Elizabeth, to have use of and live on during her natural life without being accountable to any heir or any other person for such disposition as she may think fit to make of any personal estate.

Third: I will and direct that any part of my said estate that may be left at her decease after her just debts and funeral expenses be paid, to be sold and equally divided among my children or their lawful heirs, share and share alike.

Fourth: My second named executor shall not take any action on my said estate during the life of my said wife, Elizabeth.

Fifth: I do hereby make and ordain my beloved wife, Elizabeth (Fluke) Bowser, and my son, Abraham Bowser, executors of this my last will and testament in witness whereof, I, Valentine Bowser, the testator, have to this my will written on one sheet of paper set my hand and seal this ninth day of March, 1851. Signed, sealed and delivered in the presence of us who have hereunto subscribed in the presence of each other.

His
Valentine (X) Bowser.
mark

Wm. Noble,
Geo. Noble.

Probated March 15, 1852.

III. Valentine Bowser, Sugar Creek Township. In the name of God, Amen, ... I bequeath to my sons John and Samuel

Bowser and my daughters Cristina Bowser (Smail) and Margaret Bowser (Sites) ...... tract of land, etc., 1836. Joseph Bowser. I bequeath to (1) heirs of my son Moses Bowser the farm given to Moses. (2) Jonathan to have the farm he lives on. (3) James to have $1,000. (4) John, $1,000. (5) Catherine and Barbara the farm I now live on. (6) Grandson Joseph, $75.00. (7) Grandson Emanuel, $75.00.

Book, p. 278.

Probated January 28, 1792.

IV. 13th of March 1784 "I John Bowser of Washington County and State of Md., being sick, and weak in body"—I do order that my Exect' which I shall hereafter Name After my Decease, to sell and dispose of all my real and personal estate on Bublick Vandue and to give a Good a Lawfull Convayns for my real estate and then to Aquent or to inform my friends in Germanie thereof, that if my well beloved Brooder Jacob Bausser and my well beloved Sisters Barbara and Feronica in the Canton Bassel and County of Faspurg and village called Damiken or either of their heirs, and it is further my will that after my debts and funeral charges are paid, then I give and bequeathe to my well beloved Bruder or to his heirs, at first Fifty Pounds of good and lawful money of this State, and after I order that he or his heirs shall go in an equal sear with my two Sisters Barbara and Feronica or with their heirs after such discharge is made which I shall mentions. It is further my will and I give and bequeath to the reformed Prispetarianer Congregation in Hagerstown Fifty Pounds of good and lawful money for the use of finishing the meeting house or towards the Ball and said sum of money shall be paid by my Executor three years after my decease and it is further etc. gives to Executor one hundred Pounds for his trouble, order and constitute "Doct Henry Schnebely to be my Executor.

Wit. LAWRENCE PROTZMAN,
JOHN CRUMBACK,
WILLIAM CONRAD.

His
JOHN (X) BAUSSER.
mark

INVENTORY

1 large Bible 35/ 1 large history 20/ 1 large book 10/ 11 small old books 22/6 2 old books 6/ some pewter, 1 old cythe (the largest item)

2 stills both hold 190 gallons @ 41c a gallon		38.00
14½ bushels of rye @ 3/6		21.09
also Indian corn, oats, buckwheat "very sorry" wheat.		
1 old Syder mill.		
23 old still tubs	Total	83.1019

dated April 3, 1792.

V. Will of John Bowser of Hopewell Township, Bedford County, registered in Bedford, September 3, 1813. The last will and testament of John Bowser, of Hopewell Township, in the name of God, amen, I, John Bowser, in a weak state but sound in mind, in memory, having thought it proper to make a divide of my property: 1. All my lawful debts to be paid. I bequeath to my loving wife Mary three hundred dollars, one cow and bed and bedding and one pat one saddle. I bequeath to my son John ten pounds, I bequeath to my son Jacob ten pounds, I bequeath to my son Mathers (Mathias) ten pounds, I bequeath to my son Valentine ten pounds, I bequeath to my son Samuel ten pounds, I bequeath to my son Nicholas ten pounds, I bequeath to my son Peter ten pounds. I do request that my property be sold and equally divided between my sons before mentioned and my daughter Mary, and my daughter Elizabeth, and my daughter Catherine Kline and my daughter Uley (Julia Ann), and my daughter Barbara. I do appoint Theodoris Inorsberger and John Piper of Yellow Creek (Hopewell) my lawful executors. Signed and sealed this 19th day of June in the year of our Lord 1813 in the presence of John Kay and William Williams.

His
JOHN (X) BOWSER.
mark

VI. Will of Andrew Bowser, York County, B. U. 154. Andrew Bowser of Manheim Township. Mentions his wife Margaret—plantation in Manheim Township containing 254 acres of land. After said land is sold I bequeath $100 to my brother Adam Bowser (afterward in Armstrong County) and if any is left $91.81 to Andrew Bowser, son of Joseph Bowser; and if any remains equally divide between Adam Bowser's children and Joseph's children and Benjamin Bowser's children and Isaac Bowser's children.

His
ANDREW (X) BOWSER.
mark

VII. Benjamin Bowser's will. Son of Daniel, B. K. S. 394. Died April 18, 1844: I, Benjamin Bowser, devise, that my plantation, situated in Maryland, Baltimore County, shall be sold as soon as convenient after my death, the widow, Catherine B., shall have kitchen and house furniture, also two cows, if she choose: order that the remainder of my estate be sold at vendue and my son Benj. Bowser and son Samuel, late dwelling in Shrewsbury Township, York County, all my heirs shall share alike: Elizabeth M., Joseph Kaufman, George Bowser, Daniel Bowser, Catherine M., Peter Ulrich (went to Ohio), Benj. Bowser and Samuel Bowser and appoint Benj. Bowser and George Bowser sole executors. George Bowser died aged 85 in Stark County, Ohio, will probated 1873.

Daniel Bowser will dated 1878, Stark County, Ohio. Benjamin Bowser, Samuel Bowser, Catherine Bowser, Michael Ulrich, died at Wyandotte, Ohio, aged 85. Elizabeth, married Isaac Kaufman, died Morrow County, Ohio, aged 86. These children of Benjamin Bowser went before the Justice of the Peace in Stark County and Wyandotte, Ohio, and made an acknowledgment that they received their full share of Benjamin's estate.

His
BENJAMIN (X) BOWSER.
mark

VII. Will of Daniel Bowser, York County, B. K. L. 446, April 20, 1807. Wife Elizabeth Bowser. Children: Magdalena M., Nicholas Miller, Elizabeth M., Conrad Keppenheffer, Benj., Esther, Joseph, Mary, Isaac, Jonas, Solomon and Adam.

VIII. John Bowser St. Clair Township, Bedford County, B. K. L. 270. I, John Bowser, give my plantation and tract of land whereon I now live, containing 180 acres, to my son George, he paying thereout 670 pounds lawful money to my other children, Michael, Elizabeth m. to John Mack, Ann Elizabeth m., Henry Beckley, Eve m., John Arthurs 152 pounds, 10 shillings each, and 60 pounds to the children of my daughter Madalena Swoveland (except John). Geo. Imler, Ex. 1808. (This property John Bowser bought from Starcher. See deed.)

IX. Will of David Bowser, Bedford County Wills, Book 1, page 340. St. Clair Township. Date of probate, March 22, 1813. . . . Give and bequeath unto wife Elizabeth one-third of my real and personal estate during the time she remains my widow, no sale to be made of estate during the time she remains my widow; after her decease to be equally divided between my children, viz.: Catraut Bowser, Elizabeth Bowser, Mary Bowser, Catharine Bowser, Valentine Bowser, John Bowser, Easter Bowser, and my grandson John Mock. . . . Appoints James Clark, Sr., and William Clark, Esq., executors. "Set my hand and seal," 19th day of October, 1810.

His
DAVID (X) BOWSER.
mark

CHAPTER XI

BOWSERS WAR RECORD

Revolutionary War

The ancestors of the Bowsers sprang from the pioneers and founders of democracy.

History has recorded the influence of the far-visioned prophets of liberty, Oliver Cromwell, William of Orange, William Penn and Roger Williams; but the cradle of democracy was rather on the continent, among the Huguenots of France, the Mennonites of Switzerland and the Anabaptists of Germany. We can readily understand why the Palatine natives came to Pennsylvania in such predominating numbers. The "Holy Experiment" of the noble Penn found an echo in their souls. The Bowsers have always borne their full share in the various wars for liberty, and promptly marched to battle under the Stars and Stripes at the call of Washington and Lincoln and McKinley and Wilson. Many of them gave their lives and today repose in graves forever honored.

At the opening of the Revolution, 1775, able-bodied citizens of Pennsylvania formed themselves into military companies and were known as Associators. Five battalions were organized in York County. No complete muster is now known to be in existence. The 7th Battalion of York County Militia, organized under the state constitution of 1776, was commanded by David Kennedy, Colonel, with James Agnew, Lieutenant Colonel; John Means, Major; page 271, muster roll for this battalion, 1777-1778, privates: Jacob Bowser, Noah Bowser, Daniel Bowser, Abram Bowser.

Page 274—3d Co., 5th Battalion, 1780: Daniel Bowser, John Bowser.

Page 275—6th Co., 5th Battalion: Michael Bowser.

York County, Penn. Arch. 6th series, Vol. 2, a list of the 3d Co., 5th Battalion of York County Militia, October, 1780. Capt. Peter Zolinger, 5th class: Daniel Bowser. 7th class: Jacob Bowser. Returns of the 3d Co., Paradise Township, August 29, 1781-2: Jacob Bowser, Daniel Bowser, John Bowser.

Muster roll of the 7th Co., 7th Battalion, October, 1785. Capt. John Wampler: Christian Bowser, Jonnas (Jonas) Bowser.

Sixth Co., 1785. Capt. Andrew Former: Samuel Bowser.

Capt. Adam Shoffer's Co., 5th Battalion, York County Militia, private: John Bowser.

Muster roll, 1785, of Hanover Township, Capt. Simon Clear: Joseph Bowser.

Associators and Militia, Capt. Andrew Balley, privates: Michael Bowser.

Militia, 1782, David Jamison, Colonel: Henry Bowser.

Archives, 6th series, York County Militia, Camp Security, December 21, 1781: "This is to certify that Jacob Bowser has served his full time of duty agreeable to the law in the 7th class of York County Militia, under the command of Capt. Pennington, and is discharged by me, George Gyselman, Capt.

Associates and Militia of York County, Capt. Zahniger: Abram Bowser, Daniel Bowser, Noah Bowser, Jacob Bowser.

Penna. Archives, 6th series, Vol. 2. Associates and Militia, York County: "This is to certify that John Bowser, associate, has served in my company from May 4, 1782, to June 21, 1783." Peter Ford, Captain.

Penna. Archives 2d series, Vol. 1.

Associators and Militia: William Bowser.

Vol. 2, series 14, Bensalem Township, Associated Co.: Henry Bowser.

Sixth Battalion, Berks Co. Militia, 1780, Sergeant: Peter Bowser.

Page 666, Capt. Paxton's Ranging Co., Bedford Co., 1781, 3: Jacob Bowser.

1—William Bowser, ——————, 10th Pennsylvania.
2—Jacob Bowser, 1777-78, 7th Battalion, York County Militia.
3—Michael Bowser, about 1782, 5th Battalion, York County Militia.
4—Noah Bowser, 1777-78, 7th Battalion, York County Militia.
5—Abraham Bowser, 1777-78, 7th Battalion, York County Militia.
6—Daniel Bowser, 1781, 1777-78, 7th Battalion, York County Militia.
7—Peter Bowser, Ranger on Frontier, Northumberland County, 1778-83.
8—Andrew Bowser, 1777, 5th Battalion, Philadelphia Militia.
9—Christian Bowser, 1781, 7th Battalion, Lancaster County Militia.
10—Jonas Bowser, 1785, 7th Battalion, York County Militia.
11—Henry Bowser, 1783, York County Militia, Col. David Jamison.
12—Joseph Bowser, 1785, Hanover Co., York County Militia.
13—Samuel Bowser, 1785, 6th Co., York County Militia.
14—Joseph Bowser, 2d Lt., 1776, 3d Battalion, 7th Co., Northumberland County Militia.
15—John Bowser, 1781, 3d Co., Paradise Township, York County Militia.

Associators and Militia, York County: "This is to certify that John Bowser has served in my company from May 4, 1782, to June 21, 1783. Peter Ford, Captain."

Mathias Bowser, Jr., lived in Paradise Township, York County, and since Jacob, Samuel, Noah and Abram Bowser are recorded in the same township, they evidently were his sons.

Bowsers in the Civil War

Addison H. Bowser, 39th Ohio Inf., 2nd lieutenant.
Alex D. Bowser, 137th Pa., private.
Benjamin S. Bowser, 12th Ohio Vol. Cav., corporal.
Aaron J. Bowser, 103d Pa., private.
Daniel Bowser, 103d Pa., private.
Daniel L. Bowser, 55th Pa., private.
David Bowser (cousin of Daniel L.), 55th Pa., private.
Emanuel Bowser, 37th Pa., private.
Hezekiah Bowser (son of Noah and Catherine), 78th Pa., private.
James M. Bowser (son of Daniel and Hannah), 29th Ind., private.
Joshua Crawford Bowser, 103d Pa., musician.
Mark C. Bowser (son of Noah and Catherine), 78th Pa., private.
Mathias P. Bowser, 78th Pa., private.
Mathias A. Bowser, 78th Pa., private.
Nicholas Bowser, 55th Pa., private.
Peter O. Bowser, 78th Pa., sergeant.
John G. Bowser (son of Jacob and Rachel), 12th Ohio Vol. Cav., corporal.
John W. Bowser (son of Michael), 12th Ohio Inf., 2nd lieutenant.
Henry Bowser (son of Jacob of Ohio), 2d Calif. Cav., private.
Samuel A. Bowser, 104th Pa., 2nd lieutenant.
George and Wm. R. Bowser, of Michigan.
Eli, James and Christian Bowser, of Ohio.
John G. Bowser, 78th Pa., private.
Thomas H. Bowser, 62d Pa., corporal.
William H. Bowser (son of Jacob of Maryland), 12th Ill. Inf., 2nd lieutenant.
William J. Bowser, 78th Pa., private.
William Bowser, 78th Pa., private.
Washington R. Bowser, 78th Pa., private.
Alex M. Bowser (son of John), 139th Pa., private.
John R. Bowser, 139th Pa., private.
Jacob F. Bowser (son of John), 139th Pa., private.
John F. Bowser, 159th Pa., private.
Jeremiah Bowser, 76th Pa., private.
John W. Bowser (son of Henry and Emily of Kosciusko Co., Ind.), 74th Ind., private.
Adam Bowser, 12th Md. Inf., private.
Chas. W. Bowser (son of Adam of Maryland), 3d Reg't Potomac Home Brigade Inf., private.
Samuel Bowser (son of John and Elizabeth), 4th Ohio Vol. Cav., corporal.
Jacob Bowser (son of John and Elizabeth), 4th Ohio Vol. Cav., private.

Elwood Bowser (son of John and Elizabeth).
John W. Bowser (son of John and Elizabeth, born 1829), 187th Ohio Vol. Inf., private.
John Bowser, 195th Pa. Vol. Inf., private.
George W. Bowser, Co. F, 76th Reg't Pa. Vol. Inf., private.

—*From Chas. A. Bowser.*

Bowsers in the World War

Wayland Stanley Bowser, 1st lieutenant..................France
Frank Excell Bowser, sergeant....................Rahway, N. J.
Arda J. Bowser, marine aviation..................Boston, Mass.
Corbin Wayland Wyant, sailor.................New York City
Roy Frick Booher..................................France
Ford W. Frick....................................France
Orville Frick..............................Cape May, N. J.
William Clyde Bowser...............................France
Lewis Bowser ....Arizona
Sylvester Hyndman Smith...........................France
William Calvin Bowser......................Oglethorpe, Ga.
Hyatt Hawk ....France
Edward Gumbert ....France
Hollace Gumbert ....Georgia
Jay Finley Wyant..................................Georgia
Herman Schreckengost ....Georgia
William Arthur Bowser..............................France
Ralph John, buried on Bowser Day.
Edward E. Evans, captain.........................Pike, Ark.
Frederick Bowser ....France
Charles Bowser ....France
Paul Crytzer ....France
Wade Bailey Bowser.................................France
Orman Younkins ....France
Blair Toy ....Georgia
Kirneal Mechling ....Georgia
Clarence Bowser ....Georgia
Edgar Westlake ....France
Howard Westlake ....France
Clement Arthur Cox.................................France
Harry A. Bowser....................................France
William A. Bowser..................................France
Guilford C. Brown.........................Camp Lee, Va.
Eugene M. Brown....................................France
Mabel G. Hudson, nurse.............................France

Catharine Leone Bowser, nurse ....France
Paul Lawson Bowser...............................France
John Thoburn Beck.................................France
George H. Chappell................................France
Pressie M. Hooks..................................France
Harry L. Kegg.....................................France
William Thomas Bowser.............................France
Harry Ed. Bowser..........................Honolulu, H. I.
Casper Bowser ....Navy
Bryan B. Bowser, corporal.........................France
Henry A. Hudson, sergeant.........................France

Old Mechling Hotel, Kittanning, Pa.
By courtesy of the Kittanning Daily Leader-Times

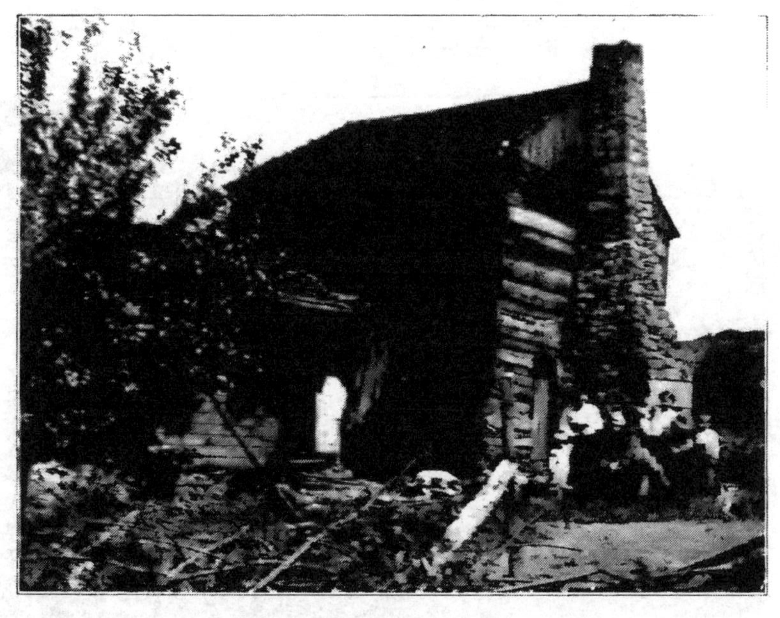

House Built by Martin John, 1808
Washington Township, Armstrong County, Pennsylvania

"NEXT STOP, HOPEWELL"

HOPEWELL, BEDFORD CO., PA.

GOOD ROADS IN BEDFORD CO., PA.
Between Reynoldsdale and Alum Bank

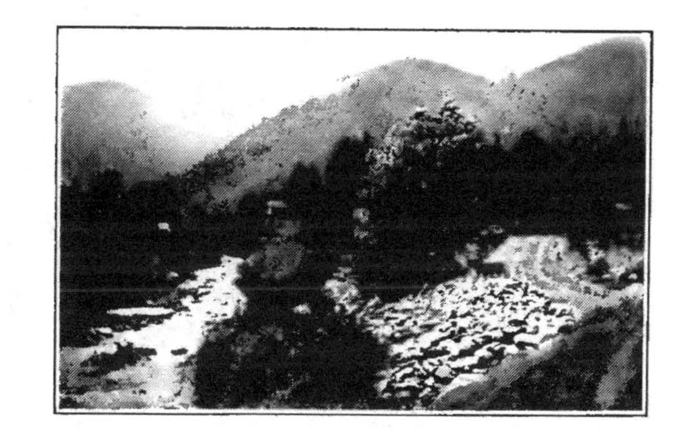

SCENE IN THE BLUE KNOB

To A. B. Bowser
with the salutations and good
wishes of a kinsman.
Warren G. Harding

The President

FLORENCE KLING HARDING

Doctor Andrew Robert Elmer Wyant

WARREN G. HARDING

In June, 1920, the news was flashed around the world that Harding and Coolidge were the nominees of the Republican convention for the presidency and vice-presidency of the United States. The fall election gave them the most overwhelming triumph in the history of the nation. Again the people asserted their confidence in the predominant type of an American president—a man born in the common ranks and elevated to greatness by his own efforts and the integrity of his character. His election for the supreme office of the country was not a chance or the accident of a political exigency. He stood a towering personality before the aspirants to the presidency. Like all famed men of history, like Lincoln and Grant, he was ready when the summons to duty called. Twenty years ago my father wrote me the prophecy: "Some day Warren will be president of the United States." President Warren G. Harding was born at Corsica, Morrow County, Ohio, November 2, 1865, son of Dr. George Tryon and Phoebe Elizabeth (Dickerson) Harding, grandson of Mary Ann (Crawford) and Charles A. Harding, and great-grandson of Sophia (Stevens) and Joshua Crawford, thus linking him with our Bowser family on the maternal side. Sophia Stevens was a sister of Mary Stevens, who married Abram Bowser. President Harding was educated in the public schools and the Ohio Central University at Iberia, Ohio. In 1871 Dr. Harding moved from Blooming Grove to Caledonia, and soon after started a country newspaper. Here Warren picked up a knowledge of typesetting and managing a newspaper, an important step in his career. In 1882 Dr. Harding moved again, this time to Marion, an enterprising, growing interior city now known over the world. Here the future President found his opportunity as reporter, manager, editor and publisher of the "Marion Star," now one of the most influential dailies in the state. He soon gained the attention of the political leaders of the state and was elected to the Ohio State Senate in 1900. In 1904-6 he was lieutenant governor and in 1914 he was elected to the Senate of the United States. At the National Republican Convention, 1912, he nominated President Taft for the presidency and in 1916 was chairman of the convention, and his address gave the keynote of the campaign. In 1891 he married Florence Kling of Marion, whose portrait appears wiith that of her famous husband, a woman whose intelligence and good judgment have been potential factors in his success. By her natural grace and kindliness, and like her husband "possessed of a preëminent gift of friend-making," she has gained more than applause—the esteem of all classes. President Harding came into office in a difficult time, in the after-sludge of the World war—stagnation, high prices, demoralized commerce and general moral breakdown. But he has fulfilled the pledges he made to the people and today stands in the full confidence of the nation—an humble, kindly, wise, Christian president of all the people. Aside from the constructive policies of his administration, now beginning to bring order out of chaos, the one inspired master move—his summoning the civilized nations to a conference on disarmament and its complete success—will be sufficient to make his fame immortal.

Hon. Adam Martin Wyant

ADAM MARTIN WYANT

Hon. Adam Martin Wyant (2299) was born on a farm near Montgomeryville, Armstrong County, Pennsylvania, September 15, 1869, a son of Christian Yerty and Elizabeth (John) Wyant. He was one of a family of six children whose parents provided for them the highest educational advantages. After finishing in the public school course, he taught one year prior to entering Reid Institute, Reidsburg, Clarion County, Pennsylvania, where he spent a year, and in the spring of 1889 entered the Western Pennsylvania Classical and Scientific Institute at Mount Pleasant, Pa., where he graduated in 1890. The three succeeding years he was at Bucknell University, but relinquished his work there to finish his course in the University of Chicago. He taught at the Mt. Pleasant Institute where he had previously been a student, during 1894-95, and was graduated at the University of Chicago, 1895, with the degree of A. B. While in the academy and college he won distinction throughout the country in the athletic field. He maintained a high rank in scholarship, taking the college entrance prize of $300, as well as the prize in oratory at Mount Pleasant. In 1896 he was elected principal of the public schools of Greensburg, Pa., and after serving two months as principal, a superintendency was created, and he was elected for two terms of three years each.

Having decided to follow the legal profession, he registered as a law student with Hon. Willis D. Patton of Kittanning, and J. M. Hunter of Pittsburgh, and during vacations prepared for admission to the bar. He was admitted to the Allegheny County Bar on December 21, 1901, and to the Westmoreland County Bar on May 5, 1902, and immediately took up his practice at Greensburg. He has been admitted to the practice of law in the Appellate courts of Pennsylvania and also the United States Federal courts.

In March, 1911, he formed a partnership with Hon. Edward E. Robbins, which continued until the death of Senator Robbins on January 25, 1919, and then formed a partnership with Paul J. Abraham, January 2, 1921, of which firm he is the senior member.

Shortly after his admission to the bar he began the manufacture of coke and the mining of coal, and at present is extensively engaged in the business, acting as secretary and treasurer for the several companies with which he is connected. He also has a large interest in several banking institutions in his county and serves as a director in the Safe Deposit and Trust Company, of Greensburg, Pa.

In 1920 he was a candidate for Congress in the Twenty-second District of Pennsylvania and was elected by the largest majority ever given a Republican for Congress from that district. In 1922 he received the nomination without opposition.

On December 1, 1909, he married Katharine Nelson Doty, daughter of Hon. Lucien Wilson Doty, judge for several terms of the Westmoreland County Common Pleas Court. They have two children: Anna Moore, born June 23, 1912, and Adam Martin, Jr., born September 1, 1917.

His record in Congress has confirmed the confidence of his constituents and justified his election to so exalted a position of responsibility in the nation.

Sheriff Chambers Frick

ANDREW ROBERT ELMER WYANT

Andrew Robert Elmer Wyant, A.B., A.M., B.D., Ph. D., M.D., son of Christian Y. and Elizabeth (John) Wyant, was born on his father's farm near Montgomeryville, Armstrong County, Pennsylvania, May 20, 1867. He acquired the rudiments of an education at the old Ruffner school, where the three R's were taught nearly a century ago. Heredity and wholesome hard work on the farm gave him a stalwart physique and proportionate stamina. He entered Reid Institute, with the writer as his chum, in April, 1880. While a student at Reidsburg he united with the Baptist Church, and was there licensed to preach. For four years he taught school, then returned to study at Bucknell Academy, from which he graduated in 1888. He entered Bucknell University in the fall of 1888 and graduated with the highest honors in 1892, taking scholarship prizes in literature, mathematics, oratory, psychology and philosophy; graduated from the Divinity School of the University of Chicago in 1895, with historical fellowship honors; received the degrees of master of arts and doctor of philosophy for post-graduate work; member of Phi Gamma Delta fraternity; college tennis champion; played football for seven years against colleges from the Atlantic to the Pacific, and was the first captain of the University of Chicago team. He gave the commencement oration at Bucknell, 1917, choosing as his subject "Football and Preparedness." While at Bucknell and Chicago he was student pastor, and was pastor of the Morgan Park Baptist Church, Chicago, and continued for over ten years during which period he received into membership 594 and erected a new edifice; edited the "Baptist Record" and author of "The English Reformation and Puritanism," based upon the lectures of his father-in-law, Dean Hulbert. Doctor Wyant went abroad in 1900 and witnessed the Passion Play. He has given more than 200 lectures on that religious drama. He belongs to the Masonic order. Doctor Wyant took the course in medicine at the Chicago College of Medicine and Surgery, graduating in 1908, and is now well known and successful in his profession. His articles on Modern, Mental and Religious Cults have attracted wide attention. He is a member of the American, Illinois and Chicago Medical Associations, Red Cross war physician; on Chicago hospital corps, and responds to calls for lectures and public addresses on religious and current subjects. Always a hard worker with a definite plan, he is an example and challenge to the boy on the farm, of what can be won by industry, native talent and perseverance. Doctor Wyant married Louise Hulbert, daughter of Dean Eri B. Hulbert, of the Divinity School of the University of Chicago. They have two children, Florence and Elizabeth.

WILLIAM H. BOWSER

William H. Bowser was born in Kittanning, Pa., February 16, 1857, a son of William Fluke and Margaret E. Bowser, grandson of Christian and Susana (Fluke) Bowser, great-grandson of Jacob Bowser, the oldest son of "Hopewell" John. Mr. Bowser was reared in Kittanning and has always lived there. He attended the public schools of North Buffalo Township and Kittanning, and Pritner's Academy. He has been a successful business man and conspicuous in the social and political affairs of the town and county. The people expressed their confidence in him by giving him a great majority in his election (1919) to the office of county commissioner. He married (1) Clara W. Moul of Allegheny, and (2) Ida B. Bowser of North Buffalo Township.

Sylvanus F. Bowser

SYLVANUS F. BOWSER

Mr. Bowser was born August 8, 1854, eight miles north of Fort Wayne, Ind. His father was John H. Bowser and his mother's maiden name was Eliza Kariger.

About three months of elementary instruction in the district school was the extent of his school experience. Later, however, self-instruction gave him some knowledge of primary arithmetic.

Chopping wood, delivering ice and other rough labor served as his introduction to the business of earning a livelihood. He traveled for some time as salesman for a paper house.

At the age of 31 (1885) he conceived the idea of a self-measuring pump for coal oil. With the aid of his brother and his nephew, Allen A. Bowser, he built the first device, and continued to build others from that time on. Likewise, he sold the products of the embryo shop, was its bookkeeper and general manager until the business was started and was its president for thirty-seven years. January 1, 1922, he was elected chairman of the board of directors.

The company which grew out of such a small beginning has branched out and expanded until today S. F. Bowser & Company, Inc., employs about twenty-five hundred people; has two subsidiary companies (S. F. Bowser Co., Ltd., Toronto, Canada, and S. F. Bowser & Co. of Texas, Dallas, Tex.); has a manufacturing plant at Milwaukee, Wis.; has warehouses in Albany, N. Y.; Dallas, Tex., and San Francisco, Calif.; tank assembly plants at Albany, Dallas, San Francisco and Sydney, Australia, and offices and salesmen in all of the principal cities of the world.

The company is valued at approximately ten million dollars, has a payroll of two and one-quarter million dollars per year and is enjoying steady growth and development.

As stated, Mr. Bowser is now chairman of the board of directors, and Allen A. Bowser, who helped start the business, and Harry M. Bowser, his son, are vice-presidents.

Mr. Bowser was married in 1877 to Sarah F. Russell and to this union six children were born: Harry, Eva, William Hugh, Albert, Verne and Mildred. Mr. Bowser is enjoying vigorous health in his sixty-eighth year and gives promise of many years more of active business life.

Doctor Mortimore Copsy Hawk

CHAMBERS FRICK

Sheriff Chambers Frick, son of Abraham and Delilah (Bowser) Frick, was born at Montgomeryville, Armstrong County, Pennsylvania, November 26, 1852. He is a sturdy type of the self-made man. The start of an education he received in the public schools. His broader, practical knowledge he has acquired by his own effort. He early learned the value of efficiency in whatever sphere he was placed. If he was set to a task with a bunch of men, he was soon their foreman. He has mastered several trades; kept store for many years; was justice of the peace, mine foreman, bank director, United States Labor Board official, and sheriff of Armstrong County, Pennsylvania. In 1871 he entered the employ of the Montecello Furnace Company, three miles north of Kittanning on the Allegheny River. One year later he was given charge of the company's coal mines and coke yards, with a daily "pot" of 4,000 bushels of coal, at that time the largest iron furnace in that part of the state. In 1878 he went to Dixonville, Pa., and opened a coal mine for his uncle, Dr. M. S. Bowser. In 1881 he opened a mercantile business in the village of Montgomeryville, Pa., and continued for twenty-five years until elected sheriff in 1906. At present he is a director of the Merchant's National Bank of Kittanning, president of the Limestone company, and conducts a wholesale and retail flour and feed store. He married Nancy Flenner, November 3, 1870. They have the following children: Mary Delilah, Ada Jane, Rose Lee, Lottie Belle, Lillian Helen, James H., Florence, Chambers F., and Rufus S. Chambers Frick is one of our executive committee and has served as treasurer and in various capacities. He has had a great interest in the publishing of this history, and it is in part to his effort the book could be printed promptly when it was ready.

ISAAC BOWSER

Professor Isaac Bowser, son of Benjamin and Elizabeth Bowser, was born November 23, 1841, near New Freedom, York County, Pennsylvania. Early in life he discovered a love of music in his soul and began to study its science, both vocal and instrumental. At the age of 18 he was teaching singing schools when not at work on his father's farm. A few years later he began instructing brass bands, and since that beginning he has had over 2,000 pupils under his instruction. At the age of 29 he bought a farm of 33 acres near the homestead and has resided there ever since. He married Anna Flory, daughter of Jacob H. and Mary Flory, of Canton, Ohio. Those who were at the Bowser Reunion (1921) will never forget the genial, bright-eyed man "from New Freedom, York County," apparently in middle life, who held them with his happy address and entertained them with a song.

MORTIMORE COPSY HAWK

Dr. Mortimore Copsy Hawk, son of John M. and Anna Elizabeth (Bowser) Hawk of Kittanning, Pa., was born January 11, 1873, at St. Petersburg, Clarion County, Pennsylvania, one of eighteen children, thirteen of whom are living. He was educated in the public schools, Kittanning Academy and Reid Institute, Reidsburg, Pa., and took his medical degree at the University of Pittsburgh, Pa., class of 1896. He married Pearl E. Strayer of Colorado. Doctor Hawk went to Chicago after his graduation from the university and located there, and has enjoyed a fine practice. Although enamored of his location, the lure of the scenes of his boyhood and love of his family draw him in repeated visits to his parents and friends in Armstrong County. His residence is at Blue Island, Ill.

Doctor Jay Crawford Booher

JAY CRAWFORD BOOHER

Dr. Jay Crawford Booher, son of Jacob and Sarah Ann (Bowser) Booher, was born on his father's farm in Washington Township, Armstrong County, Pennsylvania, March 20, 1867. He is one of nine children, four sons and five daughters. (See picture group.) Doctor Booher began his education in the public schools in Armstrong County, later becoming a student in Reid Institute and Clarion State Normal School, Clarion, Pa., and preparing for his profession in the medical department of the Western University of Pennsylvania, which he entered in 1889, and was graduated in 1892. Immediately after his graduation he located at Falls Creek, Pa., and since has enjoyed an extensive practice, his talents and culture having gained for him an honorable position in the medical fraternity. Shortly after Doctor Booher located at Falls Creek there appeared a disease among the workers of the tanneries that baffled the older physicians. Four cases died in a few days, and Doctor Booher made the diagnosis as anthrax, which proved to be correct. Under his treatment the patients began to recover. Since then he has treated more than a thousand cases and only lost four. His fame as specialist in anthrax has spread throughout the United States. He is consulted in the largest hospitals in the country and his success in treating this dread disease has not been surpassed in the history of medicine. He has given special attention to the schools of his town and has been instrumental in making many improvements. He is a member of the Jefferson County Medical Society, American Medical Association and the Pennsylvania State Medical Society, the Pennsylvania Railroad Surgeon's Association; also consulting surgeon to the Adrian Hospital, Punxsutawney, Pa.; Central Leather Company, New York; staff surgeon of the Maple Avenue Hospital, Dubois, Pa., and surgeon for the Pennsylvania Railroad Co. He is also an enthusiastic adherent of the Masonic fraternity, being a member of Garfield Lodge No. 559 of Dubois, Pa.; Jefferson Royal Arch Chapter No. 25 of Brookville; charter member Bethany Commandery No. 83 of Dubois; charter member of Williamsport Consistory, Acacia Club, and a charter member of Jaffa Temple, A. A. O. N. M. S. of Altoona. He prizes a jewel (25 year) presented by the Falls Creek Lodge No. 957, I. O. O. F. In college days he won great fame as an all-round athlete. He won the football team immediately upon entering the university and remained with the team during his full course. He also was in the champion class in wrestling, boxing and broad-jump. For a number of years he has been engaged in raising the best bred pacers and trotters. His horses and trained bird dogs and gun provide him the diversions he most enjoys. Doctor Booher married Sara Jane Carrier, daughter of J. E. Carrier, a prominent business man of Falls Creek. He has a daughter, Sara.

DALLAS D. BOWSER

Dallas D. Bowser, son of Mathias Bowser of Manor Township, Armstrong County, Pennsylvania, was born February 20, 1857. Like all his brothers and sisters, he received a good education and specialized in agriculture and stock-raising. He was recognized as the most extensive breeder of fine horses in the county. After suffering great financial losses through incendiary fires, he moved to Warren, Ohio, where he continued the same business until recently. He married Mary Myrtle Kettering and has two children, Mary, born November 12, 1892, and Casper Findley, born August 14, 1894. Casper married Katharine Portevus. They have one child, Elizabeth Jean, born October 31, 1920. Casper and Mary attended the country schools, later the schools of Warren, Ohio. After their graduation from the high school, Mary took a course in the University of Chicago. Casper enlisted in the navy May, 1917, and was in active service until discharged in July, 1919.

S. F. Booher

SAMUEL FURMAN BOOHER

Sheriff Samuel F. Booher is a native of Armstrong County, Pennsylvania, and a descendant of Bartholomew Bucher, an emigrant from Switzerland, who owned considerable land in Frederick County, Maryland, and died there. His will is recorded in Frederick County. He had at least three sons, Bartholomew, Jr., Peter and Mathias Bucher. Bartholomew, Jr., and Mathias received land in Bedford County, Pennsylvania, by their father's will, October 21, 1791. Deeds to this land are recorded in the court house at Bedford. This tract was surveyed in 1767 and contained 317 acres, and was purchased by Bartholomew in 1777. Bartholomew, Jr., lives on his half of the above land near Bedford. He had the following children: Frederick, Elizabeth, Christina, Catharine, Juliana. They received by his will, dated October 26, 1822, 541 acres—Elizabeth 137 acres, the others 96 each. Frederich Bucher married Elizabeth Wyant. In 1830 he sold his two farms at Everett, Bedford County, Pennsylvania, and moved to Armstrong County near Montgomeryville. Frederich Bucher was the grandfather of the subject of this sketch. (See Dr. J. C. Booher.) Samuel F. Booher has attained a commanding position in Armstrong County and in the state, a position he has gained by his own efforts and intelligence. He began as a farmer and storekeeper at Sherrett, Pa. He was elected sheriff of Armstrong County in 1894, and county treasurer in 1902. He was twice county chairman of the Armstrong County Republican organization, and two terms postmaster at Kittanning, being reappointed the second term by President Taft. He has been engaged in stockraising and has bred some of the fastest horses in the state. He has erected and owns the most valuable apartment houses in Kittanning. Besides his town properties he owns a tract of more than 700 acres of land near the place where he was reared in Washington Township. He married (1) Sarah Titley, daughter of Walter Titley of Sherrett, Pa., and (2) Demps Beighley, daughter of Samuel J. and Hannah (Rowe) Beighley, of Vandergrift, Pa.

Martin Luther Bowser

MARTIN LUTHER BOWSER

Martin Luther Bowser, son of Martin L. and Nancy (McGinnis) Bowser, and a grandson of Mathias Bowser (133), was born at Woodsfield, Monroe County, Ohio, June 26, 1859. Mathias Bowser, son of "Hopewell" John Bowser, was the first of John's children to move to Armstrong County, in 1798, and purchased land now incorporated in the town of Kittanning. Martin L. Bowser, son of Mathias, and father of Martin L., was born in 1814, and died in 1888. He was given a medical education but never practiced, his inclinations leading him to agriculture and lumbering. For several years he lived in Ohio, then moved to Pike County, W. Va. Martin L., the subject of this sketch, attended the public schools of his section and later taught school in Tyler and Wetzel counties, W. Va. In 1886 he went to Pittsburgh, where he was employed as a clerk. After two years he took up similar work with A. Grow in a general store at Fairview, Butler County, Pa., remaining two years. Another period of two years were spent in the store business at Duke Centre, Pa. On May 31, 1890, he married Edith Krotzer, who died June 24, 1897, daughter of David Krotzer of Smethport, Pa. In 1890 he located in Butler, Pa., where he was engaged in the grocery and bakery business for two and a half years; in 1893 he returned to Pittsburgh and became a salesman in the large shoe house of W. M. Laird and remained for two years. By this time he had learned many business details necessary for successful merchandising, especially in the shoe business, and in 1895 he came to Kittanning, where he settled permanently and opened a shoe store of his own in the most desirable location on Market street. He was eminently successful and four years ago erected a large buff brick building on the opposite side of the street, where he is now located in the largest shoe store between Pittsburgh and Buffalo, doing both wholesale and retail business. There were two children by his first marriage: Winnifred L., m. James A. Gault, II, and Cecil Edith, m. John P. Roberts. On August 1, 1899, he married Mary M. Krotzer. They have had three children: Elizabeth C., Jeane Rebecca, and Martin Kenneth.

His residence at Applewold, just across the river from Kittanning, formerly the property of Hon. Calvin Rayburn, is attractive both in architecture and its location. Mr. Bowser and his family are active members of the Presbyterian church of Kittanning.

Bowser Reunion Executive Committee, 1918

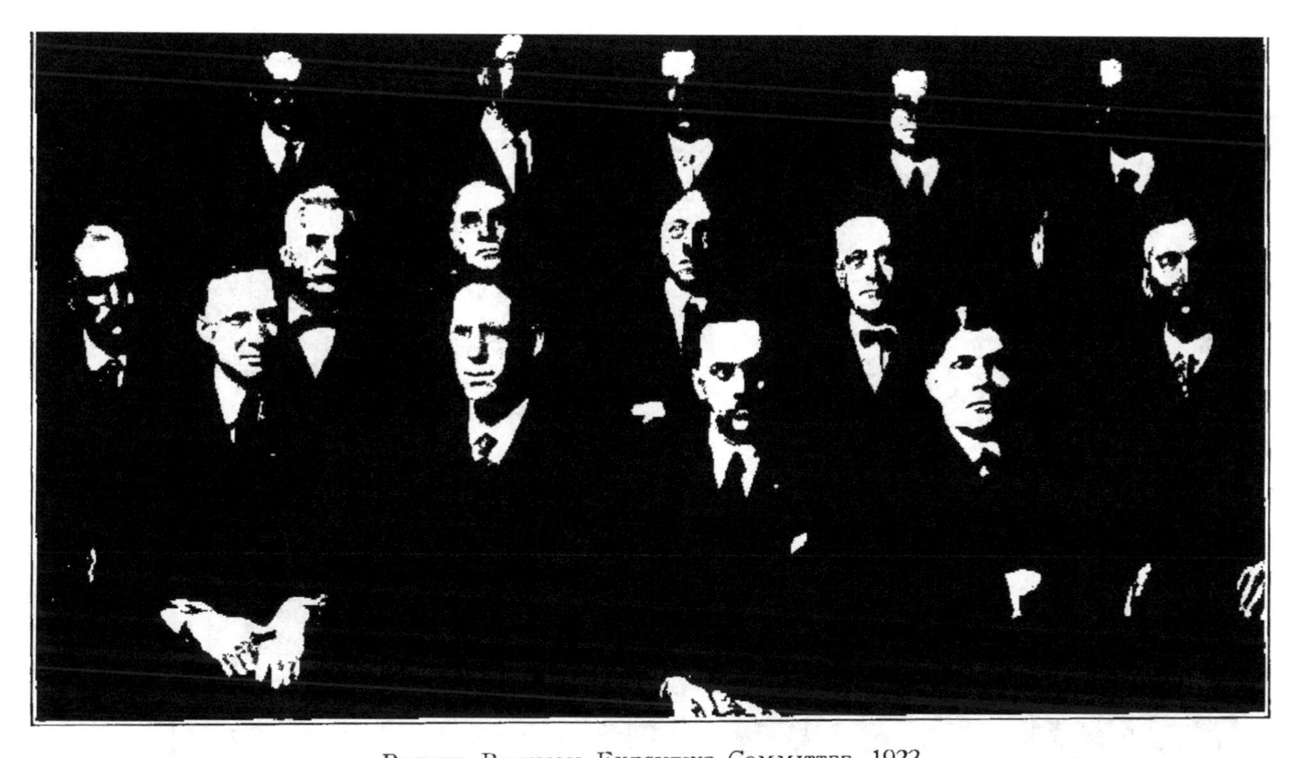

Bowser Reunion Executive Committee, 1922

Top row, left to right—Lee Toy, B. W. Wyant, Dr. J. B. F. Wyant, M. L. Bowser, H. S. Bowser.
Middle row—Miller Bowser, Chambers Frick, J. H. Bowser, A. B. Bowser, Amos T. Fair, C. Y. Bowser
Lower row—Mervin C. Hawk, Abram Wolfe, Dr. E. C. Winters, H. H. Claypoole

Jacob and Sarah Ann (Bowser) Booher Family

JACOB AND SARAH ANN (BOWSER) BOOHER FAMILY

Sarah Ann Bowser, daughter of Abram and Mary (Stevens) Bowser, was born near Walk Chalk, Pa., August, 1830, and died March 2, 1916. She married Jacob Booher, son of Frederick and Christina (Wyant) Booher, born September, 1830. Shortly after their marriage, Mr. Booher bought the Reed farm in Washington Township, Armstrong County, Pennsylvania. After a residence there of about five years he purchased the Simon Fair farm near Sherrett, Pa., which he still owns. On this farm, Mr. and Mrs. Booher reared their family of eleven children, eight of whom are living. By the intelligent methods applied to the land upon which they lived, and extensive stock raising, their farm became conspicuous in the county. They were industrious, hospitable to all their friends, and, like all of their children, members of the Baptist church. Mr. Booher is still living at the advanced age of ninety-two, and, except failing sight, has all his faculties perfectly preserved. They had the following children: Abram, Mary Catharine, Evaline, Melissa Jane, Samuel Furman, Frederick F. B., Leah Amanda, Rosanah, Joshua Crawford, Sophia Elizabeth and Lydia Ann.

CHARLES A. BOWSER

Charles A. Bowser is the son of William W. and Nettie (Tague) Bowser. His father was born in Indiana in 1849, a son of Daniel Bowser, born in Somerset County, Pennsylvania, in 1812. Charles A. was educated in the Kansas State Normal school and the University of Southern California. He married Alice M. McMinn, a descendant of the Lancaster County, Pennsylvania, McMinns. Mr. Bowser has spent several years, starting in 1902, in collecting data for a complete "Genealogy of the Bowser Family." He has traveled extensively and visited many states in his quest for Bowser records, especially of York and Somerset counties of Pennsylvania, and of Maryland, Ohio and Indiana Bowsers. The writer of this work received valuable assistance from him and was pleased to give such information as he could in return. In May, 1922, Mr. and Mrs. Bowser moved from Pittsburgh to Los Angeles, where he will go into business.

John M. and Eliza Ann (Bowser) Hawk Family

RIED FRAMPTON SHIELDS

Rev. Ried Frampton Shields (147), son of Emma Margaret (Bowser) and Samuel Frampton Shields, was born at Allerton, Iowa, March 1, 1893. He attended the public schools of this city, graduating from the high school in 1908. He took a secretarial course in the Capital City College, Des Moines, graduating in 1909, and entered Tarkio College, Tarkio Missouri, in 1910, where he graduated with the B. S. degree in 1914. He then took up his theological studies in the theological seminary of his church at Pittsburgh, graduating in 1917, and was ordained in June of that year by the Des Moines Presbytery of the United Presbyterian Church as a missionary to the Anglo-Egyptian Sudan. He sailed for his station in October, 1917, and has been located since that time at Omdurman, the old Dervish capital, and has been director of the American mission schools in the Sudan. He is now on furlough at his home in Allerton, Iowa, where his mother lives.

JOHN M. AND ANN ELIZA (BOWSER) HAWK FAMILY

John M. Hawk, a great-grandson of Esther (Bowser) John, was born August 6, 1848. He married Ann Eliza, a daughter of Benjamin S. and Elizabeth (Yerty) Bowser, born November 18, 1848. Mr. Hawk spent his early life on a farm in the great pine timber belt of Indiana County, Pennsylvania, five miles from Punxsutawney. His father was both farmer and lumberman, having a large saw mill on his place, and his boys all became expert woodmen. After his marriage Mr. Hawk settled in the Armstrong and Clarion County oil fields and worked at his trade, that of carpenter, changing locations as the oil booms shifted. About 1875 he bought a farm near Montgomeryville, Pa., where he lived for several years, later removing to a house he built on the west bank of the Allegheny River near Kittanning, where he now lives. Mr. Hawk is a well-known contractor and builder, erecting buildings of every size and for every purpose; remarkably vigorous, quick in judgment and a speedy workman. Mr. and Mrs. Hawk have had sixteen children: Benjamin S., Dr. Mortimore C., Jennie Roduska, Hattie May, William E., Flossie Ora, Elizabeth Lee, John Herbert, Rachel C., Grace A., Mervin C., Mildred Florence, Annalee, David Boggs, Hyatt L. The worthy parents of this great family are esteemed members of the First Baptist Church of Kittanning, where he holds the office of senior deacon.

GEORGE B. BOWSER

George B. Bowser was born March 22, 1868, near Montgomeryville, Armstrong County, Pennsylvania, son of J. Crawford and Kisiah Bowser. Went to Jefferson County in 1878. After a course in the country school he engaged in mining till 1895, when he embarked in the mercantile business at Rathmel, Pa., which has been his vocation up to this time. He was appointed postmaster in 1897, and served in that capacity till 1913. Mr. Bowser belongs to the following lodges: F. & A. M. No. 536: I. O. O. F.; K. of P. He married Jennie McIntosh, daughter of Mr. and Mrs. Alexander McIntosh of Rathmel, Pa., December 19, 1900. They have five children: Ralph, died August 20, 1905; George, died March 16, 1915; Belva, senior in Reynoldsville high school; Helen, freshman in Reynoldsville high school; Alexander, now in the public school at Rathmel. He and his family are members of the Presbyterian Church of Reynoldsville.

George and Delilah (Wyant) Boylestein Family

GEORGE AND DELILAH (WYANT) BOYLESTEIN FAMILY

George Boylestein came from Germany when a young man and learned the trade of cabinetmaker. He married Delilah, daughter of Adam and Sophia (Bowser) Wyant. They lived first at Montgomeryville, Pa., and later at Ford City and Kittanning, Pa. Characteristic of German thoroughness, Mr. Boylestein became exceptionally proficient at his trade and held a responsible position in the great Pittsburgh Plate Glass Company at Ford City. They had the following children: Archibald, married Elizabeth Serene; George L., married Kate Hanes; Elizabeth, married J. B. Greer; Katharyn, married William Gess; Sarah, married J. C. Douglas; Daisy, married George Edward Hanley; Sophia, died young.

G. W. W. AMICK

Rev. G. W. W. Amick, son of George B. and Mary (Hinsling) Amick, and grandson of Peter and Eve (Bowser) Amick, was born at St. Clairsville, Pa., the home of the Amicks, April 16, 1861; attended the public schools, graduated at Gettysburg, 1883, as one of the honor men, and from the theological seminary, 1887. He was professor and taught for several years at Selinsgrove, Pa., and then went into the ministerial labors, beginning at Johnstown, Pa., where he established the Trinity Lutheran Church. He remained with this congregation ten years and then became a missionary of the Lutheran Home Mission Society in Kansas and Iowa; served as pastor four years in New York state, "and now," he writes, "I expect to spend the rest of my days in my native state of Pennsylvania." He is now pastor of the Brick Church (Lutheran) near Kittanning, Pa. He married twice: (1) Florence Philips, and (2) Virgie Walters, and has two children, Arthur Park and Walter.

William and Catharine (John) Hays Family

WILLIAM AND CATHARINE (JOHN) HAYS AND FAMILY

William Hays, son of William Hays II, was born in Donegal County, Ireland, and came to this country with his parents when 16 years of age, and immediately took a position with the American Furnace Co., at Rimerton, Pa. In July, 1861, he enlisted in the army with Co. E, 62d Reg., Penn. Vol., and served three years. He was in the battle of Gettysburg and the other battles fought by his regiment. On his return from the war he married Catharine John and bought the homestead of her grandfather, Peter John, where he spent the remainder of his life. He was twice elected auditor of Armstrong County; member of the John Foster G. A. R. Post; Activity Lodge of I. O. O. F., and Grange No. 593, P. of H. Mr. and Mrs. Hays had sixteen children, all of whom except two lived to grow to manhood and womanhood. They were given the example by their parents of an inflexible code of honor and integrity. The group picture shows William and Catharine Hays in the center, the scenes of the childhood of Mrs. Hays are in view. A corner of the old loghouse built by her grandfather Peter John nearly a hundred years ago can be seen. The children then living are grouped there at their doorway, with little apprehension of the fate which overtakes united households. That picture is today chiefly a memorial, for only about one-half of the persons present there are now living. After the death of Mr. Hays in 1908 his widow made her home with her daughter, Mrs. Ruth Crisman, at West Kittanning, until her death in 1918.

JOSHUA CRAWFORD BOWSER

Joshua Crawford Bowser, son of Abram and Mary (Stevens) Bowser, was born in 1846 near Walk Chalk, Pa. His boyhood was spent on his father's farm until his fourteenth year, when he slipped to the recruiting station at Kittanning and offered himself to his country. His widowed mother brought him home. That night the embryonic soldier crept out of the window and started for Kittanning. After following the company to the South he was accepted as a real soldier and enrolled with Co. D, 103d Regt., Penna. Vol., to serve three years; musician, August 30, 1862; discharged at Pittsburgh, June 2, 1865. In subsequent years he has had an aversion to talk "war," but one experience he has dared to tell—that when he was captured and sent to Andersonville Prison he weighed 180, and weighed 80 when he got out and was two years in the invalid corps as a consequence. He married Kiziah, daughter of Jacob and Mary (Moore) Bowser. They had three children: Ulysses Selby; George B., and Maud B. Mr. Bowser is now retired and lives at Columbus, Ohio.

Doctor Ira D. Bowser

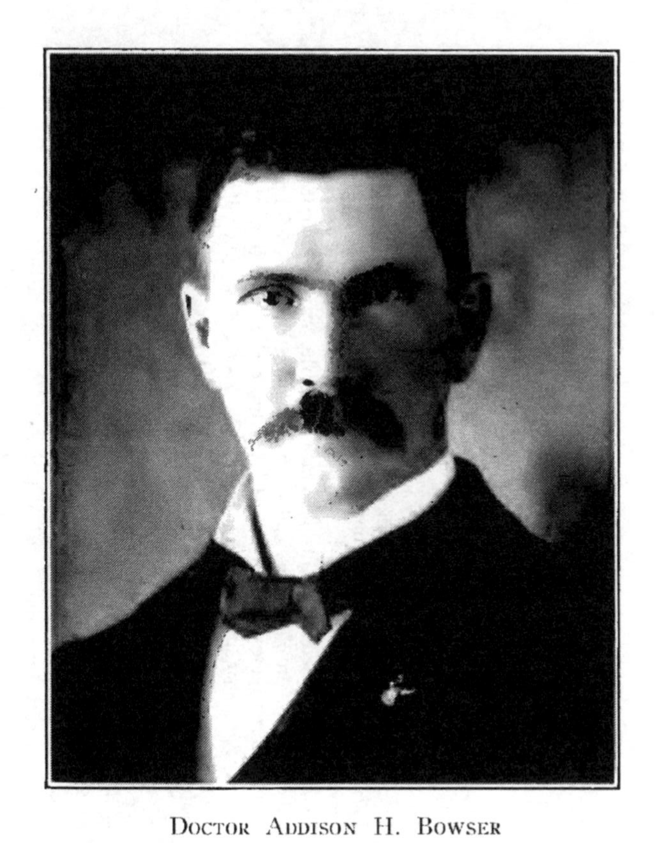

Doctor Addison H. Bowser

ADDISON HARVEY BOWSER

Dr. Addison Harvey Bowser was born near Walk Chalk, Armstrong County, Pennsylvania, February 18, 1862. He was a son of David S. and Lydia (McCollum) Bowser. Dr. Bowser acquired his education in the public schools and Reid Institute, Clarion County, Pennsylvania. He entered the medical department of the Western Reserve University, Cleveland, Ohio, and was graduated February 25, 1885. He began the practice of his profession in Venango County, Pa. After five years he located permanently at Reynoldsville, Pa., and built up a substantial general practice, which continued until his death in 1914. He was an active and devoted member of the Baptist church, serving as president of the board of trustees; member of the school board of his town, president of the Jefferson County Medical Society, and member of the Pennsylvania and American Medical Societies, and also affiliated with the I. O. O. F. Doctor Bowser married Sara Hannah Booth, daughter of Rev. Jacob Booth, a Baptist minister. They had three children: Dr. Ira D., Bertha E. and Addison W.

IRA D. BOWSER

Dr. Ira D. Bowser, son of Dr. Addison H. annd Sara Hannah (Booth) Bowser, was born in Clarion County, Pennsylvania, November 29, 1883. He was educated in the public schools and graduated from the high school of Reynoldsville, Pa. He early became attracted to the profession in which his father had won signal honor and success and accomplished this ambition by entering the medical department of the University of Pittsburgh, graduating there with the class of 1906. For six years he followed his profession at Rathmel, Jefferson County, Pa., then moved to Reynoldsville, and became associated with his honored facher. After the death of his father he assumed the latter's practice and his recognized ability enabled him to retain his father's former patrons and to extend his practice to even broader limits. He is a close student and brings to his work the most approved and modern methods both in medicine and surgery. The doctor is identified with the following organizations besides being an active member and trustee of the Baptist church, the Jefferson County Medical Society, Pennsylvania State Medical Society, and the American Medical Association, the Independent Order of Odd Fellows, Knights of Pythias, Patriotic Sons of America and the Independent Order of Red Men. Politically, he is a staunch Republican and is affiliated with all local social and educational interests, now serving as a director of the school board. In 1902 he was married to Laura E. Wheeler, daughter of David Wheeler, a representative farmer of Jefferson County. They have six children: Albrey; Sara H., now a student at Beaver College; Martha Jane; Mary Katheryn; Alma Esther and Ira David, Jr.

WILLIAM R. BOWSER

William R. Bowser, son of Frederick R. and Elizabeth F. Bowser, was born on his father's farm in Washington Township, Armstrong County, Pennsylvania, April 4, 1859. He devoted his life until recently to the farm. He attended the public school in his neighborhood and worked on the farm till he was grown up. For a short period he worked for his brother-in-law, Amos T. Fair, at the carpenter trade. He married Martha J. Campbelle, March 4, 1879. They had one daughter, Gertrude, married to Leroy Bargerstock, and three grandchildren: Ralph, Harland and Helen. Shortly after his marriage William R. settled on a farm at Cowansville, Pa., where he remained until recently, when he erected a fine residence near the village where he now lives.

Children of Abram and Mary (Stevens) Bowser, Founders of the Bowser Reunion

ARDA JOSHUA AND NELLIE (CRAFTS) BOWSER

Rev. Arda J. Bowser was born at Rural Valley, Pa., in 1868, son of Rev. M. S. and Elizabeth (Booher) Bowser. He attended the public schools of Indiana and Butler counties and finished his education at Dennison University, Granville, Ohio, and Crozer Theological Seminary, Upland. Pa. After his graduation from the seminary he took charge of the Baptist church, Reedsboro, Vt., where he was ordained. He has served with much success also the churches of Saltsburgh and Bellwood, Pa., Vincennes, Vt., Windsor, Vt., and is now pastor of the First Baptist Church of Delaware, Ohio. He married Nellie May Crafts of St. Marys, Ohio, who has been a valued helper and sympathizer in his ministry. She was educated in the city schools of St. Marys. They have had two children, Harry Addison, born in 1890, and Erma Elizabeth, born 1892, died in 1893.

Armstrong County Trust Company, Kittanning, Pa.

ARMSTRONG COUNTY TRUST COMPANY

The Armstrong County Trust Company was incorporated in 1902 with a paid in capital of $125,000.00 which was afterwards increased to $150,000.00. The growth of the Armstrong County Trust Company has been marvelous as at the present time its total assets amount to over four and one-half million dollars ($4,500,000.00) and besides being the largest bank in Armstrong County it is considered one of the strongest banks in the state. A bank is considered as strong as its board of directors and the personnel of this bank's board consists of many of our leading business men, namely, Harry R. Gault, O. W. Gilpin, J. R. Einstein, D. B. Heiner, S. H. McCain, Dwight C. Morgan, Floy C. Jones, W. A. Louden and H. G. Gates.

The Armstrong County Trust Company pays 4 per cent. interest on savings accounts, acts as executor, administrator, guardian, etc.

The active executive of the Armstrong County Trust Company for the past seventeen years is Mr. Herbert G. Gates, who has devoted his entire time in making this bank a strong, safe bank where service is the motto.

Elizabeth (Fluke) Bowser

Mary (Stevens) Bowser

ELIZABETH (FLUKE) BOWSER

Elizabeth Fluke was the oldest child of John Fluke, who moved from the eastern section of the state to Bedford County, Pennsylvania, and settled at Hopewell, where we found many of his descendants (1921). She married Valentine Bowser, son of John Bowser, frequently mentioned in this history as "Hopewell" John. In 1815 they moved to Armstrong County, Pennsylvania, and settled on a 50-acre farm near Walk Chalk, now known as the Dougherty farm. They spoke only the Palatine German language. Elizabeth was born in 1782 and died at the home of her daughter Margaret, wife of Jonas Bowser, in Washington Township, Armstrong County, Pennsylvania, at the age of 97.

MARY (STEVENS) BOWSER

Mary Stevens, daughter of Benjamin and Sarah Ann Stevens, was born October 5, 1805. While the Stevens family were living at Beaver Falls, Pa., Mary, in company with another girl friend, visited the vicinity of Walk Chalk, a place that had become the center of a large Bowser settlement. She was but fifteen years of age but she met her destiny in the person of Abram Bowser, son of Valentine and Elizabeth (Fluke) Bowser. He returned with her to the Stevens home in Beaver Falls and finally won her parents' consent to marry the young lady. Abram Bowser was an industrious and upright man and soon became a well-to-do farmer as well as a successful stone mason. Mary Stevens was the sort of wife for a man of ambition and a Christian character. She intensified his ambition and steadied and inspired his religious life. The writer is glad to acknowledge with reverence his father was one of the children of this talented and devoted Christian woman and sturdy, Godfearing nobleman. She was 15 years of age when she was married and Abram was eighteen. He was killed in 1852 by the fall of a tree. She eventually married John P. Davis and thereafter lived at Montgomeryville, where her body now rests surrounded by many of her beloved.

William R. Bowser

George B. Bowser

JOHN F. BOWSER

John F. Bowser, son of Rebecca (Swigart) and Mathias Bowser, was born near Kittanning, Pa., September 5, 1867. He was educated in the public schools and Reid Institute, Reidsburg, Pa. For twenty-five years he has followed a mercantile business. For four years he was an employee of the Buffalo, Rochester and Pittsburgh Railroad Coal Company's store at Rathmel, Pa.; for seventeen years he was manager of the L. W. Hicks Coal Company's store at Avonmore, Pa., and for the last five years, owner and manager of a general store at Summerville, Pa. For twenty-three years he and his wife have been active members of the Presbyterian Church; in Avonmore and at Summerville he has held the trusted position of a "ruling elder." His two children, Louisa and Daniel, are also active members of the church of their parents. Mr. Bowser is active in all local affairs and at present burgess of Summerville.

READY FOR THE BOWSER REUNION

From left to right: ADDISON B. BOWSER, PROF. ISAAC BOWSER, MR. and MRS. JACOB C. BOWSER, and daughters, MARCIA and KATHLYN.

HENRY P. BOWSER, center, JOHN FLUKE, his son-in-law, at left, are standing on the burial place of John Bowser, Hopewell, Pa.

HIRAM F. BOWSER

HIRAM F. BOWSER

Hiram F. Bowser was born near Kittanning, Pa., September 29, 1874. son of Lewis and Eva (Snowden) Bowser. He attended the public schools until early young manhood, when he went into business. He went to Blairsville, Pa., and established a general store, and is today one of the leading merchants of the place. On June 10, 1903, he was married to Pearl A. Cribbs, a popular young woman of Blairsville. Mr. Bowser has been much interested in our Bowser history. His grandfather, Peter Bowser, was six weeks old when brought by his parents, Valentine and Elizabeth (Fluke) Bowser, to Armstrong County, Pa.

JAMES QUINTER BOWSER

James Quinter Bowser, son of Jacob and Margaret (Claar) Bowser, was born on the foothills of the Allegheny Mountains in Union Township, Bedford County, Pennsylvania, September 29, 1856. Born of poor parentage he had to make his own way in life when quite young, and among strangers. When about fourteen years of age he began chopping wood for Hopewell, Sarah and Springfield charcoal furnaces. A few years later he began huckstering to Altoona, Pa., and continued for about five years. In 1884 he took up farming and followed that pursuit until 1919, when he retired. By his industry and skillful management he acquired the possession of four fine farms in the beautiful Morrison's Cove. Bedford County, Pennsylvania. His address is Baker Summit, Pa. He married Rebecca Walter. Their children are: Rosco C., Sarah O., John W. and Anna M.

CATHARINE LEONE BOWSER

Catharine Leone Bowser, daughter of J. Miles and Elsie (Clever) Bowser, was born at New Kensington, Pa., October 27, 1893. She received her education in the public schools in Wisconsin and Armstrong County, Pa., and Dayton Academy, Dayton, Pa. She took training as a nurse in the West Penn Hospital of Pittsburgh, Pa., where she was graduated and registered July 10, 1917. She volunteered into the service of her country and for a short period was stationed at Camp Upton. She sailed for France on the Megantic, June 12, 1918. On her arrival at the war zone she was stationed at Base Hospital No. 1, thence transferred to Chamanit. She returned to her home land on the S. S. Agamemnon, May 15, 1919.

Catharine Leone Bowser

William Patton Bowser

James Quinter Bowser

Rev. Wellington Bowser, A.M.

JAMES B. FINLEY WYANT

Doctor James B. Finley Wyant, was born on the Wyant homestead, in Washington Township, Armstrong County, Pa., on August 7, 1862, son of Adam and Sophia (Bowser) Wyant. He attended the public schools of his locality, and after he had received whatever advantages they offered, he entered Reid Institute, a Baptist academy at Reidsburg, Clarion County, Pa., established before the Civil war. Several circumstances are encountered here of great consequence in his subsequent life. First of all, he remained in this excellent school for a period of five years, except two or three short terms in which he was engaged in teaching; and then, it was during his course in Reid Institute that he registered as a medical student and began a course of preparation for his chosen profession, which he completed at the University of Pittsburgh, graduating in 1889. And lastly, while engaged in teaching in the Institute, immediately after he had graduated there, he married the younger daughter of the principal, Prof. C. A. and Sarah F. Gilbert, Louise Gilbert, who has been a cultured and sympathetic help-meet in the home, church and also his profession. Prof. C. A. Gilbert, A. M., was one of the foremost educators in the state, and many men and women of Western Pennsylvania, now filling honored and useful places, owe the slender chance they had to acquire a good education to the paternal care and scholarship of this great man. .After the death of Professor and Mrs. Gilbert, the writer had the satisfaction of gathering funds from their former students to erect a beautiful monument to their memory, which now stands at their graves in the Baptist cemetery at Montgomeryville, Armstrong County, Pennsylvania. For ten years, Doctor Wyant practiced medicine at Templeton, Pa., after which he moved to Kittanning, Pa., where he still lives highly successful and honored in his profession. He has served as secretary of the Armstrong County Medical Society continuously since 1901; a member of Pennsylvania Medical Association; the I. O. O. F. and Royal Arch Masons, Kittanning, Pa. Doctor and Mrs. Wyant have had the following children: Sophia Irene, Sarah Alleine, Margaret C., Corbin Wayland and Mary Louise. Corbin Wayland Wyant, who is with his father in the picture, is now a senior in Bucknell University. He enlisted in the Marine service in the World war and made numerous voyages to France on the transports. When the war closed he returned to his studies at the university.

WILLIAM PATTON BOWSER

William Patton Bowser, son of Benjamin S. and Elizabeth (Yerty) Bowser, was born at the old Bowser homestead near Kittanning, Pa., May 9, 1854. Leaving the farm at quite an early age, he was engaged for some time in carpenter work, rig building and oil field labor in the vicinity of Rimerton, Parkers Landing, and other places in Armstrong and Butler counties. During 1874 he married Margaret Sindorf. Seven children were born to this union, as follows: Parma, Park, Celeste, Saida, Clema, Clarence and Wayne. After a few years following his marriage he moved to Cattaraugus County, N. Y., where he was employed in the great Bradford oil field. In 1890 he went to the Turkeyfoot field in West Virginia as field manager for John Coast of Olean, N. Y., his former employer. His employer gave him a responsible position in 1893 in the oil field of Wood County, Ohio, where he acquired an interest in the property. Following the sale of this property he returned to Armstrong County, Pennsylvania, and bought the old Bowser homestead near Walk Chalk, still in the hands of his heirs. After a few months he returned to the oil district near Weston, W. Va., where he was employed for seventeen years as superintendent of the Fink District, by the South Penn Oil Co. He relinquished this position in 1915 on account of ill health and accompanied by his wife, made a trip to Florida, and thence to Oklahoma to visit the family of his wife's brother, John Sindorf. While there he received tidings of the death of his daughter, Parma (Mrs. W. J. Tapp), at Portville, N. Y. After the funeral of his daughter he returned to his home in West Virginia. His health continuing to decline, he entered the Hillsview Sanitarium, Washington, Pa., where he died December 16, 1916. His body was taken to Montgomeryville, Pa., he having expressed a desire to have his remains placed there by the last resting place of many relatives and old friends in the cemetery connected with the Baptist church of which he was a member.

Old Hague Hotel
Built by Mathias Bowser, Kittanning, Pa.

Doctor James B. Finley Wyant and His Son,
Corbin Wayland Wyant

JACOB BOWSER

Jacob Bowser, son of John Bowser, grandson of Samuel Bowser (19) and great-grandson of Mathias, Jr. (2), was born January 30, 1841. Jacob and his three brothers, John, Samuel and Elwood, were in the Civil war and all lived through its perils to return home, but not without bearing their share of its hardships, as indicated by Jacob's biography. He enlisted September 16, 1861, with Co. C, 4th Ohio Cavalry. Honorably discharged January 3, 1864, at Pulaski, Tenn. Re-enlisted next day (Jan. 4). Captured at Atlanta, Ga., and sent to the infamous Andersonville Prison, July 22, 1864, where he endured the horrors of that notorious starvation camp for nine months; at the time of his release, April 28, 1865, his weight was 80 pounds, having lost 110 pounds. He was mustered out of service, June 30, 1865, at Columbus, Ohio. In 1867 he married Jane Ann Chilton, a neighbor's daughter. In 1873 he moved to Indianapolis, Ind., where he continued to live until the time of his death, July 30, 1914. He was an invalid for three years prior to his death, but with mind unimpaired. Mr. Bowser, during those three years of physical inaction, gave much of his time to reminiscences and much of historical interest and value was gleaned, and now cherished by his family. For children, see Jane Ann (Chilton) Bowser.

JANE ANN (CHILTON) BOWSER

Jane Ann Chilton was born in Sunderland, England, December 19, 1850, daughter of Thomas Stafford and Jane Ann (Turner) Chilton. She came from England to Xenia, Ohio, with her parents in 1852. She met Jacob Bowser at the close of the Civil war, and they were married May 6, 1867, at Lebanon, county seat of Warren County, Ohio. They had three children: Carrie, who married Arthur G. Wills; Minnie, a twin of Carrie, who married G. W. Bunting, Sr., and J. Edward, deceased. Mrs. Bowser is in good health, enjoys the society and comfortable home of the family of her daughter, Mrs. A. G. Wills, in Indianapolis, and is active in the Eastern Star organization and philanthropic bodies. The writer is grateful to Mrs. Bowser and daughter, Mrs. Wills, for valuable information which finally enabled us to determine the place of Samuel Bowser (19) in our line.

Jacob Bowser

Jane Ann (Chilton) Bowser

Jacob C. Bowser

William H. Bowser

JACOB C. BOWSER

Jacob C. Bowser was born November 8, 1870, on a farm in York County, Pennsylvania, about one mile west of the town of New Freedom and joining the farm originally purchased by his great-grandfather, Benjamin Bowser, son of Daniel Bowser, who came to this country and landed at Baltimore, Md., in the year 1733. He spent the first fifteen years on his father's farm and attended country school in the winter, and after finishing public school attended a few terms at Shrewsbury Academy. January, 1888, he entered Huntingdon Normal School (now Juniata College) at Huntingdon, Pa. In his junior year at Huntingdon he became interested in penmanship, pen art and shorthand, and in the fall of 1889 he completed a course in penmanship at the G. W. Michael Pen Art School at Delaware, Ohio, then considered the leading pen art school in the country. After completing his course at Delaware he went to the Zanerian Art College, Columbus, Ohio, and took an additional course in penmanship and art to prepare himself for teaching in this particular line. In January, 1890, he started teaching penmanship in a business college at Watertown, N. Y. At this time business colleges were in a very flourishing condition throughout the country, and was the connecting link between common or high schools in preparing young men and women for business positions. He taught in various business colleges throughout the country, not only teaching penmanship, but also branched out and taught shorthand and all commercial branches. He also did considerable work along the pen art line and was considered at that time one of the leading pen artists and instructors of penmanship in the country.

In 1896 he entered the employ of J. H. Wasson & Sons, of Columbus, Ohio, as private secretary and general office man and remained with them for four years, or until the Salt Trust was formed which put this firm out of business. In November, 1900, he entered the employ of the Erie City Iron Works, at Erie, Pa., and has been with this firm ever since in various capacities, being auditor for the past ten years.

In 1895 he was married to Miss Rose Mead, of Erie, Pa. They have two daughters, Kathlyn and Marcia.

Loben R. Bowser

Adam and Sophia (Bowser) Wyant

Esther Jane (Bowser) Fair

Amos T. Fair

LOBEN R. BOWSER

Loben R. Bowser, son of Peter and Jane Bowser, was born on his father's farm near Walk Chalk, Pa., April 23, 1849. He married Catharyn Fair, and after his marriage bought a farm in Madison Township, Clarion County, Pa., and lived there until his death, on September 23, 1916. They had four children: an infant child died in 1881; Emmett Bowser, living near Rimersburg, Pa., Harry Bowser, living near Emmett, and Mrs. Edward Conner, living on the homestead at Kissinger's Mill. Address: Rimersburg, Pa., R. D. No. 2.

ADAM AND SOPHIA (BOWSER) WYANT

Sophia Bowser, daughter of Abram and Mary (Stevens) Bowser, was born on the "Bowser" farm, one mile west of Walk Chalk, Armstrong County, Pa., May 27, 1828. On Saturday, May 27, 1922, her children and their descendants gathered at the home of Mrs. Emma T. Wolfe, near Mahoning, Pa., to celebrate her 95th birthday. It was another great day for "Aunt Sophia." These anniversaries have brought her children to her side annually since 1889, and this one was the first of the thirty-three birthdays thus observed when all of her children were not present. Her oldest son, Eli, of Steubenville, Ohio, was not able to attend. Aunt Sophia, despite her ninety-five years, was as happy as a school girl. She sat with her family at the table as she had always done; and while the after dinner program progressed, she was in her arm chair and heard the songs, the prayer, and the complimentary and loving words spoken. She is no doubt the oldest living Bowser, and retains all her faculties to a remarkable degree—memory, hearing, eyesight, and general good health and a genial happy spirit. She married Adam Wyant, son of Martin and Christina (Booher) Wyant. They lived on the Wyant homestead in Washington Township, Armstrong County, Pa., and there reared their family of ten children, all living except the oldest two, Mary and Delilah. The living children are: Eli Fluke, Christina, Benjamin W., Emma T., Catharine, Dr. J. B. Finley, Margaret and Susanette.

AMOS T. FAIR

Amos T. Fair, son of Leonard and Mary Magdalena (Helm) Fair, was born on the Fair homestead near Montgomeryville, Pa., March 23, 1853. He attended the public schools until he was old enough to handle carpenter tools; learned the trade with his father, and in a few years was recognized as one of the most competent carpenters in the country. When the great Pittsburgh Plate Glass Company began building their works at Ford City, Pa., in 1887, now the largest in the world, they appointed Mr. Fair foreman of the carpenters, a position he has held ever since. He has held office as councilman or school director ever since the town became organized, and has served as burgess for eight years. He married, (1) Adaline Bowser, and had the following children: Frederick Lee, Clara Myrtle, Daisy Delcine, Leonard Augustus, Elizabeth Araminta, and Olive Lenore. He married (2) Esther J. Barbor.

ESTHER J. FAIR

Esther J. Bowser, daughter of Rev. M. S. and Elizabeth (Booher) Bowser, was born February 4, 1860. She attended the schools of Rural Valley, Pa. In 1876 she was married to Robert O. Barbor of Cookport, Pa. They had the following children: Verner L., Delmong C., James R., and Mina Ruth. She married (2) Amos T. Fair, Ford City, Pa., November 28, 1905. Mrs. Fair has devoted her life to religious and philanthropic work.

Benjamin S. Bowser

Dr. Mathias S. Bowser

Elizabeth F. Bowser

John F. Bowser

MATHIAS STEVENS BOWSER

Mathias Stevens Bowser, M. D., was born in a log house three miles west of Kittanning, Pa., May 14, 1837, a son of Abram and Mary Stevens Bowser. He worked on his father's farm in summer and attended public school in winter, until he was seventeen years of age, when he attended "Select" school, later finishing his education in Elder's Ridge Academy at Dayton, Pa., and Reid Institute, at Reidsburg, Clarion County, Pa. He was endowed with a rare voice and was widely known as a leader of musical conventions. At twenty-two he was ordained to the Baptist ministry and served several churches in successful pastorates. In 1877 he took up the study of medicine under the tutelage of Dr. George Tryon Harding, father of President Warren G. Harding, at Caledonia, Ohio, completing his medical course in the University of Cleveland. He resides at Lima, Ohio, where he has enjoyed a large practice. He married (1) Elizabeth Booher, of Adrian, Pa. There were the following children: Addison B., the author; Hettie J., Mary Bell, David Elmer, Rev. Arda J., Elizabeth L. and Arlington R. He married (2) Mrs. T. A. Ruff, of Caledonia, Ohio. Doctor Bowser has been closely identified with civic and educational work in his city, and is frequently invited to make addresses on social and religious subjects on prominent occasions. He is called the "Grand Old Man cf Lima."

ELIZABETH F. BOWSER

Elizabeth F. Bowser, oldest daughter of Abram and Mary (Stevens) Bowser, was born on the Bowser farm near Walk Chalk, Pa., December 8, 1825. She received such education as the public schools afforded and supplemented it in later years by her own efforts. She married Frederick R Bowser, and with her husband settled on a farm near Montgomeryville, Pa. Her husband died there, August 11, 1874. Subsequently the farm passed into the possession of her youngest son, Jacob L. Bowser (one of our Bowser committeemen now deceased), with whom Mrs. Bowser continued to live until her death, November 27, 1908. Mrs. Bowser was well acquainted with the hardships and endless labor of the generation to which she belonged, the days of the spinning wheel and the great oak loom. She was known as Aunt Betsey and was loved and respected by all who knew her, a good mother, a diligent housewife and a conscientious Christian.

George E. Hanley

Daisy Jeannette (Boylestein)
Hanley

GEORGE EDWARD AND DAISY JEANNETTE (BOYLESTEIN) HANLEY

George Edward Hanley, son of John and Winnefred Hanley, was born at Lynn, Mass., April 19, 1881. Mr. Hanley received a liberal education in the schools of his city and took up a business calling in which he has been eminently successful. In 1917 and 1918 he was president of the Pennsylvania Shoe Travelers Association. At present he is the manager of a large shoe establishment in Pittsburgh. On February 15, 1915, he married Daisy Jeannette Boylestein, daughter of George and Delilah (Wyant) Boylestein, of Kittanning, Pa. Mrs. Hanley was born April 7, 1891, at Ford City, Pa. Mr. and Mrs. Hanley are well known in the best social ranks of Pittsburgh.

BENJAMIN S. BOWSER

Benjamin S. Bowser, oldest child of Abram and Mary (Stevens) Bowser, was born on his father's farm near Walk Chalk, Pa., December 20, 1823. He married (1) Elizabeth, daughter of Joseph D. Bowser, who died soon after their marriage. He married (2) Elizabeth Yerty and settled on land he bought in Washington Township, Armstrong County, Pennsylvania, where he spent the remainder of his life. He was one of the foremost farmers of his section. During the days of the Brady's Bend Furnace, he was constable of his township and recognized as the fearless foe of evildoers, especially the vagrant and criminal classes who frequently haunt a public works. There were five children of the second marriage: Eliza Ann, Catharine, Rachael, Christian Y., and William P. He married (3) Catharine Yerty. Of this union there were seven children: Mervin C., Steven, Abraham, Denny D., Ellen, Sophia and Rose. He was the first president of the Bowser Reunion—loved by everyone and known throughout the county as Uncle Benny. He died in 1915.

VERNER L. BARBOR, ESQ.

DELMONT A. BARBOR

MINA RUTH (BARBOR) MYGRANT AND DAUGHTER, JANE

JAMES ROBERT BARBOR

ELIZABETH (BOOHER) BOWSER

Elizabeth Booher, a daughter of Bartholomew and Esther (Helsel) Booher, was born on her father's farm, Washington Township, Armstrong County, Pennsylvania, September 6, 1841. She is a descendant of the great Bucher family, found through Switzerland, France and Germany, of Palatine origin. One branch of this family has been traced to Klaus Bucher, a nobleman of Switzerland, 1535. The first of the family of Elizabeth was Bartholomew Bucher, who came to America through Baltimore, and settled in Frederick County, Maryland, where he died in 1791. Elizabeth (mother of the author) was one of five children. Her eldest brother, Emanuel Booher, was killed in the Battle of Fair Oaks, in the Civil war. Isabelle, married Abner Bonner; Henry, recently deceased, and Mary, who married Jacob Frick, now living at Norwalk, Calif. She married Rev. M. S. Bowser, son of Mary (Stevens) and Abram Bowser, and had the following children: Addison B., David Elmer, Esther J., Mary Belle, Arda Joshua, Elizabeth Lulu, and A. Reed. Two of her sons are ministers and one a teacher. Among her grandchildren are doctors, lawyers, chief accountants, real estate dealers, merchants, and four were in the World war. She married (2) Martin Bowser. They had one child, Jennie Templeton, who married George Rickle.

CHILDREN OF ESTHER JANE (BOWSER) AND ROBERT O. BARBOR

VERNER L. BARBOR

Verner L. Barbor, Esq., was born at Cookport, Indiana County, Pennsylvania, March 21, 1877. He finished his public school course at Wilmerding, Pa., then entered Grove City College. After his graduation from college he took up the study of law in Pittsburgh, where in due course he was admitted to the bar. He married Edith Davis, daughter of William and Cora Belle (Hover) Davis. They have three children: Cora Belle, Delmont and Verner, Jr.

DELMONT A. BARBOR

Delmont A. Barbor was born at Cookport, Pa., December 14, 1878. He was educated in the public schools of Indiana, Pa., and Wilmerding. When he had completed his course in school, he took a position in the Westinghouse Air Brake Works, of Wilmerding. His natural adaptability and steadiness were rewarded by advancement in the institution until today he has charge of the vast real estate interests of the company. He married Anna Wise. They have one child, Verner H.

JAMES ROBERT BARBOR

James Robert Barbor was born October 18, 1887. James attended the public schools and before he was out of his teens, went to work in the Westinghouse Air Brake Works, where, like his brother, Delmont, soon held a highly responsible position. He married Jennie Parker. They have three children: Robert, William and Isabelle.

MINA RUTH BARBOR

Mina Ruth Barbor was born September 17, 1891. She attended the public schools of Wilmerding and Ford City, Pa. She married Harry R. Mygrant. About 1914 they moved to Los Angeles, Calif., and in 1920 Mr. Mygrant accepting a position there, they took up their residence in San Francisco, where they now live. They have had six children: Elizabeth Jane, Clifford, Richard, Robert, Miriam Ruth and Glee.

Rev. Arda Joshua Bowser

Nellie (Crafts) Bowser

Elizabeth (Booher) Bowser

Harry Addison Bowser

HARRY ADDISON BOWSER

Harry Addison Bowser, son of Rev. Arda J. Bowser, was born at St. Marys, Ohio, 1890. He was educated in the public schools of St. Marys, Cleveland, and the Dennison University, Granville, Ohio. He married Rose Nitchman, of Schenectady, N. Y. They have two children. Harry was in the World war and saw most of its worst features and endured all of its perils. He went to France, May 28, 1918, and returned to America, May 10, 1919. He was with Battery E, 309th Field Artillery, 78th Division, 1st Army Corps, and was in the following battles: Toul Sector, St. Mihiel, Preny Raid, Meuse-Argonne, and Grand Pre. He is living at Schenectady, New York.

Furman T. Bowser

Ella (Lyle) Bowser

Archibald W. Bowser

In Memoriam
John F. Bowser
Born September 6, 1887
Died February 5, 1889

FURMAN T. AND ELLA (LYLE) BOWSER

Furman T. Bowser, son of Archibald and Rosannah Bowser, was born at Montgomeryville, Pa., August 18, 1861. He secured the first grades in the public school and then, while still in his teens, went to work. In his early years he learned the value of application to the task in hand, and by his industry and upright life has won success in business and a good name. He is an esteemed and active member of the Baptist Church of Galeton, Pa., where he lives, and belongs to the Masonic lodge, F. and A. M. No. 252. He married Ella Lyle, daughter of William and Mary Lyle of Barclay, Pa., and much of his success has to be attributed to the intelligent and faithful helpfulness of his wife. Besides her activities in her church, she is devoted to the interests of the Order of the Eastern Star. They have had three children: Archibald William, Daisy and John Fluke Bowser, the portrait in memoriam of the latter appears in this work.

ARCHIBALD W. BOWSER

Archibald W. Bowser, son of Furman T. and Ella (Lyle) Bowser, was born at Olean, N. Y., November 16, 1885. He received his education in the schools of Olean, and prepared himself for a business career, and now holds a responsible position with the Union Tank Car Co., of New York City. His address is, room 1402, 21 East 40th St., New York. He married Emma Goodrich, of New York City. He is a member of the I. O. O. F. of Galeton, Pa.

Family of Mary Jane (Hays) and Joseph Leigh Barber

Nina E. Barber
Lettie O. Barber Mary O. Barber
Sarah Kathern Barber

CHILDREN OF MARY JANE (HAYS) AND JOSEPH LEIGH BARBER

LETTIE O. (BARBER) TICE

Lettie O. Barber was born November 10, 1889, at Dubois, Pa. She married Oliver C. Tice, born May 12, 1886, at Cogley, Pa. Mr. Tice attended a business college in Dubois, Pa., and the Clarion State Normal School. He was an official in the National Bank, New Bethlehem, Pa. Later he moved to Yukon, W. Va., where he is employed as bookkeeper for the Pocahontas Coal Company. They have the following children: Mary Elaine, Martha Jane and Frances Leigh.

MARY O. (BARBER) GILLIAM

Mary O. Barber was born in Dubois, Pa., May 23, 1891. She attended the public schools and the high school of Dubois. In 1915 she moved to West Virginia where she met her future husband, Marion W. Gilliam. They were married on June 14, 1918. Mr. Gilliam was chief clerk of the local board of Williamson, W. Va., during the World war. He is at present chief electrical and mechanical engineer with the West Virginia Engineering Company at Williamson, W. Va. They have one child, David Marshall Gilliam, born December 6, 1919.

NINA E. (BARBER) BILGER

Nina E. Barber was born at Dubois, Pa., August 22, 1893. She married Dr. Frederick W. Bilger, who was born at Curwensville, Pa. He was educated in the public schools of his native place, and attended a medical school in Philadelphia, and later, a medical college of Louisville, Ky., graduating from the latter institution. He settled in Maybeury, W. Va., where he now lives and has established a large practice.

SARAH KATHERN (BARBER) PRESTON

Sarah Kathern Barber was born at Dubois, Pa., May 20, 1898. She married Seaton Tinsley Preston, born at Bristol, Va., 1892. Mr. Preston received a high school education and graduated from the Virginia Polytechnic Institute in electrical engineering. He served as captain in the United States Army in France during the World war. After the war he took up the work for which he had prepared himself, accepting a position as electrical engineer with the West Virginia Engineering Company. In 1920 he was made assistant district manager of the Kentucky and West Virginia Power Company, at Pikeville, Ky., where he now resides. They have one child: Seaton Tinsley Preston, Jr.

Lieut. Wayland Stanley Bowser, Arda Crawford Bowser, Sgt. Frank Excell Bowser.
Sons of the Author

FRANK E. BOWSER

Frank Excell Bowser, son of Addison B. and Ella Z. Bowser, was born at Watsontown, Pa., October 31, 1892. He graduated from the Ingram, Pa., public schools, 1908, and the Crafton (Pittsburgh) high school, 1912. Entered the University of Pittsburgh Science School in 1913. Two years later he entered the junior class at Bethany College, W. Va., and graduated from that institution in 1915, receiving the degree of bachelor of science. He attained a high standard in scholastic and athletic circles. For two years he was halfback on the Bethany football team. After graduation he enlisted in the medical corps of the U. S. Army at Fort Oglethorpe, Ga. After three weeks he was transferred to the U. S. Army General Hospital No. 3, Rahway, N. J., where he was made a sergeant. From Rahway he was transferred to the Central Officers' Training School for Infantry Officers at Camp Lee, Va. After his discharge from the army following the armistice, he entered the University of Pittsburgh Medical School, where he is a senior. He will receive his degree in June, 1923. He was president of the Sophomore class in the medical school; member of Phi Beta Pi (medical) and Beta Theta Pi (collegiate) fraternities; member of the Cap and Gown Club; Glee and Banjo clubs of the University; leader of the College orchestra, Bethany, two years; president Bethany College Literary Society and vice-president Bethany Chemical Club.

WAYLAND S. BOWSER

Lieut. Wayland Stanley Bowser, son of Addison B. and Ella Z. (Stebbins) Bowser, was born at Danville, Pa., March 29, 1894. He attended the public schools, graduating with his brother Frank in the Crafton high school, 1912. He enlisted in the Officers' Training Corps August 27, 1917, and was stationed at Fort Oglethorpe, Ga., receiving his commission of first lieutenant in the infantry November 26, 1917; assigned December 15, 1917, to Co. D, 325th Infantry, 82nd Div., at Camp Gordon, Atlanta, Ga.; transferred December 23, 1917, to the 5th Div., Regular Army, at Camp Logan, Houston, Texas: assigned to Co. B, 5th Military Police; left Houston for France April 20, 1918, and sailed April 30 on the S. Niagara; arrived at Bordeaux, France, May 11, 1918. He was in service in the Vosges mountains, St. Mihiel offensive, Meuse, Argonne, Luxembourg and Germany. He was transferred to the 42nd Division, March 15, 1919, and assigned to the 42nd Military Police Co., and left Germany April 6, 1919; arrived at New York on the Leviathan April 18, 1919; discharged at Camp Dix, N. J., May 1, 1919. He was wounded in the battle at Romagne, France. After his discharge from the army he entered the University of Pittsburgh and is now (1922) a member of the senior class.

ARDA C. BOWSER

Arda Crawford Bowser, son of Addison B. and Ella Z. (Stebbins) Bowser, was born at Danville, Pa., January 9, 1899. He attended the public schools at Millville, N. J., Crafton, Pittsburgh, and graduated from the Ford City high school June, 1917. After spending one term at Bethany College, West Virginia, he enlisted in the United States Navy Flying Corps and was sent to the training camp at Boston, Mass. When the World war came to an end he was released from service (finally discharged in 1921) and entered the freshman class at Bucknell University, where he is now a Junior. On his entrance at college he was placed on the Varsity football team and at once was given the position of fullback. In his sophomore year he was recognized by the majority of critics as the greatest fullback in the country. In the 1921 season he was captain of his team. He was chosen as the best fullback in the state and was also the choice of many writers for all-Eastern honors and was mentioned by Walter Camp as an all-American. He married Elsie Laura Reitler of Ford City, Pa., August 26, 1921.

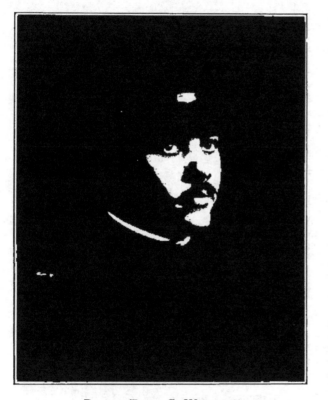

Doctor Ellis C. Winters

Isabelle (Bowser) Winters

WELLINGTON BOWSER

Rev. Wellington Bowser, A. M., was born on a farm near Echo, Armstrong County, Pa., September 13, 1852, son of Loben and Martha Jane (Oliver) Bowser. He worked on the farm and attended the public school of his district until fifteen years of age, when he entered an academy. After he had finished courses in the academy and college, he taught school for several years and then went to India as a missionary, where he remained for seven years. On account of breaking health, he returned to America and held pastorates in the states of Washington, Oregon and Idaho. Compelled to relinquish the arduous labors of the ministry, he located at Pasadena, Calif., where he is now living. He has been keenly interested in our preparation of the Bowser history and has furnished valuable assistance. He married Fannie Waid. They have the following children: Vincent Earl, born at Rurki, India, under the shadows of the Himalaya Mountains; Ethel Maude, born at Karachi, a seaport on the Arabian Sea, and Genevieve Irene, born at Spartansburg, Pa. (See 1108, 1109, 1110.)

ISABELLE (BOWSER) WINTERS

Isabelle Bowser, only daughter of Addison B. and Ella Z. (Stebbins) Bowser, was born at Danville, Montour County, Pa., February 14, 1896. She received her education in the public schools of Danville, Pa., Millville, N. J., and Ingram, Pa., graduating from the Crafton (Pittsburgh) high school. After her graduation she taught the Sherrett, Pa., school one term; then took charge of the music department in the Wilmerding, Pa., schools, where she remained three terms, until her marriage to Dr. Ellis C. Winters, June 24, 1920. During the time she was teaching school she was studying voice under Doctor Savage, of Pittsburgh, who is recognized as one of the most widely known voice teachers in the state.

ELLIS CALVIN WINTERS

Dr. Ellis C. Winters, son of Elmer E. and Emma (Machamer) Winters, was born at Watsontown, Northumberland County, Pa., January 17, 1889. He attended the public schools and graduated from the Dewart High School; a student at the Muncy Normal School, Bucknell University and the Medico-Chirurgical of Philadelphia, Pa., where he graduated in 1914. He was resident physician in the Western Pennsylvania Hospital, Pittsburgh, for one year. In 1915 he located at Ford City, Pa., where he immediately established a large practice. He served eighteen months in the United States Army, thirteen months of which were spent overseas. After his discharge from the army, he resumed his practice in Ford City. He married Isabelle Bowser, daughter of Addison B. and Ella Zelima (Stebbins) Bowser, at Ford City, June 24, 1920. They have one child, James Elmer, born August 26, 1921. Doctor Winters is a member of the Veterans of Foreign Wars; American Legion; Armstrong County Medical Society; the Pennsylvania State Medical Society and a fellow of the American Medical Association.

Addison Bartholomew Bowser

Ella Zelima (Stebbins) Bowser

ADDISON B. AND ELLA ZELIMA STEBBINS BOWSER

The author of this book was born near Montgomeryville, Armstrong County, Pennsylvania, May 22, 1858. He was educated in the public schools of Rural Valley, Pa., Reid Institute, Bucknell University (graduating with the class of 1888 with the B. A. degree) and Crozer Theological Seminary. He also holds the A. M. degree from his alma mater. He was pastor of the Third Baptist Church of Philadelphia, Pa., where he was ordained in 1890; the First Baptist Church of Danville, Pa.; the First Baptist Church of Millville, N. J.; the First Baptist Church of Crafton (Pittsburgh, eleven years) and now of the First Baptist Church of Ford City, Pa. He was president for eighteen years of the Bowser Reunion. He is a son of Rev. M. S. and Elizabeth (Booher) Bowser. During his pastorate in Philadelphia he married Ella Zelima Stebbins of Watsontown, Pa., daughter of Achilles R. and Emily (Baker) Stebbins, born December 10, 1869. She was educated in the public schools of Watsontown and Bucknell University. Mrs. Bowser is a descendant on her mother's side of Samuel Gorton, proprietary governor of Rhode Island. A genealogy of the family of that illustrious friend and mentor of Roger Williams has been made, embracing more than 13,000 names. Her father's people were also English emigrants who settled in Tioga County, Pennsylvania. They have had four children: Frank Excell, Wayland Stanley, Isabelle and Arda Crawford, and one grandchild, James Elmer Winters.

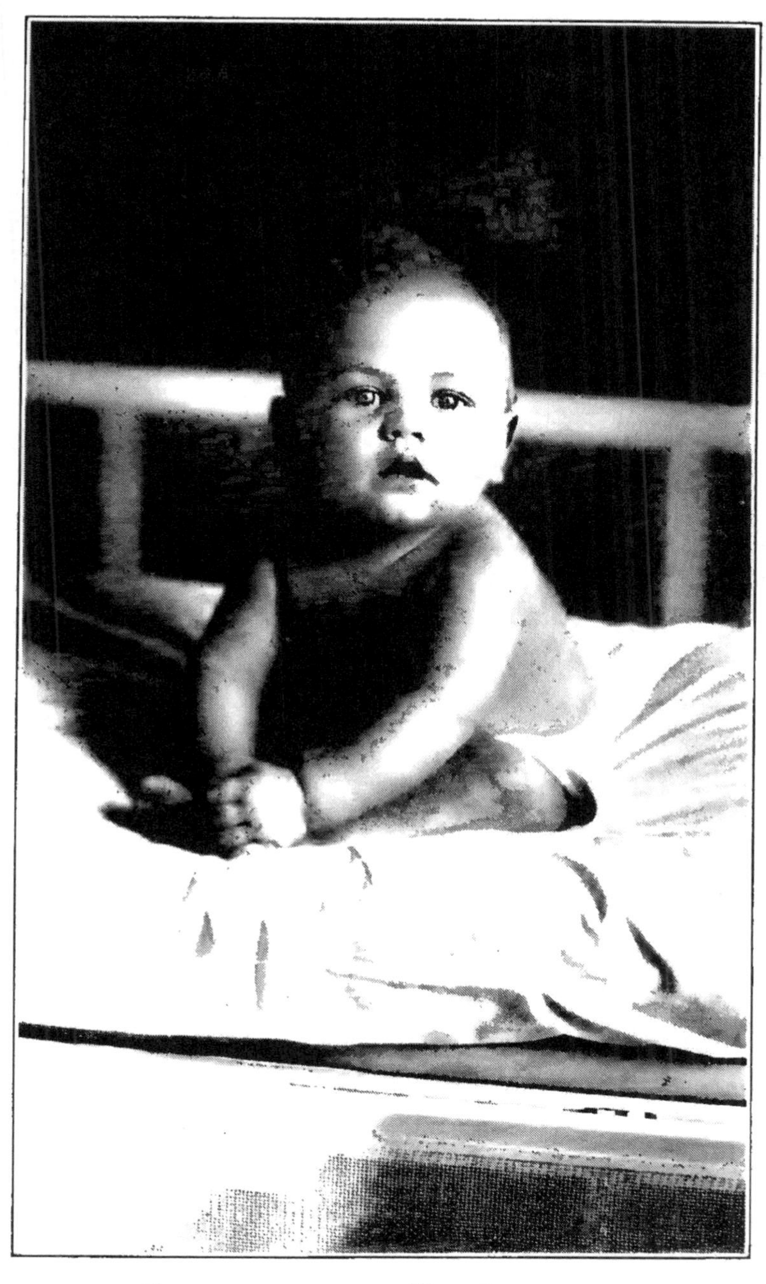

REPRESENTATIVE OF A NEW GENERATION

JAMES ELMER WINTERS, born August 26, 1921, son of Doctor Ellis C. and Isabelle (Bowser) Winters, and first grandson of the author.

THE BOWSERS IN AMERICA

In the Pennsylvania Archives, 2nd series, Vol. 17, are the names of foreigners who took the oath of allegiance to the Province and State of Pennsylvania. "Palatines: September 28, 1733, Brigantine, Richard and Elizabeth, Christopher Clymer, Master, from Rotterdam, last from Plymouth."

Passengers, 44 males above 16.
Passengers, 34 females above 16.
Passengers, 24 males under 16.
Passengers, 35 females under 16.

Mathias Bausser, aged 63; Mathias Bausser, Jr., aged 22; Christian Bausser, aged 18; also Daniel Bausser, under 16, took the oath September 28, 1733; i. e. on the day of their arrival. Along with the three given above there are the names of Esther Bausser, aged 49; Anna Elizabeth Bewser, aged 20; Jacob Bewser, aged 9½; Magdalena Bewser, 7½; Anna Maria Bewser, 4; Anna Catherina Bewser, 1½; Anna Elizabeth Bewser, 7; Anna Maria Bewser, 17 weeks.

The clerk of the court evidently made errors both in spelling the names and in the ages. Esther was the wife of Mathias, Sr., and Anna Elizabeth of Mathias, Jr. Anna Catherine, aged 1½ years, and Anna Maria, aged 17 weeks, were doubtless children of Mathias, Jr., and Anna Elizabeth.

In this list of family names we include as children of Mathias, Sr., several whose ages evidently were wrongly transcribed.

ch.—children
m.—married
b.—born
d.—died
} abbreviations.

MATHIAS BAUSSER, SR., BRANCH

1. MATHIAS BAUSSER, SR., b. 1670; m. Esther, b. 1684.
   Children:
   2. Mathias Bausser, Jr., b. 1711; m. Anna Elizabeth, b. 1713.
   3. Christian Bausser, b. 1715.
   4. Daniel Bausser, b. 1722.
   5. Jacob Bausser, b. 1724.
   6. Magdalena Bausser, b. 1726.
   7. Anna Elizabeth Bausser.
   8. Anna Maria, b. 1729.

2. MATHIAS, JR. (2); MATHIAS, SR. (1).
   Children:
   9. Anna Catherine Bausser, b. 1731.
   10. Anna Maria Bausser, b. 1733.
   11. Anna Margaret Bausser, baptized in Lancaster May 12, 1739.

12. David Bausser, b. 1738; m. Elizabeth; d. 1813.
13. John Bausser, b. 1740; d. 1813; m. Mary.
14. Jacob Bausser, b. 1745; d. 1834; m. Elsie Kal.
15. Noah Bausser, b. 1748; m. Eunice Ditto.
16. Valentine Bausser, b. 1750; d. in Armstrong Co., 1836.
17. Abraham Bausser, b. 1758; d. about 1853-5.
18. Esther Bausser, b. 1758; m. Martin John.
19. Samuel Bausser, b. about 1755.

12. DAVID (3); MATHIAS, JR. (2); MATHIAS, SR. (1). David Bowser was in Maryland in 1785. In 1798 he sold land in Frederick County, Md., and was living in Bedford County the same year. Mr. G. W. Bowser of Osterburg, Bedford County, relates that David Bowser, his great-grandfather, settled on the farm upon which he lives, 1½ miles west of Osterburg, and cleared the land; and a small burial place on the same land shows that he was 75 years old when he died; 1813: that he had come from some place in the east towards Philadelphia. "He had three sons. John Bowser, my grandfather, was born about 1784." David Bowser was therefore a year old and his sister Anna Margaret no doubt an infant when they were baptized in the Reformed Church of Lancaster, Pa., May 12, 1739. David married Catherine. In his will he mentions seven children: Catrout, Elizabeth, Mary, Catharine, Valentine, John and Esther; also a grandson, John Mock. Bedford County History says David also had a son David who went west.

Children:

20. Catrout Bowser, a female, was buried in the ancient burial place on the David Bowser farm; never married.
21. Elizabeth Bowser.
22. Mary Bowser.
23. Catharine Bowser. m. John Berkheimer.
24. Valentine Bowser, m. Mary; lived in St. Clair Township in 1821. In the census reports of 1820 St. Clair Twp., Bedford County, he and his wife are recorded as aged between 26 and 45; no children; farmer. Valentine probably died in 1830 or shortly before. The census of 1830 does not give Valentine, but Mary, no doubt his widow, aged 40 to 50 years. In her family are 6 males and 3 females.

    Children:

    a24. Valentine Bowser, b. 1819; d. 1891; m. Catherine ——, b. 1824; ch.: Mary, b. 1848; Joseph, b. 1851; m. Eve, b. 1854; Henry, b. 1857; Jacob, b. 1860; Valentine, b. 1862; m. William.

    b24. Samuel Bowser, b. 1824; d. Dec. 20, 1896; m. Ann ——, b. 1824; ch.: Alexander, b. 1850; Michael, b. 1851; Elizabeth, b. 1853; Matthias, b. 1854; m. Lucinda; Susan, b. 1856; Rachel, b. 1860; Samuel, b. 1864.

25. John Bowser, m. Mary Helm, Daughter of John Helm of Bedford County.
26. —— (Mother of John Mock). The will of Peter Mock of St. Clair Township, dated 1815, mentions his grandson John Mock, who was a son of his son Jacob Mock. Therefore it is probable that a daughter of David married Jacob Mock.
27. Esther Bowser, m. —— Mock.
28. David Bowser.

23. CATHARINE (4), DAVID (3), MATHIAS, JR. (2), MATHIAS, SR. (1). Catharine Bowser, m. John Berkheimer. Catharine is an important personage in our history, as she becomes the connecting link between

two branches of Bowsers in the marriage of her daughter Sarah to Isaac Bowser, a descendant of John and Eve.

Children:

29. William Berkheimer, m. Hannah Mock.
30. Peter Berkheimer, m. Margaret Bowser, daughter of George, Sr., and Margaret (Swartz).
31. Moses Berkheimer, m. Elizabeth Furney.
32. John Berkheimer, m. Sarah Shatzer.
33. Sarah Berkheimer, b. in 1804; m. Isaac Bowser, b. in 1798.
34. Joseph Berkheimer. Never married.
35. Jacob Berkheimer, b. March 6, 1806; d. July 9, 1874; m. Catharine Bowser; b. June 17, 1808; d. Oct. 19, 1866.

29. WILLIAM and HANNAH BERKHEIMER.

Children:

36. Joseph Berkheimer, m. Mary Earnest; ch.: William, m. Florence Kneisly; Dr. George; Bessie, m. M. A. Davis; Hannah Mary, m. Ellis Holsinger.
37. Amos Berkheimer, m. Hannah Honestine; ch.: Sarah, m. Edward Mason; Emma, m. O. S. Acher; Hannah, m. Harvey Brown; Dollie, m. Elmer Claycomb.
38. Sarah Berkheimer, m. Joseph Riddle; ch.: G. W. Riddle, m. Emma Oster; Shannon Riddle, m. Florence Potter; Hannah Mary Riddle, m. Frank Oster.
39. Dorothy Berkhkeimer, m. William Oster; ch.: Sarah, m. David Shaffer; Amanda, m. Dr. Conrad.

30. PETER and MARGARET BERKHEIMER.

Children:

40. John Berkheimer.
41. George Berkheimer, m. Jane Christ; ch.: Jacob Berkheimer, m. Flora Fitler.
42. Samuel Berkheimer, m. Griffiths.
43. Jacob Berkheimer.

31. MOSES and ELIZABETH BERKHEIMER.

Children:

44. Hannah Mary Berkheimer, m. Huston.
45. Matilda Berkheimer, m. James Grindle.
46. Oliver Berkheimer, moved to Ohio.
47. Alonza Berkheimer, m. Mollie Barley.
48. Andrew Berkheimer.
49. Aaron Berkheimer.
50. Emma Berkheimer.
51. Agnes Berkheimer.
52. Elmyra Berkheimer.

32. JOHN BERKHEIMER and SARAH SHATZER.

Children:

53. John Berkheimer, m. Jane Christ.
54. Alexander Berkheimer, m. Elmira Claycomb.
55. Frank Berkheimer, m. Moses.
56. Mandilla Berkheimer, m. John Brown.
57. Mary Berkheimer, m. John Smith.
58. Sarah Berkheimer, m. Thomas Way.

33. SARAH and ISAAC BOWSER (son of George).

Children:

59. Joseph Bowser, b. Sept. 13, 1824; d. 1905.
60. George W. Bowser, b. Nov. 1, 1825; d. June 25, 1898; m. Frances Matilda Gillett, b. Feb. 18, 1839; d. Dec. 10, 1911. See (17) under "John and Eve."
61. Catharine Bowser, b. Mar. 3, 1827; d. 1910. Single.
62. Hannah Bowser, b. May 17, 1828; d. June 24, 1891; m. George Bollinger, b. 1838; d. 1910 in Sioux City, Ia.; ch.: Elizabeth, m. Joseph Bates, Detroit, Mich.
63. John Bowser, b. Oct. 25, 1829; m. Mary Echert, d. at Claysburg, Pa., Sept. 1, 1907; ch.: Mary, Laura, Amanda.
64. William Bowser, b. Jan. 7, 1831; d. 1907; m. Elizabeth Trees; ch.: William, Bernice, Martha, Emma, Ida, Ada.
65. Eve Bowser, b. Aug. 7, 1832; d. 1906. Single.
66. Isaac Newton Bowser, b. Dec. 25, 1833; d. Feb. 21, 1901; m. Annie M. Smith. Dr. Isaac Bowser was a well known dentist and lived at Woodbury, Bedford County, Pa. Later lived at Martinsburg, Blair County, Pa. Ch.: Seward, Howard, Sarah, Haller.
67. Henry Bowser, b. June 10, 1835; died aged about 14 yrs.
68. Margaret Bowser, b. Jan. 18, 1836; m. John W. Cunningham, b. Oct. 9, 1820; d. Dec. 3, 1886. Margaret d. Nov. 2, 1878. Ch.: Charles, John, Bruce, Belle, Bess.
69. David Porter Bowser, b. June 30, 1838; d. Apr. 3, 1882; m. Elizabeth Lyons, b. July 20, 1835; d. Jan. 14, 1912. (See John and Eve) (22).
70. Sarah Jane Bowser, b. Oct. 10, 1840.
71. Solomon Bowser, b. Sept. 13, 1842; died in Civil War.
    a70. Frederick Bowser, b. Dec. 8, 1844.

60. GEORGE and FRANCES MATILDA (Gillett) BOWSER. See John and Eve (17) for children.

a71. Matilda Bowser.
72. Gilbert Bowser.
73. Charles T. Bowser (eldest son), b. Sept. 25, 1858; d. May 12, 1906; m. Mary Snyder, b. Apr. 28, 1863.
74. Samuel H. Bowser, b. July 16, 1860, m. Crecie Belle Nesbit, b. Sept. 3, 1862.
75. Thomas L. Bowser, b. Nov. 6, 1863; d. Aug. 5, 1901. Grocer with his brother Charles.
76. Sadie E. Bowser, b. July 28, 1870; m. Jesse J. Sankey. Live in Sunbury, Pa.

69. DAVID PORTER and ELIZABETH.

Children:

77. Catharine V. Bowser, b. Jan. 2, 1874; m. (1) Elmer E. Casiber, (2) John S. Schreyer; address, Crafton, Pa.
78. Alpha L. Bowser, b. Feb. 28, 1876; m. Gertrude E. Cox, Crafton, Pa.; ch.: James Robert, b. Apr. 4, 1906; Alpha Lyons, b. Aug. 21, 1910; Margaret Elizabeth, b Jan. 25, 1917.

35. JACOB and CATHARINE BERKHEIMER.

Children:

79. Margaret Berkheimer, b. 1877; d. 1893; m. Michael Stambaugh, b. 1824; d. 1899.
80. Catharine Berkheimer, b. 1829, d. 1910; m. John H. Bowser, b. 1814, son of "Davie" John.
81. Mary Berkheimer, b. Aug. 9, 1831; d. July 21, 1919; m. Jacob Iches.
82. Sarah Berkheimer, d. single, aged 73.

83. John Berkheimer, d. aged 70; m. Catharine Claycomb.
84. George Berkheimer, d. aged 71; m. Rebecca Acker, d. aged 59.
85. Annie Berkheimer, b. 1845; d. Dec. 6, 1867; m. David C. Ling.,
86. Matilda Berkheimer, b. Oct. 10, 1847; lives at St. Clairsville, Bedford Co., Pa.; single.
87. Alexander Berkheimer, b. 1861; d. Sept. 20, 1862.
88. Elizabeth Berkheimer, d. 1841.

80. CATHARINE and JOHN H. BOWSER.

Children:

89. Quitman Bowser, b. 1851; m. (1) Emma Rock; (2) King.
90. John F. Bowser, b. 1853; m. Mary Dougherty.
91. Mary Bowser, b. 1855; m. Michael D. Smeltzer.
92. Alexander Bowser, b. 1857; d. 3 yrs. of age.
93. Jacob Bowser, b. 1859; m. (1) Sarah Oster; (2) Amanda Schroyer.
94. Leander H. Bowser, b. 1861; m. Minnie Crisman.
95. William Bowser, b. 1863; m. (1) Sadie Claycomb, (2) Maud Wolf.
96. George W. Bowser, b. 1866, living on his great-grandfather David Bowser's farm near St. Clairsville, Bedford Co., Pa. A slate stone picked from the hillside marks David Bowser's grave in the old cemetery on his farm with the year of his death, 1813, aged 75 years.
97. Alice Bowser, b. 1867; m. Jacob Dively.
98. Charles C. Bowser, b. 1871; m. Bessie Imes.

25. JOHN (4), (DAVID (3), MATHIAS (2), MATHIAS, SR. (1).

Children:

99. Jacob H. Bowser, b. Nov. 6, 1808; d. May 22, 1887; m. Margaret Hillegas, b. 1814.
100. David H. Bowser, b. Dec. 21, 1810; m. Charlotte Potts, dau. of Rev. Jephthah and Mary Potts.
101. John H. Bowser, b. Aug. 14, 1814; d. 1889; m. Catharine Berkheimer. See children under Catherine and John H. (80).
102. Elizabeth Bowser, b. 1816; m. Charles W. Colvin, of Bedford Co., Pa.
103. George W. Bowser, b. 1820; d. 1885; m. Rebecca L. Burns, b. 1832; d. 1870. They lived in Napier Township, Bedford Co., Pa.
104. Alice Colvin, m. John Gerlinger. See 121.

99. JACOB H. and MARGARET BOWSER.

Children:

105. John Bowser, b. 1839; m. Jane Chilcott; ch.: Nora, Alice, Annie, Lulu, Blanche, Ray
106. Elizabeth Bowser, b. 1837; m. A. J. Kegg.
107. Amanda Bowser, b. 1842; m. George Marshall; ch.: Mamie, Ward.
108. Matilda Bowser, b. 1857; m. Jacob Blackburn; also known as Hester M.; ch.: Ada, Carrie, Clifford.

a108. Emma M. Bowser, b. 1848; m. Thomas Alstatt; address, Windber, Somerset Co., Pa.; ch.: Millie, Keiffe.

109. George Polk Bowser, b. 1845; m. Mary J. Clark.

109. GEORGE POLK and MARY J. BOWSER. Address, Alum Bank, Bedford Co., Pa.

Children:

110. Jacob Bowser; m. Carrie Blackburn; ch.: Harold, Walter, Ruth, Charles.
111. Elmer Bowser; m. Carrie Hoover; ch.; Rayford, Dorothy, Gladdys, Paul.
112. Myrtle Bowser; m. John Heinze; ch.: Charles.

113. Sewell Bowser; m. Ada Barefoot; ch.: Kenneth, Warren, Russel, Carl, Aline.
114. Carrie Bowser; m. Harry Schrock; ch.: Vera.
116. Harry Bowser; m. Mattie Ellison; ch.: Ruth, Viola, Stanley, Evelyn, Alton.
117. Emerson Bowser.
118. Jerl Bowser.
119. Helen Bowser.

100. DAVID H. and CHARLOTTE BOWSER.

Children

120. Dr. Alexander J. Bowser, b. Nov. 27, 1862; d. Apr. 11, 1906; m. (1) Louie O. Mock; (2) Mary P. Amick.* ch. by second marriage, Georgia A.; David P., d 1897; Alex J. Jr., d. 1906.

*Daughter of George B. and Mary P. Amick of St. Clairsville.

102. ELIZABETH (BOWSER) and CHARLES W. COLVIN.

Children:

121. Alice Colvin, m. John Gerlinger.
122. George Colvin, m. Belle Williams.
123. Charles Colvin, m. Wishers.
124. John Colvin, m. Kerr.
125. William Colvin.
126. Frank E. Colvin, Esq.; m. Effie Wilhelm.
127. Blanche Colvin, m. Roy Stauflet.

103. GEORGE and REBECCA BOWSER.

Children:

128. James S. Bowser, b. 1860; m. Kerr.
129. Harry Bowser, b. 1864; m. Harvey.
130. Ralph Bowser, b. 1867.

13. JOHN (3), MATHIAS, JR. (2), MATHIAS, SR. (1). John Bowser, a soldier of the Revolutionary War, bought land on Yellow Creek, Hopewell Twp., Bedford County, Apr. 5, 1797. Deed Book Vol. I, page 479: "Know that I, Jos. Haines of Hopewell Twp., made an improvement on a tract of land in March, 1796, joining lands with Melor and Jos. Snyder and Tusseys Mountain in Hopewell Twp. and on Apr. 5, 1797, for the sum of 26 lbs. ten shillings, to me in hand paid by John Bowser, did sell improvement and to warrant and defend it from me and my heirs forever unto said John Bowser of Woodbury Twp., County of Bedford." Signed in German.* Here, on these fertile acres, John Bowser and Mary, his wife, lived until his death in 1813. (See his will). His great-grandson, Henry P. Bowser, lives in Hopewell Twp. about three miles east of the old John Bowser homestead.

*The signature is that of Joseph Haines, the grantor, not of John Bowser and Mary.

Children:

131. John Bowser, b. before 1770.
132. Jacob Bowser, b. 1770.
133. Mathias Bowser, b. Dec. 16, 1773; d. at Kittanning, Pa., Jan. 4, 1830; m. Christianna Loy.
134. Valentine Bowser, b. 1777; d. 1852; m. Elizabeth Fluke of Hopewell, b. 1782; d. 1879, near Montgomeryville, Pa.
135. Samuel Bowser, b. 1778; m. Catharine Snyder.
136. Nicholas Bowser, b. 1781 or 1782; d. 1862 at Hopewell; m. Elizabeth ———.

137. Peter Bowser, b. 1786; d. 1879; m. Sarah Russell, b. 1787.
138. Mary Bowser, m. John Burnhamer.
139. Elizabeth Bowser, m. Abram Swigart.
140. Catherine Bowser, m. Peter Kline.
141. Julia Ann Bowser, m. David Flenner.
142. Barbara Bowser, m. Joseph Bowser, b. 1791; d. 1873.

133. MATHIAS (4), JOHN HOPEWELL (3), MATHIAS, JR. (2), MATHIAS, SR. (1). Mathias Bowser was the first of John Bowser's family to settle in Armstrong County. He came to Kittanning five years before the town was organized and bought a tract of land now lying within the city limits. Later he moved to Kentucky. He returned to Kittanning some years afterward, where he died in 1830. He built the first brick house in Kittanning. The old Hague Hotel building on Market Street, still standing and in good condition, attesting the honest workmanship of its builder, was erected by Mathias Bowser in 1826. It was built very early in the history of the town and on the very site of the ancient Indian town destroyed by Colonel John Armstrong in 1756. Mrs. Margaret Bowser, wife of Jonas Bowser, a niece of Mathias Bowser, frequently, when a child, visited the house of her uncle in Kittanning, which was the above-mentioned hotel, and saw Indian beads which the children of Mathias had found when the yard of their house was spaded. Mathias Bowser was married to Christianna Loy, daughter of Martin Loy, a wealthy land owner and merchant of Loysburg, Bedford County, Pa. Loysburg lies 4 miles west of the John Bowser homstead in Hopewell Twp. On the well-preserved tombstones marking the resting place of Mathias and his wife Christianna in the old burying ground in the heart of the town we noted the following:

(1) Mathias Bowser, b. Dec. 16, 1773; d. Jan. 4, 1830.

"Far from afflictions, toil and care
Thy happy soul is fled;
The breathless clay shall slumber here,
Among the silent dead."

(2) Christianna L., wife of Mathias Bowser, b. May, 1787, d. April 13, 1855, aged 67 years and 11 months.

(3) Catharine Bowser, b. Feb. 17, 1811; d. Dec. 16, 1830. Daughter of Mathias and Christianna Bowser.

(4) George Augustus, b. Sept. 30, 1832; d. April 5, 1833. Son of Dr. G. A. Meeker and Mary (Bowser), daughter of Mathias and Christianna Bowser. (Mary Meeker died in Tennessee.)

Children:

143. Catherine Bowser, b. Feb. 17, 1811; d. Dec. 16, 1830.
144. Rebecca Bowser.
145. Nancy E. Bowser, m. Steven B. Young.
146. Martin L. Bowser, b. 1814 in Armstrong County, Pa.; d. Jan. 23, 1888, in W. Va.; m. Nancy McGinnis, d. 1892.
147. William A. Bowser, b. 1816, a physician, lived at Callensburg, Pa. He had a son Heber (d.) and 3 daughters; d. in 1865.
148. Mary Bowser, m. George A. Meeker; d. in Tennessee.
149. Emanuel Bowser, b. 1824, a physician and surgeon in Civil War; d. at Houston, Tex.; single.
150. Albert I. Bowser, b. 1826; d. young.
151. Margaret Bowser, m. Elisha D. Barrett; lived in Muskingum, Ohio; d. 1849.

146. MARTIN LOY (5), MATHIAS (4), JOHN (3), MATHIAS (2), MATHIAS (1). Martin Loy Bowser and Nancy McGinnis lived in Kentucky; d. 1892.

Children:

152. Flora T. Bowser, b. Mar. 10, 1846; m. Aaron Klipstein; d. Apr. 20, 1912; ch.: Augustus, Loy, Catharine.
153. Christianna Bowser, b. Nov. 28, 1842; m. Samuel Fluharty; are living in W. Va.; ch.: Minnie, Nancy, Della, Virgil (d.).
154. Martin Luther Bowser, b. June 26, 1859; m. (1) Edith Krotzer; (2) Mary M. Krotzer; ch.: Winnefred L. Bowser, b. Dec. 30, 1894; m. James A. Gault, Jr., II, (ch.) James A. Gault, III, b. May 9, 1918; Cecil Edith Bowser, b. July 18, 1897; m. John P. Roberts of Ford City, Pa.; (ch.) John Martin Roberts, b. Apr. 13, 1922; Elizabeth Claire Bowser, b. Sept. 14, 1900; Jeane Rebecca Bowser, b. July 11, 1902; Martin Kenneth Bowser, b. Feb. 1, 1905.
155. William W. Bowser, b. July 4, 1849; d. in California; never married.
156. Cleora C. Bowser, b. Mar. 7, 1851; living at Sardis, Ohio; m. Lively Fluharty; ch.: Oscar, Huber.
157. Virgil M. Bowser, b. June 7, 1852; lives at Ravenwood, W. Va.; m. Nancy Fluharty; child: Nancy.
158. Homer Loy Bowser, b. Jan. 6, 1854; d. May 9, 1919; m. Marietta Jenkins; ch.: Ora, d.; Ella living in Akron, Ohio; Orin, living in Huntingdon, W. Va.; William living in Paden City, W. Va.
a158. Belle I. Bowser, m. J. W. Morgan.
160. Adda Liletta Bowser, b. Aug. 7, 1857; m. John Watkins; living in W. Va.; ch.: Jessie, Earnest, Stephen, Gaeta, Dassie, John.
161. Heber O. Bowser, b. April 26, 1862; m. ——— Pipher; ch.: Philip, b. 1902; Michael, b. 1908.
162. Gaeta Bowser, b. Nov. 28, 1863; d. July 30, 1918, at Little Rock, Ark.; m. Ella Champion. He was a business man of large interests and owner of the Bowser Company Furniture Store.
163. Minnie M. Bowser, b. Sept. 6, 1865; m. James Feist; lives in W. Va.

147. WILLIAM ALEXANDER (5), MATHIAS (4), JOHN (3), MATHIAS (2), MATHIAS (1). Dr. William Alexander Bowser was born Feb. 22, 1822; d. Nov. 29, 1865. He lived in Callensburg, Pa.; m. (1) Anna MacDowell, d. May 21, 1848.

Children:

147. Emma Margaret Bowser, b. Apr. 23, 1846; m. Samuel Frampton Shields, b. Jan. 27, 1840; d. Aug. 17, 1919. They lived near Callensburg, Clarion County, Pa., until 1875, when they moved to Allerton, Iowa, where Mrs. Shields still lives.

Children:

(147) Frank Bowser Shields, b. May 15, 1867; m. Stella Brown; address: Denver, Colo.; ch.: Gussie Margaret Shields, b. Apr. 23, 1893; Cecil Helen Shields, b. Mar. 1, 1895, m. Findley George; Howard Samuel Shields, b. Mar. 8, 1897; served in inf. in World's war; Kathleen Margaret Shields, b. June 6, 1899.

(147) Edward Arthur Shields, b. Feb. 13, 1869; d. July 4, 1870.

(147) Anna Adella Shields, b. Jan. 4, 1871; m. Joshua Davis; address: Reeder, Colo.; ch.: Caroline Margaret Davis, b. June 4, 1898.

(147) Sallie Ellen Shields, b. Aug. 11, 1872; single.

(147) Mary Core Shields, b. Feb. 17, 1874; m. James E. Moore, d. 1908; ch.: Howard Shields Moore, b. Mar. 16, 1901; Harold Boise Shields, b. Dec. 17, 1904.

(147) Ida Nan Shields, b. May 9, 1875; m. Judge James P. Hewitt; address: Des Moines, Iowa; ch.: Ruth Georgia Hewitt, b. May 27, 1903; Elizabeth Nan Hewitt, b. Jan. 26, 1905; James Randolph Hewitt, b. Nov. 27, 1906; Edwin Shields Hewitt, b. Apr. 16, 1908.

(147) Heber Rex Shields, b. Dec. 21, 1876; m. Susan McNab; d. May 8, 1921; address: Vega, Tex.; ch.: Vernon Frampton Shields, b. Sept. 27, 1897; served in the Marine Corps in the World's war; Elbert Kent Shields, b. Nov. 10, 1899; Edith Claire Shields, b. Sept. 24, 1901; Rachel Ethel Shields, b. 1903; Emma Margaret Shields, b. June 6, 1905; Susan Rexine Shields, b. Feb. 6, 1914.

(147) John Craig Shields, Jr., b. Oct. 6, 1878; veteran of the Spanish-American War, Co. H, 51st Iowa Reg.; m. Othelia W. White; address: Fort Yates, N. D.; ch.: John Frampton Shields, b. July 7, 1921.

(147) Minnie Emma Shields, b. Aug. 2, 1880.

(147) Harlan Samuel Shields, b. April 19, 1882.

(147) Edith Zella Shields, b. Feb. 22, 1885; m. Dr. Fred S. Wells; address: Des Moines, Iowa; ch.: Frederick L. Wells, Jr., b. Apr. 27, 1920.

(147) Benjamin Prentiss Shields, b. Dec. 2, 1888; m. Mary Karlinski; address: Mobridge, S. D.; ch.: John Craig Shields, b. June 9, 1918.

(147) Rev. Ried Frampton Shields, b. Mar. 1, 1893; see Biographies.

B147. CHRISTIANNA LOY BOWSER, b. May 17, 1848; m. JAMES MONTGOMERY CLUGH, b. Sept. 11, 1843; d. Nov. 5, 1920; address: Bloomington, Neb.

Children:

(147) Anna Belle Clugh, b. July 14, 1869; d. Apr., 1872.

(147) William Bowser Clugh, b. Jan. 28, 1871; m. May Kerrivan; ch.: William, Jr., b. June 25, 1901; Francis, b. Oct., 1904; Ramona Belle, b. May 30, 1902.

(147) Kate Emma Clugh, b. June 30, 1873; m. Walter Lloyd Hayden, b. Mar. 25, 1867; ch.: Josephine Maxine, b. Apr. 12, 1901; Catharine Eleanor, b. Oct. 14, 1902.

(147) Francis Loy Clugh, b. Sept. 2, 1875; m. Mar. 16, 1901.

(147) Nancy Eleanor Clugh, b. Feb. 17, 1877; m. Clarence E. Harman, b. 1877; ch.: Frederick Clugh, b. Nov. 21, 1902; Virginia Clare, b. July 20, 1907.

(147) Mary Eva Clugh.

(147) Thomas Clugh.

(147) Heber Clugh, b. Jan. 23, 1883; m. Rose Farmer; ch.: Dorothy, b. Feb., 1908; Heber, Jr., b. May, 1911.

147. DR. WILLIAM ALEXANDER BOWSER, married (2) NANCY ELEANOR BRANDON, d. Nov. 1905.

Children:

(147) Alice Bowser, b. July, 1864; m. David A. Moore; address: Newcastle, Pa.; ch.: Eleanor Moore, b. 1900.

(147) Mary Bowser, b. Apr., 1852; m. William English.

(147) Heber B. Bowser, b. 1853; d. 1895; attorney.

(147) Nancy Ellen Bowser, b. May, 1858; d. Sept., 1886; m. David A. Moore; ch.: Phillip A., b. 1883.

134. VALENTINE (4); JOHN (3); MATHIAS (2); MATHIAS (1). Valentine Bowser, the fourth son of John Bowser (Hopewell), b. 1777, d. March, 1852, m. Elizabeth Fluke, oldest child of John Fluke of Hopewell, about 1800. He was reared on the farm of his father, John Bowser, Hopewell Twp., about 4 miles west of Hopewell on the Loysburg road. He

came to Armstrong County, Pa., with his wife and seven children, in 1815. His son Peter was born Oct. 20, 1815, a few weeks after their arrival. They crossed the Allegheny River 2½ miles north of Kittanning, and traveled up the ravine now known as Furnace Run, and took up land one mile north of Walk Chalk, now owned by Dougherty heirs, and there raised a family of eleven children. Valentine and his wife adhered to the use of their native speech, the Palatine German. Elizabeth (Fluke) was born in 1782 and died in the home of her daughter Margaret Bowser (Jonas) Washington Twp., Armstrong County, Pa., 1879, aged 97.

Children:

164. Abram Bowser, b. 1802; d. 1852; m. Mary Ann Stevens, b. 1805, a relative of Alexander Stevens, vice president of the Southern Confederacy.
165. Elizabeth Bowser, b. 1804; m. Henry McAninch.
a165. Jacob Bowser, b. Aug. 5, 1805; d. May 21, 1883; m. Mary Moore, b. July 14, 1806; d. May 21, 1883.
166. Delilah Bowser, b. Nov. 15, 1808; d. April 17, 1887; m. Peter Toy, b. Feb. 8, 1805; d. Oct. 6, 1898.
167. Mary Bowser, b. 1810.
168. Catharine Bowser, b. Oct. 13, 1809; d. 1906; m. Noah Bowser, b. Dec. 1, 1806; d. Oct. 31, 1878.
169. Peter Bowser, b. Oct. 20, 1815; d. Jan. 29, 1879; m. Jane Bowser, b. Dec. 21, 1821; d. Jan. 22, 1900.
170. Margaret Bowser, b. July 30, 1818; m. Jonas Bowser, b. July 13, 1811; d. June 11, 1891.
171. Mathias Bowser, b. Aug. 6, 1820; d. April 22, 1889; m. Rebecca Swigart, b. July 25, 1823; d. Oct. 27, 1901.
a171. William Bowser, b. Nov. 20, 1813; d. Feb. 3, 1898; m. Mary Ann Bowser, b. June 7, 1820; d. Apr. 8, 1906.
172. Valentine Bowser, b. Sept. 28, 1822; d. April 28, 1875; m. Elizabeth Stephenson, b. April 2, 1828; d. July 18, 1900.

164. ABRAM (5); VALENTINE (4); JOHN (3); MATHIAS (2); MATHIAS (1). Abram Bowser was a stone mason by trade. He was also a prosperous farmer. He was killed by the fall of a tree, 1852. His farm was located four miles west of Kittanning and is now owned by the heirs of his grandson William P. Bowser. The children of Abram Bowser inaugurated the Bowser Reunion in Armstrong County in 1899 (see Reunions). He was buried in the Pine Hill cemetery on the hill on the west side of Kittanning—the first burial place in the county west of the Allegheny river. His grave was not marked and the spot is now unknown. He married Mary Stevens, a relative of Alexander Stevens, vice-president of the Southern Confederacy. She was a daughter of Benjamin and Sarah Ann Stevens, who lived at Beaver Falls, Pa., and conducted a hotel. After the death of her husband she married John P. Davis and moved with her husband to Montgomeryville, Armstrong County, Pa., where she died Aug. 8, 1874. She had a liberal education and devoted her talents to beneficent works. She and her husband Abram, as also her second husband, were staunch supporters of the Baptist Church. She was buried in the cemetery of the Montgomeryville Baptist Church. Mary Stevens had two brothers, Vachel and Moses, and one sister, Sophia. Vachel Stevens lived in the South. He owned a large sugar plantation and a great number of slaves. Moses Stevens moved to Ohio. For Sophia see page 151.

Children:

173. Benjamin Stevens Bowser, b. Dec. 20, 1823; d. Dec., 1915; m. (1) Elizabeth Bowser; (2) Elizabeth Yerty, d. 1855; (3) Catharine Yerty, b. Mar. 13, 1835; d. 1914.

174. Elizabeth F. Bowser, b. Dec. 8, 1825; d. Nov. 27, 1908; m. Frederick R. Bowser, b. May 12, 1821; d. Aug. 11, 1874.
175. Sophia Bowser, b. May 29, 1828; m. Adam Wyant, b. July 4, 1813; d. May 28, 1882.
176. Sarah Ann Bowser, b. Oct. 17, 1830; d. March 2, 1916; Jacob Booher, b. Sept. 20, 1830.
177. Delilah Bowser, b. Nov. 27, 1833, d. Mar. 15, 1873; m. (1), Abram Frick, b. Jan. 24, 1830; d. Oct. 7, 1862; (2) John D. Wolf.
178. Eli Bowser, b. Jan. 29, 1835.
179. Mathias Stevens Bowser, M.D., b. May 14, 1837; m. Elizabeth Booher, b. Sept. 6, 1841.
180. Rosana Bowser, b. April 4, 1840; d. Aug. 18, 1880; m. Archibald Bowser, b. Nov. 1, 1836; d. Nov. 12, 1889.
181. Jane Bowser, b. April 15, 1842; d. July, 1892; m. Adam Grantz, b. March 25, 1837; d. April 22, 1905.
182. Joshua Crawford Bowser, m. Kiziah Bowser, b. Dec., 1841.
183. Nancy Bowser, d. in infancy.
184. Susan Bowser, d. in infancy.
185. James Hindman Bowser, b. June 7, 1852; m. (1) Amanda J. Bowser, b. May 5, 1855; (2) Alberta Olevia Anylock, b. 1855.

173. BENJAMIN S. (6), ABRAM (5), VALENTINE (4), JOHN (3), MATHIAS (2), MATHIAS (1). Benjamin S. Bowser devoted his life to the soil. He was well known throughout the county (Armstrong, Pa.). His beautiful country home was a popular resort to his hosts of friends. He lived to the unusual age of 92 and was familiarly known as "Uncle Benny." He was president of our Bowser Reunion from its organization until his death. He was buried near his home and church at Montgomeryville. See biographies.

173 (2). Children by his second wife, Elizabeth Yerty:
186. Catharine Bowser, b. Feb. 17, 1846; d. June 20, 1892; m. Ezekiel Ekis, b. March 21, 1839; d. Oct. 4, 1900.
187. Ann Eliza Bowser, b. Nov. 18, 1848; m. John M. Hawk, b. Aug 6, 1848.
188. Rachel Bowser, b. 1850; m. (2) Lee Stoops, (1) Gideon McGreggor
189. Christian Yerty Bowser, b. Jan., 1853; m. (1) Sadie J. Helm, b. Nov., 1853; d. March 7, 1910; (2) Delilah Salsbury.
190. William P. Bowser, b. May 9, 1854; d. Dec. 16, 1916; m. Margaret Sindorf, b. July 25, 1857.

173 (3). Children by his third marriage, Catharine Yerty:
191. Mervin C. Bowser, b. 1858; m. Pearl B. Kern. They live on the old Benjamin S. Bowser farm, Adrian, Pa.
192. Ellen Bowser, b. 1860.
193. Abram Bowser, b. 1862; m. Nancy Jack, b. May 20, 1872.
194. Sophia Bowser, b. Mar. 9, 1864; m. (1) Daniel Giles; (2) Grant Coggan.
195. Rosa Bowser; d. in infancy.
196. Stephen Bowser, b. 1866; m. Sally Wible.
197. Denny D. Bowser, b. June 6, 1868; d. Aug. 10, 1920; m. Olive J. Jack, b. May 19, 1869.

186. KATHARINE (BOWSER) and EZEKIEL EKIS.

Children:
198. Henry A. Ekis, b. Sept. 23, 1866; d. Nov. 3, 1905.
199. Benjamin S. Ekis, b. Feb. 17, 1869; d. April, 1898; m. Jennie Foye.
200. Levi B. Ekis, b. June 17, 1870; m. Bertha Bowser.
201. William R. Ekis, b. Dec. 11, 1872; m. Laura S. Keene.
202. Blair C. Ekis, b. May 31, 1875; d. May 1, 1907; m. Ella King.

203. Minnie Ekis, b. Mar. 11, 1877; m. Frederick C. Wehling, b. Feb. 20, 1871; present address: 3029 Owen Ave., Brentwood Boro., Pittsburgh; ch.: Clarence Wehling, b. Oct. 29, 1897; Viola Wehling, b. Dec. 25, 1899; Beulah Wehling, b. Feb. 23, 1900; Leslie Wehling, b. Jan. 12, 1902; Grace Wehling, b. Sept. 21, 1905 Ida Mae Wehling, b. Oct. 24, 1912; Frederick Wehling, Jr., b. June 12, 1916.
204. Mary L. Ekis, b. Mar. 21, 1879; m. Harry Heighley.
205. John C. Ekis, b. Jan. 10, 1881.
206. Katharyn Ekis, b. June 12, 1883.
207. Wilda E. Ekis, b. Apr. 24, 1885; d. Oct., 1899.
208. Tillie B. Ekis, b. June 2, 1899; m. Lee Householder.
209. Charles Ekis, b. June 3, 1892; d. 1892.

187. ANN ELIZA (BOWSER) and JOHN HAWK.

Children:

210. Benjamin S. Hawk, b. Feb. 9, 1871; m. Lina Craig.
211. Dr. Mortimore C. Hawk, b. Jan. 11, 1893; m. Pearl E. Strayer of Colorado.
212. Jennie Roduska Hawk, b. Oct. 7, 1874; m. J. W. Gumbert.
213. Hattie May Hawk, b. March 28, 1876; m. J. Hays McDonald.
214. William E. Hawk, b. Aug. 31, 1877; m. Edith Baum.
215. Flossie Ora Hawk, b. Dec. 26, 1878; m. H. A. Waugaman.
216. Elizabeth Lee Hawk, b. May 27, 1880; m. Homer Ruff.
217. John Herbert Hawk, b. Nov. 12, 1881; m. Dollie Steinbeck.
218. Rachel C. Hawk, b. May 17, 1883; m. Chates Simson.
219. Grace A. Hawk, b. Jan. 23, 1885; m. Guy Albright.
220. Mervin C. Hawk, b. July 6, 1886; m. Mabel Matin.
221. Mildred Florence Hawk, b. Sept. 17, 1888; m. Clifford Rechards.
222. Anna Lee Hawk, b. Sept. 17, 1892; d. Feb. 24, 1921; m. David Boggs.
223. Hyatt L. Hawk, in World war, b. April 8, 1896; m. Jennifer E. Shaul, b. Sept. 26, 1898; ch.: Edward Stanley, b. Dec. 23, 1920. Ann Eliza (Bowser) Hawk and husband, John M., live in West Kittanning. He is a prominent contractor and builder. See biographies.

189. CHRISTIAN YERTY and SADIE J. (HELM) BOWSER. Christian Y. Bowser is an extensive farmer of Washington Twp., Armstrong Co., Pa.; address: Cowansville.

Children:

224. Ralph D. Bowser, school teacher, b. March, 1883; d. Feb., 1905.
225. Vima E. Bowser, b. July, 1884; m. Curtis Toy.
226. Mabel Sidney Bowser, b. Jan., 1886; d. Feb., 1914; m. Blair Gumbert.
227. Anna Arminta Bowser, b. Oct., 1887; m. R. M. Collier, b. March, 1888.
228. B. S. Watson Bowser, b. Oct., 1889; m. Essie R. Tarr.
229. Polly Irene Bowser, b. July, 1894; m. H. L. Benton.
230. Spurgeon Bowser, b. June, 1898.

190. WILLIAM P. and MARGARET (SINDORF) BOWSER. William P. Bowser during his entire life held a responsible position with the Standard Oil Company. At the time of his death he was living in Parkersburg, W. Va.

Children:

231. Parma Bowser, b. May 14, 1876; d. June 5, 1916; m. William J. Tapp.
232. Park Bowser, b. Nov. 2, 1877; m. Alta Barker.
233. Celesta Bowser, b. Dec. 9, 1879; m. John D. McCutchan.
234. Sadie Bowser, b. Feb. 14, 1882; m. Ami V. Barker.
235. Clema Bowser, b. Oct. 17, 1883; m. Clyde B. Ross.
236. Clarence Bowser, b. May 6, 1889; m. Bertha Linder.
237. Wayne Bowser, b. May 6, 1892; m. Bessie Means.

193. SOPHIA BOWSER m. (1) DANIEL GILES, b. Feb. 3, 1871; d. Sept. 6, 1895.

Children:

238. Homer Giles, b. Feb. 4, 1891; m. Minnie Ludwig, b. Jan. 9, 1892; ch.: Charles, Phyllis and Grace.
239. Goldie Giles, b. June 2, 1892.
240. Mervin Giles, b. Dec. 3, 1893; d. Oct. 26, 1901.
241. Sheridan Giles, b. Feb. 16, 1895; m. Rose Tarr, b. July 26, 1897.

(2) m. Grant Coggan, b. Feb. 13, 1866. Ch.:

242. Herbert Coggan, b. May 22, 1902.
243. Joseph B. Coggan, b. Jan. 14, 1904.
244. Kenneth Coggan, b. Dec. 27, 1907.

194. ABRAM and NANCY (JACK) BOWSER. Carpenter. Address: West Kittanning, Pa.

Child:

245. Ward Bowser, student.

196. STEPHEN and SALLY (WIBLE) BOWSER.

Children:

246. Clinton Bowser.
247. Clyde Bowser.
248. Raymond Bowser.
249. Margaret Bowser.
250. Ruth Bowser.
251. Naomi Bowser.

197. DENNY D. and OLIVE (JACK) BOWSER.

Children:

252. Lenora B. Bowser, b. Mar. 11, 1893; m. W. A. Chaplain, b. Oct. 22, 1894.
253. Bernetta C. Bowser, b. Sept. 11, 1897; m. Elmer Gaiser, b. Sept. 15, 1895; ch.: Harold Geiser, Virginia Gaiser, Lois Gaiser.

174. ELIZABETH BOWSER (6), ABRAM (5), VALENTINE (4), JOHN (3), MATHIAS (2), MATHIAS (1).

Children:

254. Chambers T. Bowser, b. Oct. 17, 1846; d. Sept. 17, 1915; m. (1) Margaret Cook, b. Nov. 30, 1844; d. Oct. 24, 1895; (2) Margaret McCausland, b. May 31, 1853.
255. Adaline Bowser, b. June 24, 1854; d. Mar. 13, 1904; m. Amos T. Fair.
256. David J. Bowser, b. Sept. 24, 1856; m. Kathryn Vensel, b. July 3, 1863; d. July 26, 1909.
257. William R. Bowser, b. Apr. 4, 1859; m. Martha Campbell, b. May 4, 1861. See biographies.
258. Ann Elizabeth Bowser, b. April 23, 1864; m. Lee Guthrie, b. April 10, 1859.
259. Frederick Bowser, b. Jan. 18, 1862; m. Eva Schaffer.
260. Jacob L. Bowser, b. Dec. 23, 1866; d. Aug. 14, 1919; m. Nellie Frederick, d. Sept. 22, 1916; ch.: Frederick, Alene.
261. Mary R. Bowser, b. April 15, 1849; d. March 15, 1854.
262. Margaret Jane Bowser, b. Jan. 15, 1852; d. March 4, 1854.

254. CHAMBERS and MARGARET (COOK) BOWSER.

Children:

263. Francis S. Bowser, b. Aug. 2, 1876.
264. Amos S. Bowser, b. April 10, 1870; m. (1) Matilda D. Kunkle, b. Jan. 19, 1873; d. March 4, 1908; m. (2) Jennie R. Groves, b. Sept. 12, 1874.

265. Elizabeth C. Bowser, b. Mar. 22, 1876.
266. Jessie W. Bowser, b. July 5, 1874.
267. Bertha Bowser, b. July 1, 1879.
a267. Matilda J. Bowser, b. April 20, 1872.
b267. Minnie C. Bowser, b. April 3, 1882.

255. ADALINE BOWSER, m. AMOS T. FAIR, b. March 23, 1853.
Children:
a255. Frederick Lee Fair, b. July 8, 1874; d. Sept. 17, 1893.
b255. Clara Myrtle Fair, b. March 6, 1877; d. March 5, 1881.
c255. Daisy Delcine Fair, b. Oct. 20, 1881; m. Frank Croyle.
d255. Leonard Augustus Fair. b. Oct. 28, 1884; m. Anna Rhodes.
e255. Elizabeth Ariminta Fair, b. Sept. 15, 1887; d. April 14, 1893.
f255. Olive Lenore Fair, b. July 25, 1892; d. Nov. 11, 1918; m. Ray Snyder.

256. DAVID and KATHRYN VENSEL BOWSER.
Children:
268. Frederick H. Bowser, b. Dec. 13, 1882; m. Eleanor Friskorn, b. Jan. 23, 1888; ch.: Glen, b. Dec. 14, 1911; John Nenry, b. March 2, 1913; Clair, b. March 14, 1918.
269. Pearl Bowser, b. July 16, 1887; m. Ulysses Lasher, b. Aug. 15, 1883; d. March 30, 1914; ch.: Edna, b. Aug. 12, 1905; Kenneth, b. Oct. 9, 1907; Robert, b. June 20, 1912; Donald, b. July 8, 1914.
270. Viola Bowser.
271. Sarah Bowser, b. Jan. 24, 1892; m. Nelson McClay, b. Sept. 6, 1894; ch.: June McClay, b. April 16, 1916.
272. Calvin Bowser, b. Sept. 26, 1895; in Prov. Motor Amb. Co. No. 618 Reg., World war.
273. Mary Bowser, b. Feb. 20, 1900.
274. Oliva Bowser, b. May 10, 1903; m. Andrew Edwards, b. Oct. 18, 1901; child:
275. Doris Edwards, b. July 23, 1920.

257. WILLIAM R. BOWSER and MARTHA CAMPBELL.
Child:
276. Gertie Bowser, b. Aug. 15, 1880; m. Leroy Bargerstock, b. Feb. 7, 1877; ch.: Ralph, b. Dec. 9, 1905; Harland G., b. Jan. 26, 1912; Helen C.

258. ANN (BOWSER) and LEE GUTHRIE.
Child:
277. Elizabeth Guthrie, b. May 20, 1892.
278. Ira D. Guthrie, b. Oct. 15, 1897; m. Grace Bierline, b. May 27, 1896; ch.: John Darwood Guthrie, b. May 31, 1920.
279. Adelynne L. Guthrie, b. Aug. 3, 1899.

264. AMOS S. and MATILDA D. (KUNKLE) BOWSER. Amos S. Bowser is a farmer of Washington Twp., Armstrong Co., Pa.
Children:
a264. Florence E. Bowser, b. Sept. 13, 1891; m. Jay Yerty, b. April 7, 1890.
b264. Edward T. Bowser, b. Aug. 29, 1893.
c264. Lewis S. Bowser, b. July 17, 1899; m. Violet Rice.
d264. Clarence E. Bowser, b. Jan. 2, 1902; d. July 26, 1909.
Amos S. and (2) Jennie R. (Groves).
Children:
a264. Chambers A. Bowser, b. Oct. 12, 1911.

175. SOPHIA WYANT (6), ABRAM (5), VALENTINE (4), JOHN (3), MATHIAS (2), MATHIAS (1). Sophia (Bowser) Wyant is the third child of Abram and Mary Ann Stevens Bowser. She was reared in Franklin Twp., Armstrong Co., Pa.; m. Adam Wyant, March 25, 1847, a prominent farmer. Mrs. Wyant is still living at the remarkable age of 94 and retains the full use of her mental faculties. She has been able to attend all the Bowser reunions since the first one in 1899. For more than twenty years her children and descendants have gathered at her home on May 29th in the celebration of her birth.

Children:

280. Mary Wyant, b. March 2, 1848; m. Albert H. Rea; ch.: Albert W., b. Nov. 6, 1876; m. Elizabeth Bandi, b. Feb. 21, 1878; (ch.: Ira S., Merl W.; Floyd, Enza E., Alton O.); Tillie Belle, b. 1875; d. 1884.
281. Delilah S. Wyant, b. Sept. 23, 1849; m. George Boylstein, b. July 28, 1845; d. April 10, 1910.
282. Eli Fluke Wyant, b. Aug. 9, 1851; m. Parmelia Sindorf, b. Dec. 27, 1853.
283. Christina Wyant, b. March 13, 1853; m. Thomas Jack, b. May 11, 1844; d. March 24, 1915.
284. Benjamin Wyland Wyant, b. Sept. 4, 1855; m. Cynthia A. Dickey, daughter of Samuel H. and Diana (Wolfe) Dickey, b. June 26, 1853.
285. Emma T. Wyant, b. Feb. 4, 1858; m. Frank L. Wolfe, b. Jan. 1 1858; d. Sept. 6, 1915.
286. Catharine Wyant, b. April 13, 1860; m. Isaac F. Kramer, b. Jan. 17, 1865; ch.: Margaret, b. Jan. 12, 1896; d. July 30, 1896; Frederick, b. Sept. 12, 1898; d. May 1, 1920.
287. Dr. Jay B. F. Wyant, b. Aug. 7, 1862; m. Mary Louise Gilbert, b. May 11, 1864. See biographies.
288. Margaret Wyant, b. Sept. 2, 1868; m. (1) Labana Wolfe; (2) Thomas Cramer.
289. Susanette Wyant, b. June 3, 1869; m. William Manross, b. 1865.

281. DELILAH S. and GEORGE BOYLSTEIN.

Children:

290. Archibald Boylstein, b. 1869; d. Jan. 12, 1910; m. Elizabeth Serene; ch.: May.
291. George L. Boylstein, b. 1871; m. Kate Haines; ch.: Jessie, Elsie, James, Jean, Frederick, Daniel, Hainer.
292. Elizabeth Boylstein, b. 1875; m. James Boyd Greer; ch.: Mary Louise.
293. Alma Kathryn Boylstein, b. 1879; m. John William Gess; ch.: John W., Jr.
294. Sarah Boylstein, b. 1887; m. John Clayton Douglass.
295. Daisie Jeannette Boylstein, b. 1891; m. George Edward Hanley.
296. Sophia Boylstein.

282. ELI FLUKE and PARMELIA WYANT.

Children:

297. Alma Wyant, b. May 11, 1874; m. William Anderson.
298. James Ray Wyant, b. Dec. 25, 1875.
299. Stella Mindon Wyant, b. Feb. 2, 1877.
300. Reno Curtis Wyant, b. 1879; d. young.
301. Ray Finley Wyant, b. Nov. 11, 1880; m. James.
302. Sophia Isabelle Wyant, b. Oct. 8, 1884; m. Howard Butcher.
303. May Wyant, b. 1886; m. Roy Krebs.

283. CHRISTINA WYANT and THOMAS JACK.

Children:

304. Laura M. Jack, b. May 9, 1876; d. May 24, 1900; m. Harve Mechling, b. 1876; ch.: Hazel, Neal.
305. Margaret Jack, b. Nov. 27, 1876; m. Herbert Summers; ch.: Edwin, Homer, Ira, Howard, Thomas.
306. Robert Jack, m. Alice Stringer, b. Apr. 11, 1880; ch.: Daisey, Lillian, Mary, Louise, Martha, Jean.
307. Rose Jack, b. Jan. 10, 1880; m. Frank Burdett; ch.: Thelma, Saidie Louise.
308. Milton Jack, b. Aug. 5, 1881; m. Dorothy Wolfe, b. May 11, 1892; ch.: Charles, Helen, Ruth.
309. Labana Jack, b. Dec. 29, 1890; m. Marie Bish, b. Jan. 22, 1891; ch.: Wallace, Uda, Neil.

284. BENJAMIN W. and CYNTHIA WYANT.

Children:

310. Finne Lula Wyant, b. Aug. 25, 1878; d. Aug. 30, 1879.
311. Mary Josephene Wyant, b. May 22, 1880; m. Horace E. Nichols.
312. Ch.: Kenneth W. Nichols, b. Feb. 12, 1907.
313. John Finley Wyant, b. July 7, 1883.
314. Samuel B. R. Wyant, b. May 3, 1886.
315. Anna Sophia Wyant, b. Jan. 16, 1890; m. Joseph Leard.
316. Ch.: Finley Arthur, b. Nov. 14, 1915.
317. Ruth L., b. Jan. 26, 1912.
318. Benjamin F. Wyant, b. June 26, 1892; m. Lottie May Wolfe.
319. Ch.: Harding Ashley, b. Nov. 16, 1915.
320. Muriel Josephine, b. Oct. 6, 1917.
321. Gaynell Isabell, b. Feb. 23, 1920.

285. EMMA and FRANK L. WOLFE.

Children:

322. Daniel W. Wolfe, b. Aug. 29, 1877; m. Pearl Lias, b. April 11, 1882; ch.: Vernon, Pauline, Theone, Sidney, Marian.
323. A. Weldon Wolfe, b. Dec. 22, 1880; d. Apr. 16, 1911.
324. Orca May Wolfe, b. Apr. 22, 1884; m. (1) George McAuley; (2) Victor S. Say, b. Feb. 18, 1887.
325. Clifton Wolfe, b. July 27, 1895; m. Margaret Gilbert, b. Mar. 14, 1895; ch.: Iris, Edward, Claris, Allen.
326. Milburn Wolfe, b. Dec. 25, 1901.

287. DR. J. B. F. and LOUISE (GILBERT) WYANT.

Children:

327. Sophia Irene Wyant, b. Oct. 12, 1886; d. Oct. 8, 1904.
328. Sarah Alleine Wyant, twin of Irene; m. Doctor Edward E. Evens, a prominent physician of McKeesport, Pa.
329. Ch.: Finley Edward.
330. Anna Louise.
331. Margaret C. Wyant, b. Mar. 13, 1890; m. William C. Kline, in banking business New York City.
332. Ch.: Robert Wyant Kline, b. Sept. 15, 1916.
333. Corbin Wayland Wyant, b. Mar. 23, 1896; student Bucknell Univ.
334. Mary Louise Wyant, b. July 20, 1902.

288. MARGARET (WYANT) and LABANA WOLFE (1).

Children:

335. Hazel Wolfe, m. Kenneth Costello; ch.: Mildred, Margaret, Sophia.
336. Kramer Wolfe, b. Oct. 16, 1898; m. Charlotte Raub, b. Sept. 11, 1902.

289. SUSANETTE (WYANT) and WILLIAM MANROSS.
Children:
337. George Manross, b. Sept. 18, 1890; d. Aug. 12, 1908.
338. Luetta Manross, b. July 21, 1894; m. H. B. Phillips, b. Apr. 19, 1888; ch.: Evelyn, Dudley.
339. Benjamin T. Manross, b. Nov. 18, 1900; m. Marie Wolfe, b. 1900; ch.: Betty L.
340. William Manross, b. Sept. 7, 1908.
341. Finley Manross, b. Dec. 27, 1902.
342. Eli Manross, d.
343. Ira Manross, b. Aug. 17, 1892; m. Marie Cochoran.
344. Ch.: William D.

176. SARAH ANN BOWSER (6); ABRAM (5); VALENTINE (4); JOHN (3); MATHIAS (2); MATHIAS (1). Sarah Ann Bowser m. Jacob Booher and lived near Sherrett, Armstrong Co., Pa. They resided on their farm until 1915 when they made their home with their daughter, Mrs. Wilson Fair, W. Kittanning, Pa.
Children:
345. Abram Booher, b. Sept. 26, 1849; d. Aug. 3, 1911; m. Hannah Wyant, b. Dec. 5, 1848.
346. Mary Catharine Booher, d. June 26, 1922; m. William Wyant.
347. Evaline Booher; m. John Frick.
348. Malissa Jane Booher; m. Francis M. Painter.
349. Samuel Furman Booher, m. (1) Sarah Titley; (2) Demps Beighley.
350. Frederick B. Booher; m. Rebecca Crawford.
351. Leah Amanda Booher.
352. Rosanah Booher.
353. Joshua Crawford Booher, M. D.; m. (1) Blanche Taylor (2), Jane Carrier.
354. Sophia Elizabeth Booher; m. Thomas N. Hazlett.
355. Lydia Ann Booher; m. Gideon W. Fair.

345. ABRAM and HANNAH (WYANT) BOOHER. Abram Booher was a resident of Armstrong County, Pa., engaged in stock raising and farming.
Children:
356. Jacob Booher; m. (1) Annie McGlaughlin; ch.: Sarah Pearl; (2) Elizabeth Elder; ch.: Hazel, William, Ellsworth, Erma, Mildred.
357. John Booher; m. Rose Leonard.
358. Edward Booher; m. (1) Jennie June; ch.: Josephene, June, Catharine Gladdys (2) Catharine Harker; ch.: Gertrude, Florence, Lillian.
359. Sadie Booher; m. Finley Shrader; ch.: Herman, Helm.
360. Harry Booher, U. S. Army, Philippines.
361. Samuel Booher; m. Vernie Rickle; ch.: Harold, Delmar, Doris M.
362. Frederick Booher; m. Annie Shrader.

347. EVE (BOOHER) and JOHN FRICK. John W. Frick is a foreman carpenter and bridge builder with the Pennsylvania Railroad—Allegheny Division—a position he has held for nearly 40 years. For several years after his marriage he resided in Armstrong County, Pa., but later moved to Verona, near Pittsburgh, where he has since lived. He and Mrs. Frick were given a memorable Golden Wedding in 1920. The author had the honor of "performing the ceremony."
Children:
363. Charles M. Frick; m. Carrie Starr.
364. Daisy D. Frick; m. James B. Shaw.
365. Katharine M. Frick; m. Edward J. Null.

366. Homer J. Frick; m. Laura Carrier.
367. Gertrude M. Frick; m. Charles P. Donahue.
368. Ford F. Frick. In World War.
369. Orville H. Frick; m. Julia Kent. In World War.
370. Norman E. Frick; m. Belle Candren.
371. Josephine E. Frick; m. Harry A. Depp.
372. John W. Frick, Jr.
373. Carrie L. Frick; d. Jan. 16, 1879.

363. CHARLES M. and CARRIE FRICK; address: Verona, Pa.
Children:
374. Walter M. Frick; b. July 26, 1905.
375. Richard L. Frick, b. April 10, 1913.

364. DAISY D. and JAMES B. SHAW; address: Verona, Pa.
Children:
376. Stanley A. Shaw, b. Sept. 9, 1906.
377. Alexander Shaw, b. Aug. 14, 1908.
378. James B. Shaw, Jr., b. Apr. 26, 1913.

365. KATHARINE M. and EDWARD J. NULL.
Child:
379. David C. Null, b. Aug. 19, 1897.

366. HOMER J. and LAURA FRICK; address: Verona, Pa.
Children:
380. John J. Frick, b. Oct. 8, 1913.
381. Jack Frick b. June 28, 1915.
382. William P. Frick, b. June 30, 1919.

367. GERTRUDE M. and CHAS. P. DONAHUE; address: Wilkinsburg, Pa.
Children:
383. Evelyn Donahue, b. July 26, 1912.
384. Clyde Donahue, b. Nov. 9, 1915.

368. FORD F. FRICK served in the A. E. F. in France as sergeant-major from May 20, 1918, to May 28, 1919. Headquarters, 80th Division.

369. ORVILLE H. FRICK served in the Machine Gun Platoon, Second Cavalry, Philippines, Nov. 18, 1910, to Nov. 18, 1913. Also in the U. S. Naval Reserves, July 3, 1918, to Dec. 10, 1919.

370. NORMAN E. and BELLE FRICK.
Children:
385. Norman E. Frick, Jr., b. Feb. 22, 1913.
386. Wesley Frick, b. Dec. 23, 1920.

348. MALISSA JANE (BOOHER) and FRANK M. PAINTER. Address, Wilkinsburg, Pa.
Children:
387. Edward F. Painter b. June 7, 1878; m. Adalaide Neckerman; ch.: Jay Crawford, b. Aug. 31, 1912; Norman Harding, b. Oct. 16, 1920.
388. Sarah Ann Painter, b. Aug. 9, 1881.
389. Jay Crawford Painter; m. Irma McDonald, b. Dec. 1892.
390. Frank M. Painter, Jr., b. Sept. 23, 1886; d. June 8, 1908.
a390. Mable Alverda Painter, b. Aug. 21, 1890; d. Jan. 24, 1895.

349. SAMUEL FURMAN BOOHER. (See Biographies.)

350. FREDERICK F. B. BOOHER; m. REBECCA CRAWFORD. Farmer. Resides at Cowansville R. D. Armstrong County, Pa.
Children:
391. Mona Viola Booher, d. Dec. 25, 1918; m. C. F. Fair.
392. Flora Belle Booher; m. W. F. Porterfield, d. Oct. 29, 1918.
393. Jay C. Booher; m. Beatrice T. Smith.
Children:
394. Brayden Sherwood Booher, b. Feb. 23, 1916.
395. Frederick Smith Booher, b. June 25, 1917.
396. Mona Viola Booher, b. Feb. 21, 1919.

353. DR. JOSHUA CRAWFORD BOOHER. Doctor Booher is a graduate of Reid Institute and the medical department of the University of Pittsburgh. He is located at Falls Creek, Pa., where he has established a large practice. He made discoveries in the treatment of anthrax which gave him a reputation throughout the country. He married (1) Blanche Taylor; (2) Jane Carrier.
Child:
397. Sarah.

354. SOPHIA ELIZABETH BOOHER, b. July 4, 1868; m. THOMAS N. HAZLETT, b. Apr. 13, 1879. Address: McKeesport, Pa.
Child:
398. Edwin N. Hazlett, b. Jan. 8, 1905.

355. LYDIA ANN BOOHER, m. G. WILSON FAIR. Mr. Fair is a railroad carpenter. Residence at Apple Wold, Kittanning, Pa.
Children:
399. Jacob Clifford Fair.
400. Simon A. Fair.
401. Frederick Booher Fair.

177. DELILAH BOWSER (5); ABRAM (4); VALENTINE (3); MATHIAS (2); MATHIAS (1). Delilah Bowser, b. Nov. 27, 1833; d. ——; m. (1) Abram Frick. Lived at Adrian, Pa.; (2) John D. Wolfe.
Children:
402. Chambers Frick, b. Nov. 26, 1852; m. Nancy Flenner, daughter of David Flenner b. Nov. 23, 1850. (See Biographies.)
403. Catharine Frick, b. Apr. 21, 1854; m. Wyland Lasher, b. Mar. 4, 1850. Address: Adrian, Pa.
404. John Wesley Frick, b. 1860; d. 1862.
405. Luther Frick, d. Dec. 1881.
406. Michael Frick, d. Dec. 1902; m. Leana Wolfe.
407. Charlotte J. Frick, b. Feb. 3, 1862; m. David Booher, b. Aug. 18, 1858. Address: Kittanning, Pa.
408. (2) Dr. William Wolfe, b. 1865; m. Louise Miller. Address: Omaha, Neb.
409. John Wolfe, b. July 8, 1866; d. Sept. 18, 1912; m. Lottie Booher, b. Feb. 28, 1867. Address: Adrian, Pa.
410. Jeannette Wolfe, b. 1869; d. Dec. 11, 1894; m. Samuel Schrechengost.
411. Abram Wolfe, b. Mar. 4, 1871; m. Gertie Henan, b. Sept. 5, 1875.

402. CHAMBERS and NANCY (FLENNER) FRICK. Ex-sheriff Chambers Frick was born and reared near Adrian, Armstrong County, Pa. For years a merchant at Adrian and at present at the same place in mercantile

business with his son, Chambers Frick, Jr. He served one term as sheriff of Armstrong County, Pa. Nancy (Flenner) Frick is a grand-daughter of Julia Ann Bowser, daughter of "Hopewell" John Bowser.

Children:

412. Mary Delilah Frick, b. Sept. 27, 1871; m. George Lasher, b. Sept. 29, 1867. Address: Adrian, Pa.
413. Ada Jane Frick, b. Nov. 24, 1873; m. Edward Montgomery; ch.: Florence, b. Aug. 29, 1902; m. Chas. W. Morgan—ch.: Jane. Frank, b. Aug. 27 1905; Ralph, b. Apr. 10, 1907; Roy, b. March 24, 1908; Anna, b. May 7, 1911; Paul, b. July 18, 1913; Irene Pearl, b. Apr. 29, 1917.
414. Rose Lee Frick, b. Apr. 18, 1876; m. Tony Martin. New Kensington, Pa.
415. Lottie Belle Frick, b. Oct. 31, 1878; m. Sherman Bowser, son of Robinson Bowser. Address: West Kittanning, Pa.
416. Lillian Helen Frick, b. Mar. 7, 1881; m. (1) Joseph Toy; (2) David Achard.
417. James M. Frick, b. Aug. 24, 1883; m. Lettie Montgomery. Address: Adrian, Pa.
418. Florence Frick, b. Dec. 27, 1885; m. Charles Thompson. Address: West Kittanning, Pa.
419. Chambers F. Frick, b. Feb. 28, 1892; m. Mary Serene, b. Oct. 1, 1896. Address: Adrian, Pa.
420. Rufus S. Kank Frick, b. Apr. 13, 1894; m. Erman Tennent, b. May 24, 1893.

403. CATHARINE (FRICK) and WYLAND LASHER. Farmer at Adrian, Pa.

Children:

421. Cora J. Lasher, b. Nov. 10, 1872; m. Doctor Ernest Holtzhauser.
422. Arda J. Lasher, b. July 4, 1875; m. Minnie Croyle.
423. James H. Lasher, b. Jan. 21, 1880; m. Mary Robinson.
425. Maud D. Lasher, b. Oct. 24, 1882; m. Ambrose Bowser.
426. William L. Lasher, b. Mar. 14, 1884; m. Annie Renn.
427. John H. Lasher, b. June 29, 1886; m. Margaret Humes.
428. Dr. Lem A. Lasher, b. Aug. 5, 1889; m. Julia Blosam.
429. Lowen B. Lasher, b. Nov. 9, 1890; m. Mary Engleman.

406. MICHAEL and LEANA FRICK. Michael Frick was killed by the explosion of a boiler.

Children:

430. Dora Frick m. Walter Holmes.
431. Amanda Frick m. Ernest Fair.
432. Charles Frick.

407. CHARLOTTE and DAVID BOOHER. David Booher, son of Bartholmew and Margaret (Bowser) Booher of Adrian, Pa. Carpenter. Address: West Kittanning, Pa.

Children:

433. Nellie Booher, b. Aug. 29, 1880; d. June 18, 1889.
434. Herbert Booher, b. June 9, 1882; m. Violet Crissman, b. Aug. 4, 1882. Contractor and builder of Kittanning, Pa. Ch.: Cecil R., b. Aug. 9, 1907; Herbert, b. Nov. 25, 1910, d. Jan. 5, 1911; Alberta, b. Sept. 8, 1912; Fonda Pearl, b. Aug. 24, 1915; d. Oct. 22, 1916.
435. Bertie Booher, b. June 28, 1884; d. Mar. 9, 1886.
436. Chambers Booher, b. Aug. 16, 1886; d. June 28, 1887.

437. Elmer Booher, b. Nov. 6, 1888; m. Flow Mast, b. Sept. 14, 1891. Ch.: Charlotte L., b. Feb. 2, 1916; Betty W., b. July 28, 1918; Sarah M., b. Apr. 1, 19920. In banking business, Kittanning, Pa.
438. Margaret Booher, b. Feb. 17, 1891; m. Reed Stoops, teacher. Ch.: Glenn, b. June 13, 1912; Reed, b. May 31, 1918; Harold, b. June 6, 1920.
439. Roy Booher, b. July 6, 1893. In World war.
440. Blanche Booher, b. July 4, 1898.
441. Richard Booher, b. July 26, 1900; m. Lucy Harmon, b. Mar. 7, 1899; ch.: Roy F., b. Mar. 15, 1920; Muriel Jane, b. Aug. 8, 1921.
442. John Hartzell Booher, b. Mar. 22, 1903.

408. (2) DOCTOR WILLIAM W. and LOUISE (MILLER) WOLFE. Doctor William is also known as William W. Bowser.

Children:
443. Dell Wolfe.
444. Frederick Wolfe.
445. Robert Wolfe.

409. JOHN and LOTTIE (BOOHER) WOLFE. Address: Adrian, Pa.

Children:
446. Elsie Wolfe, b. May 8, 1893; m. Ira McAuley, b. Oct. 13, 1889; ch.: Lottie, b. Aug. 12, 1913. Address: Adrian, Pa.
447. Bert Wolfe, b. June 27, 1895; medical student; m. Ruth Fitzgerald.
448. Emanuel Wolfe, b. July 12, 1901. Teacher. Adrian, Pa.
449. Larry Wolfe, b. Oct. 8, 1905. Teacher. Adrian, Pa.

410. JEANNETTE and SAMUEL SCHRECKENGOST.

Children:
450. Sannis Schreckengost.
451. Edith Schreckengost.
452. Forest Schreckengost.
453. Viola Schreckengost.
454. Herbert Schreckengost.

411. ABRAM and GERTIE (HENNAN) WOLFE. Abram Wolfe is an iron worker. Residence, W. Kittanning, Pa.

Children:
455. Ethel Wolfe.
456. Naoma Wolfe.
457. Irene Wolfe.

179. DR. MATHIAS STEVENS and ELIZABETH (BOOHER) BOWSER. (See Biographies.)

Children:
458. Addison Bartholomew Bowser, b. May 22, 1858; m. Ella Zelima Stebbins, b. Dec. 10, 1869. (See Biographies.)
459. Esther Jane Bowser, b. Feb. 4, 1860; m. (1) Robert O. Barbor, b. Mar. 4, 1855; (2) Amos T. Fair. Address: Ford City, Pa.
460. Mary Belle Bowser, b. Feb. 24, 1862; m. Solomon Bowser, b. Jan. 9, 1859, d. Apr. 26, 1920.
461. David Elmer Bowser, b. Sept. 23, 1866; d. Oct. 20, 1882.
462. Arda Joshua Bowser, b. July 21, 1868; m. Nellie Craft, b. 1870.
463. Elizabeth Lula Bowser, b. Dec. 14, 1870; m. John Rebolt, b. Sept. 28, 1865.
464. Arlington Reed Bowser, b. June 11, 1875; m. (1) Margaret McCollums, b. Feb. 22, 1881; d. Oct. 20, 1917; m. (2) Mrs. Alice Dougherty.

458. ADDISON B. and ELLA ZELIMA (STEBBINS) BOWSER. (See Biographies.)

Children:

465. Frank Excell Bowser, b. Oct. 31, 1892. Medical student University of Pittsburgh. In Med. Corps and later in training at Camp Lee. World War.
466. Wayland Stanley Bowser. Student University of Pittsburgh. Served as 1st Lt. in France from ——— until ———. In Battle of St. Mihiel.
467. Isabelle Bowser, b. Feb. 14, 1896; m. Dr. E. C. Winters, b. Jan. 17, 1889. (See Biographies.) Ch.: James E. Winters, b. Aug. 26, 1921.
468. Arda Crawford Bowser, b. Jan. 9, 1899. Student at Bucknell; m. Elsie Laura Reitler, b. Oct. 27, 1902.

459. ESTHER JANE (BOWSER) and (1) ROBT. O. BARBOR.

Children:

469. Verner L. Barbor, b. Mar. 21, 1877; m. Edith Davis. Attorney, Pittsburgh, Pa.

Children:

a469. Corabelle Barbor.
b469. Delmont Barbor.
c469. Verner L. Barbor, Jr.
470. Delmont A. Barbor, b. Dec. 14, 1878; m. Anna Wise. Real estate, Wilmerding, Pa.

Children:

471. Verner H. Barbor.
472. James Robert Barbor, b. Oct. 18, 1887; m. Jennie Parker; ch.: Robert, William, Isabelle.
473. Mina Ruth Barbor, b. Sept. 17, 1891; m. Harry R. Mygrant; ch.: Robert, Meriam, Ruth, Elizabeth Jane, Clifford R. d. in San Diego, Cal., Nov. 21, 1913.

460. MARY BELLE and SOLOMON BOWSER. Adrian, Pa.

Children:

475. Margaret E. Bowser, b. May 22, 1882; d. Oct. 3, 1882.
476. Lydia M. Bowser, b. Oct. 30, 1883; m. Andrew Bowser, b. May 14, 1875. Address: Adrian, Pa. Ch.: Wilbert R., b. Apr. 21, 1901; Stanley S., b. June 12, 1903; Herman A., b. Sept. 9, 1905; Kenneth A., b. Dec. 13, 1910; Paul R., b. Sept. 3, 1913.
477. Gracia E. Bowser, b. May 1, 1886; d. May 3, 1887.
478. Sally R. Bowser, b. May 5, 1889; m. Robert Lemmon, b. July 6, 1870; address: Adrian, Pa.; ch.: Russell J., b. July 27, 1908; Sarah E., b. Sept. 3, 1911; Earl W., b. Jan. 16, 1914; James R., b. Sept. 26, 1920.
479. Clarence S. Bowser, b. Nov. 2, 1897. Address: Adrian, Pa.
480. Mathias E. Bowser, b. Jan. 26, 1901. Address: Adrian, Pa.
481. Ella M. Bowser, b. Jan. 30, 1902. At home.

462. ARDA JOSHUA and NELLIE (CRAFT) BOWSER. Rev. Arda J. Bowser was educated at Dennison College and Crozier Theological Seminary. Pastor of the Baptist Church at Delaware, Ohio.

Children:

482. Harry Addison Bowser, b. 1890; m. Rose Nitchman. Served in the late World War, in France, from May 28, 1918, to May 10, 1919, with Battery E, 153d Brigade, 78th Div. 1st Army Corps. Battles: Toul Sector, St. Mihiel, Preny Raid, Meuse Argonne and Grand Pre. Ch.: Jack.
483. Erma Elizabeth Bowser, b. 1892; d. 1893.

463. ELIZABETH LULU and JOHN REBOLT. Address: Templeton, Pa.

Children:

484. Charles Rebolt, b. June 17, 1890; d. Nov. 16, 1910.
485. Frank Rebolt, b. Jan. 19, 1894; m. Florence M. Gray, b. Feb. 21, 1892; ch.: Elizabeth Marghreta, b. Aug. 1, 1919. Address: Templeton, Pa.
486. Genevieve Rebolt, b. June 24, 1908. At home.

464. ARLINGTON REED and MARGARET BOWSER. Teacher, Sherrett, Pa.

Children:

487. Catharine Elizabeth Bowser, b. Jan. 7, 1911.
488. A. Gerald Bowser, b. July 24, 1912.

180. ROSANNAH and ARCHIBALD BOWSER. Archibald Bowser was an iron worker for a number of years in Kittanning, Pa. Later he moved with his family to Dubois; he subsequently removed to Olean, N. Y., where he died, Nov. 12, 1889.

Children:

489. Rhinaldo M. Bowser, b. Jan. 14, 1858; m. Alice Lindsey, b. Apr. 9, 1862. Merchant. Olean, N. Y.

Children:

490. Archibald Milton Bowser, b. Aug. 17, 1884.
492. Beatrice Ileine Bowser, b. Nov. 18, 1896.

492. Adoniram Judson Bowser, b. Sept. 25, 1859; m. (1) Della M. Frye, b. Sept. 7, 1866, d. 1884; (2) Mary H. Miller, b. May 18, 1859, d. 1899; (3) Jeannette G. Byrne, b. Oct. 19, 1871. Prof. Adoniram J. Bowser, music teacher and band leader, resides at Butler, Pa.

Children:

493. Rosanah Mabel Bowser, b. Sept. 18, 1887.
494. Hazel Adelaide Bowser, b. May 27, 1889.
495. Adrian Rupert Bowser, b. Aug. 10, 1894; d. 1895.

496. Furman T. Bowser, b. Aug. 18, 1861; m. Ella Lyle, b. Feb. 13, 1863 Resides at Galeton, Pa.

Children:

497. Daisy Bowser, b. Aug. 27, 1884; d. same year.
498. Archibald William Bowser, b. Nov. 16, 1885; m. Emma Goodrich, b. 1881. Address: New York City.
499. John Fluke Bowser, b. Sept. 6, 1887; d. Feb. 5, 1889.

500. Mary Margaret Bowser, b. June 2, 1863; d. June, 1909; m. Charles Richardson; ch.: Charles Barnes, b. Aug. 10, 1886, d. Jan. 2, 1887.
501. Jacob Fluke Bowser, b. Aug. 31, 1865; m. Ida Coonrod, b. 1871. Resides in Rochester, N. Y.
502. Benjamin Stevens Bowser, b. Dec. 23, 1867; d. Jan. 5, 1870.
503. Rosanah Francis Bowser, b. Oct. 31, 1869; d. Sept. 28, 1891.
504. Ermeda Belle Bowser, b. Nov. 12, 1871; m. Silas Hughes; ch.: Dorthea Irene, b. June 21, 1894, m. Bylgardes; Ester, b. Mar. 19, 1897, m. Arthur E. Doyle.
505. Lillie Myrtle Bowser, b. Apr. 27, 1874; d. Dec. 7, 1911; m. Chester Osterhoudt.
    (a) Ch.: Richard Isaac, b. June, 1897.
    (b) Avanail Lillian, b. Oct. 7, 1904.
506. Lottie Arvilla Bowser, b. Jan. 27, 1878; d. Feb. 26, 1880.
507. Joshua Crawford Bowser, b. Aug. 6, 1880; d. Aug. 28, 1880.

181. JANE (BOWSER) and ADAM GRANTZ. Adam Grantz, blacksmith. Residence, Adrian, Pa. Died in Westmoreland Co., Apr. 22, 1905.

Children:

a507. Alice Grantz, b. Mar. 26, 1860; m. Henry Spang, b. Aug. 17, 1844, d. July 15, 1919. Residence, Leechburg, Pa. Iron worker.
508. Benjamin Grantz.
509. Mary Elizabeth Grantz, b. Sept. 17, 1865; m. John C. Marks, b. Oct. 16, 1864. Railroad engineer. Residence: New Kensington, Pa.
510. Rosa Agnes Grantz, b. Dec. 15, 1867; m. Peter H. Kline, b. Nov. 9, 1857. Photographer, Leechburg, Pa.
511. George Grantz, m. Elizabeth Stahl.

507. ALICE (GRANTZ) and HENRY SPANG.

Children:

512. Smith McKee Spang, b. July 12, 1877; m. Mary Belle Eschelman, b. Mar. 10, 1886; d. Nov. 21, 1918.

Children:

a512. Grant McKee Spang, b. Jan. 16, 1907.
b512. George Henry Spang, b. Jan. 16, 1907.
c512. Beatrice A. R. Spang, b. Dec. 3, 1908.
d512. Mabel Prudence Spang, b. Nov. 12, 1910.

513. William Ernest Spang, b. May 25, 1899; m. Celia McCauley.

Child:

a513. Doyle Henry Spang, b. June 15, 1898.

514. Jesse Bibson Spang, b. Dec. 31, 1884; m. Mattie P. Lascoe.

Children:

a514. Kenneth Earl Spang, b. Apr. 1, 1906.
b514. Dorothy May Spang, b. 1908.
c514. Harold Henry Spang, b. July 31, 1909.
d514. Arthur Spang, b. May, 1914; d. May, 1916.

515. Alfred Spang, b. Sept. 17, 1887; d. Apr. 21, 1890.
516. Harold Henry Spang, b. July 22, 1895. Salesman.

509. MARY ELIZABETH (GRANTZ) and JOHN C. MARKS.

Children:

517. Edith Josephine Marks, b. Jan. 9, 1884; m. William Hardie Ikler, b. July 3, 1872.
Ch.: 517. Helen Elizabeth Ikler, b. Jan. 30, 1909.
518. Muriel Agnes Marks, b. Oct. 21, 1889; m. Henry William Heyer, b. May 4, 1884.
Ch.: 518a. Henry William Heyer, Jr., b. May 13, 1909.
518b. Mary Elizabeth Heyer, b. Jan. 24, 1916.
519. John E. Marks, b. Nov. 24, 1899; m. Mary Cohen, b. Oct. 2, 1900.
520. Helen Elizabeth Marks, b. May 17, 1906.

510. ROSA AGNES (GRANTZ) and PETER H. KLINE.

Children:

521. Ethel Irene Kline, b. July 31, 1891; m. A. O. Kinter.

Child:

522. Marion Agnes Kline, b. Apr. 27, 1916.

523. Marion Rebecca Kline, b. Jan. 9, 1899.
523. Harold Eugene Kline, b. Feb. 13, 1905.

182. JOSHUA CRAWFORD BOWSER, b. 1846; m. Kiziah Bowser, b. Dec. 1, 1842. Joshua Crawford Bowser enlisted in the beginning of the Civil war at the age of 13, and served to the end as a drummer. He

re-enlisted at the close of the war and was stationed first at Sacketts Harbor, N. Y., later at Columbus, Ohio, where he is at present retired.

Children:

524. Ulysses Selby Bowser, m. (1) Annie Lordel; ch.: George, Paul, Louisa, Jay. (2) May Callen; ch.: Agnes, Elizabeth, Annie, Mary and Jacob.

525. George Bowser, b. Mar. 22, 1868; m. Jennie McIntosh, b. Apr. 24, 1880.

Children:

a525. Ralph B., b. Nov. 5, 1902; d. Aug. 20, 1904.
b525. Belva J., b. Jan. 22, 1905.
c525. Helen K., b. Jan. 17, 1908.
d525. Alexander G., b. Nov. 17, 1910.
e525. George, b. Mar. 10, 1915; d. Mar. 16, 1915.

526. Maud B. Bowser, b. May 18, 1870; m. William H. Bowser, son of Mathias and Rebecca; b. Apr. 17, 1865; d. Mar. 19, 1920.

Children:

527. Nula K. Bowser.
528. Ruth R. Bowser, b. Jan. 8, 1893; m. Perry Hampton, b. July 14, 1891; ch.: Helen H., Ardel.
529. William A. Bowser. Enlisted in World War Dec. 21, 1917. Honorably discharged Aug. 12, 1919. Served with No. 405 Third Army Corps. Battles in the Meuse and Argonne Sectors.
530. Margaret Bowser. Student.
531. Harry M. Bowser. Student.

185. JAMES HINDMAN and AMANDA J. BOWSER. James Hindman Bowser was born at the Bowser homestead near Walk Chalk, Armstrong County, Pa., and has resided in the county ever since; at present in West Kittanning. He is president of the Bowser Reunion, which meets annually near Kittanning.

Children:

532. Jessie May Bowser, b. 1873; m. Captain C. A. Smith.
533. Tillie Vereta Bowser, b. 1877; m. Philip T. Bowser.
534. David S. Bowser, b. 1880; d. July 29, 1922.
535. James Herby Bowser, b. 1882; m. Louise.
536. Cozy Belle Bowser, b. 1885; m. John G. Helm.
537. Mary Ivine Bowser, b. 1890; m. (1) Frank C. Wylie; m. (2) Frank C. Ross.

164. SOPHIA (2); BENJAMIN STEVENS (1). Sophia Stevens, sister of Mary Stevens Bowser (see 164), married Joshua Crawford of Baltimore, Md. Benjamin and Sarah Ann Stevens had four children, two sons and two daughters. Vachel was a successful Southern planter and a slave-holder. Moses went from Ohio to Missouri where we lose all trace of him. Mary, grandmother of the writer, spent all her married life in Armstrong County, Pa. She was the mother of 12 children, three of whom died in infancy. Many of her descendants have made honorable careers. But to Sophia Stevens and Joshua Crawford, Providence granted the great distinction of giving a great-grandson to the Presidency of the Nation.

Children:

a(164) Mary Ann Crawford, b. 1826, d. 1896; m. Charles A. Harding, b. 1820, d. 1876.
b(164) Benjamin Crawford, m. Sarah Miller.
c(164) John Crawford, m. Elizabeth Bixby.
d(164) Matilda Crawford, b. 1840; m. Rev. Warren G. Bancroft.
e(164) Catharine Crawford, m. Seth Arborgast.
f(164) Elmira Crawford, m. Rev. Joseph Matlock.

g(164) Travis Harding, m. Jennie Close.
h(164) Louise Crawford, m. Shed Johns.
i(164) Frances L. Crawford, m. Dr. Smith.

a164. MARY ANN (CRAWFORD) and CHARLES A. HARDING.

Children:
j(164) George Tyron Harding, M. D., b. 1844; m. Phoebe Elizabeth Dickerson, b. 1843, d. 1910.
k(164) Phobe Harding, m. Thomas Mitchell.
l(164) Sophia Harding, m. Simon A. Numbers.
m(164) Callie Harding, m. Daniel Marshman.
n(164) Frances L. Harding, b. 1852, m. Rev. Andrew Wyant.
o(164) Ella H. Harding, m. Albert Wheeler Dickerson.

j164. DOCTOR GEORGE TRYON and PHOEBE (DICKERSON) HARDING. Doctor George Tryon Harding was married and lived in the village of Blooming Grove, Morrow County, Ohio, adjacent to the farm where he was born. It was here his illustrious son, Warren G. was born. In 1871 Doctor Harding moved to Caledonia, a neighboring town. Here he remained eleven years. When he had fully gained his stride as a physician and man of various enterprises, he located permanently in Marion, a growing, enterprising town, now a city known around the world.

Children:
p(164) Warren Gamaliel Harding, President of the United States, b. Nov. 2, 1865, m. Florence Kling.
q(164) Charity Harding, b. 1867, m. E. E. Remsberg.
r(164) Mary Harding, b. 1868.
s(164) Abigail Harding, b. 1872.
t(164) Dr. George Tryon Harding, Jr.
u(164) Caroline Harding. For years a missionary in India.

m164. CALLIE (HARDING) and DANIEL MARSHMAN. The children of Callie and Daniel Marshman were born at Blooming Grove. Later they moved to Galion. They now reside in Marion.

Children:
v(164) John T. Marshman; professor at the Wesleyan University, Delaware, Ohio.
w(164) Charles Marshman.
x(164) Benjamin Marshman.
y(164) Frank Marshman.
z(164) Warren Marshman.

n164. FRANCES L. (HARDING) and ANDREW WYANT; address: Sawtelle, Calif. Mr. Wyant was a native of Armstrong County, Pa. He was a veteran of the Civil War. In the early days of the oil development in western Pennsylvania he was a successful producer at Parker's Landing, Pa. He later moved to Ohio, thence to Sawtelle, Calif., where his widow and their son Harding reside. Mr. Wyant died while on a trip to his native state about 1914.

Children:
n(164) Maud E. Wyant, b. 1872; d. 1905; m. Walter Ludington, b. 1871; d. 1906.
n(164) Pearl C. Wyant, b. 1874; d. 1900; m. Vincent L. Frank, b. 1869; child: Marine Frank, b. 1898; d. Jan. 1900.
n(164) Charles Harding Wyant, b. 1876; m. Carolyn Osborne, b. 1879.

165. JACOB BOWSER (5), VALENTINE (4), JOHN (3), MATHIAS, JR., (2), MATHIAS, SR. (1); farmer; died in Washington Twp., Armstrong Co., Pa.

Children:

538. Rachel Bowser, b. Oct. 25, 1829; d. March 5, 1912; m. Samuel Harrison Bowser, son of Peter and Elizabeth; resided at Walk Chalk, Armstrong Co., Pa.; died there.
539. William Bowser, b. March 3, 1831; m. Delilah Frick; farmer; resides at Kittanning, Pa.
540. Eliza Bowser, b. March 1, 1833; m. George Helm.
541. Hannah Bowser, b. Feb. 14, 1835; m. William Henry.
542. Archibald R. Bowser, b. Nov. 1, 1836; m. Rosanah Bowser, b. April 4, 1840; d. Aug. 18, 1880. See (180) for children.
543. Valentine Bowser, b. Oct. 1, 1838; m. *Anna John. He died about 1914.
544. Mary Ann Bowser, b. Nov. 1, 1840; d. March 12, 1853.
545. Kiziah Bowser, b. Dec. 1, 1842; m. Joshua Crawford Bowser. (See 182.)
546. John Bowser, b. April 1, 1844; m. Jane Flenner; d. May 30, 1870.
547. Jacob Bowser, b. April 26, 1847; d. May 27, 1865.
548. Susan Bower, b. July 11, 1849; m. W. L. Bowser (son of Jacob F.), b. June 15, 1856.

543. VALENTINE and ANNA (JOHN) BOWSER.

Children:

(543) John A. Bowser, m. Mamie ——; address: Dubois, Pa.; ch.: Wesley M., Robert Kenneth, Nellie G., Etta V., Marie.
a543 Jacob W. Bowser.
b543 Frederick Bowser.
c543 Jeremiah Bowser.
d543 Richard Bowser.
e543 Charles W. Bowser, b. May 3, 1881; m. Elsie Treser; address: Turtle Creek, Pa.; child: Belva L., b. June 26, 1919.
f543 Susan Bowser, m. Lewis Strawmeyers; address: Clarion, Pa.
g543 Ella Nora Bowser, m. James D. Owens; address: Braddock, Pa.
h543 Blanche Bowser, m. James Purdy; ch.: Helen, Isetta, Lee, Genevieve; address: Susquehanna, Pa.
i543 Elizabeth Bowser, m. John Anderson; address: Dubois, Pa.
j543 Katharine Bowser, m. Charles Anderson; address: Dubois, Pa.
k543 Adam Bowser, d. in infancy.
l543 Lonie Bowser, d. in infancy.

539. WILLIAM and DELILAH BOWSER.

Children:

549. Anna J. Bowser, b. Sept. 11, 1857; m. Elijah Crisman; ch.: Lillie, Alice, Viola, Pearl, Ernest.
550. Mary L. Bowser, b. Sept. 8, 1859; m. G. F. Mixer.
551. Elizabeth Bowser, b. May 26, 1861; m. John M. Dickey.
552. Rachel M. Bowser, b. Sept. 23, 1863; d. August, 1864.
553. Roland S. Bowser, b. July 15, 1865; m. Tillie Wolfe.
554. Laura A. Bowser, b. Aug. 25, 1867; m. Howard Claypoole.
555. Delilah L. Bowser, b. Nov. 7, 1869; m. Lobean Gibson.
556. William Arda Bowser, b. Feb. 11, 1871.
557. Bertha L. Bowser, b. Oct. 18, 1873; m. Levi Ekis.
558. Daisie J. Bowser, b. April 2, 1876; m. Wilson Bouch.
559. Uriah F. Bowser, b. Oct. 14, 1878; m. Bertha McMillon.
560. Carrie Pearl Bowser, b. May 11, 1881.

550. MARY L. and G. F. MIXER.
Children:
561. Frederick F. Mixer, b. Sept. 13, 1898; m. Getha Carder.
562. Delilah F. Mixer, b. May 14, 1900.
563. Nellie Pearl Mixer, b. Jan. 18, 1903.

551. ELIZABETH and JOHN M. DICKEY.
Children: Hattie, Grace, Ethel.

553. ROLAND and TILLIE BOWSER.
Children: Bessie, Ada, Effie, Erma, Raymond, Warren, William, Ernest.

554. LAURA A. and HOWARD M. CLAYPOOLE; address: Adrian, Pa.
Children:
564. Mona Claypoole, b. March 12, 1892; d. Feb. 18, 1893.
565. Vera M. Claypoole, b. July 26, 1893; d. June 3, 1919.
566. Homer H. Claypoole, b. Jan. 8, 1895.
567. Aida F. Claypoole, b. June 9, 1896.
568. Lloyd M. Claypoole, b. June 25, 1898.
569. Hazelle M. Claypoole, b. May 20, 1900.
570. Mary Belle Claypoole, b. Sept. 10, 1906.
571. Clinton Y. Claypoole, b. Jan. 7, 1909.
572. Alice D. R. Claypoole, b. Aug. 28, 1911.

555. DELILAH L. and LOBEAN GIBSON.
Child:
573. Joy Gibson, b. Nov. 24, 1893.

557. BERTHA L. and LEVI EKIS.
Children:
574. Gertrude Ekis, b. Jan., 1896.
575. Ward Ekis, b. June, 1898.

558. DAISY J. and WILSON BOUCH.
Child:
576. Pearle Bouch, b. Nov. 4, 1902.

559. URIAH F. and BERTHA BOWSER.
Children:
577. Grant Bowser, b. Feb. 10, 1904.
578. Lena Bowser, b. July 25, 1905.
579. Joy Bowser, b. April 21, 1907.
580. Margaret Bowser, b. Nov. 15, 1909.
581. Glen Bowser, b. Oct. 12, 1911.
582. Grace Bowser, b. Oct. 8, 1913.
583. Lenora Bowser, b. Jan. 20, 1915.
584. Zelia Bowser, b. Sept. 21, 1916.
585. Charlotte Bowser, b. Sept. 11, 1918.

540. ELIZA and GEORGE HELM. Live on a farm near Cowansville, Pa.
Children:
586. Mary Helm, m. Alexander Shea.
587. Conrad Helm.
588. Jacob Helm, m. Anna Fair.
589. Nancy Helm, m. Thomas Ross.
590. Catharine Helm, m. William Dickey.

591. Wilson Helm.
592. Ada Helm, m. ——— Bonny.
593. Harvey Helm, m. ——— King.
594. Curtis Helm, m. ——— King.

541. HANNAH and WILLIAM HENRY.

Children: Valentine, Jacob, John, Jane, Hannah.

543. VALENTINE and ANNA BOWSER.

Children: John A., Fred V., Catharine, Elizabeth, Adam, Jacob W., Susan, Jerry M., Ella, Richard, Blanche, Gertrude, Charles W.

546. JOHN and JANE BOWSER.

Children:

595. Archibald Bowser, m. ——— Kelly.
596. Kiziah Bowser, m. ——— Mechling.

548. SUSAN and W. L. BOWSER; address: Robinson, Pa.

Children:

a597. Mary Bowser b. Sept. 1, 1877; m. Mack Shaffer; ch.: Arthur Shaffer, b. Jan. 30, 1900; Burwell Shaffer.
598. Sadie M. Bowser, b. Oct. 9, 1882; m. John Dias.
599. H. J. Bowser, b. July 29, 1884; m. Laura Duncan, b. July 6, 1885; ch.: Dorothy Bowser, b. Aug. 28, 1911; Bernice Bowser, b. Aug. 29, 1914; Phillis Bowser, b. July 12, 1918.
600. Burwell Bowser, b. April 12, 1888; d. Aug. 21, 1901.
601. Archibald Bowser, b. Aug. 29, 1890; m. Bessie Pierce; ch.: William, Louise, Orpha, Helen, Susan.

166. DELILAH (5), VALENTINE (4), JOHN (3), MATHIAS (2), MATHIAS (1), DELILAH (BOWSER) and PETER TOY. Peter Toy, farmer, Walk Chalk, Armstrong Co., Pa.

Children:

602. Michael Toy, b. Nov. 15, 1808.
603. Catharine Toy, b. March 21, 1827.
604. Margaret Toy, b. Aug. 11, 1828.
605. James Toy, b. March 11, 1829; m. Rebecca Findley.
606. Abram Toy, b. Oct. 20, 1831; m. Margaret Bowser; ch.: Peter, Elizabeth, Harvey.
607. Peter Toy, b. May 5, 1834; m. Ellen Dout; ch.: Charles, Edward, Dolly, Thomas, Albert, William.
608. Elizabeth Toy, b. Nov. 23, 1834; m. James Burford, b. April 27, 1832; d. August 21, 1920.
609. Esther Toy, b. April 5, 1837; m. David Lemon; ch.: James, Ross, Margaret.
610. Valentine Toy, b. April 18, 1839; m. (1) Julia A. Cornman, (2) Christine Achison.; ch.: John, Lemuel, Benjamin.
611. Mary Toy, b. April 15, 1841; m. Lemuel Porterfield; ch.: Annie, Katie, Myrtle, Alice, Bert, Edith, Cara.
612. Ellen Toy, b. Feb. 8, 1843; m. Adam Steinmetz; child: Mary.
613. Delilah Toy, b. Dec. 23, 1844; m. Hamilton D. Bowser, b. 1843; d. 1913.
614. Benjamin Lee Toy, b. May 10, 1847; m. Rachel Hollobaugh; address: Walk Chalk, Pa.; ch.: Rosie, Hamilton, Belle, Hannah, Mollie, Bert, Curtis.
615. Ross Toy, b. Sept. 5, 1849; m. (1) Katharine Steinmetz, b. Sept. 26, 1865, (2) Margaret King; address: Ford City, Pa.

605. JAMES and REBECCA TOY.

Children:

605. Alonza Toy, m. Shumaker.
    (605) William Toy, m. Sadie McGreggor.
    (605) James Toy, m. Annie Fonner, ch.: Mary J., m. J. S. Claypoole; ch.: Findley Sloan; Homer H., m. Wilda Rowland; ch.: Rowland Sloan, Margaret J.
    (605) Frank Toy.
    (605) Harry Toy, m. Kittie Wells.
    (605) Samuel Toy.
    (605) Mary Toy, m. Clem Adams.
    (605) Daisy Toy.
    (605) Clara Toy.

608. ELIZABETH TOY and JAMES BURFORD. James Burford was a miller and for many years operated the grist mill at Walk Chalk on the site of the mill first built in that part of the country by Samuel Bowser, son of "Hopewell" John.

Children:

616. John F. Burford, b. Nov. 8, 1856; m. Annie Heckman.
617. Parks P. Burford, b. Nov. 4, 1858; m. Edith Wible. In hardware business in Kittanning, Pa. Ch.: Arthur Fennimore, b. 1886; Elizabeth Irene, b. 1891.
618. Ida A. Burford, m. William Rumbaugh; ch.: Joseph J., Della, Ralph.
619. Dora E. Burford, m. John Buzzard; ch.: Claire, Charles.
620. James T. Burford, m. Flora Swigard; ch.: Roy, Day, Hallie, Harry.
621. Charles C. Burford, m. Eva Crawford; ch.: Annie, Margaret.

615. ROSS and CATHARINE (STEINMETZ) TOY.

Children:

622. Mary D. Toy, b. Feb. 2, 1871; m. Frank M. Fries.
623. Anna E. Toy, b. Dec. 3, 1873; m. William K. Brown.
624. Margaret E. Toy, b. Jan. 10, 1875; m. George Emminger.
625. Elmer J. Toy, b. March 4, 1877; m. Minnie Beck.
626. Dora E. Toy, b. Feb. 26, 1879; m. James Gould.
627. Catharine W. Toy, b. Oct. 30, 1881; m. George Striker.
628. Alice L. Toy, b. Aug. 13, 1884; m. William Quinn.
629. Florence V. Toy, b. Sept. 7, 1889.
630. Charles W. Toy, b. Aug. 14, 1893; d. Jan. 15, 1894.
631. Raymond H. Toy, b. April 17, 1895; m. Helen Russell.

168. CATHARINE BOWSER (5), VALENTINE (4), JOHN (3), MATHIAS (2), MATHIAS (1). Catharine and Noah Bowser resided at Clinton, Armstrong Co. She survived all of the other children of Valentine and Elizabeth (Fluke) Bowser. She died in 1906 at the remarkable age of 97.

Children:

632. Alexander B. Bowser, b. June 10, 1828; d. May 10, 1914; m. Susan Malone, b. Nov. 21, 1832; d. March 10, 1904.
633. Hezekiah Bowser, b. Oct. 13, 1829.
634. Valentine Bowser, b. Nov. 11, 1831; d. Jan. 1, 1895; m. Mary A. McNabb.
635. Lucy Ann Bowser, b. Sept. 11, 1833; d. Oct. 28, 1894; m. Samuel C. Babb, b. Feb. 24, 1834.
636. Simon Peter Bowser, b. June 4, 1835; m. (1) Susan McNabb; (2) Vina Shriner, d. 1909.
637. Isabelle C. Bowser, b. Oct. 10, 1837; d. Aug. 24, 1842.

638. Elizabeth Bowser, b. June 26, 1839; m. William Mahaffey, b. May 9, 1830; d. Dec. 9 1903.
639. Mark C. Bowser, b. Aug. 9, 1842; d. March 18, 1862; death caused by wounds received in Civil War.
640. Henry C. Bowser, b. Dec. 9, 1845; d. 1916.
641. Mary Jane Bowser, b. March 4, 1847; d. Dec. 15, 1893; m. Edward Camp.
642. Millie Rachel Bowser, b. Dec. 15, 1849; m. George McCausland.
643. Sarah Rebecca Bowser, b. July 22, 1851; d. 1854.
644. Katharine Bowser, b. Oct. 14, 1854; d. Jan. 19, 1902; m. James M. Hudson, b. March 15, 1852.
645. Steven Girard Bowser, b. May 22, 1857; m. Minnie McNabb.

632. ALEXANDER and SUSAN BOWSER. Alexander Bowser was a soldier in the Civil War, serving with the 154th Pa. Reg. Vol. Died at Burgettstown, Pa., March 10, 1914. (See Bates History for army record.)

Children:
646. Anna C. Bowser, b. 1868; d. 1908.
647. Carson A. Bowser, b. April 1, 1866; m. Nora Jackson, b. 1878.
648. Margaret A. Bowser, b. 1868; m. B. D. Malone.
649. Millicent M. Bowser, b. 1870; m. Wm. Bristol.
650. Mary Bowser, b. 1872; m. F. B. Vance.
651. Blanche Bowser, b. 1874; m. U. H. Creighton.
652. Carrie L. Bowser, b. 1876; m. Robert Phillips.

634. VALENTINE and (1) MARY A. BOWSER.

Children:
653. William A. Bowser, b. Aug. 8, 1856.
654. Thomas N. Bowser, b. April 24, 1859; d. Dec. 10, 1917; m. Annie Jane Slagle. She resides in Kittanning. Ch.: Mary, Thomas M., Flur B., Nellie.
655. Margaret Bowser, b. April 13, 1863; m. Samuel Latham.
656. Ebert Bowser, b. Jan. 3, 1865; m. Mollie Poorman, b. May 8, 1866.
657. Ada M. Bowser, b. Nov. 15, 1866; m. John E. Carns.
658. Quigly S. Bowser, b. March 5, 1878; address: Ellwood City, Pa.
659. Harry J. Bowser, b. March 5, 1869; m. Ida Baker.

634. VALENTINE m (2) SOPHIA ESSENWINE.

Children: Beulah, Frank, Rachel.

635. LUCY ANN and SAMUEL C. BABB.

Children:
660. James F. Babb, b. May 18, 1858; m. Malinda Jane Swigart; address: Ford City, Pa.; ch.: Arthur, b. April 15, 1891.
661. Catharine C. Babb, b. Oct. 5, 1860; m. Scott Wilson.
662. Mary E. Babb, b. June 22, 1862; d. July 21, 1895.
663. Sarah Isabelle Babb, b. Sept. 20, 1866.
664. Ella Fulton Babb, b. Aug. 23, 1869; d. Oct. 16, 1896.
665. Samuel Lindsay Babb, b. Oct. 18, 1872; d. Aug. 14, 1879.

636. SIMON PETER and SUSAN (McNABB) BOWSER.

Children:
666. Ross Bowser, resides in West Kittanning, Pa.
667. Kiziah Bowser, m. John Thubron.
668. Mark Bowser.

638. ELIZABETH and WILLIAM MAHAFFEY; address: Tarentum, Pa.
Children:
669. Maude Mahaffey, b. Feb. 5, 1871; m. Harry C. Brown, b. May 28, 1871; d. March, 1902; address: Tarentum, Pa.
670. Miner Mahaffey, b. July 23, 1872; d. March 12, 1873.
671. Luella E. Mahaffey, b. Dec. 23, 1873; d. June 8, 1880.
672. Harry A. Mahaffey, b. Dec. 17, 1879; m. Pearl Tucker, b. Apr. 27, 1879; ch: Thelman, b. Jan. 25, 1903.

669. MAUDE and HARRY C. BROWN.
Children:
673. Guilford C. Brown, b. Nov. 27, 1896.
674. Eugene M. Brown, b. Feb. 22, 1899.
675. Graham L. Brown, b. Jan. 16, 1902.
Guilford served in the World war s. d. f. Co., Camp Lee, August 30, 1918 to Dec. 15, 1918.
Eugene M. served with the Fifth Marine Machine Gun Company in France and Germany, June 8, 1918, to August 18, 1919.

644. CATHARINE and CAPT. JAMES M. HUDSON. Captain Hudson retired; residence, Maple Ave., Kittanning, Pa.
Children:
676. Charles F. Hudson, b. May 15, 1877; m. Emma Speece.
677. Thomas N. Hudson, b. Oct. 11, 1878; m. Elizabeth Simpson, d. 1909.
678. Herbert P. Hudson, b. Nov. 18, 1880; m. Margaret Anderson.
679. Mabel G. Hudson, b. Dec. 11, 1883; Red Cross nurse overseas in Unit L, Allegheny Gen. Hospital Corps, 1918-19.
680. James Grover C. Hudson, b. Nov. 23, 1887; m. Maude Linnon.
681. Sgt. Henry A. Hudson, b. March 24, 1891; m. Edith McGlaughlin. He served in the World war Co. A, 305th Engineer Corps; rank as sergeant.

169. PETER BOWSER (5), VALENTINE (4), JOHN (3), MATHIAS (2), MATHIAS (1). Peter Bowser owned a large farm near Walk Chalk, one mile from his father Valentine (4) Bowser's farm. His son Harry resides on the homestead. Died Jan. 29, 1879.
Children:
682. Alfred Bowser, d. in infancy (1842).
683. Adeline Bowser, b. March 15, 1844; m. John Cravenor, b. 1838; d. November, 1902.
684. Lewis Bowser, b. Nov. 23, 1846; d. June, 1922; m. (1) Eva Snowden, b. Jan. 23, 1852; d. Sept. 11, 1889; m. (2) olly Noble, d. 1916.
685. Loben R. Bowser, b. April 26, 1849; m. Catharine Fair, d.
686. Andrew Bowser, b. 1854; m. Mary E. Kribbal, b. 1855.
687. Malinda Bowser, b. 1855; m. Ormond Berry, b. July 8, 1845.
688. James M. Bowser, b. 1857; m. Evaline Stewart, b. 1858.
689. Amelia Bowser, b. July 7, 1859; m. John Collier, b. April 7, 1852.
690. Ross Toy Bowser, b. May 11, 1861; m. Cora Peat, b. May 28, 1876.
691. Harry Bowser, b. June 27, 1863; m. Minnie Rupert, b. Oct. 10, 1871.
692. Melancthon Bowser, b. March 6, 1868; m. Nettie Swartzlander, b. June 28, 1874.

683. ADELINE and JOHN S. CRAVENOR.
Children:
639. Addison Peter Cravenor, b. July 8, 1865; m. Nancy T. Dickey.
694. Elizabeth Jane Cravenor, b. Oct. 25, 1866; m. William Richardson.
695. Amelia Ann Cravenor, b. August 11, 1868; m. Harry De Vore.

696. Laura Etta Cravenor, b. June 25, 1871; m. Joseph Green.
697. William Anthony Cravenor, b. May 30, 1874; d. April 7, 1875.
698. Mary Jemima Cravenor, b. Oct. 2, 1876; m. John E. Schoop, b. March 21, 1872.
a698. Charles J. Jessup Cravenor, b. Dec. 29, 1879; d. May 26, 1881.

698. MARY JEMIMA (CRAVENOR) and JOHN E. SHOOP. Address: McCrann, Pa.
Children:
b698. Ruth Shoop, b. 1896; d. Oct. 21, 1896.
c698. Elizabeth A. Shoop, b. Oct. 28, 1897; m. Wilbert J. Funk, b. April 17, 1897; child: Wilbert James, b. March 9, 1922.
d698. Pearl A. Shoop, b. Aug. 24, 1899; m. Ira C. Crytzer, b. Oct. 14, 1896; child: Eleanor Pearl Crytzer, b. Dec. 17, 1918.
e698. Edith A. Shoop, b. Oct. 10, 1901; m. John E. Scott, b. Feb. 2, 1900; child: Dorise A. Scott, b. Aug. 27, 1920.
f698. Elinor M. Shoop, b. Oct. 2, 1903.
g698. Earnest L. Shoop, b. Sept. 20, 1905; d. Feb. 22, 1922.
h698. William Addison Shoop, b. Dec. 19, 1910.
i698. Sara A. Shoop, b. Feb. 17, 1912; d. March 28, 1913.

685. LOBEN R. and CATHARINE BOWSER; farmer in Clarion Co., Pa.
Children:
a685. James Emmitt Bowser, b. June 9, 1879; m. Beulah Shaugenkaupt.
b685. Harry Herbert Bowser.
c685. Carrie Emelia Bowser, m. Edward Conner.
d685. Eva Jane Bowser, died when aged 8 months.

684. LEWIS and (1) EVALINE SNOWDEN BOWSER.
Children:
699. Ervin C. Bowser, b. June 17, 1874; m. Lydia Troutner.
700. Hiram F. Bowser, b. Sept. 23, 1875; m. Pearl Cribbs, Blairsville, Pa.
701. Oren T. Bowser, b. Dec. 5, 1876; d. June 11, 1905.
702. Jerry F. Bowser, b. May 16, 1878; m. Margaret Christy, Blairsville, Pa.
703. Florlola J. Bowser, b. Oct. 8, 1879; m. David Shearer, Blairsville, Pa.
704. Nicholas Clark Bowser, b. Dec. 10, 1880; m. Emma Powell; ch.: Carl, Rebecca, Teressa, Paul, Edgar.
705. Olga B. Bowser, b. May 15, 1882; m. John Swigart; residence: Worthington, Pa.
706. Jesse M. Bowser, b. March 28, 1883.
707. Wilbert C. Bowser, b. Jan. 15, 1885; m. Marie Ellenberger.
708. Bessie Bowser, b. July 8, 1886; m. Charles Rosborough, Blairsville, Pa.
709. Roy P. Bowser, b. Sept. 21, 1887; m. Nellie Powell; ch.: Louise, b. 1910; Jeanette, b. 1912; Rosanah, b. 1904; Richard, b. 1917. Residence; 232 High St., Kittanning, Pa.

686. ANDREW J. and MARY BOWSER.
Children:
710. Edward M. Bowser, b. 1877.
711. Mert R. Bowser, b. 1879.
712. Charles Bowser, b. 1881.
713. Clyde Bowser, b. 1883.
714. George Bowser, b. 1887.
715. Maude Bowser, b. 1889.
716. Dean Bowser, b. 1892.
717. Harry Bowser, b. 1895; d. 1895.
718. Iva Bowser, b. 1898.

687. MALINDA and ORMOND BERRY.

Children:

Lewis D., Elizabeth J., John P., George I., Alma V., Ada A., Mintic L., Lottie G., Harry H., Prior B., Aroya.

689. AMELIA and JOHN COLLIER. Live near Petrolia, Pa.

Children:

719. Annie Jane Collier, b. May 14, 1882; m. William Parker; ch.: Richard, Edward.
720. John Herbert Collier, b. Jan. 7, 1884; m. Alta Jamison; ch.: Eugene, Geraldine.
721. Amelia Belle Collier, b. Nov. 15, 1885; m. Bert Ellenberger.
722. Harry Emmitt Collier, b. Oct. 14, 1887; m. Ella Irman; ch.: Lester, John, Thelma, Lillian.
723. Clyde Olden Collier, b. March 10, 1889; m. Ethel Foster; ch.: Gertrude, Bertha.
724. James Milton Collier, b. Nov. 1, 1890; m. Celia Waltman; child: Milford.
725. Laura Agnes Collier, b. Dec. 9, 1892; m. Roy McElravy.
726. Ross Nelson Collier, b. Feb. 1, 1895; m. May Irman.
727. Floyd La Vere Collier, b. Jan. 22, 1897.
728. Etta Florence Collier, b. April 8, 1899.
729. Dorothy Eaton Collier, b. April 10, 1903.

691. HARRY and MINNIE BOWSER. Live on the homestead, Walk Chalk, Pa.

Children:

730. Arthur Bowser, b. May 7, 1892; d. 1912.
731. Laura Bowser, b. June 2, 1894; m. H. A. Wible, b. Jan. 2, 1894; ch.: Arthur Floyd.
732. Homer Ross Bowser, b. Nov. 18, 1896.
733. Freda Bowser, b. May 5, 1900; m. W. B. Clark, b. Nov. 11, 1900; child: Richard.
734. Claude Bowser, b. Feb. 23, 1902.
735. Mabel Bowser, b. June 16, 1905.
736. Vera Bowser, b. Jan. 2, 1910; d. 1918.

692. MELANCTHON and NETTIE BOWSER: address: Butler, Pa.

Children:

737. Raymond J. Bowser, b. Jan. 27, 1896; m. Gertrude Foster; ch.: Elsie, Verda.
738. Clifford Bowser, b. Aug. 20, 1897; d. March 20, 1898.
739. Pauline Bowser, b. May 10, 1901; m. W. F. Davis.
740. Gertrude Bowser, b. Dec. 19, 1904.
741. Hulda Bowser, b. Jan. 30, 1906.
742. Melvin Bowser, b. March 1, 1914.
743. Robert Dean Bowser, b. July 31, 1918.

170. MARGARET (5), VALENTINE (4), JOHN (3), MATHIAS (2), MATHIAS (1), MARGARET and JONAS BOWSER. Margaret and Jonas lived in Washington Twp., Armstrong Co., Pa.; occupied until their death May 5, 1898, and June 28, 1891, a log house built in 1808 by Martin John, husband of Esther Bowser. The property is now in possession of their heirs. See picture of log house.

Children:

744. Eliza Ann Bowser, b. May 16, 1836, m. (1) Alexander Bowser, killed in Civil War; (2) John Southworth.

745. William Harvey Bowser, b. April 5, 1838; d. Nov. 25, 1840.
746. Alonza H. Bowser, b. July 25, 1841. Veteran of the Civil War. Capt. E. S. Jones, Co. B, 1st Reg., Penna. Mounted Volunteers; d. Nov. 9, 1920; m. Mary Ellen Yerty, b. May 12, 1835; d. Aug. 2, 1906.
747. Manuel Bowser, b. Dec. 25, 1843; d. 1844.
748. Rebecca Jane Bowser, b. Feb. 28, 1845; m. William King.
749. James Franklin Bowser, b. March 25, 1848; m. Jane Jack, b. 1843; d. 1920; address: Kittanning, Pa.
750. Ephriam B. Bowser, b. 1851; m. Catharine Gray; address: Kittanning, Pa.
751. Martin Bowser, b. Oct. 14, 1855; m. Elizabeth Bowser, b. Sept. 6, 1841; address: Adrian, Pa.
752. Solomon R. Bowser, b. Jan. 9, 1859; d. April 26, 1920; m. Mary Belle Bowser, b. Feb. 24, 1862.

744. ELIZA ANN and (1) ALEXANDER D. BOWSER.
Children:
753. John R. Bowser, b. August 15, 1859; m. Lydia Ann Booher.
754. Mary Bowser, b. May 15, 1862; m. Benson Wolfe.

744. m (2) JOHN SOUTHWORTH; lived at Worthington, Pa.
Children:
755. Sarah Southworth, b. Dec. 20, 1864; d. March 15, 1887.
756. Rebecca Southworth, b. April 14, 1862; m. William Simmers.
757. Otis Southworth, b. July 23, 1878; m. Elizabeth Birk.
758. Phoebe Southworth, b. May 7, 1875; m. Isaac Simmers.
759. Jennie Southworth, b. Nov. 30, 1879; m. Los Demly.

753. JOHN and LYDIA (BOOHER) BOWSER.
(753). Mollie M. Bowser, b. June 5, 1888; m. Frank Kunkle; b. May 5, 1884; ch.: Bernice Alberta, b. May 12, 1908; Hattie Jane, b. Jan. 18, 1910; Josephene Frances, b. Sept. 12, 1912; John William, b. April 10, 1914; Florence Irene, b. Sept. 5, 1915; Lydia Ann, b. July 13, 1918.
(753). Hettie Jane Bowser, b. July 20, 1890; d. August 25, 1911.
(753). Catherine Ann Bowser, b. April 10, 1893; d. Feb. 8, 1896.
(753). David Alexander Bowser, b. Oct. 18, 1897; d. Jan. 25, 1919; m. Emma Miller.
(753). Clara Rebecca Bowser, b. June 4, 1902; d. Oct. 30, 1902.

746. ALONZA H. and MARY ELLEN BOWSER.
Children:
760. Harvey S. Bowser, b. Dec. 18, 1860; m. (1) Lily M. Barnetto, b. July 4, 1870; d. April 23, 1902; address: Kittanning, Pa.
Child:
761. Ralston H., b. Aug. 2, 1896; (m.) Mary M. Belles, b. Jan. 31, 1877.
762. Christian Bowser, b. Sept. 21, 1862; m. Martha E. Crothers; address: Vandergrift, Pa.
763. Jonas Bowser, b. Dec. 10, 1864; d. July 25, 1865.
764. Margaret Bowser, b. April 5, 1865; d. Oct. 28, 1913; m. William Hoon; ch.: Hannah, William, Ellen, Alice, Viola, Evedell, Alonza, Isabelle, Deemer, Raymond.
765. Catharine Bowser, b. Jan. 2, 1868; d. Feb. 23, 1872.
766. E. Shenandoah Bowser, b. March 12, 1870; m. Esther Jane Edwards, b. Aug. 7, 1875; ch.: Chas. Kelley, b. Nov. 30, 1895; m. Hazel Robinson.

a766. Elmer Ellsworth, b. Oct. 28, 1897; Murry W., b. July 8, 1903.
767. Minnie Bowser, b. Feb. 22, 1872; m. Chambers S. Bowser, b. 1867 (See 1749.)
768. Ralston Bowser, b. March 21, 1874; d. April 17, 1874.
769. Etta Bowser, b. April 2, 1876; m. Frank K. Bowser, b. March 16, 1876; ch.: Dwanie, Elizabeth, Bepulah, Leroy.
770. Rosey Bowser, b. April 3, 1878; d. Jan. 31, 1891.
771. Cena M. Bowser, b. July 24, 1880; m. R. C. Kerr, b. Feb. 11, 1881.

771. CENA M. and R. C. KERR.
Children:
772. Beulah A. Kerr, b. Feb. 20, 1907.
773. Theodore C. Kerr, b. Jan. 5, 1909.
774. Charles W. Kerr, b. May 2, 1911.
775. Ethel E. Kerr, b. Oct. 24, 1912.
776. Russell Alonza Kerr, b. August 5, 1914.
777. Ida Helen Kerr, b. Sept. 14, 1915.
778. Clyde E. Kerr, b. April 19, 1917.
779. Stanley J. Kerr, b. August 6, 1918.
780. Paul Kerr, b. Nov. 8, 1920.
1781. Pauline Kerr, b. Nov. 8, 1921.

748. REBECCA JANE and WILLIAM KING.
Children:
782. Harriet Anna King, b. Nov. 15, 1864.
783. Hannah King, b. Jan. 16, 1866; m. Alexander McCullough; farmer and merchant in Kittanning, Pa.
Children:
a783. William McCullough, b. May 16, 1890.
b783. James McCullough, b. August 19, 1892.
c783. Alexander McCullough, Jr., b. Jan. 21, 1897.
d783. Mary McCullough, b. June 15, 1899.
e783. Margaret McCullough, b. May 10, 1903.
784. Lyman King, b. Jan. 28, 1870.

749. JAMES FRANKLIN and JANE BOWSER.
Children:
785. Laura L. Bowser, b. March 9, 1868; m. W. Burleigh Edwards, b. Oct. 26, 1865; address: Kittanning, Pa.
786. Margaret Ann Bowser, b. July 9, 1870; d. 1905; m. John C. Salsbury, b. April 25, 1869; ch.: Laura Fay, b. April 20, 1893.
787. Emma R. Bowser, b. Oct. 18, 1872; m. Samuel Densmore, b. March 25, 1875; address: Kittanning, Pa.
788. Elizabeth, twin of Sophia Catharine.
789. Sophia Catharine Bowser.
790. Elsie M. Bowser, b. Oct. 12, 1878; m. Z. H. Shuster, b. Jan. 22, 1873.
791. Chambers E. Bowser, b. 1880; d. 1882.
792. Florence Bell Bowser, b. April 2, 1883; m. W. E. Miller, b. July 29, 1879.
793. Jonas O. Bowser, b. July 19, 1885; m. Hilda P. Swiger, b. Sept. 29, 1889.

785. LAURA L. and W. BURLEIGH EDWARDS.
Children:
794. Elmer T. Edwards, b. Sept. 1, 1887; d. Dec. 19, 1918.
795. Robert B. Edwards, b. Sept. 12, 1889; d. Dec. 9, 1914.
796. Nancy Jane Edwards, b. August 7, 1891.

797. Adam F. Edwards, b. Nov. 15, 1895.
798. Elsie Edwards, b. Feb. 25, 1898; d. Dec. 26, 1898.
799. Charles Edwards, b. Jan. 3, 1900.

790. ELSIE M. and Z. H. SHUSTER.
Children:
800. Julia Catharine Shuster, b. Oct. 19, 1898; d. Oct. 28, 1898.
801. Mathias H. Shuster, b. Dec. 18, 1899.
802. Howard F. Shuster, b. March 18, 1901.
803. Zella B. Shuster, b. Nov. 23, 1906.
804. Edgar B. Shuster, b. April 23, 1909.

792. FLORENCE BELL and W. E. MILLER.
Children:
805. Zellers C. Miller, b. Sept. 20, 1904.
806. Dorothy M. Miller, b. Nov. 10, 1908.

793. JONAS O. and HILDA P. BOWSER.
Children:
807. Revena G. Bowser, b. Oct. 5, 1909.
808. Oran J. Bowser, b. July 15, 1911.
809. Elmer S. Bowser, b. March 30, 1918.

751. MARTIN and ELIZABETH BOWSER.
Child:
810. Jennie Templeton Bowser, b. Sept. 29, 1882; m. George Rickel, b. Oct. 30, 1873.

752. SOLOMON R. and MARY BELL BOWSER.
Ch.: See under No. 460.

810. JENNIE TEMPLETON and GEORGE RICKEL.
811. Flora Rickel, b. Nov. 27, 1905.
812. Martin Rickel, b. Nov. 4, 1909.
813. Catharine Elizabeth Rickel, b. Dec. 21, 1911; d.
814. Lulu Rickel, b. Oct. 19, 1916.

171. WILLIAM (5), VALENTINE (4), JOHN (3), MATHIAS (2), MATHIAS (1). William Bowser, farmer, Walk Chalk, Armstrong Co., Pa.; two years old when his father moved from Bedford County to Armstrong; m. Mary Ann Bowser, a daughter of "Steam" John Bowser; d. at the age of 84, Feb. 3, 1898.
Children:
815. Wilson Bowser, b. Jan. 4, 1841; d. Jan. 10, 1918; m. Sarah Milligan, b. Jan., 1840; d. April 11, 1916; farmer; lived near Cowansville, Pa.
Children:
a815. Andrew Lee Bowser, b. Aug. 16, 1870.
b815. William Park Bowser, b. Sept. 25, 1873.
c815. Ida Bowser, b. Sept. 24, 1875; m. C. A. McClay.
d815. Edward W. Bowser, b. Jan. 16, 1878; m. Jennie Helm; b. June 27, 1882; ch.: Florence, b. July 19, 1902; Hazel, b. March 25, 1905; Ray, b. Feb. 21, 1912.
816. Robert Bowser, b. Oct. 24, 1842; d. May 3, 1906; m. Martha H. Craig.
817. Francis S. Bowser, b. Nov. 18, 1844; m. Anna Davidson of Cowansville, Pa.; moved to Iowa; d. May 25, 1916; ch.: Mona, Myrtle, Robert, Herbert, Albert, Dr. William, Orlando L.

818. Elizabeth Bowser, b. Aug. 30, 1846; d. Aug. 26, 1908; m. William Wiley; ch.: Edward, Eva, Laura, John, Cora, Maud, Blanche, Boyd.
819. Curtis Bowser, b. Nov. 19, 1848; m. Rose Noble; farmer, Walk Chalk, Pa.; ch.: Alice, Earl, Violet.
820. Jane Bowser, b. Sept. 30, 1850; m. John Wolford, Ambridge, Pa.; ch.: William, Mollie, Della, Nellie, Lulu.
821. J. Albert Bowser, b. Jan. 21, 1853; m. Ellen Weamer, merchant, Rural Valley, Pa.
822. Mary Bowser, b. April 27, 1855; d. March 16, 1910; m. M. S. Kerr; lived at Worthington, Pa.; ch.: Ora, James, Robert, Ray.
823. Emma Bowser, b. Dec. 10, 1857; d. Nov. 27, 1913; m. H. McGeary.
824. Calvin Bowser, b. Oct. 4, 1861; m. Nancy A. Hays, b. Jan. 11, 1876; live on the homestead, Walk Chalk, Pa.

Children:
825. William D. Bowser, b. Nov. 14, 1898.
826. Albert F. Bowser, b. Jan. 2, 1902.
827. John Kenneth Bowser, b. Aug. 12, 1906.
828. Mary C. Bowser, b. Oct. 7, 1914.

171. MATHIAS (5), VALENTINE (4), JOHN (3), MATHIAS (2), MATHIAS (1). Mathias Bowser was an iron worker; died near Kittanning April 22, 1889.

Children:
829. Emanuel Bowser, b. April 24, 1847; d. Nov., 1860.
830. George Bowser, b. June 4, 1849; d. Jan. 27, 1901; m. Julia Flenner; ch.: Ella, Rose, Dolly, Wood, Anna, Berby, Charles.
831. Sarah Bowser, b. Feb. 4, 1851; m. Archibald Wyant; address: New Kensington, Pa.; ch.: Ida, Christopher, Rebecca, Harry S., William, Robert, John.
832. Elizabeth Bowser, b. Feb. 8, 1853; m. James Thompson; ch.: Sarah, Carrie, Harry.
833. Catharine M. Bowser, b. Oct. 23, 1855; m. Joseph Brown; ch.: Carrie, Lottie, John.
834. Robert Bowser, b. March 7, 1858; m. Elizabeth Carr; ch.: Myrtle, Margaret, John, Rebecca, Susan, Catharine, Pearle.
835. Jane Bowser, b. June 24, 1860; m. Edward Hughes; address: Rathmel, Pa.; ch.: Laura, George, James, Irene, John, Edwin.
836. Margaret Bowser, b. Dec. 26, 1862; d. Nov., 1863.
837. William Harvey Bowser, b. April 17, 1885; d. March 19, 1900; m. Maud Bowser. (See 526.)
838. John Franklin Bowser, b. Sept. 5, 1867; m. (1) Louisa Callaway; d. Dec., 1897; ch.: Louisa M., Daniel R.; m. (2) Myrtle Haven (nee Cochran), b. July 24, 1874; merchant, Summerville, Pa.

174. VALENTINE (5), VALENTINE (4), JOHN (3), MATHIAS (2), MATHIAS (1).

Children:
839. Harvey Bowser, b. July 2, 1846; d. April 3, 1901; m. (1) Hannah Claypool, b. 1847; d. Feb. 20, 1873; (2) Mary A. Toy.
840. Elizabeth Bowser, b. July 11, 1848; d. Oct. 15, 1863.
841. Mary Ann Bowser, b. July 11, 1848; (twin of Elizabeth); d. Feb. 13, 1885; m. Felix Bowser, farmer and stock raiser, Walk Chalk, Pa.
842. Valentine Bowser, b. Mar. 20, 1852; d. Mar. 11, 1910; m. (1) Martha Bouch; (2) Jennie Claypool.
843. Jacob Bowser, b. May 4, 1854; d. Nov. 6, 1863.
844. Samuel Bowser, b. Mar. 13, 1857; d. Nov. 7, 1863.
a844. Lurenna Bowser, b. Sept. 11, 1859; m. Frederick Bowser (son of "Big" Fred).

845. Miller Bowser, b. Aug. 4, 1863; m. Adeline Schrecengost, b. Dec. 4, 1864.
846. Sarah Malissa Bowser, b. Dec. 11, 1869; m. James K. Lafferty.

839. HARVEY and (1) HANNAH BOWSER.

Children:
847. Nelson Bowser, b. July 6, 1867; m. Mary E. Miller, b. Aug. 19, 1880; address: Ford City, Pa.; ch.: Annabel Bowser, b. Jan. 30, 1907; d. Feb. 24, 1920; Elizabeth Bowser, b. July 4, 1909; Millard Bowser, b. June 6, 1911.
848. Minerva Bowser, b. 1878; m. Wilson Gillam.

839. HARVEY and (2) MARY A. TOY.

Children:
849. Cora Bowser, m. William Shaffer.
850. Luie Bowser m. William Lytle.
851. Luther Bowser, m. Lydia Bouch.
852. Valentine Bowser, single (1920).
853. Wilbert Bowser, m. Goldie Hooks.
854. Jessie Bowser, m. Edward Bouch.
855. Elizabeth Bowser, m. George Montgomery; ch.: Henry R., Emily C., Lillie G., Elnora E.

841. MARY ANN and FELIX BOWSER.

Children:
856. Ella Bowser, m. Hamilton Toy.
857. Elizabeth Bowser, m. Wilbert Lewis.
858. Ambrey Bowser, m. Maud Lasher.
859. Emmit Bowser, m. Maud Brown.
860. Harry Bowser, m. Elizabeth Brown.
861. Charlotte Bowser, m. Frederick Beckwith.
862. Newton Bowser.

842. VALENTINE and (1) MARTHA (BOUCH) BOWSER.

Children:
863. Anna Bowser m. Charles Claypoole.
864. Daniel Bowser, m. Della Miller.
865. Frank Bowser, m. Maud Bruner.
866. Valentine Bowser, m. Cora Roudabush.

(2) JENNIE CLAYPOOLE.

Child:
867. Raymond Bowser, m. ——— Bowser.

845. MILLER and ADALINE BOWSER; farmer; near Adrian, Pa.

Children:
868. Edwin J. Bowser, b. Apr. 4, 1888; m. Sarah L. John, b. Sept. 29, 1893; ch.: Freda, Rebecca, Richard.
869. Albert S. Bowser, b. Jan. 31, 1896.
870. Frank L. Bowser, b. Sept. 26, 1898; m. Minnie Hooks, b. Apr. 5, 1900; ch.: Isabel, Mildred, Berton.
871. Clifford J. Bowser, b. Sept. 8, 1902.
872. Chambers Bowser, b. Dec. 3, 1884; d. Sept. 15, 1899.
873. Jennie Bowser, b. Nov. 14, 1891; d. Nov. 20, 1891.

a844. LURENNA and FREDERICK BOWSER.

Children:

874. Laura Bowser, m. Jacob Bowser, son of David.
875. Florence Bowser, m. Herbert Grafton.
876. Sarah Bowser, m. Plummer Kepple.
877. Merl Bowser, m. Viola Bowser.
878. Helen Bowser m. Edward McKelvey.

133. SAMUEL (4), JOHN (3), MATHIAS (2), MATHIAS (1). Samuel Bowser, son of "Hopewell" John, b. 1777, came to Armtsrong County in 1805 and bought land at the "Falls" of Glade Run, now known as Walk Chalk, at the junction of the two branches of that stream. He cleared the land and erected a grist mill which ground the grain of that section until recent days. A portion of his land is still in the hands of some of his heirs. He married Anna Catharine, a daughter of John "Snider," an early settler in Bedford County, Pa. He was the progenitor of a large family whose children have borne the characteristics of his industry and religious zeal. He died Aug. 7, 1861. Anna Katharine Snider, b. 1871, d. Feb. 7, 1873.

Children:

879. Peter ("Sheriff") Bowser, b. Apr. 4, 1806; d. 1864; m. Betsey White, b. 1809; d. 1905.
880. Isaac Bowser, m. Catharine, dau. of "Steam" John Bowser. (a1811).
881. Susanna Bowser, b. Oct. 16, 1819; d. May 10, 1904; m. Solomon Abe Bowser, son of Nicholas, son of "Hopewell" John, b. 1820; d. May 16, 1896.
882. Samuel Bowser, m. Margaret McGraw.
883. Lucinda Bowser, m. Daniel Slagel.
884. David S. Bowser, b. June 10, 1822; m. Lydia McCullum, b. Sept. 22, 1834.
885. Jacob Bowser.
886. Catharine Bowser, m. John Slagel.

879. PETER and BETSEY BOWSER; lived in Ohio.

Children:

887. Samuel Harrison Bowser, b. 1832; d. in 1908; m. Rachel Bowser (538); resided at Walk Chalk, Pa.
888. Sarah Bowser, b. Aug. 25, 1834; d. May 5, 1911; m. S. S. English.
889. David J. Bowser, b. 1841; m. (1) Jane Dickson; child: William H.; m. (2) Caroline Rosenberg; child: Laura; m. (3) Susan Houser; ch.: Harvey, Grant, Elizabeth; m. (4) Hattie Houser; m. (5) Hattie S. Welling.
890. Benjamin F. Bowser, b. 1845; m. Margaret I. Cornman, 8. 1844; address: Dayton, Ohio.

Children:

891. John E. Bowser, b. 1872; m. Florence Walls, b. 1874; ch.: Margaret, Raymond, Milford.
892. W. S. Bowser, m. Margaret Sherman; child: Ida.

893. Thompson P. Bowser, Feb. 12, 1850; m. Jennie E. Sloan, b. Dec. 9, 1856; address: Wickboro, Kittanning, Pa.

Children:

a893. Charles F., b. May 12, 1880; m. Jennie Bestine, b. Mar. 4, 1880; ch.: Mable, Margaret, Charles F., Jr.
b893. Orlo F., b. Aug. 23, 1881; m. Catharine McSherson, b. Apr. 8, 1882; d. Aug., 1918.
c893. Alma R., b. Dec. 18, 1883; d. Mar. 15, 1902.
d893. Jennie P., b. Jan. 22, 1889; d. Mar. 26, 1902.
children in this family. All died in infancy except the above six.

880. ISAAC and CATHARINE BOWSER; lived at Walk Chalk; moved to Pike Co., Ohio; died there.

Children:

895. Addison Bowser, b. 1837; vet. of the Civil War; 2d Lt. 39th Ohio Vol. Inf.; 1865.
896. Amos Bowser, b. 1839.
897. Samantha J. Bowser, b. 1845.
898. Samuel Bowser.

882. SAMUEL S. BOWSER, b. Jan. 21, 1817; d. June 28, 1900; m. Margaret McGraw, b. Apr. 28, 1816; d. Apr. 7, 1890; they came to Pittsburgh in 1853

Children:

899. Nancy Bowser, b. Dec. 19, 1842; m. Robert Jones; ch.: Mary Jane, Fannie, Margaret, Nellie, William C., Rebecca, Robert, Bertha, Lonella, Nancy.
900. John Bowser.
900. Margaret Ann Bowser, b. May 24, 1846; d. May 20, 1880; m. Joseph Maitland; no children.
900. Rebecca J. Bowser, b. Mar. 24, 1849; m. Peter Hyer.
900. Sarah Bowser, b. Apr. 19, 1852.
900. Emma Bowser, b. Aug. 27, 1854; d. in 1896; m. Charles Gardner.

884. DAVID S. and LYDIA BOWSER. David S. Bowser, farmer, lived on the Abram Bowser homestead near Walk Chalk; eventually he sold this property and moved into the village where he died. His widow is still living. David, his wife Lydia, and all of their children, were members of the Baptist Church of Walk Chalk.

Children:

912. Matilda A. Bowser, b. Sept. 24, 1851; d. Apr. 6, 1878; m. Rev. Chambers T. Jack, Baptist minister; Rev. Jack is located at Linesville, Pa.; ch.: Almeda, m. Zigler; address: Linesville, Pa.; Lulu m. Daniel Lacy; ch.: Jack, Jeanette.
913. Robert M. Bowser, b. July 7, 1853; d. July 5, 1854.
914. Amanda J. Bowser, b. May 14, 1855; d. 1918; m. James Hindman Bowser, b. June 7, 1852. (For children see 185.)
915. Anna M. Bowser, b. Sept. 14, 1857; m. Lebbius Russell, b. Apr. 14, 1856; address: New Kensington, Pa.

Children:

916. John B. Russell, b. July 1, 1879; m. Laura Pierce.
917. Claude M. Russell, b. Dec. 28, 1880.
918. Glendora Russell, b. Oct. 29, 1882; m. George L. Hays.
919. Charles O. Russell, b. Feb. 5, 1885.
920. Edna J. Russell, b. July 23, 1893; m. Owa McKinney.
a920. Wilda M. Russell, b. Jan. 18, 1898; m. Harry Varner.
b920. Willard J. Russell, b. Jan. 18, 1898; d. July 1, 1898.
921. Samuel S. Bowser, b. Nov. 8, 1859; m. Ida J. Booth, b. Oct. 12, 1865; in automobile business, Ford City, Pa.

Children:

922. Herbert Jacob Bowser, b. Sept. 22, 1884; m. Lulu Campbell, b. Jan. 18, 1885; in business with his father, Samuel S.; ch.: Sharon Kenneth, b. May 7, 1907; Dorothy May, b. Dec. 25, 1909; Herbert, b. Oct. 20, 1911; Mildred, died in infancy; Ida, d. ———; Walter, b. May 20, 1914; George, b. Jan. 18, 1917.
923. Harry Bowser, b. Feb. 22, 1890; d. Mar., 1900.
924. Samuel Dwight Bowser, b. July 4, 1902; d. Nov. 22, 1918.
925. Dr. Addison H. Bowser, b. Feb. 18, 1862; d. 1914; m. Sarah H. Booth, b. 1862; address: Reynoldsville, Pa.

Children:

926. Doctor Ira D. Bowser, Reynoldsville, Pa.; b. Nov. 29, 1883; m. Laura C. Wheeler.

a926. Bertha E. Bowser, m. Deible.

927. Addison W. Bowser, b. July 7, 1897; m. Tillie Hughes.

928. Ollie E. Bowser, b. Jan. 9, 1865, d. May 24, 1922; m. Chambers M. Fair, b. May 22, 1863; live in the homestead at Walk Chalk, Pa.

Children:

a928. Edith M. Fair, b. Jan. 2, 1888; m. Robert A. Ober.
b928. Stella B. Fair, b. July 29, 1889; m. Arch. L. Austin.
c928. Merl L. Fair, b. May 5, 1891, d. Aug. 23, 1892.
d928. Earl C. Fair, b. June 1, 1893; m. Mary Montgomery.
e928. Norman P. Fair, b. Oct. 8, 1896; m. Magy Stoner.
f928. Olive B. Fair, b. Apr. 11, 1899; d. May 4, 1921; m. Carl Crozer.
g928. Vernie K. Fair, b. Apr. 12, 1901; m. William Walters.
h928. Neubert W. Fair, b. Mar. 7, 1905.
i928. Ralph S. Fair, b. July 12, 1909.

929. Sarah B. Bowser, b. June 29, 1867; m. Arthur Cooper.

Children:

930. Charles Cooper.
931. David Cooper.
932. Arnold Cooper.

933. Ella D. Bowser, b. June 8, 1869; m. (1) John M. Russell; (2) Thomas H. Johnson; address: Ford City, Pa.

Child:

934. Carl Russel, b. Oct. 1893; m. Susan Bouch; in business, Ford City, Pa.; ch.: Eldora, Margaret, William.

935. Almeda M. Bowser, b. May 7, 1872; m. David Cochran.

936. Lydia K. Bowser, b. Oct. 27, 1874; m. R. L. Wylie.

Children:

937. Wanda Lee Wylie.
938. Charlotte Wylie.

939. Stella M. Bowser, b. June 9, 1877; m. Abram S. Harman; d. May 12, 1921; address: Brownsville, Pa.

Children:

940. Norma Harman.
941. Harlow Harman.

881. SUSANNA and SOLOMON ABE BOWSER, son of Nicholas (136). Of this union were born twelve children, seven of whom died in infancy. Those living are:

942. Lucinda Bowser, b. 1840; m. Michael McCoy; ch.; Matilda, m. Emery Snyder; Mary, m. William Downey; James, m. Jennie Forsythe; Ella, m. Richard Bray; Elizabeth, m. George Reibold.

943. James C. Bowser, m. Jennie Keys; ch.: Ernest, m. Anna Klinglesmith; William; Ida, m. William Smith; Flora, m. Edward Kramer; Pearl.

944. Margaret Bowser, b. 1849; m. John Roberts.

945. Mary C. Bowser, b. 1847; m. William McClain; ch.: John; Ida, m. R. C. Scott; address: Fairview, Pa.; ch.: Chambers, Kenneth, Theodore.

946. Samuel Henry Bowser, b. Jan. 29. 1856; m. Malissa Jane (1906), b. July 8, 1859; d. Oct. 25, 1901; (daughter of "Sadler" John Bowser); address: Vandergreft, Pa.

Children:

a946. Jessie, b. Jan. 30, 1878, d. Feb. 4, 1913; m. Sherman Edward Kennedy; ch.: Mendal Edward, b. May 7, 1902; Grace Elizabeth, b. Sept. 10, 1903; m. Edward Silk; Helen Rachel, b. June 22, 1906.

b946. Samuel H., Jr., b. Oct. 12, 1881.

c946. Pearl Clifford, b. Feb. 19, 1884; m. Oliver R. Long; ch.: Aceneth; Rachel Ellen, b. June 3, 1919.

d946. Gladys Susana, b. June 3, 1888; m. John Weitzel; ch.: Charles Raymond, b. Apr. 27, 1911; Isabelle Marian, b. July 9, 1913; Bernice Catharine, b. Apr. 25, 1915; Herbert Francis, b. Aug. 3, 1917.

e946. Harry David, b. Apr. 13, 1890; m. Margaret Albaugh; ch.: Harry Leon, b. May 18, 1911; William Francis, b. Oct. 4, 1912; Samuel Lawson, b. Mar. 28, 1916; Robert Leroy, b. May 24, 1919.

f946. Estella Mary, b. Oct. 17, 1891; m. Charles W. Wangler; ch.: Hildreth Harry, b. Jan. 26, 1915; Helen Florence, b. Aug. 10, 1918.

g946. Hazel Sarah, b. Aug. 22, 1894.

h946. Paul Lawson, b. June 15, 1897; enlisted in World War service, Aug. 23, 1917, Co. H, 111th Reg., 28th Div.; participated in the battles of the Chauteau Thierry, Argonne and St. Mihiel; was discharged May 13, 1919.

i946. Ruth Augusta, b. Dec. 19, 1899; m. John Fennell; address: Butler, Pa.

883. LUCINDA and DANIEL SLAGLE.

Children:

952. Lemuel Slagle, m. Catharine Hyle; ch.: Fluke, Flur.

953. Chambers Slagle; died young.

954. Miles Slagle.

955. John Slagle, m. Emma Holder.

956. Mary Alice Slagle, b. Aug. 7, 1855; m. Mathew McCollum, b. Aug. 7, 1854; address: Ford City, Pa.

Children:

a956. Charles McCollum, b. Oct. 28, 1894; m. (1) Mildred Culp; (2) m. Kunkle; ch.: Harry, Edward, Ralph, Charles.

b956. Lilly McCollum, b. Jan. 22, 1877; m. Samuel Rupert; ch.: Earl, Garland, Frederick, George, Ernest, Gladys, Floyd, Frank, Alice, Mary, Ruth.

c956. Daisey McCollum, b. Apr. 23, 1879; m. (1) John Walker; (2) Abe Stivason; ch.: Annie, George, Virginia, Clarence, Dorothy.

d956. Minnie McCollum, b. Mar. 9, 1881; m. Charles Heilman; ch.: Bert, Ruth.

e956. Carrie McCollum, b. Jan. 26, 1883; m. William Fair; ch.: William, George, Susan, Roy, Harry Hayle, Annie.

f956. Arthur McCollum, b. Mar. 4, 1885; m. Mary Thierry; ch.: Lucy, Freda, Dorothy, Rovena, Mildred.

g956. Ocie McCollum, b. Apr. 9, 1887; m. Jacob Moore; ch.: Kenneth, James.

h956. Grace McCollum, b. June 16, 1889; m. (1) Edward Burdette; (2) Archy Stivason; ch.: Dorothy, Clarence, Kathleen, Ruth, Fay.

i956. Roy McCollum, b. June 7, 1892; m. Florence Stivason; ch.: Gertrude, Ruth, Frances, Roberta, Laverne.

j956. Lulu McCollum, b. June 6, 1895; m. (1) Perry Woodward; (2) Edward Stivason; ch.: Laura, Thelma, Perry, Margaret, Teddy.
k956. Walter McCollum, b. Sept. 8, 1896.
957. Samuel Slagle, m. Jennie Leinweaver; ch.: Guss, Turrie.
958. Ann Slagle, m. Thomas Bowser; ch.: Lulu, May, Thomas, Richard, Nellie.
959. Emma Slagle, m. Cull Peters; ch.: Zetta, William, Cora, Clara, Nellie.
960. Catharine Slagle, m. Shed Starr.
Children:
961. Harvey Slagle.
962. David Slagle.
963. Ella Slagle, m. David French.

136. NICHOLAS (4); JOHN (3); MATHIAS (2); MATHIAS, SR (1). Nicholas, John and Jacob Bowser were the only members of John Bowser's family (of Hopewell) who remained in Bedford County. Nicholas' farm was located about one mile southeast of the John Bowser homestead. As his farm laid on the slope of a mountain near Hopewell he could look from his doorstep to the door of the home of his childhood. The picture shows the site of the farm. His grandson, Henry P. Bowser, of Hopewell, remembers Nicholas in the early days of the Civil War, an old decrepit man. He died about 1862. He married Elizabeth Kline. He was a member of the Dunkard Church.

Children:
964. Jacob Bowser; moved to Venango County, Pa.
965. Magdalena Bowser; moved to Worthington, Pa.; one of her daughters married George Bellus. (See No. 975.)
966. Peter Bowser, b. between 1810 and 1820; died in Armstrong Co., Pa.
967. Solomon Abe Bowser, b. 1820; m. Susan Bowser; daughter of Samuel Bowser (133); for children see Susannah (881).
968. John Bowser, b. 1805; m. Ruth Weaver, b. 1810; ch.: Henry, John, Jacob, Lily, Caroline, Martha, Rachel, James, Nicholas, b. 1842, Ashbury, Tillie, b. 1847.
969. Nicholas Bowser; in Mexican war; died in New Orleans with Yellow fever.
970. Henry Bowser, b. 1810; d. Feb. 20, 1878; m. Mary Steele.
971. Samuel Bowser; lived in Hopewell Twp., Bedford Co., Pa.
972. William Bowser.
973. Mary Bowser, m. John Grace; ch.: John W.; Daniel; Piper; Sarah, m. George Cartright; Hannah, m. John Croyle; Rebecca, m. —— Woodlock; Elizabeth, m. Heffher.
974. Hannah Bowser, m. Daniel Ritz; ch.: Henry, James.
975. Magdelena H. Bowser, m. William Brannen.
976. James Bowser, b. 1824; d. 1880; m. Elizabeth Kelley.

970. HENRY (5); NICHOLAS (4); JOHN (3); MATHIAS (2); MATHIAS (1). Henry and Mary Steele Bowser. His will in Book 5, page 351, Bedford, Pa. Henry Bowser of Liberty Township, Bedford County; wife, Mary.

Children:
977. James S. Bowser, b. 1840; d. 1917; m. Fannie S. Moore.
978. Emanuel Bowser; m. Margaret Divelbiss.
Children:
a978. Elsie Bowser.
b978. May Bowser.
c978. Preston Bowser.
d978. Roy Bowser.

e978. Mary Bowser; m. A. C. Householder; address: Johnstown, Pa; ch.: George, Bessie, Preston.
f 978. George H. and Alice Sutchall; address: Hopewell, Pa.; ch.; Edith, John, Helen.
g978. Fannie Bowser; m. M. H. Cook, 401 Main St., Niles, Ohio; ch.: Chester.
h978. Alzie Bowser; m Bou Ramie; Philadelphia, Pa.
i 978. James W. Bowser; m. Anna Plant; Youngstown, Ohio; ch.: James.
j978. Alida Bowser; m. Steven Dudley, 26 Hunter Ave., Niles, Ohio; ch.: Margaret.
k978. Robert Bowser.

979. Charles Bowser; m. Sarah Mardis.

Children:

a979. Clifton Bowser, m. Viola Troutman; Riddlesburg, Pa.
b979. Zella Bowser, m. Joseph Cleve; Liberty Twp., Bedford Co.
c979. Dorothy Bowser, m. Alvin Carbary; Liberty Twp., Bedford Co.
d979. Eliza Bowser.

980. Maria Bowser, m. John Hawkins, Riddlesburg, Pa.

Children:

a980. Mary Hawkins, m. Oliver Phillips.
b980. Rosa Hawkins, m. Irvine Bredenstine.
c980. Elizabeth Hawkins, m. Elmer Menster.
d980. Jennie Hawkins.
e980. Myrtle Hawkins.
f980. Hawkins, m. Alice Guthridge.
g980. Hawkins, m. Mary Shannon.
h980. Hawkins, m. Lena Switzer.

981. Catharine Bowser, m. John Long.

Child:

a981. Mary Long, m. John Fields.

982. Mary Ann Bowser, m. David Brunbaugh.
983. Elizabeth Bowser, m. Jacob Weyandt.
984. Harrison Bowser, m. Ida Brumbaugh.

977. JAMES S. and FANNIE S. BOWSER.

Children:

985. Mary Jane Bowser, b. 1860; m. D. N. Hanley.
986. Annie M. Bowser, b. 1865; d. 1918; m. J. H. Black.
987. Alice M. Bowser, b. 1867; d. 1901; m. W. A. Butts.
988. Rev. H. Graybill Bowser, b. 1872; m. (1) Esther Williams, (2) Viola M. Swisher; minister of the Church of God; residence near Franklin, Pa.
989. Clay M. Bowser, b. 1873; m. Estella Burtnett.
990. James S. Bowser, Jr., b. 1875; m. Elizabeth Jones.
991. Hattie T. Bowser, b. 1880; d. 1919; m. Fred Oast.

988. REV. H. GRAYBILL and VIOLA (SWISHER) BOWSER.

Children:

992. Ruth May Bowser, b. 1891; m. J. J. Cashman.
993. M. Ester Bowser, b. 1896; trained nurse.

989. CLAY M. BOWSER and ESTELLA.

994. Edna Bowser, b. 1900; teacher.
995. Irma Bowser, b. 1902.
996. Frank Bowser, b. 1904.
997. Ida Bowser, b. 1907.
998. Victory Elnora Bowser, b. 1907.

976. JAMES and ELIZABETH BOWSER.

Children:

999. Nicholas Bowser; went West; was a veteran of the Civil War; died in the West about 1910; m. Alice; one son: William.
1000. Catharine Bowser, d. 1916; m. Valentine Fink.

Child:

1001. Cinderella, m. Wood Spellman.
1002. Rev. John Bowser, minister of the Dunkard Church; d. Feb., 1907; m. Elizabeth Thistle; (2) Catharine Stair; no children.
1003. Henry P. Bowser, b. 1852; m. Catharine Smith.
1004. William Bowser; never married; died in New York State 1882.
1005. Rebecca Bowser, now living on the John Bowser homestead at Hopewell; m. Henry Cogan.
1006. Simon Bowser, m. Sara Rush; lived in the West; present residence, 2846 Blake St., Denver, Colo; child: Lena Bowser, m. ——— Jones.
1007. Jeanette Bowser, b. about 1860; m. William E. Baker; ch.: Elizabeth, Mary, John.
1008. Rufus Bowser; living in Florida.
1009. Edmund Bowser; living in Altoona, Pa.; m. Elizabeth Smith.
1010. Ch.: Chester Byron Bowser, b. May 20, 1884; d. Aug. 14, 1884.
1011. Gussie Bowser, b. Aug. 8, 1885; d. 1908; m. Charles Roop; child: Melvin E.
1012. Harry P. Bowser; m. T. E. Mertz, b. Aug. 27, 1887.
1013. Cora E. Bower, b. July 12, 1890; m. A. L. Lytle; child: Edmund B.
1014. Savilla Bowser, b. 1862; m. Oliver Parrin, farmer of Hopewell Twp.; address: Jerome, Yavapai Co., Arizona.
1015. Tobias Bowser

1003. HENRY P. and CATHARINE BOWSER. Henry P. Bowser is an extensive land owner and successful farmer. He resides one and a half miles northwest of Hopewell, and two miles from the John Bowser homestead on "Yellow Creek," so frequently mentioned in this history. His father told him that his (Henry's) great-grandfather came "from Germany"; that he brought parts of a wagon and farming implements with him from the old country, and that he was wealthy. Some of his ancestors were in the Revolutionary War. His great-grandfather, whom he believes was Mathias, made frequent trips to Philadelphia for supplies.

Children:

1017. Mary Elizabeth, m. John Fluke; living near Hopewell; ch.: Florence, m. Roy Basler; Margaret.
1018. Ella Bowser, m. Ambrose Steel; ch.: Edith, Margaret, Robert.
1019. Scott Bowser, m. Florence Eichelberger.
1020. Russell Bowser, m. Ora Cypher.
1021. James Franklin Bowser.
1022. Anna Bowser.
1023. George Bowser.

1014. SAVILLA BOWSER and OLIVER PARRIN; ch.: Clarence, m. Mary Likens; Frank, m. Della Reed; Tobias; Valentine.

1005. REBECCA and HENRY COGAN.

Children:

1024. Gertie Cogan.
1025. Charles Cogan.
1026. James Blaine Cogan.
1027. Chester Cogan, m. ——— Ham.
1028. Stella Cogan.
1029. Elizabeth Cogan.
1031. Ethel Cogan.
1030. Elsie Cogan.

137. PETER (4); JOHN (3); MATHIAS (2); MATHIAS (1). Peter Bowser, the youngest son of John Bowser, of Hopewell, Pa., came to Armstrong County, Pa., early in the history of the country and bought land on Pine Creek, two miles east of the Allegheny River. Here he reared a large family and lived to see the country of his adoption emerge from a wilderness into a land of fertile farms, schools and churches.

Children:

1032. Elizabeth Bowser, b. 1811.
1033. Mary Bowser, b. 1813; m. Abram Swigart.
1034. Martha Bowser, b. 1815; d. Oct. 12, 1877; m. Jacob Bowser (son of Joseph Bowser, son of Noah Bowser), b. 1806; d. June 9, 1868.
1035. John Bowser, b. 1816.
1036. Mathias Bowser, b. 1819; d. 1909; m. Sarah H. Baum, b. 1825.
1037. Jane Bowser, b. Dec. 21, 1821; d. Jan. 22, 1901; m. Peter Bowser (169), b. Oct. 20, 1815; d. Jan. 29, 1879.
1038. Sally Bowser, b. 1825.
1039. Margaret Bowser, b. 1826.
1040. Loben Bowser, b. July 16, 1828; d. Jan. 11, 1912; m. Martha Jane Oliver, b. Oct. 14, 1829; d. June 29, 1879.
1041. Jeremiah Bowser, b. 1832.

1034. MARTHA (5); PETER (4); JOHN (3); MATHIAS (2); MATHIAS (1). Martha and Jacob Bowser.

Children:

1042. Mathias Q. Bowser, b. Sept. 25, 1836; d. Oct. 15, 1898; m. Margaret Stockdill, b. 1847; lived at Echo, Pa.

1043. Jemima Bowser, b. Dec. 28, 1837; d. Sept. 5, 1918; m. James McCullough; ch.: Martha, Mary.

1044. Jeremiah Bowser, b. Oct. 31, 1839; m. Catharine Snyder.

Children:

1045. Harvey Bowser.
1046. Nettie Bowser.
1047. William Bowser.

1048. Joannah Bowser, b. July 27, 1842; m. Samuel Buzzard.

Children:

1049. Mary Buzzard.
1050. Ida Buzzard.
1051. Bertha Buzzard.
1052. Robert Buzzard.

1053. Caroline Bowser, b. June 9, 1844; d. Apr., 1919; m. Henry Weaver; ch.: Jennie, Miranda, Savina, Mary, Annie, Ella, Maisey, Thomas, David Wellington.

1054. Jane Bowser, b. June 10, 1846; m. William Jones.

Children:

1055. Mary Jones, m. Daniel Schreckengost; ch.: Mary, Pearl, Berton, Claire.
1056. David Jones.
1057. John Jones.
1058. Thomas Jones, m. Ida Schreckengost; ch.: Claude, Preston.

1059. Eleanor Bowser, b. July 27, 1847; d. Oct. 21, 1919; m. Uriah M. Cleaver; ch.: Fanty, Nettie, Emma, Elizabeth, John, Thomas, Mary, Belle, Bessie.

1060. Anderson Bowser, b. Nov. 15, 1849; single; resides at Manorville, Pa.

1061. Franklin P. Bowser, b. Oct. 7, 1852; d. Jan. 24, 1920; m. Catharine Swigart, daughter of Mary Bowser (1033), daughter of Peter (137).

Children:

1062. Jennie Bowser, m. ——— Downsey.
1063. Thomas Bowser, m. ——— Schaffer.

1064. Thomas Bowser, b. Oct. 10, 1854; d. Mar., 1913; m. Catharine Boyle; d. June, 1912.

Children:

1065. William A. Bowser, b. Jan. 4, 1880; m. Bessie Geiger, b. Aug. 11, 1884.

Children:

1066. Merle L. Bowser, b. Aug. 20, 1903.
1067. Ethel C. Bowser, b. Feb. 13, 1906.

1068. Prof. John A. Bowser, b. Apr. 17, 1882; m. Joan Moore, b. Mar. 16, 1884.

Children:

1069. Janet Bowser, b. Nov. 28, 1910.
1070. Dorothy Bowser, b. Apr. 18, 1920.

1071. Elmer Curtis Bowser, b. Aug. 26, 1885; m. Wilda McIntire.

Children:

1072. Laird Bowser.
1073. Sallie Bowser.
1074. Mildred Bowser.

1075. James Y. Bowser, m. Emma Harmon.
1076, Emory P. Bowser, b. Aug. 23, 1890; m. Helen Dailey.
1077. Ch.: Martha Jane Bowser, b. July 29, 1915.
1078. Jeremiah Leroy Bowser, m. Kitty Mechling; d. 1918.

1036. MATHIAS (5); PETER (4); JOHN (3); MATHIAS (2); MATHIAS (1). MATHIAS and SARAH H. (BAUM) BOWSER. Mathias Bowser settled on the homestead established by his father on Pine Creek. He was a veteran of the Civil War. During his term of service in the army his wife and children carried on his extensive farm; he was a man of intelligence and great enterprise. He died at his home in 1909 at the advanced age of 90 years.

Children:

1079. Wilson L. Bowser, b. 1845; d. 1917; m. Caroline Hollobaugh; ch.: Henry, Mary, Wilber, Arnold, Phoebe, Anna, Cora, Maude, Essie, Benjamin, Ellen, Lee, Sandy.

1080. Ross Mechling Bowser, b. 1847; m. (1) Amanda Anthony; ch.: Jessie, Harry, Frank, Floda, Forest; (2) Christina Zimmerman.

1081. Harvey Peter Bowser, b. 1849; Wickboro, Kittanning, Pa.

1082. Hettie W. Bowser, b. 1853; m. Henry Troutner.

Children:

1083. Sarah Troutner, m. Jerry Swigart.
1084. Emma Troutner, m. Charles Crawshaw.
1085. Rebecca P. Troutner, m. Charles Walker.
1086. Lydda Troutner, m. Irvin Bowser, son of Lewis Bowser (684).

1087. Philip Templeton Bowser, b. 1855; m. (1) Mary Shannon; ch.: Mabel, John; (2) Tillie Bowser, daughter of J. H. Bowser (185); child: Charles.

1088. Sally J. Bowser; single; b. 1857.

1089. Madison M. Bowser, b. 1860; d. 1912; m. Hattie Jones; ch.: Leroy, Flossie, Fern.

1090. George McClelland Bowser, b. 1862; stockraiser and miner in the West; present address unknown.
1091. James Neale Bowser, b. 1866; m. (1) Louise Bank; (2) Minerva Hull.
1092. Rebecca P. Bowser, b. 1867; m. A. S. Schreckengost; photographer; Kittanning, Pa.

1040. LOBEN (5); PETER (4); JOHN (3); MATHIAS (2); MATHIAS (1). Loben Bowser purchased land on Pine Creek, in Armstrong County, Pa., about six miles east of his father's residence, and there reared a family of fifteen children, all of whom have honored his name and maintained the best ideals of our Bowser family. He was born July 16, 1828, and died at his home near Echo, Pa., Jan. 11, 1912. He married Martha Jane Oliver, born Oct. 14, 1829, died June 29, 1829. He devoted his life to farming, the traditional occupation of nearly all of our people, and was eminently successful.

Children:
1093. Florence Young Bowser, b. May 26, 1851; died in infancy.
1094. Rev. Wellington Bowser, b. Sept. 13, 1852; m. Fannie Waid, b. Sept. 6, 1857.
1095. Sarah Emeline Bowser, b. Jan. 27, 1854.
1096. Alexander Bowser, b. Nov. 20, 1855; d. Feb. 1, 1891, in Cincinnati, Ohio; carriage painter.
1097. Wesley Smith Bowser, b. Jan. 5, 1857; d. Mar. 1, 1911.
1098. Clement Elgin Bowser, b. July 5, 1858; m. Barbara Boyle; reside at Echo, Pa.
1099. Margaret Elmira Bowser, b. Dec. 24, 1859; m. George W. Beck, b. May 15, 1859; reside at Echo, Pa.
1100. James Miles Bowser, b. Feb. 21, 1863; m. Elsie Clever; reside at Evans City, Pa.
1101. Mary Malissa Bowser, b. July 5, 1861; m. Robert S. Andrews.
1102. McClelland Ellsworth Bowser, b. May 6, 1864; m. Mary Farster.
1103. Nancy Laura Bowser, b. Aug. 26, 1866; died young.
1104. Alice Jane Bowser, b. Nov. 3, 1867; teacher.
1105. Estella Olive Bowser, b. July 31, 1871; m. W. Van Voorliss; live at Seattle, Wash.; ch.: Helen Irene.
1106. Clara Iona Bowser, b. Nov. 11, 1872; died young.
1107. Bertha Marinda Bowser, b. Sept. 6, 1874; m. Robert R. Barker, b. Nov. 9, 1871; live near Kittanning, Pa.

1094. REV. WELLINGTON and FANNIE WAID BOWSER. (See biographies.)

Children:
1108. Vincent Earl Bowser, b. at Rurki, India, under the shadows of the Himalaya Mountains, Sept. 29, 1881; m. Mary Thompson, of Pasadena, Calif.; he studied law in the University of Southern California and is now practicing his profession at El Monte, Calif.; he has four children.

1097. WESLEY SMITH and CATHARINE BOWSER.

Children:
Bertha Jane, Margaret Ann, Harvey Miles, Mary Terressa, Wilbert Lewis, Minnie Pearl, Venice Irene.

1099. MARGARET ALMIRA and GEORGE W. BECK.

Children:
a1088. Oliver Oben.
b1099. Lillian D.

c1099. John Thoburn.
d1099. Guy Raymond.
John Thoburn Beck was in service in the World War for 16 months, 12 of which were spent overseas. He belonged to 601st Co. Eng. as first class private.
1109. Ethel Maude Bowser was born in Karachi, a seaport on the Arabian Sea, Dec. 3, 1885; m. Thomas K. Hoagiand, Hermos Beach, Calif.; they have a son.
1110. Genevieve Irene Bowser, was born at Spartansburg, Pa., June 23, 1887; m. Edgar A. Lord, Los Angeles, Calif.; they have one son.

1098. CLEMENT E. and BARBARA (BOYLE) BOWSER. Clement Elgin Bowser is a farmer, located near the Loben Bowser homestead at Echo, Pa.
Children:
1111. Nannie N. Bowser, b. June 19, 1877; m. T. Talmadge Skinner, b. Jan. 15, 1877.
Child:
1112. T. Talmadge Skinner, b. Mar. 21, 1902.
1113. May E. Bowser, b. Sept. 4, 1879; m. Harry E. Olinger.
Children:
1114. Leland Olinger, b. Nov., 1898.
1115. Leroy Olinger, b. 1900.
1116. Maud Olinger, b. 1901.
1117. Freda Olinger, b. 1904.
1118. Floyd Olinger, b. 1907; d. Mar. 1921.
1119. Sadie Bowser, b. June 2, 1883; m. Harvey McCullough.
Children:
1120. Mulvene McCullough, b. July 16, 1913.
1121. Robert McCullough, b. Sept. 1915.
1122. Bert Bowser. b. Dec. 3, 1885; m. Cora Kirkwood.
Children:
1123. Chester Bowser.
1124. Kenneth Bowser.
1125. Mildred Bowser.
1126. Robert Bowser.
1127. Freda Bowser.
1128. Edith Bowser, b. Nov. 26, 1890; m. William Emmons.
Children:
1129. Relton Emmons.
1130. Donald Emmons.
1131. James Emmons.
1132. Richard Emmons.

1100. JAMES MILES and ELSIE (CLEVER) BOWSER. James Miles Bowser taught school when a young man. For the last 30 years he has been in street car work, now a conductor on the Pittsburgh, Harmony and Butler Line; address: Evans City, Pa.
Children:
1133. Nelson Bowser, b. 1891; d. 1891.
1134. Catharine Leone Bowser, b. 1893; graduate nurse; volunteered in the war service; stationed at Camp Upton; thence sailed for France on the Megantic, June 12, 1918; was stationed at Base Hospital No. 1; later at Chamanet; returned on the Agamennon May 15, 1919.
1135. Francis Bowser, b. 1896; graduate of Duff's Business College, Pittsburgh; now employed in Butler, Pa.

1102. McCLELLAND ELLSWORTH and MARY BOWSER.
Children: Blanche, m. Frederick Greybiggle; Miles, m. —— Coonart; Minnie, m. Walter Herman; Charles, m. —— Campbell; Olive, m. Nelson Shirey; Frank, Roy, Pearl, Harry, Raymond.

1100. MARY MALISSA and ROBT. S. ANDREWS.
Children:
1136. Wellington Andrews.
1137. Lucile Andrews.
1138. Gladys Andrews.
1139. Catharine Andrews.

1107. BERTHA MARINDA and ROBERT R. BARKER; address: Kittanning, R. D.
Children:
1140. Grace Elma Barker, b. Sept. 22, 1902.
1141. Relton Barker, b. Mar. 12, 1905; d. Oct. 2, 1918.
1142. Nelda Lucile Barker, b. May 23, 1902.
1143. Ferne Marie Barker, b. May 14, 1916.

138. MARY (4); JOHN (3); MATHIAS, JR. (2); MATHIAS, SR. (1).
Mary Bowser married John Burnheimer—no doubt a descendant of the Berkheimers of Bedford County, Pa. They lived near Kittanning; later moved to Ohio.
1144. William Burnheimer; lived near Kittanning.
1145. Mathias Burnheimer; moved to Jackson Co., Ohio; died there in 1862.
1146. John Burnheimer.
1147. Samuel Burnheimer; John and Samuel moved to Canton, Ohio; died there.
1148. Mary Burnheimer, b. Mar. 15, 1803; d. Oct. 20, 1880; m. Samuel D. Bowser; b. Apr. 4, 1802; d. Aug. 18, 1885.
1149. Elizabeth Burnheimer; m. Jacob Flenner.

1148. MARY (BURNHEIMER) and SAMUEL D. BOWSER. Mary and Samuel D. Bowser lived near Walk Chalk, Pa. They were members of the Dunkard Church.
Children:
1150. Elizabeth Bowser, b. 1823; d. 1896; m. John Wible.
1151. Rebecca Bowser, b. Oct. 23, 1826; d. May 22, 1903; m. John Barker, b. Sept. 28, 1822; d. Jan. 4, 1902.
1152. Robinson Bowser, b. Sept. 14, 1832; d. May 6, 1907; m. Catharine Yingst, b. Jan. 1, 1839.
1153. Sarah A. Bowser, b. Oct. 20, 1834; d. Aug. 28, 1914; m. Robert Wible, b. Dec. 26, 1831; d. Dec. 25, 1905.
1154. Nancy Bowser, b. 1836; d. 1907; m. William J. Geary, d. 1884.
1155. Julia A. Bowser, b. May 5, 1839; d. 1902; m. James Wible, b. Aug., 1829; d. Oct., 1907.
1156. Hamilton D. Bowser, b. 1843; d. 1913; m. Delilah Toy, b. 1844.
1157. Alexander J. Bowser, b. Aug. 7, 1846; d. Mar. 2, 1915; m. Emily Bowser, b. July 20, 1854.

1151. REBECCA (BOWSER) and JOHN BARKER. Lived near Kittanning. There were eight children of this union.
1158. C. W. Barker, b. Mar. 27, 1859; d. Oct. 20, 1916; m. Melvina Tyler.
1159. G. G. Barker, b. Dec. 2, 1850; m. Mary Etta Williams, b. Sept. 9, 1856; address: Britton, Okla.; child: F. M. Barker, b. Dec. 28, 1882.

1160. Anna Barker, b. Dec. 12, 1852; d. July 5, 1877; m. J. H. R. Spilman.
1161. Mary J. Barker, b. Apr. 8, 1855; m. Percy Tyler, b. Jan. 8, 1853; resides at Ute, Iowa.
1162. Sarah C. Barker, b. July 20, 1857; d. Feb. 11, 1895; m. Daniel Farrar.
1163. P. C. L. Barker, b. Oct. 23, 1859; m. Elizabeth Morse; address: Vermillion, S. D.
1164. Ida M. Barker, b. Dec. 30, 1863; d. Feb. 10, 1864.
1165. Sherman Barker, b. Jan. 20, 1866; d. Oct. 27, 1883.

1152. ROBINSON and CATHARINE (YINGST) BOWSER.

Children:

1166. Sherman Bowser, b. April 18, 1878; m. Charlotte Frick, b. Oct. 31, 1878; address: West Kittanning, Pa.; ch.: Elizabeth, Chambers, Myrtle, Grace, Harry, Helen, Rufus, Gladine, Arthur.
1167. Whitsel Bowser, b. Mar. 6, 1882; m. Maud Cramer; ch.: Rhinaldo, Clarence, Francis, Kenneth.

1153. SARAH A. (BOWSER) and ROBERT WIBLE. Samuel D. and Mary (Burnheimer) Bowser had the rare good providence of having three daughters marry three sons of a neighbor. One daughter, Sarah A., married Robert Wible and lived near Worthington, Armstrong Co., Pa.

Children:

1168. William Wilson Wible, b. Nov. 20, 1859; m. Belle Toy, b. Apr. 6, 1872.

Children:

1169. Alvin Wible, b. 1895.
1170. Hobert Wible, b. 1897.
1171. Miles Wible, b. 1901.

1172. Charlotte Wible, b. July 21, 1861.
1173. George G. Wible, b. May 13, 1863; m. Manda Summerville, b. 1864.

Children:

1174. A. Wible, b. 1890.
1175. Howard Wible, b. 1892.
1176. Richard Wible, b. 1894.
1177. Mary Wible, b. 1896.
1178. Robert Wible, b. 1900.
1179. Dorothy Wible, b. 1906.

1180. Robert Lee Wible, b. Mar. 25, 1865; m. Lydia Bowser, b. 1874.

Children:

1181. Wanda Wible, b. 1904.
1182. Charlotte Wible, b. 1909.

1183. James Elmer Wible, b. Mar. 19, 1867; d. Jan. 8, 1912; m. Lucy Smith, b. 1869; d. 1907.

Child:

1184. Harry Wible, b. 1898.

1185. Harriet Wible, b. May 23, 1869.
1186. Tillie Wible, b. July 9, 1871.
1187. James Mark Wible, b. Mar. 29, 1874; d. Sept. 15, 1904.
1188. Charles Wayne Wible, b. Nov. 23, 1876; m. Lucille Rock

Children:

1189. Charles Wayne Wible, Jr., b. 1915.
1190. Charlotte Wible, b. 1918.

1154. NANCY (BOWSER) and WILLIAM J. GEARY.

Children:

1191. John A. Geary, b. Mar. 14, 1863; m. Margaret Smith.
1192. May E. Geary, b. 1866; m. Merl Benton.
1193. Mahala Geary, b. 1867; m. W. H. Lewis.

1194. Sarah A. Geary, b. 1870; d. 1912; m. O. N. Myer.
1195. William Geary, b. 1872.
1196. Hannah Geary, b. 1874; m. Harry Bowser.
1197. Samuel Geary, b. 1877; m. Rachel Thompson.
1198. Martha Geary, b. 1880; m. Albert Toy.

1155. JULIA A. (BOWSER) and JAMES WIBLE.

Children:
1199. Nannie Wible, b. Oct. 23, 1859.
1200. Mary Wible, b. April 27, 1861; m. Marion Zillefrow, b. 1863.
Children:
1201. Grace Zillefrow, b. 1887.
1202. Julia Zillefrow, b. 1890.
1203. Hallam Zillefrow, b. 1893.
1204. Olive Zillefrow, b. 1896; d. 1899.
1205. Leota Zillefrow, b. 1898.
1206. Kenneth Zillefrow, b. 1900; d. 1912.

1207. Parker Wible, b. Jan. 10, 1863; m. Belle McCullough.
Children:
1208. Paul Wible, b. 1885.
1209. James Wible, b. 1887.
1210. Frances Wible, b. 1902.
1211. Julia Wible, b. 1905; d. 1919.

1213. Isaac Wible, b. Jan. 15, 1865; m. Margaret Richardson.
Children:
1214. Helen Wible, b. 1892.
1215. Marion Wible, b. 1900.
1216. Edith Wible, b. Mar. 9, 1867; m. Parks P Burford. See (617) for children.

1217. Effie Wible, b. June 2, 1869; m. J. P. Stewart, b. 1867.
Children:
1218. Olive Wible, b. Sept. 1, 1871; m. W. M. Seligman, b. 1873.
Children:
1219. William Seligman, b. 1902.
1220. Donald Seligman, b. 1904; d. 1907.
1221. Julian Seligman, b. 1906.

1222. Grace Wible, b. Feb. 22, 1874; m. Earnest Bartels.
Children:
1223. Earnest Bartels, Jr., b. 1913.
1224. Carl Bartels, b. 1915.

1225. Henry Wible, b. Mar. 17, 1876; m. Jennie Foster, b. 1879.
Children:
1226. Donald Wible, b. 1909.
1227. Edith Wible, b. 1918.

1228. Florence Wible, b. July 9, 1878; m. E. E. Crawford, b. 1874.
Children:
1229. Charlotte Crawford, b. 1912.
1230. Edna Crawford, b. 1916.
1231. Elizabeth Crawford, b. 1918; d. 1918.

1232. Alice Wible, b. Oct. 10, 1880; m. Bert Foster.
Children:
1233. Glen Foster, b. 1903.
1234. Rodney Foster, b. 1906.
1235. Edna Wible, b. June 1, 1883.

1157. ALEXANDER J. and EMILY BOWSER.

Children:

1236. Nannie Bowser, b. Sept. 24, 1873; m. Everett McGeary, b. Aug. 28, 1867.

Children:

1237. Melba McGeary, b. 1899.
1238. Charles McGeary, b. 1901.
1239. Florence McGeary, b. 1903.

1240. Elizabeth Bowser, b. Oct. 1, 1875.
1241. Guy Bowser, b. Sept. 13, 1878.
1242. Jay Bowser, b. Mar. 12, 1881; d. Aug. 16, 1898.
1243. Hamilton Bowser, b. May 28, 1887; m. Sadie Shepherd.

Children:

1244. Mildred Bowser, b. May 21, 1917.
1245. Grace Bowser, b. Aug. 24, 1919.

1246. Daisy Bowser, b. July 19, 1884; d. July 19, 1909; m. Frank Borland.
1247. Iva Bowser, b. March 31, 1890; m. William Smith.

Child:

1248. Virginia Smith.

1249. Roy Bowser, b. Feb. 21, 1892.
1250. Ruth Bowser, b. Jan. 27, 1894; m. Edward L. Anderson; address: Stenen, Sask., Canada.

Child:

1251. Marie Anderson, b. 1920.

1252. Warren Bowser, b. Feb. 7, 1896.

Alexander J. Bowser reared his family near New Kensington, Pa., where most of his descendants are now living.

139. ELIZABETH (4), JOHN (3), MATHIAS, JR. (2), MATHIAS, SR., (1). Elizabeth, the second daughter of John Bowser (13) of Hopewell Twp., Bedford Co., Pa., as mentioned in his will, married Abraham Swigart, of York Co., Pa. The will of Abraham Swigart, a resident of Buffalo Twp., Armstrong Co., Pa., dated March 15, 1830, was probated in Kittanning, Pa., May 23, 1832.

Children:

1253. Jacob Swigart, m. Mary Gouldinger.
1254. John Swigart, b. 1802; d. 1878; m. Sarah A. Bowser, b. 1800, d. 1876.
1255. Elizabeth Swigart, m.
1256. Abraham Swigart.
1257. Daniel Swigart.
1258. Mary Swigart, m. ——— Cornman.

1254. JOHN and SARAH A. SWIGART. John Swigart came from Bedford County, Pa., to Armstrong County about 1812. He was united by marriage to Sarah A. Bowser, daughter of Joseph D. Bowser, son of Noah and Eunice (Ditto) Bowser. He was a stone mason and brick layer, and helped to build the "Eagle" hotel and a number of the earliest brick buildings in Kittanning. He and his wife were members of the Dunkard Church.

Children:

1259. Jacob Swigart, b. 1824; d. in infancy.
1260. Abraham Swigart, b. 1825; d. 1907; m. Margaret Burnheimer, b. 1827; d. 1902.
1261. Rebecca Swigart, b. 1828; d. 1904; m. Mathias Bowser. (See 133 for children.)
1262. Elizabeth Swigart, b. 1830; d. 1860; m. Henry Bowser, son of Christian.

1260. ABRAHAM and MARY (BURNHEIMER) SWIGART. Abraham Swigart was a veteran of the Civil War. He enlisted Oct. 1, 1861, Co. A, 2d Regiment Cavalry; discharged Dec. 16, 1863; re-enlisted Dec. 17, 1863, Co. M, Penn. Mounted Corps; discharged July 13, 1865; he married Mary Burnheimer.

Children:

a1260. Sarah E. Swigart; single; b. 1849.
b1260. Mary A. Swigart, b. 1852; d. 1900; m. Oliver P. Stover, b. 1850; d. 1910.
c1260. John Swigart, b. 1854; d. 1873; single.
d1260. Clarence Swigart; b. 1857; m. Malinda Hopper; b. 1861.
e1260. Joseph F. Swigart, b. 1861; m. Margaret Delph.
1263. Joseph F. Swigart, b. 1832; d. 1912; m. Sarah A. White, b. 1834; d. 1900.
1264. Jonas Swigart; moved to California; address unknown.
1265. John Swigart, b. 1836; d. in California.
1266. Rev. Daniel W. Swigart, b. 1838; m. Margaret Starr, b. Dec. 12, 1837; d. Sept. 26, 1868.
a1266. Sarah Swigart, b. 1840; m. Robert Adams.
1267. Nancy Swigart, b. 1842; d. 1915; m. Adam Edwards.

1263. JOSEPH F. SWIGART and SARAH A. SWIGART. After his marriage settled at Mosgrove, Pa., and engaged in farming. He was a member of the Baptist Church.

Children:

1268. Malinda J. Swigart, b. 1857; m. James F. Babb, b. May 18, 1858, a son of Samuel and Lucy Ann (Bowser) Babb. Present address, Ford City, Pa.

Child:

a1268. Arthur E. Babb, b. Sept. 15, 1891.

1269. Lycurgus Swigart, b. 1858; killed on the Pennsylvania Railroad, 1898.

1270. James W. Swigart, b. 1860; m. Elizabeth Schaub.

Children:

1271. Edna Swigart.
1272. Morna Swigart.
1273. Murial Swigart.

1274. David M. Swigart, b. Aug. 15, 1861; m. Martha Serene, b. 1863.

Child:

1275. Lotta Swigart, b. Mar. 23, 1900.

1276. John B. Swigart b. Sept. 22, 1863; m. Mollie Rebecca McNeil of East Brady, Pa. In 1881 he went into the employ of the Allegheny R. R. (now the Penna. R. R.) and has continued in the railroad service. For twenty years Mr. Swigart has been a conductor on a passenger train between Oil City and Pittsburgh, Pa.; address: Kittanning, Pa.

Children:

1277. Sarah Bertha Swigart, m. Harry D. Utley.
1278. H. B. Swigart, m. Mabel Leech; reside at Ford City, Pa.
1279. Mollie R. Swigart.

1280. Anna R. Swigart, b. 1865; m. George Sheasley.

Children:

1281. Ralph Sheasley.
1282. Pauline Sheasley.
1283. Ardell Sheasley.
1284. Harold Sheasley.

1285. Wililiam Swigart, m. Maud Ellen Campbell, daughter of Samuel Lansing and Elizabeth (Lowe) Campbell, of Mosgrove, Pa. Mr. Swigart is a carpenter and lives at Ford City, Pa. He and his entire family are members of the Ford City Baptist Church.

Children:

1286. Fonda E. Swigart, b. July 23, 1890; m. Claire W. Ankeny, b. July 20, 1887; address: Clarksburg, W. Va.

Children:

1287. Jeannette Ankeny, b. Sept. 23, 1913.
1288. Ruth Ankeny, b. Dec. 12, 1914.
1289. Miriam Ankeny, b. March, 1918.
1290. Betty Ankeny, b. Feb., 1920.
1291. Larry B. Swigart, b. Oct. 16, 1896; d. Nov. 21, 1912.
1292. Mildred LaVerne Swigart, b. July 9, 1898; m. Frank Mast, son of Frank Mast, Sr., Rimerton, Pa.; address: Ford City, Pa.
1293. Maud Lucille, b. Dec. 15, 1899; m. August C. Schubert, b. May 18, 1897.

1294. Alexander Lowry Swigart, b. 1870.
1295. Sarah Alberta Swigart, b, 1875; m. Norman J. Templeton.

Child:

1297. Ruth Templeton.

1266. REV. DANIEL W. and MARGARET (STARR) SWIGART. Rev. Daniel W. Swigart was a veteran of the Civil War. At the close of the war he completed a course of study and entered the ministry. He was an able preacher and an esteemed and active pastor in the Baptist denomination until shortly before his death, which occurred at Beaver Falls, Pa., Oct. 8, 1921. By his first marriage with Margaret Starr, b. Feb. 4, 1885, d. Mar. 30, 1897, there were the following children:

1298. Ella J. Swigart, b. Mar. 7, 1861; m. Willis O. Woods, d. June 13, 1916.
1299. Emma M. Swigart, b. Nov. 10, 1863; m. Henry W. Heasley, b. July 17, 1862; d. May 22, 1918.
1300. John J. Swigart, b. Nov. 5, 1864.
1301. Frank H. Swigart, b. Apr. 12, 1866; m. Cora Slagle.
1302. Margaret I. Swigart, b. Sept. 25, 1868; m. (1) Harry McNeil, d. June, 1912; (2) John Elwood.

(2) (Second marriage) Emily Stoughton, daughter of Rev. Samuel Stoughton. She was born June 30, 1836; d. Mar. 8, 1908.

1303. Eva M. Swigart, d. March, 1904.
1304. Samuel S. Swigart, m. Bertha Cooke.

Children:

Gladys, b. July 1, 1912; Warren, b. August, 1918.

1305. Elvira Swigart, d. 1919; m. Roland Phillips.

Child:

a1305. Elenor Winifred, b. June 8, 1907.
1306. Emerson O. Swigart, d. 1903.
(3) Mary J. Thomas.

1298. ELLA J. and WILLIS O. WOODS.

Children:

Pearle E., b. Feb. 24, 1882; Walter W., b. June 14, 1884; Mabel K., b. April 2, 1886; Warren J., b. May 29, 1888; d. April 10, 1911; Clara M., b. Aug. 13, 1890; Fred E., b. April 3, 1893.

1299. EMMA M. and HENRY W. HEASLEY.

Children:

1307. Luella M. Heasley, b. Sept. 3, 1887; m. John S. McMaster, b. 1876; d. Feb. 9, 1916.
1308. Herbert W. Heasley, b. Apr. 30, 1889; m. Golda Allott.

Children:

1309. William Heasley, b. Dec. 13, 1913.
1310. Robert Hays Heasley, b. Nov., 1919.
1311. Paul Warren Heasley, b. Oct. 19, 1921.
1312. Edna E. Heasley, b. May 31, 1891; m. George H. Chappell, b. Oct. 4, 1886; address: Ford City, Pa.
1313. Wilda M. Heasley, b. May 16, 1893; m. Bennett R. Cooke.
1314. James J. Heasley, b. Aug. 19, 1897; m. Virginia Manson.

Children:

a1314. Eldora Louise, b. April, 1918.
1315. Edna, b. July, 1920.
1316. Helen M. Heasley, b. Dec. 10, 1899; m. Harry Walsh.

Child:

1317. Betty Jane, b. May, 1919.
1318. Harry E. Heasley, b. Aug. 6, 1901.
1319. Roland P. Heasley, b. June, 1905.

1266. SARAH (SWIGART) and ROBERT ADAMS.

Children:

1320. Janet Adams, m. Gilbert Wolfe.
1321. Sarah Adams, m. Abe Zillefrow.
1322. Thomas Adams, m. Sarah Schrechengost.
1333. John Adams, m. Susana Miller.
1324. George Adams, m. Molly Mohney.
1325. Robert Adams, m. Rose Smith.
1326. Norman Adams, m. Sara Williams.
1327. Abraham Adams.
1328. Alena Adams, m. John Leech.

1267. NANCY JANE (SWIGART) and ADAM EDWARDS.

Children:

1329. W. Burleigh Edwards b. 1865; m. Laura L. Bowser. (See 785 for children.)
1330. Mary A. Edwards, b. 1867; m. Jacob Schrechengost.
1331. Albert Edwards, b. 1869; m. Jennie Lasher.
1332. John Edwards, b. 1871; m. Margaret Geary.
1333. Finley Edwards, b. 1873; m. Cora Bruner.
1334. Esther Edwards, b. 1875; m. E. Shanandoah Bowser (766).
1335. Wilson Edwards, b. 1877; m. Alice Glassel.
1336. Rebecca Edwards, b. 1880; m. William King.
1337. Emmett Edwards, b. 1882; m. Jennie Fipps.
1338. Abraham Edwards, b. 1884; d. 1888.
1339. Joseph Edwards, b. 1888; d. 1907.

140. CATHARINE (4), JOHN (3), MATHIAS (2), MATHIAS, SR. (1).
Catharine Bowser daughter of John and Mary Bowser of Hopewell, Bedford County Pa.; married Peter Kline in Hopewell; her husband died there; she came to Armstrong County in 1805 with her brother Samuel; she later removed to Jackson County Ohio.

Children:

1340. Peter Kline m. Schrechengost; moved to Jackson County, Ohio.
1341. Mary Kline, m. Daniel Swigart; after her third marriage she moved to Kentucky and died there.

1342. Barbara Kline, m. Jacob Mechling; moved to Illinois; no children.
1343. Catharine Kline, m. Daniel Fish; lived at McKeesport, Pa.

141. JULIA ANN (4), JOHN (3), MATHIAS, JR., (2), MATHIAS, SR., (1). Julia Ann Bowser came to Armstrong County, Pa., between 1815 and 1820; she was united by marriiage to David Flenner; they lived and died in Washington Township, near Montgomeryville, where most of her descendants still reside.

Children:
1344. David Flenner, m. Polly Cousins.
1345. Jacob Flenner, m. Sarah Kimmel.
1346. Elijah Flenner, m. Esther John.
1347. Catharine Flenner, m. Rev. James Toy.
1348. Sarah Flenner, m. William Cousins.
1349. Mary Flenner, m. John Henry.
1350. Christine Flenner, b. 1822; d. 1884; m. Martin John, b. 1812; d. 1894.
1351. Nancy Flenner, m. Peter John.
1352. Julian Ann, m. Alexander Henry.

1344. DAVID and POLLY Y(COUSINS) FLENNER. David Flenner settled on a farm in Washington Twp., Armstrong Co., Pa., near his parents.

Children:
1353. Nancy Flenner, b. Nov. 23, 1850; m. ex-Sheriff Chambers Frick. See Chambers Frick for children (402).
1354. Sarah Jane Flenner, m. (1) Henry Whitehead, (2) John Bowser, (3) John McElravy.
1355. Catharine Flenner, m. Thomas Rutter.
1356. Julia Flenner, m. George Bowser, son of Mathias Bowser (171).
1357. Mary Flenner, m. Carnelius Henry.
1358. Harriet Flenner, d. young.
1359. David Flenner, d.; never married.
1360. Owen Flenner, m. (1) Hannah Smith, (2) Anna Bear.
1361. George Flenner, m. (1) Maggie Sharp, (2) Ella Hetrick.
1362. Thomas Flenner, m. Mollie Schrechengost.
1363. Isaac Flenner, m. Alice Lucas.
1364. John Flenner, m. Catharine Mechling.
1365. Domer Flenner, m. Clara Bryson.

1345. JACOB and SARAH (KIMMEL) FLENNER.

Children:
1366. Elizabeth Flenner, m. ——— Bowser.
1367. Julia Flenner, m. ——— Oliver.
1368. Catharine Flenner, m. ——— Oliver.
1369. David Flenner.
1370. Alexander Flenner.
1371. Rev. Jacob Flenner, minister of the Dunkard Church.

1346. ELIJAH and ESTHER (JOHN) FLENNER.

Children:
1372. Henry Flenner, m. Catharine John.
1373. Jacob Flenner, m. ——— Toy.
1374. John Flenner; never married; killed in coal mines.

1347. CATHARINE (FLENNER) and REV. JAMES TOY. Catharine and her husband lived in Washington Twp., Armstrong Co., Pa., not far from Montgomeryville, where he served as pastor of the Church of God. He was a fine type of the sturdy frontier preacher of three generations ago.

Children:
- 1375. David Toy, m. Eliza Bonner.
- 1376. Jacob Toy; never married.
- 1377. James Toy, m. Eliza Kennings.
- 1378. Peter Toy, d. in infancy.
- 1379. Margaret Toy, m. Rev. Nncholas Lasher, a conspicuous and worthy son of this large family in Armstrong County. Mr. Lasher during the week days devoted his energies to the forge or the farm; and on Sundays gave his services to the "Shoemaker Church," as it is known locally at his home near Montgomeryville, Pa.
- 1380. Julia Toy, m. John John.
- 1381. Catharine Toy, b. Oct. 14, 1844; m. Samuel Rickle, a farmer near Rimerton, Pa.; b. Jan. 3, 1835; d. June 8, 1912.

Children:
- 1382. Jacob J. Rickle, b. Oct. 1, 1871; carpenter.
- 1383.George Rickle, b. Oct. 30, 1873; m. Jennie T. Bowser.
- 1384. James H. Rickle, b. Dec. 4, 1869; teacher, Adrian, Pa.
- 1385. Catharine B. Rickle, b. July 30, 1875; at home.

1383. GEORGE and JENNIE T. (BOWSER) RICKLE. Mr. Rickle is in the employ of J. A. Gault Co., wholesale and retail merchants, Kittanning, Pa. (For children see 810.)

1348. SARAH (FLENNER) and WILLIAM COUSINS.

Children:
- 1386. Simon Cousins, m. Martha Woodrow.
- 1387. David Cousins, m. Hannah Hagenbottom.
- 1388. Elmer Cousins, m. Sarah Bowser.
- 1389. Julia Cousins, m. ——— Snow.
- 1390. Margaret Cousins, m. ——— Edwards.
- 1391. Isaac Cousins.

1350. CHRISTINE (FLENNER) and MARTIN JOHN.

Children:
- 1392. Elizabeth John, m. Emanuel French.
- 1393. Barbara Ellen John, b. 1862; m. John Hooks, b. 1859.
- 1394. Nancy John, m. John Croyle.
- 1395. Esther John, m. Emaheizer.
- 1396. Sarah John; never married.
- 1397. William John, m. Cousins.
- 1398. Christina John, m. John Oliver.

1351. NANCY (FLENNER) and PETER JOHN.

Children:
- 1399. Mary Jane John, m. Absalom Bowser (son of Levi).
- 1400. Ida John, m. Anthony Bowser (son of John, son of Joseph D.).
- 1401. Elizabeth John, m. David Wyant.
- 1402. Nancy John, m. Lee Christman, d.
- 1403. John Adams John, m. Martha White.
- 1404. Peter John, m. Catharine John.
- 1405. Frederick John, m. Harriet Bowser (daughter of John, son of Valentine).
- 1406. David Isaac John, m. Julia Ann Bowser, b. June 3, 1860; (daughter of Alexander, son of John, son of Joseph D.)

Children:
- 1407. Harvey John, b. Dec. 27, 1879; d. Feb., 1900.
- 1408. Manuel John, b. April 26, 1881.

1409. Alexander John, b. June 16, 1884; m. Anna B. Flenner, b. Aug. 23, 1884.
1410. Sharon John, b. June 26 1886; d. April, 1887.
1411. Allamay John, b. Feb. 28, 1889.
1412. Bertha John, b. Aug. 13, 1892; d. Sept., 1904.
1413. Elizabeth John, b. Sept. 13, 1895.
1414. George D. John, b. Dec. 18, 1897; d. July 28, 1914.
1415. Nancy F. John, m. French.

1409. ALEXANDER and ANNA B. (FLENNER) JOHN.

Children:

1416. Stanley John, b. Aug. 12, 1905.
1417. Genevieve John, b. Oct. 16, 1907.
1418. David M. John, b. Sept. 3, 1909.
1419. Helen E. John, b. Oct. 24, 1911.
1420. Mabel D. (H.) John, b. Oct. 18, 1916; d. Dec. 8, 1916.
1421. M. L. John, b. Sept. 18, 1919.

1415. NANCY F. (JOHN) and FRENCH.

Children:

1422. Andrew French, b. Nov. 10, 1902.
1423. David F. French, b. Dec. 22, 1904.
1424. Annice A. French. b. Mar. 13, 1906.
1425. Freda S. French, b. Feb. 28, 1908.
1426. Vernon French, b. Feb. 22, 1910.
1427. Cecil French, b. Mar. 12, 1912.
1428. Harry S. French, b. Dec. 18, 1914.

1352. JULIA ANN (FLENNER) and ALEXANDER HENRY.

Children:

1429. William Henry, m. Harriet Rutter.
1430. David Henry, d. young.
1431. Jane Henry, m. William Darling.
1432. Julia Henry, m. William Cornman.
1433. Mary Ann Henry, m. William Toy.
1434. Catharine Henry, m. Ross Lemon.

1393. BARBARA ELLEN (JOHN) and JOHN HOOKS. John Hooks is a son of William Hooks, an early settler in Washington Twp., Armstrong Co., Pa. He was an active personality in the development of the county, serving for many years as assessor. His son John has followed his father's footsteps. For thirty years he has served his neighbors in some official capacity.

Children:

1435. Nerlis M. Hooks, b. 1884; m, Elijah John, b. 1867.
1436. Amos M. Hooks, b. 1885; m. Grace John, b. 1895.
1437. Chambers M. Hooks, b. 1887; m. Mabel Lasher.
1438. Plummer M. Hooks, b. 1889; m. Pearl Cousins, b. 1884.
1439. Pressie M. Hooks, b. 1891; m. Lettie Crisman, b. 1901.
1440. Goldie M. Hooks, b. 1893; m. Wilbur Bowser, b. 1891.
1441. Adaline M. Hooks, b. 1895; m. Frederick Croyle, b. 1888.
1442. William M. Hooks, b. 1898.
1443. Christopher M. Hooks, b. 1898.
1444. Homer M. Hooks, b. 1900.
1445. Violet M. Hooks, b. 1902.
1446. Bertha M. Hooks, b. 1904.

Pressie M. Hooks served two years in the World war with the 42nd, Rainbow Division.

142. BARBARA (4), JOHN (3), MATHIAS, JR., (2), MATHIAS, SR., (1). Barbara, the youngest daughter of John Bowser of Hopewell, Bedford Co., Pa., came to Armstrong County, Pa., in 1815. She married Joseph Bowser (1503), a son of Jacob Bowser (14). They settled on a farm two miles west of Kittanning.

Children:

1448. Catharine Bowser, single; d. Dec. 14, 1888.
1449. Elizabeth Bowser.
1450. Moses Bowser, b. 1819; d. June 24, 1865; m. (1) Mary Roudabush; d. 1858; m. (2) Eve Roudabush.
1451. James Bowser, m. Mary Ann Bowser, daughter of Jacob, son of Jacob Bowser (14).
1452. Johnathan Bowser, b. Jan. 14, 1824; d. Aug. 30, 1883; m. Esther John.
a1452. Barbara Bowser.

1503. JOSEPH BOWSER, m. (2) MARY MAXWELL.

Child:

a1452. John Maxwell Bowser, m. Tillie Booher; he died in 1919.

Children:

b1452. Aramina Bowser, m. John A. Bowser.
c1452. James K. Bowser, m. Bessie Swigart.
d1452. Alvin H. Bowser, m. Lottie Claypoole; resides in Ford City.

b1452. Aramina and John A. Bowser; ch.: Sadie, m. Emmett Jordan, d.; Ida Clara; Bert, m. Nannie Richardson; Stanley K. (single); William R.; Harry; Harlon J.; Mary; Kenneth; June A.

1450. MOSES and MARY (ROUDABUSH) BOWSER.

Children:

1453. Edward Bowser, b. Mar. 15, 1849; d. June 10, 1918; m. Lydia Bowser, daughter of Jacob Bowser, son of Rock Davy.

Children:

1454. Ida Bowser.
1455. Orman Bowser.
a1455. Elmer C. Bowser.
1456. Howard Bowser.
1457. Clarence Bowser.
1458. Clark Bowser.
1459. Jacob M. Bowser, b. Mar. 16, 1851; m. Priscilla Bowser, daughter of David R. Bowser; (2) m. Sadie Morrow.
1460. Jesse Bowser, m. Bertha Geiser; ch.: Orville, Ocie, Relton, Veda, Benjamin.

1461. Susan Bowser, single.
1462. Viola Bowser, m. Merl Bowser, b. June 23, 1860.
1463. Joseph Bowser, b. Aug., 1852; m. Dorcas Phails.

Children:

1464. Kiziah Bowser, m. Thel Williard; ch.: Clark, Alton
1465. Margaret Bowser, m. Alfred Shearer.
1466. Debeah Bowser, m. Harvey Noble; ch.: Percey, Homer, Mildred, Vera.
1467. Elizabeth Bowser, m. James McKelvey.
1468. Joseph Blair Bowser, single.
1469. Laura Bowser, single.
a1469. Barbara, m. Frank Beer.
b1469. Belle Bowser, b. June 23, 1860; m. Orman Younkins.

1470. MARY ANN BOWSER, b. Aug. 12, 1854; m. HIRAM H. BOUCH, b. 1847.

Children:

1471. Joseph Bouch, d.; m. Mollie Morrow; ch.: Frank, Lois, Mathew, Sarah.
1472. Albert Bouch, m. Mary Moore.
1473. Florence Bouch, m. Jean Furgeson.
1474. Elizabeth Bouch, m. Charles Smith.
1475. William Bouch, m. Mollie Davis.
1476. Edward Bouch, m. Jessie Bowser, daughter of Harvey Bowser, son of Valentine.
1477. Anna Bouch, m. John Smith.
1478. Walter Bouch, single.
1479. Sarah Bowser, b. March 13, 1856; m. Robert Reed, b. Dec. 3, 1847; d. Nov. 3, 1917; ch.: Anna, William, John, Clifford.
1480. Manuel R. Bowser, b. Jan. 16, 1858; m. Belle Bowser, b. May 30, 1858, daughter of Jacob, son of Rock Gravy; address: R. D., Kittanning, Pa.

Children:

a1480. Milford A. Bowser, b. May 8, 1891; m. Stella Morrison, daughter of Albert Morrison, b. Sept. 10, 1895; ch.: Virginia E., b. July 7, 1914; Ralston W., b. Oct. 30, 1916.
b1480. Ethel Bowser, b. May 22, 1894.
c1480. Carmen W. Bowser, b. June 8, 1897; m. Nancy Elder, b. Oct. 11, 1889.

1450. MOSES and (2) EVE (ROUDABUSH) BOWSER.

Children:

1481. William H. Bowser, b. Jan. 31, 1862; m. Laura A. Hooks, b. Aug. 15, 1868.
1482. Amos A. Bowser, b. 1859; d. Oct., 1917.

1481. AMOS A. and LAURA A. BOWSER.

Children:

1483. Wilber O. Bowser, b. Sept. 2, 1894; m. Gertrude Miller, b. 1901; child: Rosella, b. 1921.
1484. Ruth A. Bowser, b. Sept. 15, 1896.
1485. Rhoda E. Bowser, b. Aug. 17, 1900; d. Jan. 5, 1919.
1486. Sharon Q. Bowser, b. Nov. 8, 1902.
1487. Lois M. Bowser, b. Sept. 25, 1904.
1488. Galen R. Bowser, b. Oct. 9, 1906.
1489. Amos E. Bowser, b. Dec. 1, 1912.

1451. JAMES and MARY ANN BOWSER.

Children:

1490. Catharine Bowser, m. Albert Claypoole.

Children:

1491. Boggs Claypoole, m. Sadie Bowser, daughter of Wm. J., son of Jacob, son of Rock Davy.
1492. Barbara Claypoole, m. Samuel Snyder.
1493. Grover Claypoole, single.
1494. Alfred Claypoole, m. Margaret Yount.
1495. Wilda Claypoole, m. Edward McQuinny.
1496. Raymond Claypoole, m. in Davenport, Iowa.
1497. Margaret Bowser, single.
1498. Melvina Bowser, single.

1452. JOHNATHAN and ESTHER (JOHN) BOWSER.

Children:

1499. Enos Bowser, m. (1) Mary M. Myers, d. Oct. 23, 1888; (2) Phoebe Booher, d. Nov. 25, 1903; ch.: William Bartholomew Bowser, b. Oct. 20, 1903.

14. JACOB (3), MATHIAS, JR., (2), MATHIAS, SR. (1). Jacob Bowser, son of Mathias Bowser, Jr., was born in York County, Pa. 1745, and came to Armstrong County in 1808 or 1810. He served in the Revoluntionary War. He married Elsie Kal, established his home near Centre Hill, three miles west of Kittanning, where many of his descendants are living.

Children:

1500. Christian Bowser, d. at Centre Hill, buried in a private plot on Joseph Bowser farm.
1501. John Bowser, known on account of his stalwart physique as "Big John," b. 1781; d. 1857. He married Margaret Razor, daughter of Rev. David Razor, a Dunkard minister.
1502. Catharine Bowser, never married; distinguished from the many Catharines by the nickname "Long Katie."
1503. Joseph Bowser, b. Dec., 1791; m. Barbara Bowser. (See 142 for children.) (2) m Mary Maxwell.
1504. David Bowser, called "Rock Davie," b. 1788; d. Sept. 27, 1860; m. Mary Razor, sister of Margaret, b. 1797; d. Aug. 27, 1870.
1505. Jacob Bowser, also bearing the insignia of this family as "Big Jake"; b. 1811; m. (1) Isabelle Claypoole and (2) Mary (Bucher) Galusha.

1501. JOHN and MARGARET (RAZOR) BOWSER. John and Margaret Bowser lived near the homestead at Centre Hill. He was a farmer.

Children:

1506. Mary Bowser, m. Levi Bowser. (See 348, under Daniel, for children.)
1507. Margaret Bowser, m. George Jack.
1508. Elsie Bowser, m. David Wyant.
1510. Catharine Bowser, m. Thomas Cousins.
1511. Jacob Bowser, m. (1) Isabelle Claypoole, (2) Mary Bucher.
1512. Frederick Bowser, m. Elizabeth Claypoole.

1507. MARGARET (BOWSER) and GEORGE JACK. Lived near Slatelick, Armstrong County, Pa.

Children:

1513. Catharine Jack, b. 1840; d. Dec. 22, 1921; single.
1514. Margaret Jack, m. Stofel Burns; settled near Atwood, Indiana County, Pa.; ch.: Anthony, Clark, George, Sarah.
1515. Caroline Jack, m. W. Reynolds Bowser.
1516. George Wilson Jack, m. Mary Ellen Bonner, daughter of Chas. Bonner.
1517. John Alexander Jack, single.
1518. Thomas Jack, b. May 11, 1844; d. Mar. 24, 1915; m. Christina Wyant, b. Mar. 13, 1853. (See 283 for children.)
1519. Jacob Jack, m. Betsey Jane Galusha; ch.: William, Harry.

1515. CAROLINE (JACK) and W. REYNOLDS BOWSER. Reynolds Bowser, the husband of Caroline Jack, was a well known educator. He was a prominent personality in the Armstrong County public schools. In later years he held public offices under the Government. He was one of the original committee on our Bowser History. He was called by death, however, suddenly, at Kittanning, Pa., before his valuable services on the History became available. The writer will always cherish the frequent conversations on the proposed history and the interest Reynolds had in the great family to which he belonged. He was an intelligent student of history and frequently conversed with me on the Huguenots and Palatines, and the suffering our parents endured in the homeland. He was a veteran of the Civil War.

Children:

1520. Milton Nerr Bowser, b. 1871; d. 1910; m. Margaret Lawson, of Lawsonham, Pa.
1521. Joseph Bowser, b. 1873; killed by a train at Bokerton, Ohio, in 1907.
1522. Nellie Blanche Bowser, born June 11, 1880; m. Harry S. Marsh.

Children:

a1522. Jack C. Marsh.
b1522. Philip Reynolds Marsh.

1523. Anna Bowser, b. Feb. 17, 1878; d. Jan. 27, 1903; m. Abraham Cook, b. June 7, 1876; residence: Kittanning.

Children:

1524. Nell Irene Cook, b. Feb. 21, 1901.
1525. Elizabeth Frances Cook, b. March 18, 1902.
1526. Anna J. Cook, b. Jan. 7, 1903; d. Sept. 14, 1903.

1514. MARGARET (JACK and STOFEL BURNS.

Children: Anthony, Clark, George, Sarah.

1516. GEORGE WILSON and MARY ELLEN JACK.

Children:

1529. Olive J. Jack, b. May 19, 1869; m. Denny D. Bowser, b. June 6, 1868; d. Aug. 10, 1920. (See 197 for children.)
1530. Nancy Jack, b. May 20, 1872; m. Abram Bowser. (See 194 for children.)
1531. May Jack, m. Harry Foreman; ch.: Wilbert, Louise.
1532. Belle Jack, m. George Ruth.

1508. ELSIE (BOWSER) b. Apr. 16, 1824; d. Jan. 29, 1892; and JOHN JACK, b. Mar. 20, 1810; d. June 13, 1883.

Children:

1533. Jane Jack, b. 1843; d. 1920; m. James Franklin Bowser, b. Mar. 25, 1848. (See 749 for chidren.)
1534. Letitia Jack, m. Robert Bonner, d. at Centre Hill, Pa., 1920.
1535. Rev. Chambers T. Jack, Baptist minister; veteran of the Civil War; Educated at Reid Institute, Reidsburg, Clarion Co., Pa. After his graduation he became pastor of the Baptist Church at Linesville, Pa., where he is now living. He was also the pastor of a Baptist church in Michigan for a number of years. He married Matlida A. Bowser. (See 912 for children.)
1536. Johnston Jack, m. Bella Claypoole, daughter of Joseph Claypoole; address: Bradford, Pa.; ch.: Edwin Jack, college student.
1537. Otis Jack.
1538. John Jack.
1539. Margaret Jack.
1540. Mary Jack.

1509. MAGDALENA (BOWSER) and DAVID WYANT; lived at Cadogan, where she died.

Children:

1542. Samuel Wyant, m. ——— Bowser.
1543. John Wyant, m. ——— John, daughter of Martin John.

1544. Oliver Wyant, m. ——— John.
1545. James Wyant, m. Nancy Jane Claypoole.

1510. CATHARINE (BOWSER) and THOMAS COUSINS.
Children:
1546. John Cousins, single.
1547. Alexander Cousins, single.
1548. Levi Cousins, m. Mary Bowser, daughter of Absolom Bowser.
1549. Absolom Cousins, m. Mary ———.
1550. Joseph Cousins, single.

1505. JACOB and (1) ISABELLE (CLAYPOOLE) BOWSER.
Children:
1551. George Bowser, m. Eliza Claypoole.
1552. Jacob (Rich) Bowser; lived near Slatelick; died there 1920; m. Clarissa Claypoole.
a1552. Mary Ann, m. James Bowser. (See 1451 for children.)
b1552. Margaret Bowser, m. William Bowser, son of Jacob, son of "Rock" David.

1505. JACOB BOWSER, m. (2) MARY (BUCHER) GALUSHA.
Children:
1553. Emanuel B. Bowser, m. Mary Byers.
1554. Frederick Bowser, m. Margaret McNab.
1555. Adaline Bowser, m. William Greesly.
1556. Emily Bowser, m. Jacob Bowser, son of Samuel Bowser.

1551. GEORGE and ELIZA (CLAYPOOLE) BOWSER. George Bowser lived on a farm near Montgomeryville, Pa., until his death.
Children:
1557. Henry Bowser, m. Sarah Hooks.
1558. Wilson Bowser, m. Dora Bonner.
1559. Richard Bowser; single.
1560. Cover Bowser; single.
1561. Anna Bowser, d.; m. Harvey Claypoole.
a1561. Melissa Bowser, m. Haines Zillefro.
1562. Laura Bowser, m. ——— Crisman.
1563. Elizabeth Bowser, m. Raymond Bouch.
1564. Maud Bowser.
1565. Orrie Bowser.
1566. Malinda Bowser.
1567. Emma Bowser, deceased.

1552. JACOB and CLARISSA (CLAYPOOLE) BOWSER.
Children:
1568. Laura Bowser, m. Alexander Claypoole.
1569. William H. Bowser, m. Candace Grafton.
1570. Allison C. Bowser, m. Elizabeth Snyder.
1571. Blanche Bowser, m. Guy Miller.

b1552. MARGARET (BOWSER) and WILLIAM BOWSER.
Children:
1572. Alfred Bowser, m. Wilda Wood; ch.: Carl, b. Jan. 3, 1903; Wood, b. Feb. 12, 1910.
1573. Sarah Bowser, b. Feb. 9, 1880; m. Boggs Claypoole, b. Nov. 8, 1875.
a1573. Melvina Bowser, b. Aug. 12, 1874; d. May 6, 1898; m. Loyal Claypoole.
b1573. Flora Bowser, b. Jan. 9, 1883; single.

1572. ALFRED and WILDA (WOOD) BOWSER.

Children:

1574. Carroll W. S. Bowser, b. Jan. 3, 1903.
1575. Wood J. R. Bowser, b. Feb. 20, 1910.

1573. SARAH (BOWSER) and BOGGS CLAYPOOLE.

Children:

1576. William S. Claypoole, b. Dec. 10, 1901.
1577. Hazel A. Claypoole, b. Mar. 8, 1904.
1578. Irene Claypoole, b. June 27, 1909.
1579. Margaret Claypoole, b. Aug. 4, 1912.
1580. Flora Claypoole, b. Oct. 15, 1915.

1553. EMANUEL B. and MARY (BYERS) BOWSER.

Children:

1581. Oliver Bowser, m. Pearl McDonald.
1582. Emma Bowser, m. Ross Booher, son of John Booher.
1583. Calvin Bowser, m. Lena Stitt.
1584. Clem W. Bowser, m. Pearl Hetrick.
1585. Celia Bowser, m. Charles Lytle.
1586. Lenora Bowser, m. Charles Hetrick.
1587. Cora Bowser.

1554. FREDERICK and MARGARET (McNAB) BOWSER.

Children:

1587. Leslie M. Bowser, m. Elizabeth Ober.
1588. Sarah Bowser, m. Alfred Shoop.
1589. Maud Bowser, m. Frank Shankel.

1555. ADALINE (BOWSER) and WILLIAM GREESLY.

Children:

1590. Ocie Greesly.
1591. William Greesly.
1592. Ada Greesly.
1593. May Greesly.
1594. Emma Greesly.

1556. EMILY (BOWSER) and JACOB BOWSER.

Children:

1595. Nancy Bowser, m. Everett McGeary.
1596. Daisy Bowser, d.
1597. Iva Bowser, m. William Smith.
1598. Guy Bowser, single.
1599. Hamilton Bowser, m. Sarah Shepherd.
1600. Elizabeth Bowser.
1601. Roy Bowser.
1602. Warren Bowser.
1603. Ruth Bowser.

1512. FREDERICK (5), JOHN (4), JACOB (3), MATHIAS, JR., (2), MATHIAS, SR., (1). Frederick Bowser settled near the homestead at Centre Hill, Pa. He had five sisters and one brother, "Big Jacob."

Children:

1604. David C. Bowser, m. Mary McCollum.
1605. Frederick Bowser, m. Louise Bowser.
1606. Margaret A. Bowser, m. Abraham Toy.
1607. Elsie Y. Bowser, m. Michael Younkins.

1608. Isabella Bowser, m. Isaac Bouch.
1609. Magdalina Bowser, d. 1921; m. David Bouch; residence near Montgomeryville, Pa.
1610. Elizabeth Bowser, m. Obediah Claypoole.

1588. DAVID C. and MARY (McCOLLUM) BOWSER.

Children:
1611. Hays Bowser.
1612. Minerva Bowser, m. Jacob Whitmer.
1613. Frederick Bowser; single.
1614. M——Bowser; single.
1615. Margaret Bowser; single.
1616. William C. Bowser, m. Dessie Fiscus.
1617. Pearl Bowser.

1587. LESLIE M. and ELIZABETH (OBER) BOWSER.

Children: Lloyd, Thomas, Anna, Evelyn, George.

1588. SARAH (BOWSER) and ALFRED SHOOP.

Children: Ray, Francis, William, Margaret, John, Leslie, Geraldine.

1589. MAUD (BOWSER) and FRANK SHANKEL.

Children: Omer, Harry, Leona, Frank, Leslie.

1589. FREDERICK and LOUISE BOWSER.

Children:
1618. Laura J. Bowser, m. Jacob Bowser, son of David C. Bowser.
1619. Florence Bowser, m. Herbert Grafton.
1620. Marlin J. Bowser, m. Viola Bowser, daughter of Jacob Bowser.
1621. Sarah Bowser, m. Plummer Kepple.
1622. Helen Bowser, m. Edward McKelvey.

1590. MARGARET (BOWSER) and ABRAHAM TOY.

Children:
1623. Harvey Toy, m. Emma Montgomery.
1624. Peter Toy, m. Susan Montgomery.
1625. Elizabeth Toy; single.

1591. ELSIE Y. (BOWSER) and MICHAEL YOUNKINS.

Children:
1626. Nelson Younkins.
1627. Elmer Younkins, m. Molly Benton.
1628. Mary Belle Younkins, m. Gabriel Yockey.
1629. Frank Younkins, m. Rosa Cravenor.

1592. ISABELLA (BOWSER) and ISAAC BOUCH. Mr. Bouch was a soldier in the Civil War; died shortly after the war from the effects of wounds and exposure.

Children:
1630. Frederick Bouch, m. Harriet Claypoole.
1631. Eliza Jane Bouch, m. Adam Shearer.
1632. Adaline Bouch, m. Oliver V. Claypoole.

1593. MAGDALINA (BOWSER) b. 1850; d. Mar. 22, 1921; and DAVID BOUCH.

Children:
- 1633. Park D. Bouch.
- 1634. Clarence Bouch.
- 1635. Ella Bouch, m. David McNutt.
- 1636. Elizabeth B. Bouch; single.
- 1637. Rosa Bouch, m. ——— Lasher.
- 1638. Wilson Bouch.
- 1639. Harry H. Bouch.
- a1639. Charles B. Bouch.

1594. ELIZABETH (BOWSER) and OBEDIAH CLAYPOOLE.

Children:
- 1640. Loyal Clapoole, m. (1) Melvina Claypoole; (2) Florence Kimmel.
- 1641. Alvin Bowser, m. Orpha Bowser, daughter of David C. Bowser.

1504. DAVID (4); JACOB (3); MATHIAS (2); MATHIAS (1). "Rock" Davy Bowser came to Armstrong County, Pa., in 1800, and took up a section of land near Centre Hill, Pa.; he married Mary Razor.

Children:
- 1642. Jacob Bowser, b. Mar. 2, 1818; m. Margaret Claypoole, b. 1816.
- 1643. Frederick R. Bowser, b. May 12, 1821; d. Aug. 11, 1874; m. Elizabeth R. Bowser (174) b. Dec. 8, 1825; d. Nov. 27, 1908. (See 174 for children.)
- 1644. Magdalene Bowser, m. William Walker.
- 1645. William Bowser, m. Elizabeth Roudabush.
- 1646. David R. Bowser, b. June 1, 1827; d. June 2, 1910; m. (1) Susan Yerty, b. 1830; d. 1872; (2) Elizabeth Kelso, b. Mar. 24, 1845; d. Aug. 22, 1883.
- 1647. Mary A. Bowser, single.
- 1648. Margaret Bowser, b. June 18, 1832; d. Apr. 24, 1890; m. Bartholomew Booher, b. May 1, 1819; d. Jan. 4, 1905.
- 1649. Elsie Bowser, b. 1837; m. John Booher.
- 1650. Lydia Bowser, b. 1840; m. Henry McCollum who was killed in the Civil war; (2) m. Rev. Levi Wells; ch.: Mary Ann McCollum, William McCollum.

1642. JACOB and MARGARET (CLAYPOOLE) BOWSER.

Children:
- 1650. William Bowser, b. Mar. 30, 1843; d. Aug. 15, 1918; m. Mary J. Claypoole; (2) Margaret Bowser.
- 1651. Francis Bowser, b. Apr. 24, 1847; m. Sarah Shearer, b. Dec. 25, 1858.
- 1652. Lydia Bowser, b. Sept. 26, 1855; m. Edward Bowser.
- 1653. Belle Bowser, b. May 30, 1858; m. Manuel R. Bowser.

1650. WILLIAM BOWSER and (1) MARY J. CLAYPOOLE; (2) MARGARET BOWSER. See (b1552) for children.

1651. FRANCIS and SARAH (SHEARER) BOWSER. Francis Bowser lives in the Centre Hill Bowser settlement. Perhaps there are more of our kinship in this district than can be found in a like area in the world. He and most of the large family he represents have been staunch supporters of the Dunkard Church, which stands near his house in the center of the village.

Children:
- 1654. Adam S. Bowser, b. Aug. 25, 1878; m. Eliza Chappell; ch.: George, Ralph, Mabel, Gertrude.

1655. Cora Bell Bowser, b. Sept. 7, 1883.
1656. Luella Bowser, b. Sept. 18, 1885; m. Blaney Somerville; ch.: John, Hazel, Genevieve and Beatrice (twins), Margaret, Thelma.
1657. Effie Ann Bowser, b. May 19, 1888; m. Arthur Roudabush; ch.: Isabelle, Paul, Edna, Francis, Stanley.
1658. Elizabeth Bowser, b. Aug. 31, 1890.
1659. Minerva J. Bowser, b. Apr. 24, 1894; m. Harry Toy; ch.: Clare, Vernon.
1660. Wilda May Bowser, b. Aug. 29, 1900; d. May 17, 1915

1652. LYDIA and EDWARD BOWSER.

Children:
1661. Ida B. Bowser, b. May 4, 1875.
1662. Orman J. Bowser, b. Oct. 8, 1876; m. Della M. Bouch, b. May 24, 1881; ch.: Lena B., Delbert, Stanley.
1663. Lewis K. Bowser, b. July 7, 1878; m. Ollie Walker, b. 1877; ch.: Clair, Ralph, Omer, Blaney, Harvey, Edna.
1664. Elmer Bowser, b. Nov. 12, 1881.
1665. Edward C. Bowser, b. Mar. 2, 1886; m. Margaret Younkins, b. July, 1893; ch.: Hazel, Allene, Rudell, Vera.
1666. Howard R. Bowser, b. Mar. 3, 1890.
1667. Clarence Bowser, b. Apr. 8, 1893; m. Margaret Bouch, b. Mar. 24, 1891; ch.: Esther.
1668. Clark Bowser, b. June 24, 1896.

1644. MAGDALINE (5); DAVID (4); JACOB (3); MATHIAS (2); MATHIAS (1). Magdaline Bowser married William Walker.

Children:
1644. Catharine Walker, m. Henry Cornman; ch.: Julia A, Chambers, William, Margaret, Samuel, Mabel, Laura.
1644. Mary Ann Walker, m. Samuel Nunamaker; ch.: Nancy J., Margaret, Elizabeth, Ella, Martha, Henry, Samuel, John.
1644. Lydia Walker, m. Samuel Younkins; ch.: Harrison, Jacob, Austin, William, Charles, Rose.
1644. Nancy J. Walker, m. Henry Livengood; ch.: Harvey, John, Thomas, Effie, Ruth.
1644. William Walker, m. Mary Livengood; ch.: James M., Irvin, George, John.
1644. Hamilton Walker, m. Christina Livengood; ch.: Miles, John, Joseph, Etta, Oliver, Harvey.
1644. Sarah Walker, m. William A. Fish; ch.: Ella, m. Wm. H. Klingensmith; Kelley; Jane, m. Frank Camp; Catharine, m. Charles Nicely; John, m. Lulu Shaffer; Charles, m. Bertha Beck.

1644. HAMILTON and CHRISTINA (LIVENGOOD) WALKER.

Children:
a1644. Miles Walker, m. Ollie Gillam; ch.: Bertha, m. Harvey Sipes; Nora, m. Norman Bowser; Roy, m. Elizabeth Bowser, daughter of Valentine Bowser.
b1644. John Walker, m. Elizabeth Bowser.
c1644. Christopher Walker, m. Etta Bowser, sister of Elizabeth.
d1644. Harvey Walker.
e1644. Joseph Walker, m. Ona Bowser, also a sister of Elizabeth.
f1644. Etta Walker, m. William Roudabush.
g1644. Ollie Walker, m. Lewis Bowser (son of Edward Bowser).

1644. WILLIAM and MARY (LIVENGOOD) WALKER.

Children:

h1644. James M. Walker, b. Apr. 29, 1875; m. Lydia B. Gillam, b. Aug. 25, 1876; ch.: Earnest M. Walker, b. Apr. 22, 1901; m. Marion Beer; ch.: Marshall, b. Oct. 3, 1921. Raymond Walker, b. Mar. 23, 1905; Ethel R. Walker, b. Jan. 13, 1908; Dorothy P. Walker, b. Aug. 11, 1911.

1646. DAVID (5); DAVID (4); JACOB (3); MATHIAS (2); MATHIAS (1). David R. Bowser, a prosperous farmer, lived near Walk Chalk, Pa.; he married (1) Susan Yerty.

Children:

1669. Christian Bowser, b. Jan. 16, 1853; killed by an explosion in 1880; m. Ellen Miller.
1670. Catharine Bowser, b. Feb. 28, 1855; m. Wilson Bowser.
1671. Priscilla Bowser, b. Mar. 19, 1857; m. Jacob M. Bowser. See (1459) for children.
1672. Lydia Bowser, b. Jan. 5, 1859; m. Daniel Wilcox.
1673. Ross Bowser, b. Nov. 20, 1861; m. Clara Anthony.
1674. Austin Bowser, b. July 26, 1863.
1675. Ida Bowser, b. Aug. 6, 1865.
1676. William Bowser, b. Feb. 8, 1869; d. March 3, 1902.
1677. Jacob Bowser, b. March 5, 1869; m. Laura Bowser.
1678. Rose Bowser, b. March 4, 1871; m. Frank Braun.

1646. DAVID R. m. (2) ELIZABETH KELSO.

Children:

1679. Frank K. Bowser, b. Mar. 16, 1876; m. Etta Bowser, b. Apr. 2, 1876. (See 769 for children.)
1680. Charles L. Bowser, b. Jan. 23, 1878.
1681. Orphie Bowser, b. Aug. 20, 1879; m. Alvin Claypoole, d. Mar. 10, 1920.
1682. Flora A. Bowser, b. June 1, 1882.

1648. MARGARET (5); DAVID (4); JACOB (3); MATHIAS (2); MATHIAS (1). Margaret Bowser married Bartholomew Booher, a farmer of Washington Township, Armstrong County, Pa.; grandfather of the author on his mother's side. This was Mr. Booher's second marriage.

Children:

1683. Elsie Booher, b. July 26, 1856; m. James L. Dailey, b. May 5, 1852.
1684. David Booher, b. Aug. 18, 1858; m. Charlotte Frick. See (407) for children.
1685. Catharine Booher, b. Dec. 26, 1860; m. William McCollum, b. April 24, 1854.
1686. Lydia Booher, b. Nov. 4, 1862; m. John Bowser. See (753) for children.
1687. Margaret Booher, b. Aug. 18, 1865; m. Isaac McCullough, b. June 9, 1858.
1688. Phoebe Booher, b. Apr. 16, 1864; d. Nov. 25, 1903; m. Enos Bowser. See (1499) for children.
1689. Charlotte Booher, b. Feb. 28, 1867; m. John Wolfe. See (409) for children.

1683. ELSIE (BOOHER) and JAMES L. DAILEY. Mr. Dailey is a carpenter. He gave most of his life to the employ of the Penna. R. R., where he was recognized as an efficient and faithful employe; at present he and Mrs. Dailey reside at Kelly Station, Armstrong, County, Pa.

Children:

1690. Mary Dailey, b. March 21, 1877; m. Samuel Lasher, b. May 13, 1876.
1691. Charles Dailey, b. Sept. 15, 1878; m. Clara Helm, b. 1876; d. April 28, 1921; their children are: Carl, Olive, Elsie, Theodore and Maxine; address: Kittanning, Pa.
1692. Bert Dailey, b. May 31, 1882; b. Eliza Crisman; address: Kittanning, Pa.
1693. Harry Dailey, b. Oct. 20, 1888; single.
1694. William Dailey, b. July 15, 1884; m. Lena Rereigh.
1695. James L. Dailey, b. Mar. 7, 1892; m. Vernice Weaver, b. Dec. 28, 1892.

1685. CATHARINE (BOOHER) and WILLIAM McCOLLUM. Mr. McCollum is a native of Armstrong County, Pa.; a plasterer and decorator by trade; present address, New Kensington, Pa.

Children:

a1685. Bartholomew R. McCollum, b. Dec. 15, 1879; m. Ella McCullough; d. Oct. 17, 1918; ch.: Clara Leona, b. Aug. 16, 1901; m. John McNamara; Margaret Catharine, b. Mar. 16, 1904, m. Clarence Nolte.
b1685. Margaret Jane McCollum, b. Feb. 22, 1881; d. Oct. 20, 1917; m. A. Reed Bowser. See (464) for children.
c1685. William Andrew McCollum, b. Feb. 14, 1883; m. Carrie M. Cederborg; ch.: James Andrew, b. Nov. 11, 1915.
d1685. James Henry McCollum, b. Aug. 15, 1884; d. Aug. 30, 1889.
e1685. Zetta Mae McCollum, b. Aug. 6, 1886; m. Frank J. Kline; ch.: Margaret Catharine, b. Mar. 28, 1907; William Earle, b. Oct. 10, 1909; Charles, b. Sept. 15, 1913; Luella Jane, b. Feb. 22, 1917; Phoebe Janet, b. May 22, 1920.
f1685. Phoebe McCollum, b. Nov. 23, 1887; m. Charles C. Starr; d. Apr. 17, 1913; ch.: Charles Andrew, b. May 21, 1908.
g1685. David Lee McCollum, b. Aug. 2, 1889; m. Margaret Reynolds.
h1685. Della Catharine McCollum, b. July 10, 1891; m. Frank McConnell. ch.: Vernon Franklin, b. Jan. 31, 1910; Bartholomew R., b. July 30, 1911.
i1685. Frank C. McCollum, b. Oct. 2, 1893; m. Carrie Geiser; ch.: Frank C., b. Feb. 13, 1915; Paul F., b. March 14, 1916; Mildred Ruth, b. Dec. 16, 1918.
j1685. Lydia Ann McCollum, b. Jan. 26, 1897; m. Harry E. Bowser; ch.: Kathleen Elizabeth, b. April 8, 1920; Alverta Mae, b. Oct. 16, 1921.
k1685. Ella Alverta McCollum, b. May 27, 1898; d. Sept. 29, 1899.
l1685. John J. McCollum, b. March 20, 1900; m. Lucy Hodgson; ch.: Betty Jane, b. April 25, 1921.
m1685. Elizabeth B. McCollum, b. April 18, 1904.

1687. MARGARET (BOOHER) and ISAAC McCULLOUGH. Mr. McCullough recently retired from the Pennsylvania Railroad service. After his marriage he bought property at Rimerton Station, Armstrong County, Pa., where he and his family reside.

Children:

1696. Lottie May McCullough, b. May 26, 1888; m. Mathew Fair, b. April 6, 1861; ch.: Josephine Fair, b. Feb. 22, 1910.
1697. Charles McCullough, b. Oct. 21, 1892; m. Agnes Minich, b. July 25, 1899; ch.: Margaret.
1698. Bartholomew McCullough, b. Sept. 21, 1892; m. Nora Belle Armstrong, b. Feb. 8, 1896; ch.: Lena Pearl, Mandella.

15. NOAH (3); MATHIAS (2); MATHIAS (1). Noah Bowser was a soldier of the Revolutionary War, 1777-78, 7th York Co. Militia. This battalion of York Co. Militia was organized under the state constitution of 1776. Com. Col. David Kennedy. (See chapter on York County.) "Noah Bowser came to Armstrong County, Pa., in 1807, and bought 100 acres of land west of Glade Run (near Walk Chalk). His son, Joseph D. Bowser, bought this farm from him." (Benjamin S. Bowser, notes.) He was the fourth son of Mathias Bowser, Jr., who landed in Philadelphia, Sept. 28, 1733, with his father, Mathias Bowser, Sr. Noah was born between 1748 and 1750. He married Eunice Ditto. She was a Catholic, but it was agreed between them that their children should have the utmost freedom in the choice of a religious denomination. The children all adhered to the Protestant faith. Noah Bowser died in Armstrong County, Pa. After his death his widow moved with some of her children to Mount Heathy, Ohio, where she died.

Children:

1699. Joseph D. Bowser, b. 1775; d. 1845; m. Rebecca Dull.
1700. Noah Bowser, b. about 1783; m. Catharine Bowser.
1701. Elizabeth Bowser.
1702. George Bowser, b. about 1785; m. Mary ———
1703. John ("Steam") Bowser, b. Feb. 26, 1784; d. Feb. 22, 1834; m. Elizabeth Baker, b. 1789.

1699. JOSEPH D. and REBECCA (DULL) BOWSER. Joseph D. Bowser moved from Bedford County, Pa., early in the last century and settled in Armstrong County, Pa.

Children:

1704. John Bowser, b. Nov. 1, 1796; m. ——— Shumaker.
1705. Joseph Bowser, born May 19, 1798; d. Oct. 21, 1874; m. Nancy Cole, b. Feb. 9, 1800; d. 1869.
1706. Sarah A. Bowser, b. May 25, 1800; m. John Swigart. See (1254).
1707. Samuel Bowser, b. April 4, 1802; d. Aug. 18, 1885; m. Mary Burnheimer, b. March 15, 1803; d. Oct. 20, 1880. See (1448) for children.
1709. Eunice Bowser, b. July 29, 1804; m. John Morrison.
1710. Noah Bowser, b. Dec. 1, 1806; d. Oct. 31, 1878; m. Catherine Bowser, b. Oct. 13, 1809; d. 1906. See (168) for children.
1711. Jacob Bowser, b. April 6, 1809; d. June 9, 1868; m. Martha Bowser, b. Oct. 12, 1815; d. Oct. 12, 1877. See (1034) for children.
1712. Jonas Bowser, b. July 13, 1811; d. May 5, 1898; m. Margaret Bowser, b. July 30, 1818; d. June 28, 1891. See (170) for children.
1713. Peter Bowser, born Oct. 11, 1813; d. July 13, 1899; m. Hannah Eaton, b. ———, 1829; d. Sept. 20, 1907.
1714. Elizabeth Bowser, b. June 20, 1816; m. Benjamin S. Bowser, b. Dec. 20, 1823; d. 1915. (173).
1715. Joshua Bowser, b. July 29, 1818.

1704. JOHN (5); JOSEPH D. (4); NOAH (3); MATHIAS (2); MATHIAS (1). John Bowser was a school teacher and a well known musician.

Children:

1716. Jacob F. Bowser, b. 1827; m. Sarah Hepler; lived in E. Franklin Twp., Armstrong Co., Pa.
1717. Alexander Bowser, d. 1919; m. Mary Jane Hepler, b. June 2, 1836; was with his parents in Sugar Creek Twp., Armtsrong Co., Pa.
1718. George R. Bowser, b. 1838 in Pennsylvania.
1719. Anthony C. Bowser, b. 1834 in Pennsylvania; retired; 1903 Walnut St., Murphysboro, Ill.

1716. JACOB F. and SARAH (Hepler) BOWSER. Jacob F. Bowser was a soldier in the Civil war, Co. B, 139th Reg. Pennsylvania Vol., and died in a hospital April 15, 1863, while in the service. Buried in National Cemetery, Arlington, Va.

Children:

1720. William L. Bowser, b. June 15, 1856; m. Susan Bowser, b. July 11, 1849. Present address Robinson, Pa. For children see (548).
1721. J. H. Bowser, b. March 8, 1854; m. Emma Mobly, b. Oct. 31, 1863; ch.: Eva, b. Dec. 5, 1883; Arthur, b. Sept. 9, 1893.
1722 Anthony Bowser, b. June 5, 1858; d. July 7, 1895; m. Nancy John, b. 1858; d. Sept. 25, 1911; ch.: Charles, b. Oct. 5, 1881; Edward, b. July 20, 1883; Harry, b. July 10, 1885; Oscar and Lewis, twins; William and Wilbert, twins, b. June 5, 1891; Alice, b. Aug. 31, 1895.
1723. Rev. Robert B. Bowser, b. 1861; m. Katharine Leisure, b. 1864. Ch.: John A., b. 1881; Dora Bell, b. 1884; Sarah M., b. 1887. Rev. Robert B. Bowser is a prominent minister of the Church of God denomination, located at Indiana, Pa.

1717. ALEXANDER (6); JOHN (5); JOSEPH (4); NOAH (3); MATHIAS (2); MATHIAS (1). Alexander Bowser was the father of nineteen children, five of whom are living.

Children:

1724. Ephriam Bowser, b. Dec. 19, 1853; m. Mary Ann Helsel.
1725. Loviet Clarissa Bowser, b. Mar. 23, 1858; m. James Smith.
1726. Julia Ann Bowser, b. June 3, 1860; m. David Isaac John. See (1406) for children.
1727. Ebin G. Bowser, b. Feb. 5, 1867.
1728. Ellis S. Bowser, b. Nov. 16, 1868; m. Minnie Cunningham.

1705. JOSEPH (5); JOSEPH D. (4); NOAH (3); MATHIAS (2); MATHIAS (1). Joseph Bowser bought a farm two miles west of Kittanning and resided there the remainder of his life.

Children:

1729. Joshua Cole Bowser, b. Jan. 24, 1821; d. May 20, 1875; m. Margaret Dick, b. Aug. 2, 1825; d. March 13, 1905.
1730. David Failes Bowser, b. 1827; d. 1898; m. Huldah Reyburn, b. 1829; d. 1855.
1731. James Ditto Bowser, b. 1829; d. 1880; m. Mary Rayburn, b. 1832; d. 1910.
1732. Isabelle Bowser, b. 1831; d. 1883.
1733. Peter Osborne Bowser, b. 1853; d. 1896; m. Eliza Dick, b. 1836; d. 1919.
1734. John Gilpin Bowser, b. 1836; d. 1917; m. Eliza Bradford, b. 1846; d. 1897.
1735. William Johnson Bowser, b. 1836; d. 1914.
1736. Chambers Orr Bowser, b. 1838; d. 1864.
1737. Caroline Bowser, b. 1840; m. William Cunningham, b. 1820; d. 1900.
1738. Washington Reynolds Bowser, b. 1843; d. 1918; m. Caroline Jack, b. 1856. See (1515) for children.

1729. JOSHUA COLE and MARGARET BOWSER.

Children:

1739. William G. Bowser, b. Sept. 6, 1854; d. 1860.
1740. Mary Ann Bowser, b. March 24, 1858; m. James A. Painter, b. Sept. 1, 1853.
1741. John Dick Bowser, b. July 3, 1861; m. Cora V. Kennedy.

1740. MARY ANN and JAMES A. PAINTER.

Children:

1742. William W. Painter, b. March 23, 1887; d. Oct. 30, 1889.
1743. Vernice A. Painter, b. May 25, 1889; m. Frederick Swank, b. April 12, 1890; ch.: Samuel J., b. March 1, 1915; Gladys, b. June 9, 1919.
1744. Stanley C. Painter, b. Dec. 21, 1891; m. Florence Swank, b. Dec. 12, 1895; ch.: Donald, b. Aug. 30, 1919.
1745. Margaret W. Painter, b. March 23, 1894; m. Hayes Manthe, b. July 2, 1896; ch.: Mary, b. Jan. 5, 1919; Vernice, b. Sept. 2, 1918; Hayes, b. June 30, 1920.
1746. Jessie D. Painter, b. March 28, 1896; m. John McGuire, b. May 8, 1892; ch.: Roy, b. Dec. 5, 1919.

1741. JOHN DICK and CORA V. (KENNEDY) BOWSER. Ch.: Florence, Stella, Harry, Charles, Margaret, Albert.

1731. JAMES DITTO and MARY (RAYBURN) BOWSER.

Children:

a1731. Lorenzo Dow Bowser, adopted son, m. Elizabeth J. White.

Children:

b1731. James David Bowser, b. Feb. 27, 1886; m. Ethel Hockman; ch.: Elma Margaret, b. Oct. 8, 1914; Velma Elizabeth, b. Oct. 8, 1914.
c1731. Lorenza W. Bowser, b. 1889, m. Sarah R. Stock; ch.: Clara Amette, b. Dec. 16, 1914; Sarah Elizabeth, b. May 8, 1916.
d1731. Elizabeth Rachel Bowser, b. 1887; d. Jan. 26, 1916.

1733. PETER OSBORNE and ELIZA (DICK) BOWSER. Peter Osborne Bowser enlisted in the army, October, 1861. He was sergeant of Co. G, 78th P. V. Inf.; honorably discharged, November, 1862.

Children:

1747. Isabella Bowser, b. 1858; m. Henry A. Painter.
1748. Lillian Bowser, b. 1864; m. William J. Bowser.
1749. Chambers Sirwell Bowser, b. 1867; m. Minnie Bowser.
1750. Margaretta Bowser, b. 1874; trained nurse.
1751. Sara Dick Bowser, b. 1876; m. Joseph F. Huey.

1749. CHAMBERS SIRWELL BOWSER and MINNIE (BOWSER) (767). Chambers S. Bowser resides at Wickboro, Kittanning.

Children:

1752. Earnest Edwin Bowser, b. 1891.
1753. Herman Osborne Bowser, b. 1893; m. Martha J. Helrick; ch.: Harry Arnold, b. 1917.
1754. Freda Rose Bowser, b. 1894; m. Frederick W. Wolfe; ch.: Edwin Lee, b. 1917.
1755. Margaretta Bowser, b. 1896; m. Philip Calhoun; ch.: William Sheridan.
1756. Leon Alonza Bowser, b. 1898; m. Nora Manthe.
1757. Jean Dick Bowser, b. 1902.
1758. Marion Elizabeth Bowser, b. 1904.

1709. EUNICE (5); JOSEPH (4); NOAH (3); MATHIAS, JR. (2); MATHIAS, SR. (1). Eunice Bowser was born in Bedford County, Pa., July 29, 1804. She came to Armstrong County with her parents and was married to John Morrison.

Children:

1759. Joseph Morrison, b. July 26, 1826; d. March 26, 1891; m. Lucy Zeller, b. Feb. 8, 1828.

1760. Agnes Morrison m. Neal McClafferty; ch.: Cynthia; Adalaide (d).
1761. Catharine Morrison, d. 1895; m. Edward Rial; ch.: Clara, Edward, James, Emma, Catharine.
1762. Rebecca Morrison, d. 1910; m. James Kennedy; ch.: Catharine, Ida, Elizabeth, Seward, Samuel.
1763. Hiram Morrison, b. 1844; d. Nov. 21, 1909; m. Susan Uber; ch.: Catharine, William, John Harry.
1764. Thomas Morrison, d. 1900; m. Katharine McCoy; ch.: Clara, Gussie, Eunice, Madge, Thomas, Pearl, Emma, Josephine, Francis, Sylvester.

1759. JOSEPH and LUCY (ZELLER) MORRISON.
Children:
1765. Erben Henry Morrison, b. Dec. 1, 1847; address: care of "Texas Co.," Tulsa, Okla.; m. Mary Alford; ch.: Frank, Hattie.
1766. Alice A. Morrison, b. May 21, 1850; m. John A. McCutcheon; address: 312 Central Ave., Oil City, Pa.
1767. Silas Munroe Morrison, b. Aug. 20, 1852; m. Lida Shaffer; address: R. D. No. 1, Nevada, Mo.; ch.: Mary, John.
1768. Flora Josephine Morrison, b. Nov. 15, 1854; m. William C. Manning; address: 201 Kirkpatrick St., Syracuse, N. Y.; ch.: Charles D., John A., Richard B.
1769. Eunice Catharine Morrison, b. April 7, 1857; m. (1) James Alford; (2) Eugene Freeman; address: 225 South St. Clair St., Painesville, Ohio; ch.: Alice Alford, Silace Alford, Fannie Alford, Goldie Alford, James Alford.
1770. Clara Emma Morrison, b. June 5, 1860; d. Nov. 21, 1863.
1771. Charles Munson Morrison, b. Feb. 2, 1863; d. June 13, 1864.
1772. Hannah Jeannette Morrison, b. June 9, 1865; d. Feb. 27, 1921; m. John Linton; address: 938 Fruit Ave., Farrell, Pa.; ch.: Wesley Linton, Joseph Linton, Beulah Linton, Guy Linton, Ira Linton; m. (2) Lawrence L. Newton.
1773. William Dawson Morrison, b. Feb. 23, 1868; m. Pearl Myers; address: R. D. No. 6, New Castle, Pa.; ch.: James, Evelyn.
1774. James Eaton Morrison, b. Feb. 3, 1871; m. Alice Rea; address: 1416 South Boston Ave., Tulsa, Okla.

1766. ALICE A. and JOHN A. McCUTCHEON.
Children:
1775. David Bowser McCutcheon.
1776. Jane D. McCutcheon; m. Bruce G. Eddy, Oil City, Pa.

1713. PETER (5); JOSEPH (4); NOAH (3); MATHIAS, JR. (2); MATHIAS, SR. (1). Peter Bowser, while a young man, went to Franklin, Pa., where he engaged in the tailoring business. He became one of the prominent and successful business men of the town. Later he purchased a large farm on the eastern bank of the Allegheny River and combined his town business with his agricultural interests. His death occurred at Franklin, July 13, 1899. His will, in which all his property, real, personal and mixed, was given to his wife, Hannah (Eaton) Bowser, absolutely during her natural life to be disposed of by her as she might see proper, etc., is recorded in Will Docket 9, page 380.
Children:
1777. Lycurgus Bowser, b. Dec. 16, 1848; resides with his daughter, Mrs. Harry L. Warner, Greenfield, Ind.; m. Margaret Tighe, b. 1846.
1778. Hannah Bowser, b. 1846; m. Harry L. Warner.
1779. Frederick Park Bowser, b. Aug. 24, 1850; d. Mar. 23, 1910; m Sarah M. Mayes, b. Dec. 10, 1850.
1780. Marshall Eaton Bowser, b. July, 1852; d. Mar. 22, 1907.

1779. FREDERICK PARK and SARAH M. (MAYES) BOWSER. Address: Franklin, Pa.

Children:

1781. Harry P. Bowser, b. May 7, 1875; m. Florence Wood, b. Dec. 25, 1875.
1782. Frank Mayes Bowser, b. May 5, 1877; on the staff of the Franklin Daily Herald; residence, 838 Elk St., Franklin, Pa.; m. Jane L. Tracey; ch.: Betty Jane, b. June 4, 1918.
1783. Mary Bowser, b. May 26, 1880; m. Dr. Lewis S. Rickards, b. 1870. The dwelling of Dr. Rickards stands exactly on the site of the famous French fort at the mouth of French Creek, now 1322 Franklin Ave, Franklin, Pa.; Mrs. Sarah M. Bowser lives with her daughter, Mrs. Rickards.

1781. HARRY P. and FLORENCE (WOOD) BOWSER.

Children:

1784. Allen Wood Bowser, b. Oct. 9, 1897.
1785. Sarah M. Bowser, b. Nov. 22, 1899.
1786. William A. Bowser, b. Oct. 13, 1908.
1787. Frederick Park Bowser, b. Oct. 25, 1912.
1788. Robert Lewis Bowser, b. Aug. 2, 1915.
1789. Harriet Bowser, b. May 12, 1917.

1700. NOAH, JR. (4); NOAH, SR. (3); MATHIAS, JR. (2); MATHIAS, SR. (1). Noah Bowser, Jr., lived in St. Clair Township, Bedford County, Pa., with a family of eleven, census reports 1820; not mentioned in 1830; probably moved to Ohio.

1702. GEORGE (4); NOAH (3); MATHIAS, JR. (2); MATHIAS, SR. (1). Moved to Hamilton County, Ohio, near Mount Heathy.

Children:

1790. Denny Bowser.
1791. Eli Bowser, b. 1818.
1792. Elizabeth Bowser.
1793. Anderson Bowser, b. 1822 inBedford Co., Pa.; d. at Plumville, Pa., May 8, 1876; m. Mary Templeton, b. 1829; d. 1913, daughter of Col. Templeton of Kittanning, Pa.

Children:

1794. Mary Bowser, b. 1843.
1795. Martha L. Bowser, b. 1848; m. William Davis.
1796. Thomas Bowser, single, b. 1853; d. 1891.
1797. Dr. William E. Bowser, b. Feb. 5, 1861; m. La Vinnia Pounds; died at Plumville, Pa., 1916.
1798. Nancy Bowser, b. 1862; d. 1910.
1799. Clarilla Bowser, b. 1856; d. 1879.

1795, MARTHA L. and WILLIAM DAVIS.

Children:

1800. Althea M. Davis, b. Oct. 28, 1870; d. 1909; m. J. W. Stevenson, she was a graduate of Bucknell University, 1888; ch.: Marie.
1801. Charles S. Davis, b. Mar. 29, 1873; m. Bernie Meals.
1802. Marie Davis, b. Mar. 17, 1875; m. Doctor King; ch.: Martha, Helen, Louise; address: Syracuse, N. Y.
1803. Elizabeth Davis, b. June 20, 1877; m. J. N. Harth.

1703. JOHN (4); NOAH (3); MATHIAS, JR. (2); MATHIAS, SR. (1). John Bowser moved from Bedford County to Glade Run, Armstrong County, Pa. He was a miller and built a mill on his property. He was said to have been the first miller in the country to apply the use of the steam engine to a flour mill; on that account he was known as "Steam" John.

Children:

1804. George Bowser, b. 1809; m. Elisabeth Cooper, b. 1825.
1805. Noah Bowser, b. 1816; d. 1894; m. Eunice Boney, b. 1822; d. 1912.
1806. Mary Ann Bowser, b. June 4, 1820; m. William Bowser. (See 171 for children.)
1807. Margaret Bowser, b. 1822; single.
1808. Sarah A. Bowser, b. 1825; single.
1809. Samuel A. Bowser, b. 1835; m. Gumbert (widow); no children.
1810. Barbara Bowser, b. Mar. 14, 1818; d. July 17, 1882.
1811. Elizabeth K. Bowser, b. Mar. 14, 1818; d. July 17, 1882; m. James R. Boney, b. Apr. 30, 1817; d. Apr. 13, 1897.
a1811. Catharine Bowser, m. Isaac Bowser. See (880) for children.

1804. GEORGE (5); JOHN (4); NOAH (3); MATHIAS (2); MATHIAS (1). George Bowser, like his father, was a miller. For many years he operated the Patterson mill, nine miles east of Kittanning. He later took charge of his father's mill on Glade Run and continued there until his death.

Children:

1812. Baxter Bowser, a musician, m. Margaret Coleman, b. 1858 in Strausburg, Va.; she lives in Tennessee.
1813. Jennie Bowser, b. 1860; m. Haines.
a1813. John P. Bowser, d. in infancy.
b1813. Melissa Bowser, d. in infancy.

1805. NOAH (5), JOHN (4), NOAH (3), MATHIAS, JR. (2), MATHIAS, SR. (1). Noah Bowser moved to Muscatine, Iowa.

Children:

1814. Harriet Bowser, b. 1846; m. Edward Thornton.
1815. Matilda A. Bowser, b. 1848; d. 1911; m. James Middagh, b. 1851; d. 1916.
1816. Ella Jane Bowser, b. 1849; m. John Reynolds.
1817. James Albert Bowser, b. 1851; m. Emma Warman, b. 1854; d. 1919.
1818. Sarah Bowser, b. 1852.
1819. Rachel Bowser, b. 1853; d. 1858.
1820. John B. Bowser, b. 1854; d. 1918; m. Minnie Spitznzagel, b. 1859.
1821. Samuel Wilson Bowser, b. 1857; m. Sarah H. Warman, b. 1861; d. 1895.
1822. Ann Eliza Bowser, b. 1858; m. (1) D. M. Foster; (2) George Daut.
1823. Margaret Bowser, b. 1860; m. William Kampman.
1824. Emma Bowser, b. 1861; d. 1864.
1825. Joseph Bowser, b. 1863; m. Clara Foster, b. 1872.
1826. Nora Bowser, b. 1866; m. Lewis Thomas.

1814. HARRIET (BOWSER) and EDWARD THORNTON.

Children:

1827. Roy Thornton.
1828. Nora Thornton, m. Leonard Harper; ch.: Ruth B., Edith B.
1829. James Thornton, m. Telsa H. Allen, d. 1919; ch.: Mildred Eileen.

1815. MATILDA A. (BOWSER) and JAMES MIDDAGH.

Children:

1830. Hattie E. Middagh, b. 1882; m. Claude E. Smith; ch.: Kathleen, b. 1908; Karl, b. 1912.

1831. Ella E. Middagh, b. 1804; m. Frederick Krauz.
1832. George E. Middagh, b. 1885; m. Anna Bailey; ch.: Lucile, b. 1919; Margaret M., b. 1920.
1833. William N. Middagh, b. 1886; m. Lydia Livesay; ch.: Glen E., b. 1909; Ruby M., b. 1911; Zora, b. 1913; Serena M., b. 1915.
1834. Serena I. Middagh, b. 1889; m. Floyd Hewes; child: Martha Louise, b. 1918.

1816. ELLA JANE (BOWSER) and JOHN REYNOLDS.

Children:

1835. Della Reynolds, b. 1870; m. John W. Lawrence; ch.: Zola, b. 1892; m. Wayne Menear; Percy, Ethel, Hazel, Elmer, Wilson Zona. (Zola and Wayne Meanear: child, Virgil, b. 1918.)
1836. Matilda L. Reynolds, b. 1873; d. 1912; m. ——— Pickens.
1837. Josie Reynolds, b. 1875; m. (1) Butts; (2) Peterman; ch.: Eunice Butts, b. 1893.
1838. John Reynolds, b. 1877; m. Agnes ———; child: Bessie, b. 1906.

1817. JAMES ALBERT and EMMA (WARNIAN) BOWSER.

Children:

1839. Archie E. Bowser, b. 1878; m. Minnie L. Keller, b. 1882. Archie E. Bowser is a hardware merchant, located in Muscatine, Iowa. Ch.: Carroll C., b. 1905; Lois M., b. 1909.
1840. Orson A. Bowser, b. 1896; m. Lula France; child: Delbert, b. 1912.

1820. JOHN B. and MINNIE (SPITZNAGLE) BOWSER.

Children:

1841. Mae Bowser, b. 1881; m. H. R. Vibber; child: John R., b. 1915.
1842. Noah L. Bowser, b. 1883; m. Sadie Feldman.
1843. Pearl Bowser, b. 1885; m. Edward H. Feldman; ch.: Harry E., b. 1908; Arthur B., b. 1909; Walter W., b. 1913.
1844. Raphall B. Bowser, b. 1893.
1845. Della I. Bowser, b. 1894; m. Albert T. Workman; child: Della L., b. 1920.
1846. Mattie L. Bowser, b. 1903.

1821. SAMUEL WILSON and SARAH E. (WARNIAN) BOWSER.

Children:

1847. Grace Bowser, b. 1880; d. 1881.
1848. Williard B. Bowser, b. 1883; m. Hazel M. Nures, b. 1892; ch.: Niona R., b. 1916; Imogene, b. 1920.
1849. Harley M. Bowser, b. 1885; m. Maude A. Cramer, b. 1888; ch.: Cleo L., b. 1913; Leol M., b. 1914; Harold C., b. 1917.
1850. Almira Fay Bowser, b. 1888; m. William H. Thompson; child: Archie M., b. 1910.
1851. Wilson Dale Bowser, b. 1890; m. Grace Nelson, b. 1890; ch.: Donald N., b. 1915; Howard, b. 1919.
1852. Erda E. Bowser, b. 1892; m. Frederick L. Simons, b. 1888; child: Dariel A., b. 1912.
1853. Heber E. Bowser, b. 1894; m. Josie Rickets, b. 1896; ch.: Violet L., b. 1915; Kenneth, b. 1917.

1822. ANNA E. (BOWSER) and D. M. FOSTER.

Children:

1854. Georgia E. Foster, b. 1881; m. Olney A. Keller, b. 1882; ch.: Loren O., b. 1905; Elma R., b. 1907; Albert D., b. 1909; Kenneth A., b. 1910; Eunice B., b. 1912; Herman W., b. 1913.

1855. Archie I. Foster, b. 1883; m. Arizona Watson; child: Robert, b. 1920.
1856. Guy Foster, b. 1889.
1857. Nora Foster, b. 1895; m. John Houseman; child: John H., b. 1920.

1823. MARGARET (BOWSER) and WILLIAM K. KAMPMAN.

Children:

1858. Norvie B. Kampman, m. Nettie Ronian; child: Norvie.
1859. Darrel Kampman.

1825. JOSEPH and CLARA (FOSTER) BOWSER.

Child:

1860. Marvel Bowser, b. 1896; m. Frederick Satterethwaite; child: Norma B., b. 1919.
1861. Eunice I. Bowser, b. 1898; m. Lloyd C. Shields; child: George, b. 1919.
1862. Edith Naomi Bowser, b. 1907.
1863. Marjorie R. Bowser, b. 1911.

1811. ELIZABETH (5), JOHN (4), NOAH (3), MATHIAS, JR., (2), MATHIAS, SR., (1). Elizabeth and James R. Boney lived in North Buffalo Twp., Armstrong Co., Pa.

Children:

1864. George H. Boney, b. Sept. 11, 1838; d. Nov. 4, 1913; m. Medora Frederick, b. Sept. 10, 1851.
1865. Melissa Boney, b. Jan. 13, 1840; d. Dec. 31, 1863.
1866. Adaline Boney, b. Jan. 13, 1840; d. Dec. 31, 1863.
1866. Adaline Boney, b. July 10, 1841; d. Feb. 15, 1916; m. James D. Logan, b. Oct. 1, 1838; d. May 2, 1914.
1867. David M. Boney, b. Jan. 18, 1843; d. Feb. 23, 1904; m. Ada Campbell, b. May 5, 1855; ch.: Ethel, b. Sept. 1, 1874; d. Oct. 17, 1893; Frank, m. Bertha B. Shaffer; Thad., b. Mar. 29, 1881; d. Apr. 6, 1906.
1868. Margaret Boney, b. Aug. 2, 1845; d. Feb. 12, 1916; m. Rodney Malone, b. 1843; d. 1909; no children.
1869. Sara Elizabeth Boney, b. Oct. 23, 1848; d. July 15, 1903; m. Marian Dinsmore, b. May 12, 1837; d. Dec. 28, 1899.
1870. John A. Boney, b. Jan. 23, 1854; d. Aug. 24, 1909; m. Ella House holder, Sept. 12, 1865; ch.: Earl; Zella, m. W. C. McGreggar, Hazel; Irene, m. Heman Sedwick; Alice.
1871. Robert W. Boney, b. Sept. 23, 1856; m. Mary J. Larden, b. Apr. 26 1860; d. Apr. 19, 1914; ch.: Leona, Clair, Mabel, Lulie, Mertie, Robert

1864. GEORGE H. and MEDORA (FREDERICK) BONEY. He was a cabinet maker; lived at Rural Valley, Pa.

Children:

a1864. Etta M. Boney, m. J. R. Myers.
b1864. George M. Boney; dead.
c1864. June F. Boney; single.
d1864. Charles D. Boney, m. Lulu Duncan.
e1864. James A. Boney, m. Elizabeth Mills.

1866. ADALINE (BONEY) and JAMES D. LOGAN.

Children:

a1866. Harry White Logan, d. Sept. 26, 1887.
b1866. Emerson Logan.
c1866. Carrie Logan, d. May 16, 1892.

d1866. Martha E. Logan, d. Dec. 28, 1909.
e1866. Myrtle R. O. Logan, d. Sept. 26, 1910; m. Edward E. Shaffer.
f1866. Ollfree Boney Logan; address: Kittanning, Pa.

1869. SARA E. (BONEY) and MARIAN DINSMORE.

Children:
a1869. James R. Dinsmore, m. Anna Evans.
b1869. Nellie M. Dinsmore, m. L. C. Myers.
c1869. Mary E. Dinsmore, m. G. E. Schwemm.
d1869. Anna E. Dinsmore, m. Harry Gibson.
e1869. Floronna C. Dinsmore, m. H. B. Palmer.
f1869. Marian A. Dinsmore.
g1869. Frederick E. Dinsmore.

16. VALENTINE (3), MATHIAS, JR., (2), MATHIAS, SR., (1). Valentine Bowser came from Bedford County to Sugar Creek Twp. (now Washington Twp.), Armstrong Co., Pa., eight miles north of Kittanning, Pa., in 1798, where he settled on a large tract of land. He was born in 1750 and died in 1836. He brought a number of young apple trees with him which he planted on his farm, three of which are still living. He was buried in a cemetery which he gave to the community from his land. Many of the early settlers repose in this long-neglected and desolate spot. At his death his land was parceled out to his children. He has many descendants, a number of whom have attained prominence in various professions.

Children:
1871. Margaret Bowser, m. Andrew Sites; no children.
1872. Christina Bowser, m. Samuel Smail; no children.
1873. Elizabeth Bowser, m. ——— Thompson.
1874. Henry Bowser, b. 1794; m. Mary Fish, b. 1807.
1875. Daniel Bowser, m. Annie Anders.
1876. John Bowser, b. 1785; m. Mary Edwards.
1877. Samuel Bowser, d. about 1865; single.
1878. Barbara Bowser, m. John Wyant.
1879. Mathias Bowser, m. Musselman.

1873. ELIZABETH (4), VALENTINE (3), MATHIAS, JR., (2), MATHIAS, SR., (1), ELIZABETH AND ——— THOMPSON.

Children:
1880. Mary Thompson.
1881. John Thompson, m. Mary Wyant.
1882. Christina Thompson, m. George King; child: Mary, m. William Nevell; address: Rimerton, Pa.
1883. Joshua Thompson, m. Catharine Wyant.

1874. HENRY (4), VALENTINE (3), MATHIAS, JR., (2), MATHIAS, SR., (1).

Children:
1884. Absolom Bowser, b. 1827; d. May 5, 1904; m. Mary Hershey.
1885. Thomas Bowser, b. 1848; d. 1919; m. Margaret Davison.
1886. William Bowser, b. 1835; m. Jemima Phillips.
1887. John F. Bowser, b. Dec. 12, 1825; d. May 6, 1877; m. Jane Sadler, b. May 24, 1846.
1888. Elsie A. Bowser, b. 1836.
1889. Deborah Bowser, b. 1840.
1890. Mary Bowser, b. 1833; d. 1905; m. ——— Mards.
1891. Aaron Bowser, b. 1842.

1892. Elizabeth Bowser, b. 1845.
1893. Jane Bowser, m. ——— Tanner.

Henry Bowser was killed at Rimerton, Pa., while engaged in construction work on the new Allegheny Valley Railroad.

1884. ABSALOM and MARY (HERSHEY) BOWSER. For many years Absalom was well known in the livery business at Irwin, Pa.

Children:

1894. John A. Bowser, b. 1855 at Jacksonville, Westmoreland Co., Pa.; d. 1906 at Wilmerdivg, Pa.; m. Jennie Geddings; no children.
1895. DeWitt C. Bowser, b. 1863; d. 1917 at Elwood, Ind.; m. Frances Krause.
1896. Sarah A. Bowser, b. 1862; m. David C. Hackensmith; address: Chambersburg, Pa.; ch.: DeWitt, Mervin M., Mary M., Emily, Catharine, Amy, Jeane.
1897. Rebecca M. Bowser, b. 1864; d. 1916.
1898. James M. Bowser, b. May 1, 1869; single; in restaurant business, Irwin, Pa.
1899. Harry Bowser, b. 1862; d. in infancy.
1900. Edward H. Bowser, b. 1882; m. Marie ———; ch.: Howard, Thomas, Sarah, Edna.

1886. WILLIAM and JEMIMA (PHILLIPS) BOWSER. William Bowser was a soldier in the Civil war. He was wounded in the battle at Bull Run; subsequently murdered in the South.

1887. JOHN F. and JANE (SADDLER) BOWSER. John F. was distinguished among the numerous John Bowsers as "Saddler" John.

Children:

1901. Sarah E. Bowser, b. Nov. 6, 1847; single; lives at Bruin, Pa.
1902. Lucy A. Bowser, b. Nov. 21, 1850; d. Feb. 27, 1854.
1903. Firman Duff Bowser, b. Oct. 22, 1852; d. May 1, 1900; m. Susan Stanley.
1904. John Milton Bowser, b. Nov. 21, 1854; m. Margaret Turk.
1905. E. DeWitt Lawson Bowser, b. May 5, 1857; m. Rachel Phillips.
1906. Melissa Jane Bowser, b. July 8, 1859; d. Oct. 25, 1901; m. Samuel H. Bowser, b. Jan. 29, 1856. (See 946 for children.)
1907. Anna B. Bowser, b. May 25, 1861; m. Elmer Cousins.

1903. FIRMAN DUFF and SUSAN (STANLEY) BOWSER.

Children:

1908. Clara Bowser, b. Apr. 27, 1879; d. Feb. 27, 1912; m. Thomas Forrester.
1909. Homer Bowser, b. Oct. 12, 1880; d. August, 1918; m. Elizabeth Bowser.
1910. Bessie Bowser, m. Jason Gray.
1911. Edna Bowser, m. Frederick Lasher.
1912. John Bowser.
1913. Elda Bowser.

1904. JOHN MILTON and MARGARET (TURK) BOWSER.

Child:

1914. Louisa Bowser, b. Jan. 29, 1885; m. McCormick.

1905. E. DEWITT LAWSON and RACHEL (PHILLIPS) BOWSER. Address: Vandergrift, Pa.

Children:

1915. Aida Bowser, b. Apr. 26, 1879; m. George Weitzel; child: Helen.
1916. Claud Bowser, b. June 3, 1880; m. Florence Bryan.

1907. ANNA B. and ELMER COUSINS.

Children:

1917. Edwar Cousins, m. Edith Ihenlot.
1918. Goldie Cousins, m. Ellis Artman.
1919. Lawrie Cousins, m. Minnie Flasher.

1890. MARY (BOWSER) and —— MARKS.

Children:

1920. Rhuhanna Marks, d. 1920; m. —— Turney.
1921. Jane Marks.
1922. Agnes Marks, m. —— Bell.
1923. George Marks.
1924. Samuel Marks.

1891. AARON BOWSER. A soldier in the Cicil war, Co. D, Inf., Pa. Vol. A prisoner in Andersonville prison; captured at Plymouth, N. C., Apr. 20, 1864; d. at Charleston, S. C., Oct. 10, 1864.

1875. DANIEL (4), VALENTINE (3), MATHIAS, JR., (2), MATHIAS, SR. (1). Daniel Bowser lived in Manor Twp., Armstrong Co., Pa. Census reports, 1850, his wife Ann was 55 years of age.

Children:

1925. Mathias Bowser, b. Dec. 8, 1814; d. Sept. 18, 1881; m. Margaret Williams.
1926. Valentine Bowser, b. October, 1817; d. August, 1889; m. Mariah Bowser, b. February, 1818; d. 1891.
1927. Christina Bowser, m. Abraham Slagle.
1928. Anna Bowser, m. (1) James Brice; (2) Alex Ritchey.
1929. Catharine Bowser, m. James Nolder.
1930. Philip Bowser, m. Margaret Slagle.
1931. Jacob A. Bowser, b. 1827; m. Mary Ann Murphy, b. 1832.
1932. Mary Bowser by a (2) marriage; m. Robert Hooks.
1933. Julia Bowser, m. John Allen.

1825. MATHIAS (5), DANIEL (4), VALENTINE (3), MATHIAS, JR., (2), MATHIAS, SR. (1). Mathias and Margaret (Williams) Bowser lived in Manor Twp., Armstrong Co., Pa., five miles southeast of Kittanning. He engaged in farming and became a large landholder. All the children of his large family received a liberal education. He died Sept. 18, 1881 and his wife in April, 1887.

Children:

1934. Senthelia Bowser, b. May 12, 1839; d. August, 1898; m. Amos Wilson, b. 1836; d. March, 1907.
1935. Clarissa Bowser, b. 1840; m. Isaac Wilson.
1936. Sylvester F. Bowser, b. 1842; m. Mary Curll Young.
1937. Marlin Bowser, b. Dec. 1, 1843; m. Arreta Hawkins, b. May 28, 1854.
1938. Malinda Bowser, b. 1845; m. John J. H. Truby, Leechburg, Pa.
1939. Josephus S. Bowser, b. 1848; m. (1) Susan F. Bredin; (2) Mary L. Hynson.
1940. Lyman Bowser, b. 1850; m. Laura Fennel.

1941. Albert L. Bowser, b. 1852; m. Mary B. Smiley; no children.
1942. Dallas D. Bowser, b. Feb. 20, 1857; m. Mary M. Kettering, b. Oct. 31, 1861.
1943. Harrena Bowser, b. 1856; m. William Sim; d. at Blairsville, Pa.

1934. SENTHELIA (6), MATHIAS (5), DANIEL (4), VALENTINE (3), MATHIAS, JR., (2), MATHIAS, SR., (1).

Children:

1944. Nordena Wilson; m. James B. Mates.
1945. Affa Wilson; single.
1946. Elmer Wilson.
1947. Lourene Wilson; b. Mar. 28, 1872; m. P. W. Leedam, b. July 18, 1869; wholesale merchant Oil City, Pa.; ch.: Jeanette, b. Nov. 18, 1898; Helen Elnor, b. Oct. 24, 1900.
1948. Margaret Wilson, m. John B. Grier, Esq., Butler, Pa.

1935. CLARISSA (6), MATHIAS (5), DANIEL (4), VALENTINE (3), MATHIAS, JR., (2), MATHIAS, SR., (1). Clarissa and Isaac Wilson lived in Manor Twp., Armstrong Co., Pa.

Children:

1949. Alvin E. Wilson, b. Jan. 2, 1859.
1950. Ott N. Wilson, m. Lu. Brumbaugh; prominent shoe dealer and stockman, Kittanning, Pa.
1951. Edwin Wilson, m. Ida Bayha; ch.: Mildred, Jerlina, b. 1902.
1952. Olive Wilson, d. aged 18 years.
1953. Charles R. Wilson, b. Apr. 8, 1868; m. Edith Seifert, b. Mar. 1, 1879; merchant, Erie, Pa.; ch.: Thomas N., b. Sept. 21, 1903; Robert C., b. Oct. 6, 1905; Margaret R., b. Aug. 23, 1907; John A., b. June 17, 1910; Helen G., b. Nov. 8, 1918.
1854. William F. Wilson; m. (1) Jessie Firth; ch.: Edward William, Virginia; m. (2) Ethel Barnes; child: Lloyd.
1955. Harry M. Wilson, m. Frances Lea King; ch.: Frances Gage, Harry N., Jr.
1956. Clara Kate Wilson, b. Sept. 29, 1873; m. Hugh F. Iseman; farmer; address: Ford City, Pa., R. D.

Children:

1957. Hugh Wilson Iseman, b. June 1, 1909.
1958. Robert Earle Iseman, b. Jan. 17, 1911.
1959. Lois Irene Iseman, b. June 14, 1913.

1936. SYLVESTER F. (6), MATHIAS (5), DANIEL (4), VALENTINE (3), MATHIAS, SR., (2), MATHIAS, JR., (1). At the completion of his college course, Sylvester F. Bowser studied law and was admitted to the bar at Butler, Pa., where he has earned for himself distinguished honor. He has been engaged on many of the most important cases in western Pennsylvania.

Children:

1960. Mary Edna Isabelle Bowser.
1961. George Franklin Bowser.

1937. MARLIN (6), MATHIAS (5), DANIEL (4), VALENTINE (3), MATHIAS, JR., (2), MATHIAS, SR., (1). Professor Marlin Bowser is a resident of Manor Twp., Armstrong Co., Pa.; address: Ford City, Pa., R. D. He purchased a farm near the homestead of his father Mathias and has lived there all his life. Besides carrying on extensive agricultural pursuits he taught in the public schools of his district for nearly thirty years and for two terms was superintendent of the county public schools. His versatile talents have contributed noted poems and essays on the bird life of his locality.

Children:

1962. Ella Dale Bowser, b. Mar. 30, 1878; m. Claude E. Hyfringer; ch.: Katharyn, Marlin Claude, John Earl, Paul Luther.
1963. Wilber Roy Bowser, b. Feb. 28, 1880; m. Rhetta Heilman; merchant, Ford City, Pa.; ch.: Clayton Heilman, Rhetta Grace, Florence Gail.
1964. Walter Hawkins Bowser, b. Sept. 18, 1881; m. Edna Artman; jeweler, Ford City, Pa.; ch.: Margaret Josephine, Richard Artman.
1965. Ximena Moss Bowser, b. Aug. 18, 1884; m. Mont Clare Emrich; ch.: Paul Clare.
1966. Paul Forbes Bowser, b. May 26, 1886; m. Cora Livingstone; won fame as the world's champion middleweight wrestler; in business at Newark, Ohio.

1938. MALINDA (6), MATHIAS (5), DANIEL (4), VALENTINE (3), MATHIAS, JR., (2), MATHIAS, SR., (1). Residence: Leechburg, Pa. Malinda (Bowser) and John J. Truby; address: Leechburg, Pa.

Children:

1967. John Truby.
1968. Mathias Truby.
1969. Paul Truby.
1970. Margaret Truby, m. Frank I. Gosser, Esq.; practicing law in Pittsburgh, Pa.
1971. Harrena Truby.

1939. JOSEPHUS S. BOWSER, b. 1848; m. (1) Susan T. Bredin, b. 1853; d. 1861; (2) Mary L. Hynson. Received a liberal education; well known shoe merchant at Kittanning; later general store at Franklin, Pa.; now retired; lives at Warren, Ohio.

Child: Howard P. Bowser, b. 1883.

1942. DALLAS D. BOWSER, b. Feb. 20, 1857; m. MARY M. KETTERING, b. Oct. 13, 1861.

Children:

1972. Mary Bowser, b. Nov. 12, 1892.
1973. Casper Bowser, b. Aug. 14, 1894; m. Katharine Portevus, b. Oct. 12, 1899; child: Elizabeth Jean, b. Oct. 31, 1920.

1926. VALENTINE (5), DANIEL (4), VALENTINE (3), MATHIAS, JR., (2), MATHIAS, SR., (1). Valentine Bowser lived at Sherrett, Pa., where he raised a large family. Two of his sons reside on the homestead.

Children:

1974. Emily Bowser, m. Robert Ridley.
1975. Jonathan Bowser, b. 1839; d. about 1900; m. Lucinda Booher, the only child of John Booher and Jane Bowser, daughter of John Bowser, son of Valentine (16); ch.: Maria, b. 1868; Mary; Elizabeth; Leonard; Oliver; Nancy, b. 1877; m. L. Henderson; m. (2) Mary Edwards; ch.: Joseph, Stanley, Harry, Anthony, Christina.
1976. Philip Bowser, m. Margaret Regis; ch.: Benson, James, Henry, John Jefferson, Oliver, Nelson, Elizabeth, Lulu, Ellen, Maria, Jane, Adaline.
1977. James C. Bowser, b. 1847; m. Phoebe Bowser, a daughter of Valentine ("Tine"), son of Valentine (16).
1978. David Bowser, d. Mar. 29, 1914; m. Jemima Wyant.

1979. Jackson Bowser, b. Mar. 18, 1855; m. Mahala Bowser, daughter of Reuben Bowser (2084); ch.: Jacob, Elizabeth; address: Sherrett, Pa.
1980. Jacob Bowser, b. Apr. 23, 1859; m. (1) Mary A. Swigart; address, Sherrett, Pa.; ch.: Larenz, James, Earl, Nora; m. (2) Harriett Hilliard, b. 1885; ch.: Andrew J., William, Donald, Kenneth, Homer.
1981. Sarah Bowser, b. Apr. 3, 1844; m. James Booher, son of Henry Booher and Susan (Bowser) Booher; ch.: Margaret, Jackson, Frank.
1982. Robert Bowser, d. in infancy; b. 1849.
1983. John Bowser, d. in infancy.
1984. Elizabeth Bowser, d. in infancy.
1985. Loben Bower, d. in infancy; b. 1841.

1974. EMILY (BOWSER) and ROBERT RIDLEY.

Children:

Thomas, Annie, Marie, Sara Belle, Martha, Matilda, Mary, Margaret, Harriet, Susan, Valentine, b. April 15, 1862; m. Evaline Early, b. June 20, 1867; ch.: Lulu, Eva Belle, William, Albert, John, Phoebe, Nellie, James, Walter, Lillian

1977. JAMES C. and PHOEBE BOWSER. James C. Bowser has been a successful farmer; address: Adrian, Pa.

Children:

1986. Elizabeth Bowser, m. (1) Joseph Crisman, (2) Jacob Forney; address: Adrian, Pa.
1987. Peter Bowser.
1988. Maria Jane Bowser.
1989. Catharine Bowser.
1990. David Quigley Bowser, m. Ollie Cousins: address: Kittanning, Pa.
1991. Harriet Ann Bowser, m. Frederick John; address: Kittanning, Pa.
1992. Robert M. Bowser; m. Lydia Chandler; address: Manorville, Pa.
1993. Valentine Bowser.
1994. Jacob C. Bowser, b. Aug. 13, 1882; m. Verdie I. Aaron, b. Aug. 14, 1883; address: McGrann, Pa.; merchant.

Children:

a1994. James Lewis Bowser, student; b. Apr. 5, 1903.
b1994. Charles Roy Bowser, b. Feb. 12, 1905.
c1994. Verdie Irene Bowser, b. Aug. 27, 1912.

1995. James Lewis Bowser, m. Esther Bechtel; address: Adrian, Pa.
1996. Thomas L. Bowser, m. Minnie Stover; address: Adrian, Pa.
1997. John Bowser, m. Blanche Crisman; address: Adrian, Pa.

1978. DAVID and JEMIMA (WYANT) BOWSER. Residence: Kittanning, Pa. Jamima Wyant was a daughter of Henry Wyant, who died in Andersonville prison during the Civil war.

Children:

1998. Samuel B. Bowser, b. May 9, 1871.
1999. Valentine Bowser, b. March 19, 1873.
2000. Andrew W. Bowser, b. May 14, 1875; m. Lydia Bowser. (See 476 for children.)
2001. Henry W. Bowser, b. Oct. 14, 1877.
2002. Adam Bowser, b. Apr. 27, 1880.
2003. Mary Magdalena Bowser, b. Oct. 10, 1882.
2003. Peter J. Bowser, b. Apr. 29, 1885.

2004. Catharine Bowser, b. March 17, 1888.
2005. H. Reed Bowser, b. Jan. 17, 1891.
2006. Jemima M. Bowser, b. May 4, 1894.

1927. CHRISTINA (5), DANIEL (4), VALENTINE (3), MATHIAS, JR., (2), MATHIAS, SR., (1).

Children:

2007. George Slagle, m. Rubie F. Benner.
2008. Daniel Slagle, m. Jane Lasher.
2009. Jacob A. Slagle, Templeton, Pa.; b. Dec. 15, 1844; m. (1) Mary Gamble, b. Aug. 2, 1847; d. May 30, 1908; m. (2) Mary Grafton.
2010. Melissa Slagle, m. Robert Gamble, Breckenridge, Pa.
2011. Jennie Slagle, m. R. M. Walker.
2012. John Slagle, m. Annie Kimmel, Mosgrove, Pa.
2013. Manuel Slagle, m. ——— Stewart, Lawsonham, Pa.
2014. Smith Slagle, m. Maud Dias, Templeton, Pa.
2015. Mary Slagle, m. Samuel Gamble.
2016. Malinda Slagle, m. Samuel Gamble. (Samuel Gamble married his first wife's sister.)
2017. Alice Slagle, m. Michael C. Carl.
2018. Washington Slagle, m. Sarah Hopper.
2019. Rose Slagle, m. (1) Frederick Walker, (2) John Johnson.

2009. JACOB A. and MARY (GAMBLE) SLAGLE. Rev. Jacob A. Slagle is an honored minister of the Church of God denomination; he resides on a farm near Adrian, Pa., and ministers to a church in Kittanning, Pa.

Children:

2020. Francis H. Slagle, b. Aug. 4, 1866; d. June 18, 1918; ch.: William, Eva, Ethel, Frederick.
2021. William H. Slagle, b. Dec. 22, 1869; m. Elizabeth Casper; ch.: Francis, Arthur.
2022. Samuel E. Slagle, b. March 14, 1872; m. Carrie Rowe; ch.: Mary, Andrew, Daisey, Nettie, Liah, Sarah E., Retta, Ida, Cecil.
2023. Sarah M. Slagle, b. March 30, 1874; m. John A. Hill.: ch.: Jessie, Randall, William, Edna, Russell, Dale, Samuel.
2024. Mary Elizabeth Slagle, b. April 19, 1877; m. (1) Orion Flick; ch.: Washington A., Harry Myron; m. (2) S. H. Hartman; ch.: Edward, Walter, Russell, William, Dorothy.
2025. Abraham L. Slagle, b. March 17, 1880; m. Maud Garvin; ch.: Harry, Merl, Nellie.
2026. Quintine E. Slagle, b. April 23, 1883; m. Sarah E. Bighly; ch.: Dorothy, Clyde, Arnold.
2027. George A. Slagle, b. March 22, 1889; m. Ethel J. Feh; ch.: Iola, George, Ardell.

2016. MALINDA and SAMUEL GAMBLE.

Children:

2028. Elizabeth Gambel, m. William McCoy.
2029. Frank Gamble, m. Julia Delp.
2030. Randle Gamble, m. Anna Clark.

2017. ALICE and MICHAEL C. CARL.

Children:

2031. Lee Carl, m. Annie Dyes; ch.: Luther, Minnie, Harry, Florence, Mary.
2032. Harry Carl, m. Margaret Swigart.
2033. Rose Carl, m. Howard Heckman; child: Earl.
2034. Nelson Carl, m. Lottie Reese.

2035. Anna Carl, m. Arthur Geiger.
2036. Cora Carl, m. Earl Lark.
2037. William Carl.
2038. Robert Carl.
2039. Florence Carl.
2040. Charles Carl.

1928. ANNA (5), DANIEL (4), VALENTINE (3), MATHIAS, JR., (2), MATHIAS, SR. (1). ANNA (BOWSER) and JAMES BRICE.

Children:

2041. Charles Brice, m. Ella Schumaker.
2042. Allen Brice, m. Ella Thompson; m. (2) Alexandre Ritchey.
Child:
2043. James Ritchey, m. Agnes Mechlin.

1929. CATHARINE (5), DANIEL (4), VALENTINE (3), MATHIAS, JR. (2), MATHIAS, SR. (1). CATHARINE (BOWSER) and JAMES NOLDER.

Children:

2044. Jacob Nolder, m. Hannah Moses.
2045. Robert Nolder, m. ——— Schall.
2046. David Nolder, m. Marian Anderson.
2047. Catharine Nolder, m. Jacob Nelson.
2048. Julia Nolder, m. James Norman.
2049. Susan Nolder, m. Ellis Schall.

1930. PHILIP (5), DANIEL (4), VALENTINE (3), MATHIAS, JR., (2), MATHIAS, SR., (1). PHILIP and MARGARET (SLAGLE) BOWSER.

Children:

2050. Anna Bowser.
2051. Rebecca Bowser, m. William Ramer.
2052. Margaret Bowser, m. William McCoy.
2053. John Bowser, m. Louisa Sample.
2054. Marlin Bowser, m. Ella Yates.
2055. Chambers Bowser, m. Priscilla Lasher.

1931. JACOB A. (5), DANIEL (4), VALENTINE (3), MATHIAS, JR., (2), MATHIAS, SR. (1). Jacob A. Bowser settled on a farm adjacent to the farm of his brother Mathias (1925) in Manor Township.

Children:

2056. Lafayette Bowser, b. 1857; d. 1915; m. Belle Reedy; ch.: Lydia, Essie.
2057. Mathias A. Bowser, b. 1859; m. Maggie Rogers; m. (2) Lulu Smith.
2058. Nathaniel Bowser, b. 1850.
2059. Mary Elizabeth Bowser, b. 1864; deceased.
2060. Lillian Bowser.
2061. Harriette Jane Bowser.
2062. Ella Bowser.

2057. MATHIAS A. and MARGARET (ROGERS) and LULU (SMITH) BOWSER. Mathias A. Bowser was brought up by a family related to his parents. He moved to North Fairfield, R. D. No. 1, Huron Co., Ohio, where he now resides.

Children:

2063. Lela Bowser, b. 1885.
2064. Perry J. Bowser, b. 1887.

2065. Charlotte A. Bowser, b. 1906; d. 1918.
2066. Mary Elizabeth Bowser, b. 1911.

1932. MARY (5), DANIEL (4), VALENTINE (3), MATHIAS, JR., (2), MATHIAS, SR., (1). Mary Bowser, m. Robert Hooks, son of William Hooks; they lived in Washington Twp., Armstrong Co., Pa.

Children:

2067. Elizabeth Hooks, m. Aaron Gray.
2068. Jasper Hooks, m. ——— Truett.
2069. Chambers Hooks.
2070. Madison Hooks, m. Phoebe Elder.
2071. Peter Hooks, m. ——— Walker.
2072. Annie Hooks.

1933. JULIA (5), DANIEL (4), VALENTINE (3), MATHIAS, JR., (2), MATHIAS, SR., (1).

Children:

2073. William Allen, m. Sarah McGreggor.
2074. James Allen, m. Anna Fonner.
2075. Lou Allen, m. ——— Schumaker.
2076. Frank Allen.
2077. Harvey Allen, m. Lydia Simmers.
2078. Harry Allen, m. Kittie Wells.
2079. Samuel Allen; single.
2080. Mary Allen, m. Clem Adams.
2081. Daisy Allen, m. ——— Adams.
2082. Clara Allen, m. George Anthony.

1876. JOHN (4), VALENTINE (3), MATHIAS, JR., (2), MATHIAS, SR., (1). John and Mary (Edwards) Bowser lived in Washington Twp., Armstrong Co., Pa.

Children:

2083. Johnathan Bowser, b. 1814; d. 1859; m. Matilda Edwards, b. 1824.
2084. Reuben Bowser, b. 1815; m. Sally Edwards, b. 1820.
2085. Valentine ("Tine") Bowser, b. 1809; m. Elizabeth Flenner, b. 1816.
2086. John Bowser, b. 1825; m. Nancy Slagle, b. 1830.
2087. Hettie Bowser, m. Henry Booher, b. 1810; d. 1893.
2088. Abraham Bowser.
2089. Catharine Bowser, m. Leonard Stand.
2090. Elizabeth Bowser, m. Stacy King.
2091. Jane Bowser, m. John Booher.
2092. Susan Bowser, m. (1) Christian Spiker; (2) Henry Booher; ch.: Caroline, Sophia, Christina; John, m. Mary Bowser, daughter of Lucinda (1975).
2093. Mary Bowser, m. John Booher. (Two brothers married four sisters.)
2094. Maria Bowser, m. Valentine Bowser. (See 1926 for children.)

2083. JOHNATHAN (5), JOHN (4), VALENTINE (3), MATHIAS, JR., (2), MATHIAS, SR. (1). Johnathan and Matilda (Edwards) Bowser lived in Washington Twp., Armstrong Co., Pa.

Children:

2095. Daniel Bowser, b. Aug. 9, 1840; veteran of the Civil war, Co. D, 103rd Penna. Volunteers; d. about 1916; m. Mary Ann Davis, a daughter of John P. and Elizabeth Davis.
2096. Albert Bowser, b. 1843; m. Rose Montgomery.
2097. Adam Bowser, b. 1847.

2098. Christina Bowser, m. (1) Alexandre Shrader, (2) Gus Hornberger.
2099. Mary Bowser, m. William Taylor.
2100. Sarah Bowser, b. 1845; m. James King, veteran of Civil war.

2095. DANIEL and MARY A. (DAVIS) BOWSER. Daniel Bowser was an oil producer; residence: Parker's Landing, Pa., where he died about 1916.

Children:
2101. Ola Bowser, m. Frank Claypoole, Vandergrift, Pa.
2102. Curtis Bowser.
2103. Della Bowser, m. George B. Downing.
2104. Emma J. Bowser, m. Percy A. Perrine, 6728 Kelly St., Pittsburgh, Pa.
2104. Charles Bowser.
2105. William D. Bowser, Clymer, Pa.
2106. Mathew F. Bowser, Gary, Ind.
2107. Frederick S. Bowser, m. Nora Feicht; ch.: Donald, b. Nov. 20, 1905; Phillip, b. Dec. 24, 1906; Ronald, b. May 20, 1908; Edwin, b. Apr. 6, 1910; Malcom, b. Feb. 2, 1911; Paul, b. June 6, 1910; Mary Margaret, b. Dec. 6, 1915; Ernest, b. Oct. 5, 1918; Frederick, Jr., b. Dec. 9, 1919.

2098. CHRISTINA (BOWSER) and ALEXANDER SHRADER.

Children:
2108. Finley Shrader, m. (1) Sarah Booher. (See 359 for children). (2) Mrs. Morrow.
2109. Jacob Shrader.
2110. Manuel Shrader, m. Mary Inglet.
2111. Elizabeth Shrader; single.
2112. Matilda Shrader; m. Isaac Fair.
a2112. Lydia Shrader; m. George Rickle.
b2112. Anna Shrader, m. Frederick Booher.

2099. SARAH (BOWSER) and JAMES KING.

Children: Adam, John.

2085. VALENTINE (5), JOHN (4), VALENTINE (3), MATHIAS, JR. (2), MATHIAS, SR. (1). VALENTINE and ELIZABETH (FLENNER) BOWSER.

Children:
2113. David Bowser; d. in infancy.
2114. Julia Ann Bowser; d. in infancy.
Mary, Elizabeth, Joshua, Ellen, m. (1) Frederick John; m. (2) March Hooks.; child: (1) H. Valentine Yale, m. Emma John; Phoebe, m. Lewis Bowser: ch.: Isabelle, Ida, Mildred, Lewis; (2) Austin Hooks.
2116. Christina Bowser, m. Hugh Edwards.
2117. Phoebe Bowser, m. James Bowser, son of Valentine (1926). (See 1977 for children.)
2118. Jackson Bowser; d. in infancy.
2119. Catherine Bowser, m. Peter John; no children.
2120. Elizabeth Bowser, m. Frederick Harper.
2121. Robert Bowser, m. Elizabeth John.
2122. Valentine M. Bowser, b. April 11, 1859; d. March 4, 1922; m. Caroline Stitt.

2122. VALENTINE (6), VALENTINE (5), JOHN (4), VALENTINE (3), MATHIAS, JR., (2), MATHIAS, SR., (1). Valentine Bowser, b. Apr. 4, 1859, m. Caroline Stitt, b. August 22, 1859. He was a member of the Brethren Church; buried at Centre Hill, Pa.

Children:

2123. Orlo L. Bowser, b. May 19, 1870; m. Phoebe Hooks, b. June 9, 1886; ch.: Isabelle, b. June 2, 1905; Oda, b. August 10, 1907; Mildred, b. Dec. 4, 1909; Orlo M., b. Feb. 23, 1912; Glenn A., b. Jan. 13, 1914; Eunice, b. Dec. 9, 1916; d. Feb. 6, 1917; Helen, b. May 6, 1919.
2124. Nina L. Bowser, b. Jan., 1882; d. Jan., 1903; m. Henry Bowser; child: Lewis, b. Aug. 22, 1900.
2125. Smith G. Bowser, b. Mar. 29, 1886; m. Fannie McIlsic.
2126. Owen Bowser, b. Sept. 15, 1888; d. Mar. 7, 1917.
2127. Florence Bowser, b. Nov. 16, 1894.
2128. Norman Bowser, b. June 16, 1896; m. Nora Walker; child: Bernice Geraldine.
2129. Jemima Bowser, b. Mar. 4, 1898.
2130. Alice M. Bowser, b. July 14, 1900; m. Hovie Yates; child: Elizabeth Yates, b. May 30, 1919.
2131. James Bowser, b. Apr. 4, 1905; d. May, 1905.
2132. Myrtle Bowser, b. Aug. 12, 1907.
a2132. Elizabeth Bowser, b. March, 1893; m. Roy Walker, b. Sept. 1, 1893; ch.: Clare, Melda, Flossie, Myrtle, Phoebe.

2086. JOHN (5), JOHN (4), VALENTINE (3), MATHIAS, JR., (2), MATHIAS, SR. (1). John Bowser was born 1825. He married Nancy Slagle, b. 1830, and was nicknamed "Slagle" John.

Children:

2133. Matilda Jane Bowser, b. Apr. 23, 1858; m. Bartholomew Booher, son of Henry Booher, Sherrett, Pa.
2134. Harriet Bowser, m. William Bowser.
2135. James Bowser, m. Ida Wolfe.
2136. Benjamin Bowser, b. 1866; m. Priscilla J. Walker; child: Minnie, m. Paul Stewart.
2137. William Bowser, m. (1) Jane Hamilton; (2) Alice Givens.
2138. Catherine Bowser, m. Joseph Grafton; ch.: John, Nancy Jane.

2133. MATILDA JANE and BARTHOLOMEW BOOHER.

Children:

2139. Catherine E. Booher, m. William Early; ch.: Albert, William, Margaret, Andrew, Ida, Chambers, Oscar.
2140. Lottie J. Booher, m. Chambers Spiker; ch.: Sarah, Florence, Raymond.
2141. Minnie Booher, m. Charles Spiker; ch.: Bartholomew, William, Jannie.
2142. Hannah Booher, m. William Hamilton; ch.: Kenneth, Edward, Evaline, Annie.
2143. William Booher.

2134. HARRIET and WILLIAM BOWSER.

Children:

2144. Winfield Bowser, m. Bessie Bowser, daughter of Johnathan and Lucinda; ch.: Lucile, Alberta.
2145. Mary Bowser.
2146. Alice Bowser, m. Guy Wolfe; ch.: Argie, Robert, Calvin, Vera.
2147. Elmer Bowser, m. Alice McAll; ch.: Vera, Robert, Bessie, Lloyd.

2135. JAMES and IDA (WOLFE) BOWSER.

Children:

2148. Gilmer Bowser, m. Hazel Johns.
2149. Myrtle Bowser, m. Garnet Moore.

2084. REUBEN (5), JOHN (4), VALENTINE (3), MATHIAS, JR., (2), MATHIAS, SR., (1). Reuben and Sally (Edwards) Bowser lived in Sugar Creek Twp., Armstrong Co., Pa.

Children:

2150. Charles Bowser, b. 1836.
2151. Mary A. Bowser, b. 1838; born in Ohio.
2152. William Bowser, b. 1842.
2153. Harvey Bowser, b. 1846.
2154. Matilda J. Bowser, b. 1849.
2155. Mahala Bowser.

2087. HETTIE (5), JOHN (4), VALENTINE (3), MATHIAS, JR., (2), MATHIAS, SR. (1). Hettie (Bowser) and Henry Booher lived at Sherrett, Pa. Henry accompanied his father, Frederick Bucher, from Bedford Co. to Armstrong Co., Pa., in the spring of 1831 at the age of 21; his father purchased a farm in Washington Township, then left Henry to look after the property until he should return from Bedford County. Henry improved the time during his father's absence by marrying Hettie Bowser, and was comfortably established in the log cabin when his father returned in the fall.

Children:

2156. Elizabeth Booher, m. John Edwards; ch.: Isaiah, George, Amanda, Catharine.
2157. Catharine Booher, m. John Adams.
2158. Oliver Booher, b. 1841; m. Caroline Blanchard; Oliver lived at Petrolia, Pa.; prosperous farmer; killed by a runaway team, 1883; ch.: Manual, Jay, Harry, Maud, Anna, Evaline.
2159. William Booher, m. Maria Pet, Center Hill, Pa.
2160. George Booher; single.
2161. Bartholomew Booher, m. Matilda Jane Bowser, daughter of Nancy (Slagle) and John Bowser. (See 2133 for children.) Sherrett, Pa.
2162. Mary Ann Booher, m. Daniel Greek; ch.: Wesley, Harvey, Malinda.

2090. ELIZABETH (5), JOHN (4), VALENTINE (3), MATHIAS, JR., (2), MATHIAS, SR., (1). Elizabeth (Bowser) and Stacy King lived in Sugar Creek Twp., Armstrong Co., Pa. They were buried in the old cemetery on Valentine Bowser's farm.

Child:

2162. James King.

2091. JANE (5), JOHN (4), VALENTINE (3), MATHIAS, JR., (2), MATHIAS, SR., (1). Jane Bowser married John Booher, a brother of Henry Booher.

Child:

2163. Lucinda Booher, m. Johnathan Bowser. (See 1975 for children.)

2092. SUSAN (5), JOHN (4), VALENTINE (3), MATHIAS, JR., (2), MATHIAS, SR., (1). Susan (Bowser) Spiker married (1) Christian Spiker; (see 2091 for children); m. (2) Henry Booher.

2093. MARY (5), JOHN (4), VALENTINE (3), MATHIAS, JR., (2), MATHIAS, SR. (1). Mary (Bowser) married John Booher.

Children:

2164. James Booher, m. Sarah Bowser, daughter of Valentine (1926).
2165. Frank Booher, m. Emma Wilson; Freeport, Pa.; ch.: Harry, John.
2166. Joseph Booher, m. Ann Wilson, Freeport, Pa.; child: Frank.
2167. Christina Booher, m. William Regis.
2168. Matilda Booher, m. John Maxwell Bowser. (See 1452 for children.)

2094. MARIA (5), JOHN (4), VALENTINE (3), MATHIAS, JR., (2), MATHIAS, SR., (1). Maria (Bowser) and Valentine Bowser lived at Sherrett. (See 1926 for children.)

1778. BARBARA (4), VALENTINE (3), MATHIAS, JR. (2), MATHIAS, SR., (1). Barbara Bowser was the youngest child of Valentine, son of Mathias Bowser, Jr. (1878). She married John Wyant and came to Armstrong Co., Pa., with her parents in 1798.

Children:

2169. Mary Wyant, m. John Thompson.
2170. John ("Banks") Wyant, m. when advanced in years; residence: Tionesta, Pa.
2171. Catharine Wyant, m. Joshua Thompson.

1879. MATHIAS (4), VALENTINE (3), MATHIAS, JR., (2), MATHIAS, SR., (1). Mathias Bowser died 1865; m. Christiana Musselman in Bedford Co., Pa.; moved to Armstrong Co., Pa. His wife died in 1873.

Children:

2172. Jacob Bowser, b. 1819; d. 1896; m. Margaret Claar, b. 1823; d. 1910.
2173. Mary Bowser, b. 1870.
2174. Barbara Bowser, b. 1833.
2175. Henry Bowser, b. 1838.

2172. JACOB (5); MATHIAS (4); VALENTINE (3); MATHIAS, JR. (2); MATHIAS, SR. (1). Jacob and Margaret (Claar) Bowser.

Children:

2176. Elizabeth Bowser, b. 1846; m. Thomas Claar, b. 1840; d. 1896; ch.: Delilah, Mary, Ella, Agnes, Essington, Berdine, Margaret.
2177. Margaret Bowser, b. 1848; m. Alexandre Walter; no children.
2178. Jacob Bowser, b. 1853; d. 1917; m. Anna Kell, b. 1854; ch.: Charles, Edward, Rose, Albert, George, Lawrence, Harvey, Elmer and Della (twins), William, Anna.
2179. J. Quinter Bowser, b. 1856; m. Rebecca Walter, b. 1853.
2180. Isaac Bowser, b. 1859; m. Julia Walter; no children.
2181. Absalom Bowser, b. 1863; m. Minnie Sell; ch.: Ruth, Luke, Bertha, Paul.
2182. Aaron Bowser, b. 1870; m. Linnie Brooks; ch.: Essington, Jennie, Laura.
2183. Matilda Bowser, b. 1870 (twin of Aaron); m. Miles Claar; ch.: Ada, Mazie, Mary, Walter, Merle.

2179. J. QUINTER BOWSER and REBECCA (WALTER) BOWSER. Residence, Baker Summit, Bedford Co., Pa. He writes: "My great-grandfather and his family all lived in Armstrong County. He came back to Bedford County and married a Walter (second marriage), then returned to Armstrong County. My grandfather, Mathias, came to Bedford County and married Christiana Musselman, and lived at New Enterprise. See biographies.

Children:

2184. Rosco C. Bowser, b. 1887; m. Mary Reighard, b. 1893.
2185. Sarah O. Bowser, b. 1889; m. Wilson Reffner, b. 1884.
2186. John W. Bowser, b. 1890; m. Lena Kagarise, b. 1890.
2187. Ana M. Bowser, b. 1895; m. Harrison Settlemeyer.

18. ESTHER (3); MATHIAS, JR. (2); MATHIAS, SR. (1). Esther, in her native language called Matilena Bowser, youngest child of Mathias and Anna Elizabeth, of whom we have any certain record, was born, no doubt, in Paradise Twp., York County, Pa., 1758. She was married to Rev. Martin John, a Dunkard minister, and came to Washington Twp., Armstrong County, Pa., and settled on what is now known as the Jonas Bowser farm. He erected a log house on his property, the first building in that section of the county, in 1808. This house, subsequently, had a second story added to it, and thus stood and sheltered four generations until 1918 when it was allowed to fall into ruin (see picture). Martin John died in a small log house on the farm of Henry Helsel, his son-in-law, near Sherrett, Pa., in 1847. Esther had previously died. They spoke only the "Palatine German." Their bodies repose in the small burial plot on William Hay's farm, not more than 10 rods from the writer's land which was once a part of Martin's tract—a wooded hill top—where Henry Helsel and his wife Elizabeth and a number of other early settlers were buried. These neglected graves are easily descernable by depressions in the ground, or the slanting field stones which still remain. Under the primeval oaks sleep those hardy god-fearing pioneers; their fields remain; the roads they made through the forests, and the churches they established, but the treasure of a human life is less enduring, as this forgotten burial place is a melancholy witness. With the children of Esther Bowser and Martin John we attain the end of the family of Mathias Bowser, Sr., the progenitor of the largest branch of the Bowser clan, that to which the writer belongs. There are hundreds of this branch of the Bowser family who are not recorded in this history for the reason that it is physically impossible to visit units so widely scattered in Pennsylvania, Ohio, Indiana, Illinois, Iowa, and other states, and because of the failure to elicit a response to any kind of request for data, names, and dates.

Children:

2188. John John, m. Elizabeth Crisman.
2189. Martin John, b. 1797; d. 1856; m. Mary Crisman, b. 1799; d. 1871.
2190. Peter John m. Catharine Helsel.
2191. Catharine John m. John Crisman.
2192. Elizabeth John, d. 1858; m. Henry Helsel, d. 1866.
2193. Esther John m. Simon Steelsmith.
2194. Christina John m. Peter Helsel.

2188. JOHN (4); ESTHER (3); MATHIAS, JR. (2); MATHIAS, SR. (1). John John settled two miles east of his father's farm in Washington Township and erected a large brick house which remained until 1915, when it was torn down.

Children:

2195. Frederick John m. Eva Wolfe.
2196. Adam John d. Jan. 20, 1892; m. Esther Crisman, d. Nov. 1893.
2197. Martin John m. Christina Flenner.
2198. John John, Jr. m. Ann Toy.
2199. Peter John m. (1) Nancy A. Flenner; (2) Catharine Bowser (daughter of "Tine").
2200. Samuel John m. Sarah Lasher.
2201. Isaac John m. Catharine Lasher.
2202. Henry John m. (1) Sarah A. Hooks; (2) Caroline Hooks.

2203. Phillip John m. Mary Lasher.
2204. Esther John m. (1) Elijah Flenner; (2) Johnathan Bowser.

2195. FREDERICK and EVA (WOLFE) JOHN.

Children:

2205. Adam John m. Ella Lytle.
2206. Jerry John never married.
2207. Christiana John m. Abraham Crisman.
2208. William John m. Elizabeth Geary.
2209. Ann John m. Valentine Bowser, son of Jacob Bowser (son of Valentine).

2196. ADAM and ESTHER (CRISMAN) JOHN.

Children:

2210. Jeremiah C. John, b. May 1, 1851; m. Elizabeth Fennell.
2211. Harvey J. John, b. June 10, 1853; miller; Adrian, Pa.; m. Pauline Claypoole.

Children:

a2211. Edward John, m. Iva Belle.
b2211. Earl John, m. Alda Fonner.
c2211. Esther John.
2212. Philip John, b. 1855.
2213. Martin John, b. April, 1858.
2214. John W. John, b. August, 1860.
2215. Catharine Ellen John, b. Oct. 30, 1862; m. Joseph Stivason.
2216. Adam E. John, b. May 1, 1865.
2217. Mary E. John, b. Aug. 26, 1867.
2218. Walter John, b. February, 1870.
2219. Flora A. John, b. Aug. 16, 1875; m. John Smith.

2197. MARTIN and CHRISTIANA (FLENNER) JOHN. Farmer, Washington Township, Armstrong County, Pa. Instead of a repetition of the occupation and residence of Martin and Esther John's family it may be said that most of their descendants are farmers and settled within the bounds of the township mentioned above, where they have sustained the traditions of their ancestry for industry and religious integrity.

Children:

2220. Elizabeth John, m. Emmanuel French; address: Dial, Pa.; merchant.
2221. Sarah John.
2222. Catharine John.
2223. Jane John, m. John Croyle.
2224. Margaret John, m. Oliver Wyant.
2225. Esther Ann John, m. Laban Armahizer.
2226. Christiana John, m. John Wyant.
2227. William John, m. Emily Cousins.
2228. Ellen John, m. John Hooks. See (1393) for children.

2198. JOHN and ANN (TOY) JOHN.

Children:

2229. William John, unmarried.
2230. James John, m. Adaline Hooks.

2199. PETER and NANCY A. (FLENNER) JOHN.

Children:

2231. Mary Jane John, m. Absolom Bowser, son of Levi Bowser.
2232. John A. John, m. Martha White.
2233. Julia Ann John, m. Abram Crisman.

2234. David Isaac John, m. Julia Bowser. See (1406) for children; address: Adrian, Pa.
2235. Peter John, m. Catharine John.
2236. Nancy John, m. Anthony Bowser.
2237. Ida John, m. Levi Crisman.
2238. Frederich John, m. Harriet Bowser, daughter of James.

2200. SAMUEL and SARAH (LASHER) JOHN.

Children:
2239. Rebecca John, m. Peter Crisman.
2240. Isaac John, m. Catharine Harriger.
2241. Obediah John, m. Mary Hooks.
2242. Margaret John, m. Peter Fennell of Adrian, Pa.
2243. Samuel John, m. Catharine Hooks.
2244. Isaiah John, died single.
2245. Susan John, m. Samuel Crisman; ch.: Casper, ——— Eugene, Silvi, Samuel.
2246. Ralston John, died single.
2247. Guy John, m. Eva Winecoop.

2201. ISAAC and CATHARINE (LASHER) JOHN.

Children:
2248. Margaret John.
2249. Abraham John.
2250. Martha John, m. John A. John.

2202. HARVEY and CAROLINE (HOOKS) JOHN.

Children:
2251. Caroline John, m. Adam Croyle.
2252. Manuel John, m. Julia Cousins.
2253. Emily John, m. Hugh Hooks.
2254. Ann John, m. Roland Crisman.
2255. Hugh John, m. Laura Flenner.
2256. Abner John, m. ——— Cornman.
2257. Harvey John, m. Nancy Flenner.
2258. Louise John.
2259. Rose John, m. ——— Lemon.
2260. Phoebe John, m. Ephriam Reighard.
2261. Wilson John, m. Ella John.

2203. PHILIP and MARY (LASHER) JOHN.

Children:
2261. Lee John, m. Rose Adams.
2262. William John, m. Mont John.
2263. Guy John.

2204. ESTHER (JOHN) and ELIJAH FLENNER.

Children:
2263. Henry Flenner; address: Adrian, Pa.
2264. John Flenner.
2265. Elizabeth Flenner.
2266. Jacob Flenner.

(2) ESTHER and JOHNATHAN BOWSER; lived near Adrian, Pa. See (1452) for children.

2189. MARTIN, JR. (5); MARTIN, SR. (4); ESTHER (3); MATHIAS, JR. (2); MATHIAS, SR. (1). Martin John settled on a portion of his father's tract of land two miles north of Montgomeryville, Pa., where he followed the pursuit of a farmer. He was born 1797; died 1856; married Mary Crisman, b. 1799; d. 1871. His will was dated March 8, 1856; probated, Sept. 30, 1856.

Children:
- 2267. Jacob John, died in infancy.
- 2268. Christiana John, died at the age of 18.
- 2269. Esther John, m. David Hawk.
- 2270. Ann John, b. 1830, m. (1) Jacob Crisman; (2) Thomas Craig.
- 2271. Michael John, b. 1833; m. Nancy McCollum.
- 2272. Elizabeth John, b. Oct. 6, 1834; m. Christian Y. Wyant, b. Oct. 19, 1834; d. 1910.
- 2273. Catharine John, b. Oct. 6, 1836; m. John Donnell.
- 2274. Rev. Christian John, b. Apr. 6, 1842; m. Jane Michel.

2269. ESTHER (5); MARTIN (4); ESTHER (3); MATHIAS, JR. (2); MATHIAS, SR. (1). Esther John married David Hawk. They lived near Punxsutawney, Clearfield County, Pa. He was a lumberman and farmer.

Children:
- 2275. John Hawk, b. Aug. 6, 1848; m. Ann Eliza Bowser, b. Nov. 18, 1848. See (187) for children.
- 2276. Jacob Hawk, b. 1843; m. Amana Nicaemas.
- 2277. William Hawk, b. 1845; m. Nancy Lowmaser.
- 2278. Aaron Hawk, b. 1850; m. Fanny K. Stall.
- 2279. Elizabeth Hawk, b. 1852; m. Chambers King.
- 2280. Phoebe Hawk, b. 1854; m. Isaiah Davis.
- 2281. Ann Hawk, b. 1856; m. Clark Tiger.
- 2282. Manuel Hawk, b. 1856; m. Fanny Blue.
- 2283. Catharine Hawk, b. 1858; m. Thomas Wolfe.
- 2284. David Hawk, b. 1860; m. Susan Spencer.
- 2285. Simon Hawk, b. 1860; m. Linda McGregor.
- 2286. Adam Hawk, b. 1864; m. Anna Lydick.
- 2287. Della Hawk, b. 1871.

2270. ANN (5); MARTIN (4); ESTHER (3); MATHIAS, JR. (2); MATHIAS, SR. (1). Ann John m. (1) Jacob Crisman, farmer, Adrian, Pa.; m. (2) Thomas Craig, farmer of Madison Township, Armstrong County, Pa.

Children:
- (1) 2288. Martin Crisman, d. 1919; lived near Widnoon, Pa.
- 2289. Harvey Crisman, m. Belle Davis; live near Widnoon.

Children:
- (2) 2290. Emily Craig.
- 2291. Catharine Craig.
- 2292. Wesley Craig.

2271. MICHAEL (5); MARTIN (4); ESTHER (3); MATHIAS, JR. (2); MATHIAS, SR. (1). Michael John was a stone mason and farmer. Lived near his father's farm in Washington Township, Armstrong County, Pa. Later he retired to West Kittanning where he died.

Children:
- 2293. Minnie John, m. Sherman Craig.
- 2294. Harriet John, single.

2272. ELIZABETH (5); MARTIN (4); ESTHER (3); MATHIAS, JR. (2); MATHIAS, SR. (1). Elizabeth John m. Christian Y. Wyant, son of Adam and Sarah (Yerty) Wyant, Armstrong County, Pa. Christian Wyant was an extensive farmer. Lived near Montgomeryville, Armstrong County, Pa. He died Mar. 24, 1910. Mrs. Elizabeth Wyant is living with her daughter, Dr. Florence Belle Matta, 217 Front St., Brownsville, Pa. She and Eliza Gray living near Duncanville, Armstrong County, Pa., are the only living granddaughters of Esther Bowser.
Children:
2295. Mary Ann Wyant, b. Mar. 20, 1860; m. Curtis Philips, b. Dec. 30, 1855.
2296. Rose Elvira Wyant, b. Apr. 1, 1862; m. Cassius F. Kramer, b. Apr. 10, 1861; d. July 18, 1917.
2297. Dr. Andrew R. E. Wyant, b. May 20, 1867; m. Louise Hulbert, b. Dec. 16, 1870; ch.: Florence Ethelyn, b. June 14, 1899; Elizabeth Louise, b. July 2, 1906; Eri Hulbert, b. Dec. 18, 1907, d. Jan. 3, 1908. (See biographies.)
2298. Sarah Margaret Wyant, b. Sept., 1864; d. 1865.
2299. Hon. Adam Martin Wyant, b. Sept. 15, 1869; m. Catharine Doty, b. June 14, 1875: (See biographies.) Ch.: Anna Moore, b. June 23, 1912; Adam Martin, b. Sept. 1, 1917.
2300. Dr. William Whitfield Wyant, b. May 20, 1873; m. Rachel Sanders.
2301. Dr. Florence Belle Wyant, b. July 15, 1876; m. John Matta, b. 1873.

2191. CATHARINE (4); ESTHER (3); MATHIAS, JR. (2); MATHIAS, SR. (1). Catharine (John) and John Crisman; ch.: Elizabeth, m. Harvey Gray.

2295. MARY ANN (WYANT) and CURTIS PHILIPS. Mr. Philips is a member of the well-known Philips family, producers of natural gas, supplying Butler, and other Pennsylvania cities. They live in Butler, Pa.
Children:
2302. Hollice B. Philips, b. April 19, 1888; m. Luetta Manross, b. July 21, 1894; ch.: Evelyn, Dudley.
2303. Grace Philips, b. Sept. 10, 1889; m. W. G. McIntosh; ch.: Mary Jane, b. June 27, 1915.

2296. ROSE E. (WYANT) and CASSIUS F. KRAMER. Mr. Kramer held a responsible position in the Kramer Wagon factory, Oil City, Pa., until the time of his death, about 1917. Mrs. Rose Kramer is living in Oil City.
Children:
2304. Charles Wyant Kramer, b. Jan. 8, 1887; m. Elizabeth Kern; ch.: Virginia Rose.
2305. Dr. Homer Finley Kramer, b. June 9, 1888; m. Salome Reiss.
2306. Clarence A. Kramer, b. Feb. 26, 1891.
2307. Hazel Candose Kramer, b. Sept. 25, 1892; d. April 17, 1895.
2308. Ruth Elizabeth Kramer, b. Dec. 6, 1895; m. Mathias Saxman Hartman; ch.: Betty Jane, b. Dec. 9, 1919.
2309. William Edwin Kramer, b. Feb. 11, 1898.
2310. Isabelle Louise Kramer, b. Nov. 12, 1899; m. Robert Eldridge Deyoe.

2300. DR. WILLIAM W. and RACHEL (SANDERS) WYANT. Doctor Wyant was educated in the public schools, Reid Institute and the University of Pittsburgh. After his graduation he located in Sharon, Pa., where he has established a large practice. He married Rachel Sanders of Sharon.
Children:
2311. Christian W. Wyant, b. June 1, 1910.
2312. Martha Wyant, b. March 25, 1915.

2301. DR. FLORENCE BELLE (WYANT) and JOHN MATTA. Before her marriage she practiced her profession with her brother, Dr. William W. Wyant, of Sharon. After her marriage she and her husband, John Matta, moved to Brownsville, Pa., where she is now engaged in active practice.

Child:

2313. Elizabeth Wyant Matta.

2273. CATHARINE (6); MARTIN, JR. (5); MARTIN, SR. (4); ESTHER (3); MATHIAS, JR. (2); MATHIAS, SR. (1). Catharine John, born Oct. 6, 1836, married John Donnell. John Donnell was a successful merchant at Watersonville, Pa., in the days when the Red Bank iron furnace was in operation on the opposite bank of the Allegheny. Mrs. Donnell died there about 1900.

Children:

2314. William Donnell.
2315. Edward Donnell.

2190. PETER (5); MARTIN (4); ESTHER (3); MATHIAS, JR. (2); MATHIAS, SR. (1). Peter John married Catharine Helsel, a sister of Henry Helsel, who had married Peter's sister Elizabeth. Their farms joined. The old cemetery already referred to on William Hays' farm, as the burial place of Esther and Martin John, is on the tract of land owned by Peter John, and evidently a part of the original purchase by his father, Martin. Catharine told the writer that slight excavations, marks of the old Indian town at Kittanning, were still discernable in her girlhood days; she also described the Indians with their canoes transporting goods from Pittsburgh up the Allegheny River to their towns on its head waters, their golden ear-rings flashing in the sun as their bodies swayed with the manipulation of the "pole."

Child:

2316. Martin John, m. Mary Whitaker; they lived on a farm not far from Plumville, Indiana County, Pa.

Children:

2317. Tobias John, m. Mary McGarvey.
2318. John W. John, m. Ann McGarvey.
2319. Daniel John, gave his life to his country in the Civil war.
2320. Elizabeth John, m. Thomas McGlaughlin.
2321. Catharine John, b. Mar. 5, 1843; d. Apr. 29, 1916; m. William Hays, b. Oct. 7, 1838; d. Feb. 8, 1908.

2321. CATHARINE (JOHN) and WILLIAM HAYS. See biographies.

Children:

2322. Mary Jane Hays was born at the Peter John and Catharine (Helsel) John homestead, then owned by her father, William Hays, near Montgomeryville, Pa., Sept. 25, 1866; she attended the public school of the district until she completed the course; she married Joseph Leigh Barber, of Dubois, born March 11, 1859; she and her husband established their home in Dubois, where they continued to live until the death of Mr. Barber, Aug. 18, 1899. He was a well known and highly esteemed citizen and a trusted employe of the great Dubois Lumber Mill.

Children:

2323. Lettie O. Barber.
2324. Mary O. Barber.
2325. Nina E. Barber.
2326. Sarah Kathern Barber.

2327. Letitia L. Hays, b. May 7, 1868; m. W. Curtis Marshall; address: Dayton, Pa.
2328. Catharine A. Hays, b. April 21, 1869; m. Austin Stauffer; address: Kittanning, R. D.

Children:

2329. Austin Cyrus Stauffer, b. Jan. 25, 1888.
2330. Anna Zella Stauffer, b. Sept. 20, 1889.
2331. Earl Raymond Stauffer, b. Jan. 8, 1891.
2332. Dent Fair Stauffer b. Oct. 2, 1892.

2333. Martha E. Hays, b. April 11, 1870; d. Feb. 19, 1894.
2334. Susanna Hays, b. June 2, 1871; d. March 11, 1876.
2335. Rosa B. Hays, b. June 23, 1872; d. March 29, 1883.
2336. Margaret E. Hays, b. July 15, 1873; d. Jan. 22, 1897.
2337. William M. Hays, b. Nov. 5, 1874; m. Anna Zella Smith, b. May 22, 1879; address: Adrian, Pa.

Children:

2338. John William Hays, b. Oct. 4, 1900.
2339. Nina Isabelle Hays, b. July 22, 1903.
2340. Carl Thornton Hays, b. March 15, 1908.
2341. Rebecca Catharine Hays, b. Nov. 29, 1914.

a2341. Nancy A. Hays, b. Jan. 11, 1876; m. Calvin Bowser; address: Kittanning, Pa., R. D. (See 824 for children.)
b2341. Thomas H. Hays, b. March 5, 1877; m. Katharine Fair; address: Rochester, Pa.
2342. Robert S. Hays, b. July 27, 1878; d. Feb. 6, 1907.
2343. Emily P. Hays, b. Nov. 6, 1881; m. James McAuley; ch.: John Roy, b. Dec. 20, 1901; d. Feb. 21, 1922; Martha Ruth, b. Jan. 21, 1915; address: Adrian, Pa.
2344. Mintie Hays, b. May 26, 1881; d. Nov. 29, 1883.
2345. Ruth E. Hays, b. July 4, 1882; m. Lewis N. Crisman; ch.: Estella Grace, b. Mar. 5, 1906; d. Oct. 25, 1906; William Raymond, b. Oct. 7, 1907; Robert Roy, b. March 4, 1911; Ruby Catharine, b. July 7, 1914; Dent Hays, b. June 6, 1919; Virginia Rebecca, b. March 5, 1922.

2192. ELIZABETH (4); ESTHER (3); MATHIAS, JR. (2); MATHIAS, SR. (1). Elizabeth John married Henry Helsel, a native of Bedford County, Pa. They settled near her father in Washington Township, now known as the Roudabush farm. Elizabeth died there in 1858, and Henry They had but one child, Esther.
They had but one child:

2346. ESTHER (5); ELIZABETH (4); ESTHER (3); MATHIAS, JR. (2); MATHIAS, SR. (1). Esther Helsel, born Feb. 12, 1819, died June 5, 1851; married Bartholomew Booher, born May 1, 1818, died Jan. 4, 1905; a farmer, Washington Township, Armstrong County, Pa. Bartholomew Booher was a descendant of Bartholomew Bucher who came from the Palatine, probably Switzerland, and landed at Baltimore early in the eighteenth century, and purchased land in Frederick County, Md. He became a large land owner, as he owned large tracts of land in Bedford County, Pa. In his will in Frederick County, Md., he mentions one of his sons, Bartholomew, in disposing of his Pennsylvania estates. Bartholomew Bucher, Jr., was the father of Frederick Bucher who was the father of Bartholomew Booher, husband of Esther Helsel.

Children:

2347. Emanuel Booher, b. April 3, 1840; killed in the Battle of Fair Oaks, Civil war; m. Mary Fair.

Children:

2348. Clemence Booher, single, lives at Saratoga, Tex., b. 1858.

2349. Clara Booher, b. Mar. 9, 1861; m. Austin Leard, b. Aug. 27, 1854; ch.: Elizabeth, b. Nov. 4, 1880; Edith, b. Oct. 4, 1882, d. Jan. 13, 1921; Roy, b. Aug. 30, 1885; Verna, b. May 31, 1888; Frank S., b. Sept. 4, 1890; Ida M., b. Nov. 29, 1892; John T., b. April 20, 1895, d. June 9, 1911.

2350. Elizabeth Booher, b. Sept. 6, 1841; m. (1) M. S. Bowser; for children see (179); m. (2) Martin Bowser, see (751).

2350. Harry Bowser, m. Anna Ellenberger; ch.: Raymond.

2351. Isabelle Booher, b. Feb. 3, 1844; d. Feb. 8, 1914; m. Abner Bonner, b. Oct. 9, 1838; d. May 9, 1915; Abner Bonner was a storekeeper at Adrian, Pa.

2352. Henry Booher, b. July 27, 1846; died about 1917 in Arizona; he married Mary Ann Southworth; they had one daughter, Marda; Henry Booher spent the most of his life in the West as a prospector and miner.

2353. Mary Booher, b. Jan. 1, 1849; m. Jacob Frick, b. April 6, 1843; ch.: Mamie, b. 1873; Roy, b. 1874; Millie, b. 1877; Raymond, b. 1880.

2051. ISABELLE (BOOHER) and ABNER BONNER.

Children:

2354. Ida Bonner, b. Dec. 2, 1865; d. Dec. 13, 1919; m. Harvey M. Montgomery, b. June 1, 1862.

2355. Robert H. Bonner, b. Feb. 11, 1867.

2356. Margaret Bonner, b. Mar. 7, 1868; d. Sept. 23, 1869.

2357. Bartholomew C. Bonner, b. July 2, 1869.

2358. Sarah Bonner, b. Jan. 14, 1871; m. Lee D. Quigley; ch.: Alberta, Gladys, Grace.

2359. John F. Bonner, b. Nov. 4, 1872.

2360. James Bonner, b. Nov. 11, 1874; m. Lina Hooks; ch.: Charles, Nellie, Chester, Hugh, Eva, James.

2361. Dora Bonner, b. Feb. 10, 1876; m. Wilson L. Bowser, son of George Bowser; ch.: Roy, Mabel, Clarence, Mildred, George, Frederick. Page 179.

2362. Cora Bonner, b. Mar. 2, 1878.

2363. Harry L. Bonner, b. Dec. 1, 1879.

2364. Samuel A. Bonner, b. Nov. 7, 1883.

2365. Ross W. Bonner, b. Oct. 30, 1885.

2366. Catharine Bonner, b. Mar. 23, 1887; m. Urie B. Crisman; ch.: Russell, Hazel.

2354. IDA (BONNER) and HARVEY M. MONTGOMERY; address: Dial, Pa.

Children:

2367. Robert B. Montgomery, b. Jan. 8, 1880; m. Fanny Craig, b. Sept. 30, 1889.

2368. George Finley Montgomery, b. Feb. 12, 1885; m. Elizabeth Bowser, daughter of Harvey Bowser, ———

2369. Merle Daniel Montgomery, b. Nov. 16, 1888; d. June 3, 1918; m. Della Morgan.

2370. Lulu Mabel Montgomery, b. Feb. 22, 1890.

2371. Eva Myrtle, b. April 30, 1892.

2372. Thomas Andrew Montgomery, b. Oct. 13, 1894; m. Mary Zillefrow.

2373. Margaret May Montgomery, b. Oct. 29, 1896; d. Jan. 8, 1897.

2374. Joseph Harvey Montgomery, b. Dec. 6, 1898; m. Myra Lasher.

2375. William McClelland Montgomery, b. May 17, 1900; m. Nora Tarr.

2376. Frances Isabelle Montgomery, b. April 4, 1906.
2377. Dorothy Bernice Montgomery, b. Jan. 19, 1908; d. Nov. 29, 1917.
2378. Alvin Ross Montgomery, b. June 20, 1910.

ESTHER (4); ESTHER (3); MATHIAS, JR. (2); MATHIAS, SR. (1).

2193. ESTHER (JOHN) and SIMON STEELSMITH. Immediately after their marriage Esther and her husband went with her sister Christina and her husband who also had just been married, to the State of Indiana where they settled.

132. JACOB C. (4); JOHN (3); MATHIAS, JR. (2); MATHIAS, SR. (1). Jacob C. Bowser, second son of John Bowser, of Hopewell, Bedford County, Pa., was born in York County, Pa., about 1767. He was living in Hopewell Township in 1800 with a family of four. In 1810 he had a family of eight. We have the following esteemed letter from Peter F. Bowser, of Surver, Oregon. "Surver, Oregon, July 26, 1921. Dear Cousin: I write this in answer to your letter in regard to my grandfather. His name was Jacob Bowser. Christian Bowser was my father. My grandfather, Jacob Bowser, died at my father's house in Armstrong County, Pa., when I was a young man. I do not know what year. (Peter F. was born Sept. 10, 1836. His grandfather therefore died about 1853). My father, Christian Bowser, died at my sister, Christina Beatty's house in Clearfield County, Pa., (McGees Mills), Sept. 18, 1869. My mother died at my house in Armstrong County, Sept. 2, 1877. Your Cousin, Peter F. Bowser."

Children of Jacob C. Bowser:
2389. Jacob Bowser, d. 1855.
2390. Christian Bowser, b. Sept. 27, 1798; d. Sept. 18, 1869; m. Susanna Fluke, b. Oct. 21, 1805; d. Sept. 2, 1877.
2391. John Bowser, b. 1800; m. Margaret ———, d. 1805; lived in Bedford County, 1855; in Woodbury Township, 1850; ch.: Reuben, b. 1828; Mary A., b. 1831; Jacob, b. 1832; Margaret, b. 1839; Nancy, b. 1842; William, b. 1844.
2392. Peter Bowser, m. Lucy ———; lived in Jefferson County, Pa.
2393. Sarah Bowser, m. William McElnay; lived in Blair County, Pa., in 1855.
2394. Mary Bowser, m. Jacob Shock; lived in Blair County, Pa., 1855; died intestate.

2390. CHRISTIAN (5); JACOB C. (4); JOHN (3); MATHIAS, JR. (2); MATHIAS, SR. (1). Christian Bowser came to Armstrong County, Pa., from Hopewell, Pa., in 1840. In 1851 he moved to Jefferson County, Pa., and lived at McGees Mills. He married Susanah Fluke, daughter of Henry and Christina (Snyder) Fluke. They were married Oct. 21, 1825. Christian was buried in the Brooks cemetery near Bowersville, Jefferson County, about six miles from Punxsutawney, Pa.

Children:
2395. Henry Fluke Bowser, b. Jan. 6, 1827; d. May 20, 1892; m. (1) Rebecca Swigart; (2) Catharine Marshall, b. April 7, 1834; d. Dec. 15, 1914.
2396. William F. Bowser, b. Aug. 21, 1828; d. July 31, 1893; m. Margaret C. Campbell, b. Dec. 28, 1828; d. July 1, 1908.
2397. John F. Bowser, b. 1830; d. 1851; single.
2398. David F. Bowser, b. Sept. 10, 1833; d. March 25, 1895; m. Mary Myers.
2399. Peter F. Bowser, b. Sept. 10, 1836; m. Elizabeth Brooks, b. Jan. 21, 1836; d. Oct. 1, 1900; address: McGees Mills, Pa.

2400. Christina F. Bowser, b. 1839; m. Robert Beatty; no children.
2401. Jacob F. Bowser, b. Nov. 6, 1843; d. May 22, 1911; m. Martha Rhodes, b. April 14, 1844; d. Dec. 3, 1916.
2402. Elizabeth F. Bowser, b. 1849; m. (1) T. Rolland; no children; m. (2) Milton Miller; ch.: Florence, m. John Vite.

2395. HENRY F. (6); CHRISTIAN (5); JACOB C. (4); JOHN (3); MATHIAS, JR. (2); MATHIAS, SR. (1). Henry F. Bowser was born at Waterside, Bedford Co., Pa., and moved to a farm near Smicksburg, Indiana Co., Pa., in 1840. After his death in 1872, his large farm was divided between his two sons, Wilson M. and Arnold H. Bowser, who are living there; address: Smicksburg, Pa., R. D.

Children (by his second wife):
2403. Wilson M. Bowser, b. Aug. 21, 1865; m. Lydia Welsh, b. June 9, 1866; no children.
2404. Ida Clara Bowser, b. Oct. 18, 1867; d. April 2, 1891; m. George Sink.
Child:
2405. Clara Gertie Bowser.
2406. Arnold H. Bowser, b. Oct. 1, 1871; m. (1) Idella Rarrigh, b. July 13, 1872; d. Mar. 4, 1914; m. (2) Elizabeth B. Kirkpatrick, b. Mar. 25, 1885.
Children (first wife):
2407. Herbert W. Bowser, b. Aug. 4, 1897; m. Ruth Doutt, b. April 4, 1898.
2408. Marshall R. Bowser, b. Aug. 25, 1899; d. Mar. 20, 1901.
Children (second wife):
2409. Joseph Dale Bowser, b. July 30, 1907.
2410. Adah Catharine Bowser, b. Feb. 5, 1909.
2411. Mary E. Bowser, b. Sept. 12, 1913.
2412. Dorothy Jean Bowser, b. Sept. 16, 1920.

2396. WILLIAM F. (6); CHRISTIAN (5); JACOB C. (4); JOHN (3); MATHIAS, JR. (2); MATHIAS, SR. (1). William Fluke Bowser was born at Waterside, Bedford Co., Pa.; m. Margaret C. Campbell; moved to Armstrong Co., Pa. He died at Kittanning, July 31, 1893.

Children:
2413. Margaret Ann Bowser, b. Feb. 28, 1852; m. David H. Williams; d. 1920; residence: Apollo; ch.: May, Blaine, Belva.
2414. George W. Bowser, b. Sept. 26, 1853; m. (1) Mary Karns.
Child:
2415. George W. Bowser, Jr., b. Feb. 22, 1876; m. Ella E. Lytle; m. (2) Letta R. Zimmer, b. 1865; d. 1901.
Children:
2416. Frederick Bowser.
2417. Pearl Bowser, m. ——— Cameron.
2418. Buffington Bowser, m. ——— Bean.
2419. Alice Bowser, m. ——— Shay.
2420. Oscar L. Bowser, d. 1893.
m. (3) ——— Gustavason.
2421. Robert C. Bowser, b. 1855.
2422. William H. Bowser, b. Feb. 16, 1857; m. (1) Clara Moul; m. (2) Lydia Bowser, widow of Mark C. Bowser.
2423. Mary Bowser, b. 1859. (See biographies.)
2424. Robert L. Bowser, b. Feb. 25, 1861; m. Anna F. Krider, b. Oct. 2, 1856. Robert is a skilled iron worker; address: Kittanning.
2425. John K. Bowser, b. Jan. 1, 1863; m. Trix Painter.

2426. Emma Bowser, b. Jan. 16, 1865; m. James McNerney; ch.: James, Thomas; m. (2) James McKenna; address: 3424 Penn Ave., Pittsburgh, Pa.
2427. Elizabeth B. Bowser, b. Apr. 13, 1867; d. Nov. 9, 1912; m. (1) John Donovan; ch.: Erma, Margaret, William; m. (2) —— Metzgar.
2428. Clara May Bowser, b. May 8, 1869; m. William Goff; ch.: Thomas, William, Della.
2429. James M. Bowser, b. Oct. 8, 1873; m. Lilly Rupert; ch.: Hazel, Ruth, Mabel.

2398. DAVID (6); CHRISTIAN (5); JACOB (4); JOHN (3); MATHIAS, JR. (2); MATHIAS, SR. (1). David F. and Mary (Myers) Bowser lived at Bowersville, Jefferson Co., Pa.

Children: Martha, Robert Isaac, Jacob, Miller, George, Elizabeth.

2399. PETER F. (6); CHRISTIAN (5); JACOB (4); JOHN (3); MATHIAS, JR. (2); MATHIAS, SR. (1). Peter F. and Eliza (Brooks) Bowser lived at Bowersville, Pa., where Mrs. Bowser died Oct. 1, 1900. About 1910 Peter F. went to Surver, Oregon, and made his home with his daughter, Mrs. Miles Davis. He was living there in 1921, at the age of 85.

Children:
2430. William A. Bowser, b. Nov. 29, 1860; d. Apr. 4, 1864.
2431. Henry C. Bowser, b. Aug. 26, 1862; d. Sept. 12, 1894.
2432. Margaret A. Bowser, b. Aug. 22, 1864; m. John L. Condron.
2433. Chloe M. Bowser, b. Nov. 2, 1866; m. Miles Davis, b. Sept. 13, 1859. Surver, Oregon.
2434. George T. Bowser, b. Feb. 5, 1869.
2435. Peter A. Bowser, b. July 11, 1871.
2436. Mary E. Bowser, b. Aug. 15, 1875; d. Apr. 5, 1879.

2401. JACOB F. (6); CHRISTIAN (5); JACOB (4); JOHN (3); MATHIAS, JR. (2); MATHIAS, SR., (1). Jacob F. and Martha (Rhodes) Bowser lived on a farm at Bowersville, Pa. He died there in 1911 and she in 1916.

Children:
2437. William E. Bowser, b. Jan. 26, 1871; m. Pearl Graffins, b. Jan. 26, 1877.
2438. John E. Bowser, b. July 10, 1872; m. Emma R. McCormich, b. Oct. 19, 1868.
2439. Sarah A. Bowser, b. Oct. 30, 1873; m. Charles K. Brown, b. Sept. 19, 1877.
2440. Laura E. Bowser, b. Nov. 30, 1875; m. John H. Depp, b. Dec. 14, 1875.
2441. James M. Bowser, b. Nov. 26, 1877; m. Maude Bender, b. Dec. 5, 1884.
2442. Jane Bowser, b. Aug. 7, 1879; single.
2443. Lucy Bowser, b. Mar. 17, 1881; m. Richard Lloyd, b. Feb. 11, 1878; child: Martha, b. Mar. 25, 1905
2444. Rhoda May Bowser, b. May 7, 1884; d. April 29, 1894.

2437. WILLIAM E. and PEARL S. (GRAFFINS) BOWSER.

Children:
2445. Jacob W. Bowser, b. Oct. 29, 1902.
2446. William L. Bowser, b. June 25, 1905.

2439. SARAH A. (BOWSER) and CHARLES K. BROWN.

Children:

2449. Lloyd Brown, b. July 26, 1898.
2450. James W. Brown, b. Nov. 13, 1899.
2451. Leroy Brown, b. Dec. 12, 1904.
2452. William Carl Brown, b. May 22, 1908.
2453. Martha Jane Brown, b. June 20, 1914.
2454. Glenn H. Brown, b. Mar. 31, 1917.

2441. JAMES M. and MAUD (BENDER) BOWSER.

Children:

2455. Dee J. Bowser, b. June 10, 1901.
2456. Raymond L. Bowser, b. July 19, 1904.
2457. Harold J. Bowser, b. Sept. 8, 1905.
2458. Ruth May Bowser, b. May 5, 1907.
2459. Clara Belle Bowser, b. Sept. 11, 1909.
2460. Paul E. Bowser, b. Apr. 13, 1911.
2461. Lulu L. Bowser, b. Aug. 6, 1913.
2462. Glenn Bowser, b. Nov. 30, 1915.
2463. Ralph Bowser, b. Aug. 29, 1919.

2433. CHLOE M. (BOWSER) and MILES DAVIS. Mr. and Mrs. Davis moved from Jefferson Co., Pa., to Surver, Oregon, where they are living on a farm.

Children:

2464. Clair Davis, b. Aug. 25, 1887; m Mildred M. Claypool, b. July 24, 1887.
2465. John William Davis, b. Apr. 29, 1896; m. Ella Pettit, b. Oct. 7, 1899.
2466. Harriet Elizabeth Davis, b. Aug. 5, 1899; m. Blair Douglas, b. July 28, 1894.

2464. CLAIR and MILDRED M. (CLAYPOOL) DAVIS.

Children:

2467. Thelma Elizabeth Davis, b. Jan. 6, 1914.
2468. Robt. Miles Davis, b. Aug. 11, 1915.

2465, JOHN WILLIAM and ELLA (PETTIT) DAVIS.

Children:

2469. Harriet Irene Davis, b. July 18, 1918.
2470. Margaret Lorraine Davis, b. Mar. 5, 1919.

2466. HARRIET ELIZABETH (DAVIS) and BLAIR DOUGLAS.

Child:

2471. Margaret Harriet Douglas, b. Mar. 11, 1919.

2432. MARGARET A. (BOWSER) and JOHN L. CONDRON.

Children:

2472. Thera G. Condron, b. Nov. 4, 1894.
2473. Theda B. Condron, b. Nov. 4, 1894; m. Ren L. Womer.
2474. Leo. J. Condron, b. Nov. 2, 1896.
2475. John P. Condron, b. Aug. 15, 1898.
2476. Comfort Condron, b. Dec. 13, 1901.
2477. William Condron, b. Dec. 10, 1903.

2472. THERA G. CONDRON, m. REN L. WOMER, b. May 3, 1889.

Children:

2478. Nola R. Womer, b. July 14, 1915.
2479. Nila R. Womer, b. June 19, 1921.

2402. ELIZABETH F. (6); CHRISTIAN (5); JOHN (2); JACOB (4); MATHIAS, JR. (2); MATHIAS, SR. (1). Elizabeth Bowser m. (1) T. Rolland; (2) Milton Miller.

Child:

2480. Florence Miller, m. John Vite. They live at McGees Mills, Pa.

964. JACOB (5); NICHOLAS (4); JOHN (3); MATHIAS, JR. (2); MATHIAS, SR. (1). Jacob Bowser moved from Bedford County to Venango County, Pa. He married Sarah Ann Moore. He was killed on the Pennsylvania Railroad March 11, 1896; his widow died Oct. 13, 1906.

Children:

2481. Catharine Margaret Bowser, b. Dec. 21, 1850; m. Henry Kuhls.
2482. James Washington Bowser, b. Feb. 21, 1852; m. Jane Agnes Murphy, b. Nov. 12, 1863.
2483. William Thomas Bowser, b. May 4, 1853; d. April 13, 1909; m. Margaret Mary Murphy, b. Dec. 25, 1860; no children.
2484. John Nicholas Bowser, b. May 11, 1854; m. ——— Sylves; child: Gertrude, b. October, 1898; d. March, 1915; m. John Masts.
2485. Mary Jane Bowser, b. Apr. 25, 1857; m. (1) George Fitter; ch.: James Martin, b. Apr. 1, 1882; Agnes Myrtle, b. June 3, 1883; m. Frederick Gegogene; m. (2) John Smith.
2486. Joseph B. Bowser, b. Nov. 17, 1858.
2487. Margaret Ann Bowser, b. Aug. 14, 1860; d. Oct. 13, 1900; m. John Henry Murphy; ch.: Mary, Harry, Bessie.
2488. Manuel Harrison Bowser, b. Jan. 4, 1862; address: Oil City, Pa.
2489. Martha Elizabeth Bowser, b. Jan. 6, 1865; d. May 28, 1886; m. Charles Lynch; ch.: Mary, Carrie, Martha, Elizabeth.
2490. George Jacob Bowser, b. Dec. 10, 1866; d. July 19, 1877.
2491. Charles Kennedy Bowser, b. Apr. 27, 1870.
2492. James Washington and Jane Agnes (Murphy) Bowser. James lives at 117 Charlton Ave., Oil City, Pa.

Children:

2493. John Henry Bowser, b. Sept. 6, 1883, at Oil City; m. Catharine Meehan; ch.: James Patrick, b. Nov. 8, 1907; d. Sept., 1909; John Michael, b. Dec. 27, 1909; d. June, 1911; Mary Cecelia, b. July 19, 1912; Catharine Mercedes, b. Mar. 4, 1915; Henry Girard, Mary Jane, b. Nov. 8, 1920.
2494. James Patrick Bowser, b. Nov. 8, 1885.
2495. Ella Josephine Bowser, b. Aug. 22, 1887.
2496. Charles Bowser, b. Aug. 19, 1889; d. Jan. 27, 1890.
2497. Mary Dolores Bowser, b. Feb. 2, 1891; m. Thomas Platt; ch.: James H., b. Sept. 6, 1910; d. May 2, 1911; Mary Imogene, b. Mar. 16, 1912, d. May 5, 1917; Ruth Jeannette, b. Mar. 3, 1919.
2498. Margaret Agnes Bowser, b. Apr. 19, 1893; m. William Cowan; child: Margaret Jane, b. July 16, 1920. William Cowan served six months on the Mexican border in 1916 with the 69th Reg., N. Y. National Guards. Remained with the National Guards and served over seas with the 69th Reg. Rainbow Division 23 months. He was gassed and wounded.
2499. Laurence Bowser, b. May 6, 1895, Oil City, Pa. Laurence enlisted in Co. D, 16th Reg. Inf., Pa. National Guards, June 24, 1916; served on the Mexicon border until Jan. 17, 1917.
2500. Irene Cecelia Bowser, b. Feb. 17, 1898.
2501. Sarah Ann Bowser, b. Aug. 30, 1902.
2502. Jacob Clayton Bowser, b. Sept. 21, 1905.

19. SAMUEL (3); MATHIAS, JR. (2); MATHIAS, SR. (1). Let us now go back to York County, Pa., where lived Samuel Bowser, Sr., no doubt a son of Mathias, Jr., of the preceding paragraphs. A tax list taken in 1769 of the settlers of Paradise and Jackson townships has, under the heading "Single men," the name "Bauser, Samuel Bauser, Jacob." In other tax lists of York County we find Samuel Bowser in Berwick Township in 1779, 1780, 1781 and 1782. Berwick Township adjoins Paradise Township. The latter originally included its present area and that of Jackson Township. In the muster roll of the Sixth Company (this company was from Paradise Township) of York County militia for 1785, among the privates is the name of Samuel Bowser. The next record we have of Samuel is the assessment roll of 1799 for Berwick Township. The name of Samuel Bowser is given with an assessed valuation of $528, and that of Samuel Bowser, Jr., with an assessed valuation of $52. In 1811 Samuel Bowser Sr.'s property was assessed at $2,294. At York, Pa., is this record in the Orphans' Court: "March, 1775, came into Court, John Bowser and Samuel Bowser, administrators of goods, etc., of Mathias Bowser, deceased." John was "Hopewell" John, and Samuel was certainly his brother. Samuel Bowser was Samuel, Sr., in the following records, and the father of Samuel, Jr., who went to Warren County, Ohio. (The writer gratefully acknowledges the assistance of Chas. A. Bowser in tracing the line of Samuel Bowser.—A. B. B.). We estimate that Samuel Bowser, Sr., was born about 1748. There is no way of knowing positively, but from the data we have on hand it is probable that Samuel Bowser, Jr., was born in Pennsylvania about 1776. We have no record of either father or son in Pennsylvania after 1811. We conclude that Samuel, Sr., died in Adams County, Pa. The first Ohio record of Samuel Bowser, Jr., is that he and Henry Stibbs were witnesses to a deed dated Oct. 29, 1814, by which a Jacob Bowser buys ten acres of land "on the bank of the little Miami" river in Warren County, Ohio, for $80. One point is clear that three old-time Bowser families from Pennsylvania settled within a few miles of each other in the vicinity of Dayton and Lebanon, Ohio. Henry Bowser of York and Somerset Counties, Pennsylvania, lived near Springboro, Warren County, about half way between Dayton and Lebanon. The Daniel, Sr., family lived near Dayton while the Samuel, Jr., family lived a few miles from Lebanon.

Children of Samuel Bowser, Sr.:

2503. Samuel Bowser, Jr.
2504. Margaret Bowser, b. 1780 in Pa.; d. 1865 in Ohio.
2505. Michael Bowser, b. in 17—. In 1816 in Warren Co., Ohio, bought 100 acres of land "on the little Miami river."
2506. Mary Bowser, b. 1784 in Pa; was living in Ohio in 1851.
2507. Hannah Bowser, b. 1789 in Pa.; d. 1881 in Warren Co., Ohio.
2508. Jacob Bowser, b. 17—; bought land in Warren Co., Ohio, in 1814, 1818 and 1831; d. in Turtle Creek Twp. in 1849.
2509. Sarah Bowser, b. 1791 in Pa.; was living in Ohio in 1851.
2510. Nancy Bowser, b. 1798 in Pa.; d. 1881 in Warren Co., Ohio.
2511. John Bowser, b. 1796 in Pa.; in 1831 bought 115 acres of land in Symmes Purchase "between the two Miami rivers"; lived in Turtle Creek Twp. with five of his sisters who were known as "the Bowser old maids." They never married.
2512. Elizabeth Bowser, b. about 1800 (?). Called "Betsy." She married a man named Grosscoast; nothing further heard of her. Nancy was the last of this Bowser family, she and her sister Hannah dying in March, 1881. The day after Hannah died Nancy died of grief. As each one of this family died, the property passed on to the survivors as the following will shows. It is dated March 6, 1851: Will of Margaret Bowser (daughter of Samuel, Sr., of Pa.) "Margaret Bowser to brothers and sisters—John,

Mary, Hannah, Sarah and Nancy Bowser—Real Estate in 165 acres in Warren County, in Turtle Creek Township, on which we now reside; also about 115 acres in Union Township, Warren County, being the same bequeathed to us by our brother, Jacob Bowser, deceased, and so on as long as the last one shall survive."

Probate Oct. 24, 1865. Margaret Bowser (Seal).

2503. Samuel Bowser, Jr., and family are recorded in the census of 1820 for Union Twp., Warren Co. Samuel died there in 1829. From the fact that Samuel's son Michael was a half-brother of Samuel's other children, it appears that he married twice. Samuel's second wife was Catharine, and she (his widow) is recorded by the census of 1830 as head of a family in Turtle Creek Twp. She was born about 1780 and was the mother of Michael Bowser, b. 1820 to 1825. The "Bowser maids" raised him. Michael conducted a hotel in Xenia, Greene Co., Ohio, about 1861-65. He was sheriff of Greene Co. for 18 years. He had a son Frank. Samuel Bowser, Jr.'s, other children are as follows:

2513. Margaret Bowser (eldest child) born about 1800, married Willard Smith and lived near Springfield, Ohio; the names of their children are John, Nelson, Benjamin, James, Willard, Ann, Augusta, Eliza and Catharine.

2514. John Bowser, born in Pennsylvania in 1803, married Elizabeth Chain. In 1830 they were living in Union Twp., Warren Co., Ohio. For many years a farmer near Millgrove; died in May, 1878 in this county. The following is a brief record of their children:

2515. Isabelle Bowser, b. about 1827; m. (1) Henry Williams, a surveyor; m. (2) Charles Nixon.

2516. John Bowser, Jr., b. in 1829; in Civil war was in Co. I, 187th Reg., Ohio Vol. Inf.; d. about 1910 in Ohio; m. Mary Sparks; ch.: Hal, Lauren and Hiram.

2517. Jennie Bowser, b. 1831; m. James Shawhan and lived in Anderson, Ind.; ch.: Millie, Theodosia, Howland and John.

2518. Alfred Bowser, b. about 1835; d. in Ohio in 1859; m. Linda Case and had a son Alfred.

2519. Arminda Bowser, b. about 1837; m. James D. Wallace, an attorney of Warren Co., Ohio; they had a daughter Laura who was a musician.

2520. Samuel Bowser, b. Jan. 30, 1839; never married; in the Civil war was a corporal in Co. C, 4th Ohio Vol. Cavalry; last known address was Springfield, O.; d. about 1909.

2521. Jacob Bowser, b. Jan. 30, 1841; in the Civil war he enlisted Sept. 16, 1861, in Co. C, 4th Ohio Vol. Cav.; discharged Jan. 3, 1864, at Pulaski, Tenn., but re-enlisted the next day; mustered out June 30, 1865, at Camp Chase, Columbus, O. Jacob and his brother Samuel were in the same battles. Jacob was captain under Gen. Macpherson near Atlanta, Ga. He was captured July 22, 1864, near Atlanta and sent to Andersonville prison, where he spent nine months. In 1867 Jacob married Jane Ann Chilton, who was born in Sunderland, England, in 1850. They came in 1873 from Warren Co., Ohio, to Indianapolis, Ind. He died there July 30, 1914. Their children were Carrie, Minnie and Jacob C. Carrie Bowser married A. G. Willis, and Minnie Bowser married Geo. W. Bunting, Jr. The sisters live in Indianapolis.

2522. Clarissa Bowser, b. ———; died young.

2523. Elwood Bowser, b. about 1844; in the Civil war; d. about 1902; in 1868 married Luanna Wass; their children were Mamie, Ruth, Edgar and Elwood.

2524. Samuel Bowser, second son of Samuel, Jr., b. about 1810 in Pa.; he was a blacksmith; he married Drusilla Chance; they lived at Morrow and Millgrove, Warren Co., Ohio; their children were:

2525. Cornelius Bowser, b. about 1840; m. Jane Ann Thompson; they died about 1910; their children were John, Ella M. and Frank.

2526. Emma Bowser, b. about 1845; m. Sim Williams; their children were Alfred, Myrtle, Dora, Fred, Bert and Clem.

2527. Scott Bowser, b. Dec., 1847; never married; address (1922) is Oregonia, Warren Co., Ohio.

2528. John Woodbury Bowser, b. May 17, 1850; was a carpenter; m. Alice Cunningham; Inez, Fred C., Clifford H. and Leslie M. Bowser are the names of their children. John W. Bowser is (1922) living with his daughter Inez at 232 Charles St., Pittsburgh, Pa.

2529. Georgiana Bowser, b. about 1856; never married.

2530. Adaline Bowser.

2531. Levi S. Bowser; died when a small boy.

2532. Elijah Bowser was the youngest child; his address is (1922) Morrow, Warren Co., Ohio; they have a son, DeWitt, and a daughter.

2533. Jacob Bowser, b. about 1812 in Pa.; was a shoemaker and was living near Loveland, O., about 1850; later had a small shoe factory in Cincinnati; died there; m. (1) ——— Salisbury; their children were Amanda, Hattie and Oscar; m. (2) Hulda Williams; one of their children was Albert Bowser, a painter living near Cincinnati.

2534. Martha Bowser; never married; d. in Warren Co., Ohio.

2535. Mary Bowser; m. John Seely; they had a daughter, Amanda Seely.

2536. Nancy Bowser, b. about 1818; m. Amos Paxton of Iowa; their children were Thomas, Samuel, William, Arninda, Eliza, Frank and Mary; these children lived near Montour, Tama Co., Iowa; the mother died in or before 1881.

DANIEL, JOHN AND HENRY BOUSER FAMILIES

[1] DANIEL BOUSER AND HIS DESCENDENTS

Daniel Bouser, with his two brothers John and Henry, came to America in 1733 and landed at Baltimore, Md. We assume he was a close relative of Mathias, Jr., for the following reasons: (1) They both sailed from the same port in the year 1733; (2) they settled near each other, finally in York County, Pa. Mathias came to America via Philadelphia and joined his countrymen at Lancaster, Pa., 1733. Shortly after 1739 he moved to Paradise Twp., York Co., where he permanently settled. He died there in 1775. It is to be remembered at that time, 1733, the port of sailing, Rotterdam, Holland, was crowded with hundreds and thousands of eager Palatine emigrants. When one ship had filled its quota families were necessarily separated and a part was compelled to take another ship. On this conjecture we record Daniel and his descendants with the family of Mathias, ancestor of the Bowsers thus far numbered in this history. His will was probated in York, Pa., Feb. 3, 1803. "I, Daniel Bouser, ——— bequeath to my eldest daughter, Magdalena (m. Nicholas Miller), 5 lbs.; daughter Elizabeth (m. Conrad Coppenheffer) ———; Elizabeth, my wife; son Benj. Christian; the balance to be divided between Magdalena, Esther, Joseph, Mary, Isaac, Jones (Jonas), Andrew, Solomon and Adam." He also gave to Isaac a tract of land in Baltimore Co., Md., adjoining lands of John Zimmerman and Baker. Adam and Jonas settled in Armstrong County.

Children:

2. Solomon Bowser; lived in Carroll, Co., Md.
3. Joseph Bowser; m. Barbara ———; had sons Andrew, Joseph, Leo, Solomon, b. Dec. 11, 1817, in Md.; lived at Buda, Ill.; and a daughter Charlotte; will probated 1826.
4. Benjamin Bowser, b. 1760; d. Apr. 18, 1844; m. Catharine Grome, b. 1768; d. May 22, 1840.
5. Isaac Bowser, b. 1758; m. Violet Legget in Baltimore Co., Md., 1796.
6. Andrew Bowser.
7. Christian Bowser; b. 1757; single; York Co., 1779-80-82.
8. Jonas Bowser, m. Mrs. Mary Stauffer, Center Hill, Pa.; d. 1848; will dated July 1, 1846; prob. Mar. 7, 1848; d. near Kittanning.
9. Magdalena Bowser, m. Nicholas Miller. Magdalena Miller was a widow in Manheim Twp., 1815.
10. Esther Bowser; d. single, 1882.
11. Elizabeth Bowser, m. Conrad Koppenheffer.

a11. Adam Bowser, b. 1776; d. near Kittanning 1851; m. Catharine Wacking, b. 1780.

4. BENJAMIN (2); DANIEL (1). Benjamin Bowser was a tailor. The shears he used are still in the possession of one of his heirs; lived in Shrewsbury Twp., York Co., Pa.

Children:

b11. Elizabeth Bowser, d. aged 86; m. Isaac Kaufman.

12. George Bowser, d. aged 85.
13. Daniel Bowser; went to Stark Co., Ohio; will probated 1881.
14. Catharine Bowser, d. aged 85; m. Peter Ulrich.
15. Benjamin Bowser, b. Nov. 14, 1799; d. June 18, 1885; m. Elizabeth Blaze, b. Jan. 1, 1805; d. Aug. 26, 1892.
16. Samuel Bowser, b. Sept. 14, 1804; d. 1891; m. Mary Hershey, b. July 18, 1806; d. May 17, 1889.

15. BENJAMIN (3); BENJAMIN (2); DANIEL (1).

Children:

17. Samuel Bowser.
18. Benjamin F. Bowser, b. Aug. 3, 1829; m. Elizabeth Keller, b. 1838.

19. Sarah Bowser, m. Henry Peterman.
20. Joseph E. Bowser, b. Oct. 17, 1832; d. June 21, 1919; m. Lydia Miller.
21. Isaac Bowser, b. Nov. 23, 1841; m. (1) Amanda Fair; (2) Anna Flory.
22. Eli Bowser, b. July 23, 1845; d. Mar. 29, 1873; m. Livina Peterman, b. July 19, 1847; d. May 23, 1885.

21. ISAAC BOWSER (4); BENJAMIN (3); BENJAMIN (2); DANIEL (1). Professor Isaac Bowser is a music teacher and bandmaster. It is said his brass band was the first that ever played on the White House grounds at Washington. Lives at Five Forks, New Freedom, Pa. In 1921 he visited the Bowser Reunion at Kittanning, Pa., and made the principal address.

11. ELIZABETH (3); BENJAMIN (2); DANIEL (1).

Children:
23. Joseph Kaufman.
24. Benjamin Kaufman.
25. Isaac Kaufman.
26. Samuel Kaufman.

23. JOSEPH KAUFMAN.

Children:
27. Henry Kaufman.
28. John Kaufman.
29. Levy Kaufman.
30. Leah Kaufman.
31. William Kaufman.

12. GEORGE (3); BENJAMIN (2); DANIEL (1). George Bowser died in Stark Co., Ohio; will dated 1873.

Children:
32. Catharine Bowser, m. ——— Reichart.
33. Elizabeth Bowser, m. David Stoner.
34. Samuel Bowser, m. Mandila Fuhrman.
35. Margaret Bowser, m. Jacob Stermer.
36. Benjamin Bowser, b. Aug. 24, 1824; d. Aug. 27, 1894; m. Barbara Miller, b. Dec. 26, 1822; d. Jan. 25, 1895.
37. Levi Bowser. Levi was dead (1879) as an administrator was appointed.
38. Susan Bowser, m. ——— Ebert.

32. CATHARINE (4); GEORGE (3); BENJAMIN (2); DANIEL (1).

Children:
39. Elizabeth Reichart.
40. Rena Reichart.

33. ELIZABETH (BOWSER) STONER.

Children:
42. Catharine Stoner.
43. Rebecca Stoner.

35. MARGARET (BOWSER) (4); GEORGE (3); BENJAMIN (2); DANIEL (1).

Children:
44. Lydia Stermer, m. Edward Forman.
45. Catharine Stermer.
46. Samuel Stermer.
47. Levi Stermer.

44. LYDIA (STERMER) FORMAN.

Child:

48. Leander Forman.

46. SAMUEL STERMER.

Children:

49. Elsie Stermer.
50. Horatio Stermer.

47. LEVI STERMER.

Children:

51. Mamie Stermer.
52. Emma Stermer.
53. Lilly Stermer.

36. BENJAMIN (4); GEORGE (3); BENJAMIN (2); DANIEL (1).

Children:

54. Amanda Bowser, b. Sept., 1852; m. Samuel Garbrich; no children; (2) John Warner.
55. Isreal M. Bowser, m. Emma E. Hoover.
56. Isaiah Bowser, b. Mar. 15, 1857; m. Alice Sellers; b. Nov. 10, 1857; address: McFarland, Calif.
57. George Bowser, b. Nov. 16, 1859; m. (1) Alice Gardner; (2) Catharine Falkenstein; address: Astoria, Ill.
58. Samuel Bowser, b. June 17, 1861; m. Clara A. Brehm, b. Dec. 8, 1866.
59. Jacob Bowser, b. June 23, 1863; m. Celia S. Thompson, b. 1871; address: Nampa, Idaho.
60. Anna Bowser, b. May 29, 1865; d. Jan. 17, 1913; m. Samuel Jacobs, b. Nov. 20, 1868.
61. Sarah Bowser, b. Sept. 13, 1854.

55. REV. ISREAL M. and EMMA E. (HOOVER) BOWSER. Minister of the Dunkard Church; living at R. D. No. 3, York, Pa.

Children:

62. C. Herbert Bowser, b. Apr. 25, 1887; m. Edith L. Marsh; address: York, Pa.; ch.: Milner H. Bowser, b. Feb. 25, 1912; Emerson M. Bowser, b. June 26, 1914; d. Dec. 23, 1914; Robert E., b. Oct. 12, 1916; Ralph J., b. Mar. 2, 1921.
63. Carrie M. Bowser, b. Mar. 12, 1893; m. Austin M. Martin, York, Pa.; ch.: Milton, b. Mar. 23, 1914; Austin, b. May 24, 1915; Helen, b. June 23, 1917; d. Nov. 13, 1918; Marie, b. Aug. 1, 1919.
64. Lulu C. Bowser, b. Aug. 8, 1896; m. Clarence Haubert; address: Baltimore; ch.: Robert, b. June 11, 1906.
65. Blanche G. Bowser, b. Oct. 26, 1906.
66. E. Ward Bowser, b. Oct. 12, 1890; d. Jan., 1892.

56. ISAIAH and ALICE (SELLERS) BOWSER.

Children:

67. Clara Bowser, b. Jan. 30, 1881; m. Maben Stoops; ch.: Earl, Dec. 31, 1904; Esther, b. Oct. 9, 1906; Beulah, b. Apr. 2, 1911; Elford, b. Aug. 20, 1912; Ernest, b. Feb. 17, 1919; d. May 17, 1919.
68. John E. Bowser, b. Mar. 14, 1882; m. Ethel Baker; ch.: Thelma, b. Mar. 7, 1910; Clayton, b. Mar. 4, 1914.
69. Anna Bowser, b. Oct. 19, 1885; m. Luther Hylton; ch.: Harold, b. Mar. 6, 1911; Wilbur, b. Nov. 2, 1913; A. Melvin, b. Feb. 9, 1921.
70. Jacob B. Bowser, b. June 19, 1887; m. Flossie Michler; child: Donnis T. Bowser, b. Sept., 1919.

71. W. Titus Bowser, b. Aug. 22, 1889; ch.: Lois, b. Aug. 28, 1917; Frances, b. Apr. 26, 1919.
72. Elizabeth M. Bowser, b. Aug. 26. 1892; m. N. Edward Baker; ch.: Dorris, b. July 29, 1915; Elden, b. Jan. 14, 1917; Otho, b. Mar. 26, 1920.

57. GEORGE BOWSER, b. Nov. 16, 1859; m. (1) ALICE GARDNER; (2) CATHARINE FALKENSTEIN; address: Astoria, Ill.

Children:

73. G. Beulah Bowser, b. Aug. 14, 1892; d. Feb. 20, 1906.
74. Ralph G. Bowser, b. Nov. 20, 1894; m. Anna Engle.
75. Miller W. Bowser, b. Feb. 9, 1896; d. Sept. 11, 1896.
76. Eugene L. Bowser, b. Dec. 8, 1904.
77. Ruth Charity Bowser, b. Apr. 15, 1907.

58. SAMUEL BOWSER, b. June 17, 1861; m. CLARA M. BREHM, b. Dec. 8, 1866.

Children:

78. Irene Bowser, b. July 19, 1889; m. R. A. Nafus; ch.: Velma C., b. Dec. 5, 1911; Irene M., b. Sept., 1913; Verum, b. March, 1915; Francis, b. January, 1919; Evelyn, b. January, 1921.
79. Percival Bowser, b. Mar. 29, 1892; d. Nov. 13, 1909.
80. Chloe J. Bowser, b. June 9, 1896; m. Guy Hoffstatter; ch.: Helen, b. 1918; Theodore, b. March, 1919.
81. Luella Ruth, b. June 10, 1920.

59. JACOB J. BOWSER, b. June 23, 1863; m. CELIA S. THOMPSON, b. 1871; address: Tampa, Idaho.

Children:

82. Joel O. Bowser, b. 1890; m. Ada Misler; ch.: D. Delbert, b. 1911; Verla, b. 1913.
83. Lillie E. Bowser, b. 1891.

60. ANNA BOWSER, b. May 29, 1865; d. Jan. 17, 1913; m. SAMUEL JACOBS, b. Nov. 20, 1868.

Children:

84. Dora Jacobs, b. Jan. 29, 1891; m. Leander Miller; address: New Freedom, Pa.; ch.: Richard M., b. Feb. 7, 1908; Edith C., b. July 15, 1910; d. May 21, 1911; Anna M., b. Feb. 22, 1912; Ruth E., b. Apr. 22, 1913; Oscar A., b. Mar. 23, 1914; d. Apr. 13, 1914; Ralph J., b. Feb. 15, 1915; Lucy J., b. Apr. 8, 1918; Daniel J., b. Apr. 11, 1920.
85. Charine Jacobs, b. Jan. 21, 1897; m. Arthur Hess; address: York, Pa.; child: Eva, b. Apr. 3, 1917.
86. Samuel Jacobs, b. Nov. 8, 1905; address: New Salem, Pa.

13. DANIEL (3); BENJAMIN (2); DANIEL (1).

Children:

87. George Bowser.
88. Samuel Bowser.
89. Daniel Bowser.
90. Elizabeth Bowser.
91. Catharine Bowser.
92. Tina Bowser.
93. Lydia Bowser.
94. Susan Bowser.
95. Anna Bowser.
96. Jacob Bowser.

14. CATHARINE (3); BENJAMIN (2); DANIEL (1). Catharine Bowser married Michael Ulrich.

Children:

97. Michael Uhlrich.
98. Benjamin Ulrich.
99. Samuel Ulrich.
100. Sarah Ulrich, m. ——— Thomas.
101. Catharine Ulrich, m. James Smalley.
102. Joema Ulrich, m. Columbus Cowden.
103. Amanda Ulrich, m. Peter Wittmer.

97. MICHAEL ULRICH.

Child:

104. LAVINAH ULRICH, m. La Follette.

Children:

105. Sarah La Follette.
106. Emma La Follette.
107. Margaret La Follette.
108. Nancy La Follette.
109. Ralph La Follette.
110. William La Follette.

99. SAMUEL ULRICH.

Children:

111. Benjamin S. Ulrich.
112. —————; m. ——— Boblet.
113. —————; m. ——— Bowers.
114. Reuben Ulrich.

17. SAMUEL (4); BENJAMIN (3); BENJAMIN (2); DANIEL (1). Samuel Bowser died Feb. 14, 1872.

Children (first wife):

115. Emma Bowser, b. Nov. 20, 1856; m. John J. Hershner.
116. Franklin Bowser; died when three years old.

Children (second wife):

117. T. Orrie Bowser, b. Dec. 2, 1863.
118. Samuel Oscar Bowser, b. March, 1866.
119. Anna M. Bowser, b. Feb. 23, 1868; m. Clayton Eby, Lancaster, Pa.
120. Corrie A. Bowser, b. June, 1870; m. Maud Abbot.

115. EMMA (BOWSER) and JOHN J. HERSHNER.

Children:

121. William Blaze Hershner, b. Mar. 30, 1874.
122. Franklin Bowser Hershner, b. Mar. 5, 1877.
123. Howard Freeman Hershner, b. Apr. 12, 1879.
124. James Oscar Hershner, b. Sept. 16, 1881.
125. Lula Elva Hershner, b. Dec. 17, 1887.
126. Beulah May Hershner, b. May 6, 1892.
127. Anna Isabel Hershner, b. Jan. 11, 1898; d. Nov. 25, 1902.

117. THOMAS ORRIE BOWSER.

Children:

128. Pearl Bowser.
129. Helen Bowser.
130. Edna Bowser.
131. Clarence E. Bowser.

118. SAMUEL OSCAR BOWSER.

Children:
132. Hazel Bowser, m. Ernest D. Breneman.
133. Nelson Bowser, m. Alma Downs.

120. CORRIE A. and MAUD (ABBOT) BOWSER.

Children:
134. Lilly Bowser.
135. Anna Bowser.
136. Howard Bowser.
137. Ivy Bowser.
138. Pearl Bowser.
139. Dorothy Bowser.

121. WILLIAM BLAZE HERSHNER, m. MARY PRAULL, b. Aug. 4, 1876.

Children:
140. John David Hershner, b. July 23, 1896.
141. Earl Carlyle Hershner, b. Apr. 21, 1898.
142. Florence Irene Hershner, b. Apr. 12 1900.
143. Leslie Praull Hershner, b. Apr. 16, 1903.
144. William Blaze Hershner, b. Aug. 24, 1904.
145. Ruth Estelle Hershner, b. Nov. 24, 1906.
146. Glen Endfield Hershner, b. Oct. 12, 1908.

122. FRANKLIN B. HERSHNER, m. IVY OLIVE GEMMILL.

Children:
147. Furman Carl Hershner, b. Mar. 5. 1895.
148. Lula Mae Hershner, b. Mar. 30, 1897; m. P. F. Rabenstine.
149. Margaret Elizabeth Hershner, b. Sept. 29, 1899; m. Stewart G. Grove.
150. Ann Miller Hershner, b. Nov. 4, 1901; m. Morgan E. Arnold.
151. Gemmill Franklin Hershner, b. June 9, 1904.
152. Hazel Lillian Hershner, b. June 28, 1906.

123. HOWARD FREEMAN HERSHNER, m. LOTTIE E. GLASSICK.

Children:
153. Harry Calvin Hershner, b. Mar. 23, 1905.
154. Erma Ferne Hershner, b. Nov. 10, 1906.
155. Charles Howard Hershner, b. Feb. 23, 1909.

124. JAMES OSCAR HERSHNER, m. SARAH E. GEESEY, b. Nov. 10, 1880.

Children:
156. Bessie Viola Hershner, b. Feb. 16, 1901.
157. Eveline Mae Hershner, b. Oct. 20, 1902.
158. Wilbur Francis Hershner, b. June 12, 1905.
159. Luther Eugene Hershner, b. Mar. 6, 1907.
160. Raymond C. Hershner, b. June 25, 1909.
161. Mary Jane Hershner, b. Nov. 1, 1912.
162. Florence Elizabeth Hershner, b. Oct. 29, 1914.
163. Dorothy Louise Hershner, b. Nov. 2, 1916.
164. Jessie Cornelia Hershner, b. Feb. 8, 1919.

125. LULA E. HERSHNER, m. S. RAY BAILEY.

Child:
165. Everett Hershner Bailey, b. June 13, 1913.

126. BEULAH MAY (HERSHNER) and ARCHIBEL H. GROVE.
Children:
167. Samuel Hershner Grove, b. Feb. 23, 1912.
168. Clair Archibel Grove, b. May 25, 1915.
169. John Richard Grove, b. May 18, 1917.
170. Wilma Emaline Grove, b. Aug. 17, 1920.

140. JOHN DAVID HERSHNER, m. FLORENCE KEESEY.
Child:
171. John D. Hershner.

148. LULA MAE HERSHNER, and P. F. RABENSTINE.
Child:
172. Eugene Franklin Rabenstine, b. Feb. 10, 1919.

149. MARGARET ELIZABETH HERSHNER and STEWART GROVE.
Child:
173. Nevin Hershner Grove, b. Nov. 27, 1919.

19. SARAH (4); BENJAMIN, JR. (3); BENJAMIN, SR. (2); DANIEL (1). Sarah Bowser was born May 9, 1831; died September, 1899; married Henry Peterman.
Children:
174. Saranda Peterman, b. Apr. 7, 1853; d. July 9, 1907; m. Adam Trone.
175. Lizzie Peterman, b. May 25, 1854; d. Sept. 23, 1919.
176. Jesse Peterman, b. Aug. 20, 1859.
177. Henry Peterman, b. Jan. 12, 1857; d. Feb. 5, 1862.
178. Benjamin Peterman, b. Oct. 10, 1864; d. Dec. 15, 1864.
179. Jemima Peterman, b. Mar. 18, 1868; m. Charles E. Reeling.

174. SARANDA (PETERMAN) and ADAM TRONE.
Children:
180. Ida Trone, b. July 28, 1875; m. Howard Albright.
181. Sarah Trone, b. Sept. 15, 1876; m. Martin Snyder.
182. Harvey Trone, b. Sept. 24, 1877; m. Mabel Gladfetter.
183. Cora Trone, b. Apr. 17, 1879; m. George Nace.
184. Chester Trone, b. June 22, 1880; m. Hilda Peterson; gave his life for his country; served in the World war in France; was missing on July 17, 1918; died four days later.
185. Paul Trone, b. May 27, 1882.
186. Charles Trone, b. Feb. 6, 1884; d. March, 1886.
187. Emma Trone, b. Jan. 8, 1888; m. Samuel Markle.
188. Sadie Trone, b. Sept. 1, 1892; d. Mar. 9, 1893.
189. Millard Trone, b. July 31, 1894; served in the World war.

175. ELIZABETH PETERMAN, m. JEREMIAH SMITH.
Children:
190. Jemima Smith, b. Mar. 23, 1887; m. Jerry Walker.
191. Sallie Smith, b. Sept. 5, 1888; m. Charles Boyer.
192. Sadie U. Smith, b. Jan. 15, 1893.
193. Albert L. Smith, b. Mar. 8, 1894; d. 1894.

176. JESSE PETERMAN, m. LEANNA MILLER.
Children:
194. Howard Peterman, m. ——— Bowman.
195. Verna Peterman, m. Jacob F. Keeny.

179. JEMIMA (PETERMAN) and CHAS. E. REEHLING.
Children:
196. Queenie V. Reehling, b. Nov. 10, 1889; m. William E. Nevin.
197. Alva Reehling, b. Jan. 31, 1891; m. J. Fred Artman.
198. Frances Reehling, b. Mar. 18, 1893; m. Harvey N. Kidd.
199. Ola Reehling, b. Jan. 15, 1898; m. Allen G. Trout.

22. ELI (4); BENJAMIN, JR. (3); BENJAMIN, SR. (2); DANIEL (1).
Children:
200. James P. Bowser, b. Jan. 1, 1872; m. Phoebe Bubb.
201. Lilly Bowser, m. Reuben Hampshire.

200. JAMES P. and PHOEBE (BUBB) BOWSER.
Children:
202. Beulah Mae Bowser, b. Sept. 11, 1894; m. Clinton Dubbs.
203. Mabel Geneva Bowser, b. Mar. 10, 1896; d. Aug. 26, 1898.
204. S. Marie Bowser, b. Sept. 25, 1900.
205. A. Merle Bowser, b. Oct. 9, 1902.
206. Stewart Roy Bowser, b. Apr. 15, 1905.
207. Lillie Naomi Bowser, b. Dec. 18, 1907.
208. Russel James Bowser, b. May 25, 1910.
209. Lola Pearle Bowser, b. Nov. 26, 1913.

202. BEULAH MAE (BOWSER) and CLINTON DUBBS.
Children:
210. Harold Dubbs.
211. Ada Dubbs.
212. Marie Dubbs.
213. Lloyd Dubbs.

201. LILLY (BOWSER) and REUBEN HAMPSHIRE.
Child:
214. Claudie Hampshire.

16. SAMUEL (3); BENJAMIN (2); DANIEL (1).
Children:
215. Christian Bowser.
216. Samuel H. Bowser, b. Aug. 18, 1836; d. May 10, 1866.
217. Benjamin H. Bowser, b. October, 1846; m. Laura Stamford, b. 1849.
218. Elizabeth Bowser; died single.
219. Catharine Bowser, b. 1835; m. Andrew Myers.
220. Margaret Bowser, m. ——— Stough.
221. Lydia Bowser, b. Mar. 28, 1840; d. Dec. 12, 1866.
222. Mary Bowser, m. Chas. King.
223. Julian Bowser, m. Louis Kraber.
a223. Rebecca S. Bowser, b. Oct. 4, 1834; d. May 12, 1852.

216. SAMUEL, JR. (4); SAMUEL, SR. (3); BENJAMIN (2); DANIEL (1).
Children:
224. Robert E. Bowser.
225. Samuel Bowser; died young.

217. BENJAMIN H. (4); SAMUEL (3); BENJAMIN (2); DANIEL (1).
Benjamin H. Bowser still lives on the old homestead purchased by his grandfather Benjamin. Part of the original tract is now the town of New Freedom, York County, Pa. The Benjamin (2) Bowser farm passed to his

son, Samuel, and from Samuel (3) to his son, Benjamin H. Bowser (4). It is now farmed by Howard Bowser (5), son of Benjamin H. This farm has the old "Bowser" cemetery. For some reason Benjamin (2) and his wife were not buried here, but about three miles distant. [From notes of Jacob C. Bowser (252)].

Children:
226. Clara Bowser, b. Apr. 24, 1871; m. Rolland Baughman.
227. Howard Bowser, b. May 21, 1877; m. Maud M. Bailey.

219. CATHARINE (4); SAMUEL (3); BENJAMIN (2); DANIEL (1). CATHARINE (BOWSER) and ANDREW MYERS.

Children:
228. Sally Myers.
229. Leah Myers.
230. Mary Myers.
231. Andrew Myers.
232. Samuel Myers.

222. MARY (BOWSER) and CHAS. KING.

Children:
233. Leander King.
234. Lilly King.
235. Mabel King, m. James Adam Downs.
236. Harry Gleen King.
237. Minnie King.
238. Samuel King.
239. Wayne King.
240. Arthur King.
241. Ada King.
242. Wilmer O. King.

223. JULIA (4); SAMUEL (3); BENJAMIN (2); DANIEL (1).

Children:
243. Wilbert Kraber.
244. Captain W. C. Kraber; residence: 508 W. Salem Road, York, Pa.
245. Edith Kraber.
246. Russel Kraber.
247. Luther Kraber.

18. BENJAMIN F. (4); BENJAMIN, JR. (3); BENJAMIN, SR. (2); DANIEL (1). BENJAMIN and ELIZABETH (KELLER) BOWSER.

Children:
248. Franklin Bowser, b. Dec. 1, 1864; d. Sept. 13, 1870.
249. Spencer Bowser, b. May 11, 1867; d. Sept. 9, 1870.
250. Jemima Bowser, b. Oct. 7, 1868; m. John P. Keeny, b. 1867.
251. Jacob C. Bowser, b. Nov. 9, 1870; m. Rose Mead, b. 1869. See biographies.
252. Elizabeth Bowser, b. May 26, 1873; d. Feb. 27, 1876.

250. JEMIMA (5); BENJAMIN (4); BENJAMIN, JR. (3); BENJAMIN, SR. (2); DANIEL (1). JEMIMA (BOWSER) and JOHN P. KEENY.

Children:
253. Bertha Keeny, b. Jan. 22, 1892; m. Paul B. Moyer.
254. Jacob Keeny, b. May 15, 1894; m. Verna Peterman.

251. JACOB (5); BENJAMIN (4); BENJAMIN, JR. (3); BENJAMIN, SR. (2); DANIEL (1). JACOB C. and ROSE (MEAD) BOWSER.

Children:

255. Ethelynn Elizabeth Bowser, b. Oct. 24, 1895.
256. Marcia Mead Bowser, b. July 19, 1902; attending Skidmore School of Arts, Saratoga Springs, N. Y.

253. BERTHA (6); JEMIMA (5); BENJAMIN (4); BENJAMIN, JR. (3); BENJAMIN, SR. (2); DANIEL (1). BERTHA (KEENY) and PAUL B. MOYER.

Child:

257. Paul Moyer, Jr., b. September, 1920.

254. JACOB F. (6); JEMIMA (5); BENJAMIN (4); BENJAMIN, JR. (3); BENJAMIN, SR. (2); DANIEL (1). JACOB F. and VERNA (PETERMAN) KEENY.

Child:

258. Helen Elizabeth Keeny, b. Nov. 25, 1919.

226. CLARA and ROLLAND BAUGHMAN.

Children:

259. Howard Samuel Baughman.
260. Florence Baughman, m. Gammel.
261. Alma Baughman.

227. HOWARD and MAUD M. (BAILEY) BOWSER.

Child:

262. Florine Bowser, b. Sept. 22, 1901.

236. HARRY GLEEN and ANNA ESTHER (McWILLIAMS) KING.

Child:

263. Dorothy Jane King.

235. MABEL (KING) and JAMES ADAM DOWNS.

Children:

264. Charles Thomas Downs, m. Iva Rebecca Diehl.
265. Harry Milton Downs.
266. Laura Grace Downs, m. Chester Ruby.
267. James Arthur Downs.
268. Ada May Downs, m. John Hoover.
269. William Edward Downs.
270. Mary Susannah Downs.
271. Clarence Elroy Downs.
272. Howard Elmer Downs.
273. Carrie Viola Downs.
274. Sarah Elizabeth Downs.
275. Chester Franklin Downs.
276. Ethel Marie Downs.
277. Margaret Pauline Downs.

264. CHARLES THOMAS and IVA REBECCA (DIEHL) DOWNS.

Children:

278. Kenneth Downs.
279. James Thomas Downs.
280. Charles Arthur Downs.
281. Dorothy Irene Downs.

268. ADA MAY and JOHN HOOVER.

Child:

282. Mabel Frances Hoover.

20. JOSEPH E. BOWSER (4); BENJAMIN, JR. (3); BENJAMIN, SR. (2); DANIEL (1). Joseph E. Bowser, b. Oct. 17, 1832; d. June 21, 1919; m. Lydia Miller, b. Jan. 28, 1841; d. Apr. 18, 1917.

Children:

283. Amanda Bowser, b. Feb. 26, 1862; d. Feb. 28, 1862.
284. Harriet Bowser, b. Dec. 27, 1862; d. Dec. 27, 1862.
285. Andrew Bowser, b. Feb. 8, 1864; m. Elizabeth Hollinger, b. 1863.
286. Moses M. Bowser, b. Aug. 18, 1866; m. Phoebe Ann Albert, b. 1873.
287. Daniel Bowser, b. Oct. 28, 1868; m. Mary Emma Farence, b. 1871.
288. Anna Elizabeth Bowser, b. Feb. 28, 1871; m. William A. Walter, b. 1866.
289. Catharine Bowser, b. Oct. 6, 1873; m. Wilson Lan Burgard, b. 1865.
290. Lillie May Bowser, b. May 4, 1876; m. Robert C. Kaufman, b. 1873.
291. John Joseph Bowser, b. Sept. 29, 1878; m. Ida Wiley, b. 1877.
292. Lydia Ann Bowser, b. May 21, 1881; m. William C. Hoffman, b. Dec. 16, 1871.

285. ANDREW (5); JOSEPH E. (4); BENJAMIN, JR. (3); BENJAMIN, SR. (2); DANIEL, (1). ANDREW and ELIZABETH (HOLLINGER) BOWSER.

Children:

293. Anna May Bowser, b. Sept. 9, 1889; d. Feb. 6, 1892.
294. Charles Edward Bowser, b. Dec. 11, 1890; m. Rachel Miller.
295. Bertha Rebecca Bowser, b. Aug. 28, 1892; m. Ralph B. Lehman.
296. Martha Alberta Bowser, b. Jan. 17, 1894; d. Oct. 28, 1901.
297. John Curtis Bowser, b. June 7, 1895; m. Della Elizabeth Smith.
298. Lillie Idel Bowser, b. Sept. 5, 1898; d. Oct. 19, 1901.
299. Harry Joseph Bowser, b. Nov. 30, 1899.
300. Grace Elizabeth Bowser, b. Dec. 3, 1903.
301. Wilbur Andrew Bowser, b. Feb. 18, 1905; d. Apr. 6, 1909.

294. CHARLES E. (6); ANDREW (5); JOSEPH E. (4); BENJAMIN, JR. (3); BENJAMIN, SR. (2); DANIEL (1).

Children:

302. Joseph Andrew Bowser, b. May 2, 1913.
303. Miriam Miller Bowser, b. Apr. 11, 1915.
304. Charles Donald Bowser, b. Oct. 29, 1916.
305. Margaret Adele Bowser, b. Aug. 7, 1918.

295. BERTHA REBECCA (6); ANDREW (5); JOSEPH (4); BENJAMIN, JR. (3); BENJAMIN, SR. (2); DANIEL (1).

Child:

306. Mildred Elizabeth Lehman.

297. JOHN CURTIS (6); ANDREW (5); JOSEPH (4); BENJAMIN, JR. (3); BENJAMIN, SR. (2); DANIEL (1).

Children:

307. Kenneth Andrew Bowser, b. Jan. 9, 1919.
308. Ray Martin Bowser, b. June 28, 1920.

286. MOSES M. (5); JOSEPH E. (4); BENJAMIN, JR. (3); BENJAMIN, SR. (2); DANIEL (1).

Children:
309. Eugene Albert Bowser, b. Apr. 7, 1897.
310. Margaret Lydia Bowser, b. Nov. 10, 1898.
311. Mary Ann Bowser, b. Nov. 11, 1900.
312. Herbert Nelson Bowser, b. Sept. 27, 1907.

287. REV. DANIEL, minister of the Brethren Church, York, Pa. (5); JOSEPH E. (4); BENJAMIN, JR. (3); BENJAMIN, SR. (2); DANIEL (1).

Children:
313. Ada Jane Bowser, b. Mar. 2, 1889; m. Wilbur Lehman.
314. Joseph Howard Bowser, b. Dec. 26, 1893; m. Esther Utz.
315. Anna Ruth Bowser, b. Aug. 4, 1895.
316. Oscar Sylvester Bowser, b. May 19, 1900.
317. Lydia Irene Bowser, b. Apr. 2, 1903; d. June 21, 1906.
318. Daniel Robert Bowser, b. July 8, 1904.
319. William Arthur Bowser, b. Mar. 28, 1906.
320. Raymond Edward Bowser, b. Dec. 8, 1908; d. Jan. 3, 1909.
321. Chester Leroy Bowser, b. Oct. 26, 1912; d. Apr. 28, 1917.

313. ADA JANE (6); DANIEL (5); JOSEPH E. (4); BENJAMIN, JR. (3); BENJAMIN, SR. (2); DANIEL (1).

Children:
322. James Paul Lehman, b. Sept. 8, 1912.
323. Mary Martha Lehman, b. Sept. 8, 1912 (twins).
324. Esther Mae Lehman, b. Dec. 24, 1913.
325. Lester Rae Lehman, b. Dec. 24, 1913; d. same day.
326. Thelme Ellen Moulu Bowser, b. Dec. 15, 1916.

288. ANNA ELIZABETH (5); JOSEPH (4); BENJAMIN, JR. (3); BENJAMIN, SR. (2); DANIEL (1).

Children:
327. Grace Matura Walter, b. Feb. 11, 1889; m. William D. Rineer.
328. Esther Marie Walter, b. July 7, 1897.
329. Joseph George Walter, b. Aug. 10, 1899.

327. GRACE MATURA (WALTER) and WILLIAM D. RINEER.

Children:
330. Donald Elmer Rineer, b. Feb. 27, 1913.
331. Elaine Marie Rineer, b. Aug. 20, 1916.

289. CATHARINE (5); JOSEPH E. (4); BENJAMIN, JR. (3); BENJAMIN, SR. (2); DANIEL (1). Catharine (Bowser) and Wilson L. Burgard.

Children:
332. Amelia Mae Burgard, b. Aug. 27, 1893; m. Charles M. Jones.
333. Charles Raymond Burgard, b. June 14, 1895; m. Mamie R. Cully.
334. Grace Irene Burgard, b. Apr. 8, 1898.
335. Mary Isabelle Burgard, b. Apr. 6, 1901; m. Carvin H. Reever.
336. Beulah Pauline Burgard, b. Sept. 26, 1903.
337. David William Burgard, b. July 22, 1906.
338. Eleanor Marie Burgard, b. Sept. 27, 1917.

333. CHARLES RAYMOND and MAMIE R. (CULLY) BURGARD.

Children:

339. Dorothy I. Burgard, b. Dec. 18, 1916.
340. Pershing W. Burgard, b. Nov. 10, 1918.
341. Charles C. Burgard, b. Nov. 11, 1919.

335. MARY ISABELLE and CARVIN H. REEVER.

Child:

342. Dorothy Mae Reever, b. May 7, 1920.

290. LILLIE MAY (5); JOSEPH E. (4); BENJAMIN, JR. (3); BENJAMIN, SR. (2); DANIEL (1). LILLIE MAE and ROBERT C. KAUFMAN.

Child:

343. Bessie Metura Kaufman, b. Aug. 24, 1845; m. Norman E. Nell, b. June 30, 1892.

Children:

344. Charlotte Mae Nell, b. Apr. 17, 1915.
345. Gerard Robert Nell, b. July 12, 1917.

291. JOHN JOSEPH (5); JOSEPH E. (4); BENJAMIN, JR. (3); BENJAMIN, SR. (2); DANIEL (1). REV. JOHN JOSEPH and IDA (WILEY) BOWSER. Minister of the Brethren Church, York, Pa.

Children:

346. Wiley Michael Bowser, b. Mar. 11, 1901; d. Nov. 27, 1901.
347. Edward Joseph Bowser, b. Oct. 19, 1902; dental student, University of Pennsylvania.

13. DANIEL (3); BENJAMIN (2); DANIEL (1). Daniel Bowser moved from York County, Pa., to Stark County, Ohio; m. Anna Eby. His will was dated 1878 and probated 1881. His estate amounted to $3,387.92. This was divided among his heirs as follows: Lydia Bollinger, Samuel B. Culler, Jacob O. Culler, John Culler, Daniel Bowser, Elizabeth Bromont, Christian Hesland, Mary Brubaker, Elizabeth Bowser, Lovania Surbey, George Bowser (probably a son of Daniel).

6. ANDREW BOWSER (2); DANIEL (1). Andrew Bowser lived in Manheim Township, York County, Pa. He is mentioned in the census of 1810; also in the census of 1850. In the latter census his age is given as eighty. He was born, therefore, in 1770. He married Margaret ——— who was born in Germany in 1790. Will dated June 30, 1854, at West Manheim Township, York County.

a11. ADAM (2); DANIEL (1). Adam Bowser, b. 1776, moved from York County to Armstrong County, Pa. Died there in 1852. Married Catharine Wacking, b. 1780. Will recorded Vol. 2, page 16, Kittanning, Pa.

Children:

348. Levi Bowser, b. 1803; d. 1865; m. Mary Bowser, a daughter of John and Margaret (Razor) Bowser.
349. Sarah Bowser, m. Robert Long; ch.: Mealy.
350. Rebecca Bowser, m. ——— Downsey; ch.: Jerry, Frantz.
351. Priscilla Bowser, m. James Russell; ch.: Lebbius, m. Margaret Bowser; Narcissa, m. John Shep.

348. LEVI (3); ADAM (2); DANIEL (1). Levi Bowser settled at Walk Chalk, Armstrong County, Pa., on a farm of 106 acres. Married Mary Bowser, daughter of John and Mary (Razor) Bowser.

Children:

352. Flora Bowser; d. young.
353. Van Buren Bowser, b. Nov. 13, 1840; d. Nov. 26, 1901; m. Sarah C. Chambers, b. Mar. 17, 1839; daughter of James Chambers of Jefferson County, Pa.
354. Caroline Bowser; d. in infancy.
355. Felix Bowser, b. July 9, 1846; m. (1) Mary Ann Bowser, b. July 11, 1848; d. Feb. 14, 1885; (2) Elizabeth Watterson, b. 1859.
356. Hannah Bowser, m. John McCullough.
357. Absalom Bowser, b. 1844; m. Jane John. See (1399) for children.
358. Harrison A. Bowser, b. 1849; m. Mary E. McNab, b. 1852.

a358. Wilson Bowser, m. (1) Catharine Bowser; (2) Mary R. Crisman.

353. VAN BUREN and SARAH C. (CHAMBERS) BOWSER. Residence: Center Hill, Pa.

Children:

359. Charles W. Bowser, b. Dec. 25, 1864.
360. James A. Bowser, b. Feb. 24, 1866.
361. Albert E. Bowser, b. Nov. 22, 1872.
362. Mary M. Bowser, b. May 9, 1875.
363. Van Buren Bowser, b. July 22, 1881.

355. FELIX and MARY ANN BOWSER. Farmer, Residence near Worthington, Pa.

Children:

364. Clymer Bowser, b. Oct. 11, 1866; d. Sept. 30, 1867.
365. Elizabeth C. Bowser, b. Aug. 28, 1868; m. Wilbert Lewis.
366. Mary E. Bowser, b. July 11, 1870; m. Robert H. Toy.
367. Emmit Bowser, b. June 14, 1872; m. Maud Brown, b. Feb. 20, 1877.
368. Olive M. Bowser, b. July 18, 1874; d. Sept. 11, 1885.
369. Melon Bowser, b. Dec. 16, 1876.
370. Lottie E. Bowser, b. Dec. 5, 1878; d. Feb. 18, 1920.
371. Ambrose Bowser, b. Nov. 7, 1880; m. Maud Lasher.
372. Harry R. Bowser, b. Feb. 5, 1883; m. Elizabeth Brown.
373. Effie Bowser, b. Dec. 27, 1890; m. S. M. Sarvey.
374. Myrtle Bowser, b. Apr. 25, 1892; m. Raymond Bowser.
375. Ivy P. Bowser, b. Aug. 29, 1893; m. Herbert Bish.
376. Rayburn Bowser, b. Aug. 15, 1895; m. Florence Claypoole.

367. EMMIT and MAUD (BROWN) BOWSER. Residence near Worthington, Pa.

Children:

377. Grace E. Bowser, b. Mar. 6, 1896; m. Ruben Miliron.
378. Bertha L. Bowser, b. Oct. 20, 1899; m. Vance Long.
379. Mary O. Bowser, b. Oct. 18, 1901; m. Wade Taylor.
380. Rufus C. Bowser, b. Aug. 15, 1903.
381. Dennis R. Bowser, b. Sept. 5, 1905.
382. King O. Bowser, b. Sept. 21, 1907.
383. Luther D. Bowser, b. May 2, 1910.
384. Howard C. Bowser, b. Feb. 5, 1912.
385. Anna M. Bowser, b. Apr. 16, 1914.
386. Arnold R. Bowser, b. Sept. 11, 1917.
387. Virginia C. Bowser, b. July 10, 1919.

356. HANNAH (BOWSER) and JOHN McCULLOUGH.

Children:

388. Mary McCullough, m. William Wolf.
389. Eva McCullough, m. Charles Dowling.
390. Ellen McCullough, m. Bert McCollum.
391. Wilda McCullough, m. ——— Peters.
392. Harvey McCullough, m. Lulu Bowser.
393. Charles McCullough, m. Ann Reitler.
394. Bert McCullough, m. May Boylstein.
395. George McCullough.
396. Jennie McCullough, m. ——— Wilkins.

358. HARRISON A. and MARY E. (McNAB) BOWSER. Since the founding of the Pittsburgh plate glass industry at Ford City, Pa., Harrison A. Bowser has resided there.

Children:

397. Mark C. Bowser, b. 1871; d. Nov. 22, 1903, at Ford City; m. Ida Claypoole; ch.: Wade, m. Finn; Ray, m. Fay Euings; Gilman, d. Nov. 22, 1903.
398. Loben Bowser, b. 1872; m. Nellie Claypoole; ch.: Ruth, m. Mark C. Barker.
399. Harrison A. Bowser, b. Apr. 21, 1875.
400. Carrie Bowser, b. 1877; m. William Anthony; ch.: Roy, m. Gladys Toy; Mary, m. Ray Downsey; Margaret; Hazel; Flora; Floyd.
401. Irwin Bowser, b. 1879; m. Christina Sowers; ch.: Thelma, m. Willis Walker; Bertha; Daniel; Nellie.
402. Mary E. Bowser, b. 1885; m. Harry P. Faith; ch.: Harry I.; m. Marie Klingensmith.
403. Margaret Bowser, b. 1888; m. Sylvester Murtland; ch.: Fonda.
404. Lucy C. Bowser, b. 1890; m. Alexander Meade; ch.: Helen, Goldie, Emma.
405. Flora Bowser, b. 1891.
406. Dora Bowser, b. 1892; m. R. M. Frantz.

357. ABSALOM and JANE (JOHN) BOWSER.

Children:

407. John A. Bowser, b. May 5, 1870; m. Arimina Bowser, b. 1875, daughter of John M. Bowser; ch.: Sarah L., Ida C., Bert, Goldie, Stanley K., William R., Harry C., Harlon J., Mary M., Kenneth E., June A.
408. Peter Bowser, m. Pearl Brison.
409. Agnes Bowser, b. 1869; m. Ezekiel Lasher.
410. Abram Bowser, m. Hattie McKelvey.
411. Clura Bowser, m. Bessie Slonaker.

a411. Hannah Bowser, m. Harry Wyant.

b411. Mary Bowser, m. (1) Lee Cousins; (2) Harmon J. Claypoole.

a358. WILSON BOWSER, m. (1) CATHARINE BOWSER, daughter of David Bowser; ch.: Permelia; m. (2) MARY R. CRISMAN; ch.: Lee, James, Jane, Violet, Hulda, Mamie, Sarah, Wilbert, Dwight. Residence: 36 Johnson Ave., Kittanning, Pa.

408. PETER and PEARL (BRISON) BOWSER; ch.: Edward, Absalom, Oersilla, Blanche, Ida, Permilda, Gertrude.

310. ABRAM and HATTIE (McKELVEY) BOWSER; ch.: Leroy, Gladdys, Bertha, Merle, Iona, Eugene.

411. CLURA and BESSIE (SLONAKER) BOWSER; ch.: Alexander, Violet, Mary, Olise, Virginia, Charlotte.

---

[2] HENRY BOUSSER AND HIS DESCENDANTS

There is abundant evidence that one of the three brothers who landed at Baltimore, Md., in 1733, was Henry Bowser. The will of Henry Bouser, which was probated on the 27th of August, 1806, in Washington County, Md., mentions the following children: Frederick Bouser; John Bouser; Barbara Bouser, wife of William Binkley; Anna Rickabach; Elizabeth, wife of Boyer; Mary, wife of Peter Boyer; Magdalena, wife of George Young. Signed in German, Heinrich Bousser. A deed to 140 acres in Washington County, Md., July 15, 1796, for which he paid 603 pounds, 10 shillings. In the census report of 1790 he was the head of a family of ten.

Children:

412. Frederick Bouser.
413. Barbara Bouser, m. William Binkley.
414. John Bouser, b. about 1750, in Washington County, Md.; d. in 1811.
415. Anna Bouser, m. Rickabach.
416. Elizabeth Bouser, m. John Boyer.
417. Mary Bouser, m. in 1799 to Peter Boyer, in Maryland.
418. Magdalena Bouser, m. George Young, in Maryland, 1802.

415. FREDERICK BOUSER; was living in Washington County, Md., in 1820.

Children:

419. Jacob C. Bouser, b. 1809 in Maryland; m. Delilah ———, b. 1816, in Virginia; in 1839 Jacob C. Bouser and James Story established a foundry and machine shop in Fort Wayne, Ind.; the enterprise was conducted quite successfully until 1876 when McLachlan and Olds became proprietors.
420. Henry Bouser, b. 1810, in Maryland; m. Emily Hammond; lived in Richland and Hancock County, Ohio; d. May 14, 1866, near Warsaw, Ind.
421. Lafayette M. Bowser, b. 1838, in Ohio; wife, Nancy J.
422. Sarah M. Bowser, b. 1840, in Ohio.
423. Jefferson C. Bowser, b. 1842, in Indiana.
424. Frances M. Bowser, b. 1846, in Indiana; m. James W. Pearse.
425. Madison M. Bowser, b. 1849, in Indiana.

420. HENRY and EMILY (HAMMOND) BOWSER.

Children:

426. William Henry Bowser, b. Oct. 30, 1832; d. Dec. 12, 1907, in Maryland; m. Catharine M. Kinsey; ch.: Malinda A., b. Dec. 16, 1858; Francis E., b. Feb. 1, 1861; Ethel L.; Althea L.; Orville A., b. 1868; Harry, b. 1872; Lucy J., b. Aug. 15, 1875; Maud, b. Jan. 18, 1878.
427. Anna E. Bowser, m. Jacob Thompson; ch.: William, Henry, Malinda, Minerva, Eli, Ludie, Emily.
428. Frederick Bowser, d. Dec. 21, 1914, in Indiana; m. (1) Sarah Manwill; (2) Anna R. Bowen; ch.: John A., Julia A., Henry H., William E., Alice, Frank H., Ethel, Hulda.
429. Ellen J. Bowser, m. William Burket; ch.: Alonza, Emma, Lilly, Joseph.

430. Malinda Bowser, d. single, aged 18.
431. John W. Bowser; in Civil war, Co. A, 74th Reg. Ind. Inf.; d. June 8, 1864.

414. JOHN BOUSER.

Children:

432. Jacob Bowser.
433. John Bowser.
434. Henry Bowser, b. between 1780 and 1785; settled in Allen County, Ind.; m. (1) ——— Sprinkle; (2) Catharine Williams.
435. William Bowser.
436. Peter Bowser.
437. George Bowser.
438. Noah Bowser.
439. Catharine Bowser.
440. Mary Bowser.
441. Elizabeth Bowser.
442. Nancy Bowser.
443. Michael Bowser, b. Apr. 22, 1799, at Lancaster, Pa.

434. HENRY and (SPRINKLE) BOWSER. Henry Bowser, Sr., went from Pennsylvania to Ohio about 1823. He went from Ohio to Allen County, Ind., about 1833. Died about 1873, in Allen County, Ind.

Children:

444. John H. Bowser, b. Apr. 15, 1812, in Pennsylvania; d. Mar. 10, 1879, in Indiana; m. Eliza Keiger, b. Sept. 18, 1818; d. Sept. 9, 1875.
445. Jesse Bowser.
446. Sarah Bowser, m. John Waters.
447. Eliza Bowser, m. ——— Haynes.
448. George W. Bowser, b. 1817, in Pennsylvania; d. in 1888; in Indiana; m. Margaret Keiger, sister of Eliza.
449. Henry J. Bowser, b. 1820, in Pennsylvania; m. Mary Keiger; three brothers marrying three sisters.
450. Samuel Bowser, b. about 1823, in Pennsylvania; d. about 1891; m. (1) Jane Waters; (2) Margaret Good.
451. William Bowser, b. 1824, in Ohio; d. about 1905; m. Rebecca Paff.

444. JOHN H. and ELIZA (KEIGER) BOWSER.

Children:

452. Eliza Jane Bowser, b. Sept. 18, 1837; d. 1878; m. John Culverson; ch.: Nettie.
453. Alexander Bowser, b. June 26, 1842; m. Laurinda Devilbiss; ch.: Allen A.
454. Mary R. Bowser, b. Mar. 10, 1847; m. Hiram Hutchinson; was living in California in 1920; ch.: Charles W., Alonzo, William.
455. Augustus Bowser, b. Apr. 10, 1849; d. Oct. 28, 1919, in Fort Wayne, Ind.; m. Fyanna Wireman; ch.: Laura, Estelle, Hazel, Delmore; Delmore was in the Spanish-American war.
456. Orra Jefferson Bowser, b. Feb. 16, 1852; m. Julia A. Jones; ch.: Cecil J.
457. Sylvanus F. Bowser, b. Aug. 8, 1854, in Allen County, Ind.; m. Sarah Frances Russell, b. Oct. 4, 1856; see biographies.
458. Lafayette E. Bowser, b. Feb. 11, 1857; m. Charity Bechtol; ch.: Ada, m. George E. Tibbits. Lafayette E. Bowser is consulting engineer of S. F. Bowser & Company, Fort Wayne, Ind.
459. Jessie E. Bowser, b. Jan. 13, 1859.
460. Asbury Ellsworth Bowser, b. Dec. 28, 1861; d. Aug. 4, 1901; m. Rachel Evans.

457. SYLVANUS F. and SARAH F. (RUSSELL) BOWSER.

Children:

461. Harry M. Bowser, b. Aug. 13, 1878; graduate of Purdue University, Indiana, 1905; m. Bertha M. Mitchell, b. Sept. 21, 1821; ch.: Wilda K., b. Aug. 1, 1908; Sylvanus F., b. July 14, 1910; Emily L., b. Nov. 21, 1913; Philip M., b. Jan. 14, 1919.
462. Eva C. Bowser, b. Jan. 17, 1881; m. Leland F. Johnson; ch.: Leland F., Jr., b. July 24, 1910; Robert B., b. Sept. 23, 1915.
463. William Hugh Bowser, b. Mar. 19, 1884.
464. Albert S. Bowser, b. July 26, 1886; m. Ida Pearl Kickley; ch.: Bon Silene, b. Mar. 12, 1910; Albert S., Jr., b. Jan. 21, 1913.
465. Ethelwyn V. Bowser, b. Sept. 27, 1890; m. Daniel G. Milligan; ch.: Daniel G., Jr., b. Aug. 18, 1919.
466. Mildred L. Bowser, b. Sept. 30, 1895; m. Edward O'Rourke Jr.; ch.: Edward, III, b. July 6, 1919.

448. GEORGE W. and MARGARET (KEIGER) BOWSER.

Children:

467. Normanda Bowser, m. William Keeper.
468. Louisa Bowser, m. Austin Pettit.
469. Elnora Bowser, m. Chalmer Morrison.
470. Lucinda Bowser, b. 1843.
471. Nelson Bowser, b. 1845.
472. George W. Bowser, b. Mar. 29, 1847; m. (1) Mary E. Lake; (2) Margaret Van Auken; ch.: Earnest M., Raymond E., Nelson J., Grace, William, Maynard E.
473. Sylvester S. Bowser, b. 1849; m. Elizabeth Morris; ch.: Charles W., Cora E., Nettie A., Vertie L., Edna V., Eva A.
474. Elizabeth Bowser, b. 1850; m. Neil Ryan.
475. William Bowser, b. 1852.
476. Charlotte Bowser, b. 1854; m. Addison Morrison.
477. Jesse Bowser.
478. Lucy Anna Bowser, b. 1859.
479. Lydia Bowser.

449. HENRY J. and MARY (KEIGER) BOWSER.

Children:

480. Lucinda Bowser, b. 1836; m. Solomon Duly.
481. Isaiah Bowser, b. 1837; m. (1) Elizabeth Herrod; (2) Samantha Bittner; ch.: Nelson J., m. Lucy White; Wesley; Etta; Clark E.
482. Adelia Bowser, b. 1840; m. Simon P. Stroup.
483. Elmira Bowser, b. 1842; m. James Hollopeter.
484. Alonzo Bowser, b. 1844.
485. Henry Bowser, b. 1846.
486. Wesley Bowser, b. 1848; m. Sarah Jackson.
487. Frank Bowser.
488. Theodore Bowser, m. Celia A. Gloyd; ch.: Raymond, Ivan C., Homer G.
489. Francillia L. Bowser, m. David L. Myers.
490. Mary Bowser, m. James F. Hollopeter (1881).

450. SAMUEL and JANE (WATERS) BOWSER.

Children:

491. Mary Ann Bowser, m. Nathan Wyatt.
492. Sophia Elizabeth Bowser, m. ——— Depew.
493. Sarah Jane Bowser, m. R. H. Brockaw.

494. Emily Bowser, m. Lewis Brockaw.
495. Samuel O. Bowser, m. (1) Rebecca Hiette; (2) Kansas Matheson.
496. Ella R. Bowser, b. April, 1861; m. Daniel Stoner.

SAMUEL and MARGARET GOOD.

Children:

497. Daisy Margaret Bowser.
498. Carrie Bowser.

451. WILLIAM and REBECCA (PAFF) BOWSER.

Children:

499. Sarah A. Bowser, b. 1845.
500. Jacob H. Bowser, b. 1847.
501. Lucy A. Bowser, b. 1849.
502. John Bowser, b. 1856.
503. William Bowser, b. 1857.
504. Andrew Bowser, b. 1859.
505. Isaac Bowser; address: Oakville, Calif.
506. Hattie Bowser.
507. Rebecca Bowser.

HENRY and (2) CATHARINE (WILLIAMS) BOWSER.

Children:

508. Lewis Bowser, b. Mar. 20, 1838; d. Feb., 1912; m. Elizabeth Noel; ch.: Arthur J., Edward C., Emerson L., Emily, Elizabeth, Bertrand F.
509. Maria Bowser, m. ——— Goodwin; address: Lafayette, Ind.
510. Lucy Bowser, m. (1) Benjamin Nickerson; (2) Charles Blair.
511. Martha Bowser.
512. Levi Bowser, b. 1840; m. Maria Nickerson; lived near Fort Wayne, Ind.; served in the Civil war and in the Indian campaigns in Wyoming under Col. Haggard of Logansport, Ind.; ch.: Edwin B.
513. Emma Bowser.

443. MICHAEL BOWSER. He was the youngest child. Went to Ohio and from Ohio to Missouri in 1856. His wife died in 1860 and he in 1864. He was a shoemaker.

Children:

514. Benjamin Smith Bowser, b. in Ohio, Feb. 4, 1836; m. Mary E. ——— in Missouri; lived in Compton, Calif., where his widow still resides.
515. John William Bowser, b. in Ohio, 1838; m. Hattie Cromer.
516. Catharine Bowser, m. Lewis McLean.
517. Mary Emeline Bowser, b. 1837; m. John Rineley.
518. Lewis William Bowser, b. in Ohio, Aug. 19, 1843; single; died in California.
519. Simon Philip Bowser, b. in Ohio, 1846; d. 1875; m. Mary Smith.
520. Mary Jane Bowser, m. James Stewart.

514. BENJAMIN SMITH and MARY E. BOWSER.

Children:

521. John William Bowser.
522. Mary Alice Bowser, m. ——— Brechenridge; live at Compton, Calif.
523. Emma Susan Bowser, m. D. J. Moody.
524. Lewis Martin Bowser.

515. JOHN WILLIAM and HATTIE (CROMER) BOWSER.

Children:

525. Hattie Bowser; lives at Morrison, Ill.
526. Mary Bowser; lives at Morrison, Ill.
527. John William Bowser, Jr.; lived at Los Angeles, Calif., 1903.
528. Harry Ed. Bowser; in Honolulu, Hawaii; Battery E, 11th Field Artillery; in the United States army for over 14 years.

516. CATHARINE (BOWSER) and LEWIS McLEAN.

Children:

529. Andrew McLean.
530. Michael McLean.
531. Benjamin McLean.
532. Lewis McLean.
533. James McLean.
534. Mary Jane McLean.
535. Julia McLean, m. ——— Butcher.

517. MARY E. (BOWSER) and JOHN RINELEY.

Children:

536. Daniel Rineley; lived at Fruitland, Iowa, 1903.
537. Mary Alice Rineley, m. ——— Knight.
538. Simon Rineley.
539. John Wilson Rineley.

520. MARY JANE (BOWSER) and JAMES STEWART.

Children:

540. Emma Stewart.
541. James Stewart.
542. Rachel Stewart.
543. William W. Stewart.

---

[3]

JOHN BOWSER FAMILY

by

CHARLES ARTHUR BOWSER*

*At my request Chas. A. Bowser has written this chapter on John Bowser, his ancestor, the oldest of the three brothers who landed at Baltimore. See biography of Charles A.—(Author.)

In 1733, as the compiler of this volume has told you, a few Baussers (Bowsers) arrived in Philadelphia. There is evidence that in the same year three brothers named Bauser or Bausser arrived at Baltimore from Switzerland. The name was changed to the English form, "Bowser," although the old form of the name was retained by some of the descendants until over a century later. In most of the public records the clerks and recorders wrote the name "Bowser" although wills, deeds, etc., were signed Bauser or Bausser in German script. The latest example of this was a will signed by Adam Bowser of Armstrong County, Pa., in 1850. In Europe, at the present, it is spelled Bauser.

Before and during the War of the Revolution there were many Bowsers in Pennsylvania and some in Maryland. There are few records about some of these Bowsers and their relationship is very uncertain, Now, after a great deal of study, I venture to say that the three Bauser brothers who landed at Baltimore were John, Daniel and Henry. This chapter is on John Bowser, the second of that trio.

1. JOHN BAUSER, SR.
   Children:
   2. John Bauser, Jr.
   3. Peter Bauser.
   4. Henry Bauser.
   5. Barbara Bauser.
   6. Daniel Bauser.
   a7. Elizabeth Bauser.
   b8. Anna Bauser.

George, Lydia, Rebecca, Sarah, Samuel, and others are among the descendants of John, Daniel and Henry Bowser mentioned above.

These, no doubt, were related to Mathias, Sr., Mathias, Jr., Daniel, Christian and Jacob who landed at Philadelphia in 1733. Records show that Daniel's children lived in York County, Pa. In the same vicinity lived the children of John, one of the brothers. The third brother, Henry Bowser, probably lived in York or Lancaster counties, Pa., although the first record we have of him is the census of 1790. showing that he lived in Washington County, Md., and was head of a family of ten persons. This census record does not include Henry's son, John, who probably was in Lancaster County. This John was the great-grandfather of S. F. Bowser, the great manufacturer of Fort Wayne, Ind. But more of Henry Bowser's descendants later.

Let us now take up the family of John Bowser who landed at Baltimore. Four consecutive generations of Johns followed him so we will have to watch closely so as not to get the Johns mixed. Almost nothing is known of this first John, but we may say he was the eldest of the three brothers, and estimate the year of his birth as about 1710. Leaving Switzerland they came down the Rhine River in a plank boat with sails, no doubt transferring to a larger vessel at Rotterdam, Holland. The tradition is that they were forty-eight weeks on water, partly by reason of the wind blowing the ship back, and when they landed they were so weak, some fell down and some could hardly walk.

John was married and on this long ocean voyage to them a son was born. They called him Johannes (German for John). This son was my great-great-grandfather and was the ancestor of the Bowsers of Somerset County, Pa., and Garrett County, Md.

The son John grew up, probably somewhere between Baltimore and York, married, and had a farm in York County, Pa., in Shrewsbury Township.

Shrewsbury Township lies on the Maryland line and was at one time part of Lancaster County. On account of its large area it was divided in 1767 and Hopewell formed.

The following old record, published by the Pennsylvania German Society, is of great interest:

CHURCH REGISTER

of the

UNITED REFORMED AND LUTHERAN CHURCH

Called Blimyers

in

Hopewell Township, York County, Pa.

BIRTHS AND BAPTISMS—1772

BAUSER, PETER. Parents, John and Christina Bauser. Born August 12, 1770; baptized August 16, 1772. Witnesses, the parents.

BAUSER, BARBARA. Parents, John and Christina Bauser. Born July, 1772; baptized August 16, 1772. Witnesses, the parents.

This John Bauser is the same one who was born on the ocean.

Another record of him is as follows:

1783—Shrewsbury Township. List of names from assessment roll and census report made in 1783, by a special order of the county commissioners, in order to lay a special tax to defray the expenses of the Revolutionary war.

BAUSER, JOHN, 50 acres; tax, 30 pounds; 7 persons in the family. The seven persons no doubt were: John and his wife, Christina and their children, Henry, John, Jr., Peter, Barbara, and probably Elizabeth.

1790, Census of Shrewsbury Township, York County, Pa.:

BAUSIR, JOHN, 2 males of 16 years and upward; 2 females (one of these was probably a daughter Anna).

At this time John was about 57 years of age and it seems that Henry, John, Jr., and two of the daughters had left home or married. This Henry Bauser was my great-grandfather and was born December 25, 1765, in Pennsylvania. He, as well as John Jr., probably were born in York County. They may have left York County before their parents

However, as the reader can see by referring to John Bauser, Sr., bought land in Somerset County, Pa., in 1795. Also a little further on, that my great-grandfather, Henry, and his brothers and sisters were also in Somerset County.

We will leave this family in Somerset County now, and turn back to York County to see what we can do with John Bauser, Sr.'s, brothers and their descendants. Considering the size of the pioneer families it is reasonable to believe that John (one of the three brothers) had other children than the son John who was born on the ocean. And so we will take up Daniel Bauser of Paradise Township, York County, named, no doubt, after the Daniel who landed at Baltimore. The elder Daniel lived in an adjoining township, Manheim, near the Maryland line. The younger Daniel was born about 1740. He is recorded in the tax lists of Paradise Township for the years 1779, 1789, and 1781. In 1783 Daniel had 100 acres in Cumberland Township and there were seven persons in the family.

The next record of this Daniel is the census of 1800 for "Hopewell and Woodberry townships," Bedford County, Pa. By it we see that Daniel and his wife were then "of 45 and upwards" and with them were two sons of 16 and under 26 years of age. These were George and Henry, whom we find later near Dayton, Ohio. In the same census record is Philip Bowser, another son of Daniel. Philip and wife are written "of 16 and under 26" and have a daughter under 10 years. Soon after 1800 these families went to Ohio.

6. The children of Daniel Bowser, Sr., were:
   7. Daniel Bowser, Jr., b. about 1770 to 1773; d. near Dayton, Ohio.
   8. Barbara Bowser, b. in 1774; d. in her 91st year near Dayton, Ohio.
   9. Philip Bowser, b. about 1775; d. in 1838 in Elkhart County, Indiana.
   10. George Bowser, b. about 1780; d. about 1862 near Dayton, Ohio.
   11. Henry Bowser, b. about 1785; d. in 1852 near Dayton, Ohio.
   12. There may have been another son, William Bowser. A William Bowser, born about 1785, entered land in Madison Township, Montgomery County, Ohio (Dayton is the county seat), prior to 1812 in the vicinity of where Philip and the other Bowsers located.

The First Bowser in Ohio

8. Barbara Bowser, the daughter of Daniel, Sr., no doubt was the first Bowser in the State of Ohio. She was married to David Bowman before Daniel, Sr., and family left Bedford County, Pa. The following very interesting article is taken from a "History of Montgomery County, Ohio." Under the heading "Jefferson Township" we find:

"As early as 1798 could be seen one of Jefferson Township's pioneers in the person of David Bowman, whose name will long be remembered in connection with the early religious history of this section of Ohio, drifting, as it were, with his good wife and rudely constructed raft down the Ohio, on his way to the country about the Little Miami River, whither he was going, to build a mill for parties who had preceded him."

The mill was erected, and, Bowman, impressed with the country, remained, and, after living in the locality and milling several years, removed to the neighborhood of Miamisburg, and there lived several years, thence to Jefferson Township, buying ¼ section of land. He was a minister of the Gospel, belonging to the denomination called German Baptists. He was instrumental in establishing several churches west of the Great Miami.

He was born near Hagerstown, Md., March 30, 1775, and at the age of eighteen went to Frankstown, Pa., and learned the trade of cabinet making. (Frankstown was then in Bedford County.) He was united in marriage with Barbara Bouser and there were born to them six children:

13. Esther Bowman.
14. John Bowman.
15. Polly Bowman.
16. Katie Bowman.
17. David Bowman.
18. Betsey Bowman.

4. The writer regrets that there is not space enough to tell about all the descendants of these families. Before leaving Ohio, we will briefly go over the records of Henry Bowser and Frances, his wife, and their descendants. Henry was a son of John and Christina Bauser of York and Somerset Counties, Pa. The writer (his great-grandson), besides obtaining information from relatives and other sources, has visited these counties as well as Warren County, Ohio, and collected much valuable material from the courthouse records.

In Somerset County, Pa., Henry Bowser first lived in Brothers Valley Township. A tax list of this township for 1796 includes the names of Henry Bouser and John Bouser. Henry Bowser married Frances Coleman, who lived near Berlin, in Brothers Valley Township.

Deeds dated 1798 show that Henry Bowser was in this township in 1798 and bought and sold land. The next deed shows that he was in Addison Township and bought a tract of land there called Eminent, in the year 1802. On the same date he bought a smaller tract of land in Addison Township. Two deeds dated April 1, 1815, record that Henry Bowser and wife sold these tracts of land for $2,200 and $800, respectively. At this time Henry Bowser was the father of nine children—Philip, John, George, Elizabeth, Christina, Susannah, Henry, Daniel and Sarah. These were born in Somerset County, Pa., with the possible exception of the first three, who may have been born in Allegany County, Md., as the parents lived close to the Mason and Dixon line which at that time was not settled. It is said that George Bowser was born in Allegany County.

Now, no doubt, Henry and family started on their trip down rivers and through forests to their Ohio home. Perhaps, like some others, they floated down the Ohio River on a raft to Cincinnati, then went by wagon toward Dayton. They located 36 miles northeast of Cincinnati and a few miles south of Dayton, and near Springboro, Warren County. Springboro was laid out in 1815. A Warren County deed, dated June 17, 1815, tells us that Henry Bowser paid Benjamin Kell $3,480 for 174 acres of land between the Miami rivers.

The family lived about a mile from the Little Miami River, and in dry seasons Henry watered his cattle there. He had a large orchard and dried much fruit. He took meat and other produce to Cincinnati to sell. It took one day to go and one to return.

A deed dated December 14, 1822, records that "Henry Bowser and his wife, Fanny, in consideration of the sum of 75 cents, grant to Henry Frey

Christian Null, Christian Blinn and John Philip Frey, a parcel of land for the use of the Society of the United Brethren in Christ in Warren County as a site for a meeting house." This agrees with the story my father told me many years ago, which is as follows:

"He (Henry Bowser) built a church on his place and preached until he went to Indiana. During protracted meetings people would come to Henry's house to sleep, usually lying on the floor on account of their number. The people were United Brethren. Wherever he went the house was crowded and a good meeting held."

CHILDREN OF HENRY AND FRANCES (COLEMAN) BOWSER

19. Philip Bowser, b. ———; d. in Ohio before 1832.
20. John Bowser, b. ———; d. in Ohio before 1833.
21. George Bowser, b. in 1800; came from Pennsylvania to Ohio with his parents in 1815; married Elizabeth Manning; they lived in Preble County, Ohio, from about 1830 to about 1831; he died in Centralia, Boone County, Mo., in 1884.
22. Elizabeth Bowser, b. in 1801 or before; m. John Ungery; d. in Indianapolis about 1870.
23. Christina Bowser, b. in 1802; m. Lewis Crepps; about 1895 was living in Muscatine County, Iowa.
24. Susannah Bowser, b. Dec. 1, 1804; m. about 1826 in Ohio to James Mullen; he was born in 1789 and died in 1854; she died near Indianapolis, Oct. 15, 1870; they were parents of Daniel, Jacob, John, Henry, Lemuel, Elmira, Joel, James, Nancy, Harrison, Larned, Morgan and Susan Mullen.
25. Henry Bowser, Jr., b. in March, 1810; when five years old he went with his parents from Pennsylvania to Ohio, and in 1831, migrated to Indiana and settled near Indianapolis, where he resided until his death, Oct. 18, 1883; in May, 1833, m. Mary Moore.
26. Daniel Bowser, b. March 31, 1812, in Somerset County, Pa.; in 1831 came with his father and Henry, Jr., and sister Sarah to Marion County, Indiana; his sisters, Rebecca and Barbara, and their mother, either came at this time or soon after.

21. GEORGE and ELIZABETH (MANNING) BOWSER.

Children:

27. John Duel Bowser, b. July 19, 1824; m. Nancy Miner; d. Jan. 4, 1900, in Callaway County, Mo.
28. Hannah Bowser, b. in 1828; m. a Mr. Bowman and lived in Cedar Rapids, Iowa.
29. Henry Bowser, b. June 6, 1831; m. Miriam ———; d. in El Reno, Okla., in 1900.
30. Theophilus Bowser, b. in Preble County, Ohio, July 17, 1836; m. Mary A. Scott; lived in Pike County, Mo.
31. Mary Ann Bowser, b. Sept. 1, 1833, near Eaton, Ohio, in 1850; the family started to the then Great West and settled in Illinois; m. William Young, b. in 1823 in Scotland; they were married in 1853 and came to the vicinity of Farmer City, where she resided until her death, Oct. 23, 1911.
32. Samuel Thomas Bowser, b. March 31, 1839, in Ohio; has resided in Illinois, Iowa, Missouri, and South Dakota; last was in Hillsboro, Ore.; m. Mary J. Ede in 1868; was a veterinary surgeon.

25. HENRY, JR. and MARY (MOORE) BOWSER.

Children:

33. Catharine E. Bowser, b. in 1835 and d. in 1858.
34. John W. Bowser, b. in 1837 and d. in 1858.

35. Edward Thomas Bowser, b. April 27, 1841; m. Martha J. Kitley; they were living near Indianapolis in 1920
36. Fanny Ann Bowser, b. March 27, 1843; m. John E. Myles; d. in Marion County, Ind., Mar. 19, 1888.
37. Sarah E. Bowser, b. May 11, 1845; m. William Rowney; d. in Marion County, Ind., Apr. 18, 1875.
38. William Henry Bowser, b. Oct. 13, 1847; m. Florence L. Shimer; d. near Indianapolis, Jan. 25, 1895.
39. Mary Jane Bowser, b. Sept. 11, 1850; m. Edgar Head.

26. DANIEL and HANNAH (MULLEN) BOWSER. In 1835 Daniel married Hannah Mullen, born in Warren County, Ohio, Dec. 16, 1816. In February, 1834, Daniel's father gave him 160 acres of land which was then about five miles southeast of Indianapolis. Here he lived until his death, May 21, 1876. Hannah, who was the writer's grandmother, died April 19, 1874, at the old home on the Shelbyville Pike. Here were born all their children:

40. Levi C. Bowser, b. Jan. 14, 1838; m. Caroline Dawson; the names of their children are: Charles, Harry, Thomas, Laura and Nellie; was in the grocery business about 25 years; has lived in Indianapolis about sixty years. Went with Jack Hoffman to Denver, Colo., in 1859, and was gone about six or eight months. They walked a great part of the way. One time there were buffalo around them as far as they could see. They had 14 yoke of oxen to start with but at the end of the journey only two were left. They had left a sort of cart on the hind wheels of one of their wagons.
41. Nancy Ann Bowser, b. Apr. 2, 1842; m. Robert D. Graham, a farmer; no children; he died in 1908; in 1920 Aunt Nan, as we called her, was living in Indianapolis.
42. Henry Davis Bowser, b. Dec. 14, 1844; d. Nov. 12, 1876, in Indiana.
43. Sarah Ellen Bowser, d. in infancy.
44. William Washington Bowser, b. July 4, 1849; he worked his father's farm until 1872, when he went to Kansas. Here he married Nettie Tague in 1874, then with her rode in a covered wagon back to his old home near Indianapolis; in 1882 they went to Illinois and in 1886 went from there to Southern California, where he engaged in growing oranges; he died May 11, 1914, as the result of a tree which he was cutting down, falling on him. This occurred in Arkansas. Since then Mrs. Nettie (Tague) Bowser, my mother, has resided in Los Angeles, Calif. There were four children: Charles Arthur (the writer), b. July 13, 1881, on the old farm which Henry, Sr., gave to Daniel in 1834; Emory E., b. in 1883, and d. in 1892; William Harrison, b. in California, Oct. 4, 1888; and Leslie Earl, b. in California, Dec. 31, 1890.
45. Mary P. Bowser, b. Oct. 6, 1851; m. Virgil Tevis, a Methodist minister; d. Oct. 27, 1895; ch.: Charles and Ruth.
46. James Marion Bowser, b. Feb. 28, 1840; in the 29th Ind. Inf. in the Civil war; d. single, Jan. 19, 1871, in Indiana.
47. Hannah Melissa Bowser, b. Mar. 29, 1856; a graduate of DePauw University; m. C. H. Horine, of Chicago.
48. Sarah Bowser, b. Aug. 24, 1814, in Pennsylvania; in 1833 m. John Moore of Marion County, Ind; they lived near Indianapolis until his death in 1889; Sarah d. Dec. 9, 1899, in that city; the names of their children are: Thomas, William, Margaret, Hannah, Richison, Isabelle, John, Sarah, Calvin, Catharine, Mary and Joseph.
49. Rebecca Bowser, b. Jan. 1816, in Ohio; in 1837 m. Gottlieb Beck; he was born in 1811 in Wittenburg, Germany; he died in 1897 and she died Mar. 15, 1894; their children: Henry, Elma, Maria, Sarah,

Julius, George W., James M. and John Benjamin; they lived in Johnson County, Ind.

50. Barbara Bowser, b. in 1820 in Ohio; in Marion County, Ind., Dec. 27, 1835, m. Gottlieb Beck, but died in January, 1836; he later married her sister Rebecca.

1. JOHN BAUSER, SR. and CHRISTINA.

We must now leave these families and turn back to their ancestor, John Bauser, Sr., who came from York County to Somerset County, Pa. A Somerset County deed, dated June 6, 1795, says:

"A Warrant dated 22nd December, 1784, did grant unto John Barkley 200 acres of land which by warrant dated 24th June, 1793, John Barkley then granted to Ludwick Barkley.

Ludwick Barkley, of Brothers Valley Township, for 200 pounds paid by John Bauser, granted to John Bauser said tract of land, surveyed or to be surveyed."

A Somerset County deed, dated May 7, 1817, in which John Bowser, Jr., buys 300 acres of John Bowser, Sr., mentions Henry, Peter, Anna, Elizabeth and Barbara Bowser, as brothers and sisters of John Bouser, Jr. John Bouser, Jr. agrees to pay $20.00 yearly to each brother and sister until $1,300.00 is paid. Payments to begin one year after their father's decease. John Bouser, Sr., died in Brothers Valley Township, Somerset County, Pa., in January, 1822. His widow, Christina Bouser, died in the same place, 1827, at an advanced age.
Children:

2. JOHN BOUSER, JR. (known also as John Bauser, III), b. in 1774, or earlier; married Magdalena Bittner, Nov. 8, 1796, in Brothers Valley Township. He lived in that township until 1820 or later. He died in 1841 in Somerset County, Pa. John, Jr. and his wife were the parents of several daughters and a son, John. This John was born in 1799, and died in 1860. He married Susan Hensel, born in 1801, and they lived in Greenville Township, Somerset County.

John and Susan (Hensel) Bowser's children are as follows:

51. William Bouser, b. 1833; m. Elizabeth Fluck.

a51. John J. Bouser, b. Sept. 20, 1836; blacksmith for 50 years, first in Somerset County, then in West Moreland County, Pa.; living with his daughter, Mrs. Dora M. Rose, in Braddock, Pa. (1922); m. Mary M. Lenhart; ch.: Madison L., Charles A., of Johnstown, Pa., Elsie K., Cyrus L., and Dora M.

52. Elizabeth Bowser, m. John Shultz.

53. Mary Bowser, b. in 1840; m. Conrad Stoy.

54. Levi Bowser, b. 1842; m. Amanda Fluck; d. about 1871.

55. Lewis Bowser, m. ——— Fluck.

56. Sarah Bowser, d. aged 22.

57. Eliza Bowser (youngest child), m. John Blank.

4. HENRY BAUSER, b. Dec. 25, 1865; brother of John Bauser, Jr.

3. PETER BAUSER, b. Aug. 12, 1770, in Hopewell Township, York County, Pa.; m. Elizabeth Blickensdarfer, b. in 1777; he died June 10, 1847, in Somerset County, Pa.

a7. ELIZABETH BAUSER, m. ——— Gidinger; living in Pennsylvania in 1882.

5. BARBARA BOUSER, b. in July, 1772, in Hopewell Township, York County, Pa.; m. ——— Bittner; living in Somerset County in 1822.

b8. ANNA BOUSER; probably died about 1820.

3. PETER and ELIZABETH (BLICKENSDARFER) BOUSER.

Children:

58. John P. Bowser, b. Mar. 15, 1807; d. Sept. 17, 1883; m. Barbara Beeghley.
59. Christina Bowser, b. June 7, 1801; d. Feb. 7, 1883; m. Jacob Lenhart, b. 1793; d. 1855; ch.: Barbara, Catharine, Peter J., Elizabeth, Jacob E., Kiziah, Susanna, Sarah, Livinia and Dianah.
60. Jacob Bowser, b. 1802; m. Elizabeth Sweitzer; lived in Allegany County, Md., near Selbysport.
61. Peter Bowser, m. Mary Sweitzer; killed by a falling tree about 1841.
62. Daniel Bowser, b. Dec. 14, 1814; d. Aug. 19, 1886; m. Harriet Schrack; they lived in the old log house which his father Peter built soon after 1800; this house is still standing in excellent preservation and is located in Addison Township, Somerset County, Pa., on old Peter Bowsers farm which adjoins the Maryland line. Daniel S. Bowser, a grandson of Peter, now lives in this old homestead.
63. Joel Bowser, b. Jan. 21, 1819; single; died in Somerset County, Pa., Oct. 30, 1900.
64. Susan Bowser, b. about 1821; d. October, 1884; m. John C. Diehl; lived in the Cove, Garret County, Md.
65. Elizabeth Bowser, m. ——— Bauman; lived in Maryland.
66. Catharine Bowser, b. about 1810; m. Henry Diehl.
67. Gabriel Bowser, b. 1812 in Pennsylvania; d. about 1883; m. Hettie Bittinger, farmer in Garrett County, formerly Alleghany County, Md.

Children:

a67. Mathias Bowser, d. single about 1891; kept store in Grantsville, Md.
b67. Perry Bowser, b. 1855; m. Emma Bittinger; lives near Bittinger, Md.; ch.: Edward F., Ida J., Lloyd, Anna, Cora and Winnie.
c67. James Bowser, b. 1852; m. Sophia ———; lived in Garrett County, Md.; ch.: Minnie, Della, Oma and Drussie.

58. JOHN P. and BARBARA (BEEGHLEY) BOWSER. Lived in Summit Township, Somerset County, Pa.

Children:

68. Mary Bowser, b. June 30, 1831.
69. Peter J. Bowser, b. May 2, 1833; d. Dec. 1, 1904; m. Elizabeth Spiker; they lived in Summit Township, Somerset County; their children were: Barbara, Solomon and John.
70. Jacob Bowser, b. Jan. 8, 1837; d. June 16, 1910, at Myersdale, Pa.; m. Caroline Hersh; ch.: Lydia, Lucinda, Catharine, Emanuel, John J., Anna, Milton, William, Carrie, Elizabeth and Mollie.
71. Elizabeth Bowser, b. Mar. 19, 1835.
72. Susan Bowser, b. Aug. 21, 1840; m. Moses Bauman.
73. Samuel J. Bowser, b. July 22, 1843; d. Jan. 16, 1905; m. Sarah Wegley.

60. JACOB and ELIZABETH (SWEITZER) BOWSER.

Children:

74. Peter Bowser, b. about 1830; d. about 1917; he and his wife Jane lived near Accident, Md.; ch.: Mary, Dolphus, Clara, Samuel, Ella, Anna.
75. Harriet Bowser; died young.
76. Catharine Bowser, m. Andrew Colflash; ch.: William, George, John, Emanuel, Jackson, Orville, Kate, Mary, Malinda, Lydia and Ella.
77. Joseph Bowser, b. about 1840; d. 1918; m. Ellen Logue.

78. Thomas J. Bowser, b. June 12, 1842; d. July 21, 1914; m. Catharine Heimbaugh; ch.: Robert J., Charles and Albert.
79. Daniel Bowser, m. Catharine Hileman; ch.: Harvey, John, Peter, Mary, Meshek, Archibald, Truman and Frank W.
80. Susan Bowser, m. William J. Young.
81. Hiram Bowser, m. Barbara Brown; lived near Accident, Md.; ch.: Cornelius C., Emory, Effie, Ella, Sarah.

a81. Cornelius Bowser, b. ———; m. Lucinda Livengood; ch.: Alvina, b. 1877; Joseph E., b. 1879; George; William H.; Ernest; Samuel and Jennie.

82. Ammia Bowser, b. 1850; m. Susan Bane; ch.: Stella, John C., Drusilla, Laura, Samuel, May, Charles, Pearl and Bertie.
83. Mary E. Bowser, m. Andrew Pysell; live near Deer Park, Md.
84. Jacob E. Bowser, b. 1854 in Maryland, Md.; m. Susan Brown; live at Selbysport, Md.; ch.: Wallace, Dora, Annie, William Frederick, Margaret, Sarah, Earl, Clara and Henry Oscar.
85. Annie Bowser, b. July 22, 1861; lives in Oakland, Md.; ch.: William D.

61. PETER and MARY (SWEITZER) BOWSER.

Children:

86. John W. Bowser, b. 1832 in Maryland; m. Rebecca Speicher.
87. Jacob Bowser, b. 1827 in Maryland; m. Catharine Boyer.
88. Peter Bowser, m. Minerva Turney.
89. Elizabeth Bowser, m. John C. Diehl.
90. Lydia Bowser, b. 1837 in Maryland; m. William Ross.
91. Susan Bowser, m. John Beachey.
92. William Bowser, b. about 1842; d. 1882; m. Diana Lenhart.
93. Sarah Bowser, m. Harrison Turney.

62. DANIEL and HARRIET (SCHROCK) BOWSER.

Children:

94. Mary Elizabeth Bowser, b. July 19, 1853; m. Thomas P. Green.
95. Joseph S. Bowser, b. Sept. 25, 1854; m. Mary Upholt.
96. Salina Bowser, b. Feb. 18, 1856; m. George Oester.
97. Daniel S. Bowser, b. Sept. 28, 1857; m. Agnes R. Sellers.
98. Franklin J. Bowser, b. Oct. 29, 1859; m. Lucinda Fike.
99. Harriet Bowser, b. July 8, 1863; m. William Sellers.
100. Susan Bowser, b. June 20, 1869; m. John Sellers.

JOHN AND EVE BOWSER

It is probable John Bowser of Lancaster, Pa., was a brother or a close relative of Mathias Bowser, Sr. He moved from Lancaster to Cumberland County, thence to Bedford County, Pa. Cumberland County was organized February 27, 1750. Bedford County was formed out of the western part of Cumberland March 9, 1771. Colerain Township was created by the Court of Cumberland County in 1767. Bedford, Colerain and Cumberland Townships in 1772 included the whole of the present Bedford County. It is probable John and Eve Bowser moved from Lancaster to this part of Cumberland County in 1768. The first record of any Bowser in Bedford County, after the creation of the county in 1771, is the name of John Bowser, Bedford Township, 1772, a taxable with 100 acres of land, 2 horses and 1 cow. In 1774 he had 150 acres. (Pennsylvania Arch., 3d Series, Vol. 25, page 456.) In a deed by "Miller" John Bowser (a grandson of John Bowser) of Colerain Township, to Adam Fink, the deed says: "70¾ acres thereof being a part of a tract surveyed in pursuance of a warrant dated January 13, 1774, and for which Thomas and John Penn esquires, then proprietors, of Pennsylvania, granted their patent to John Bowser, October 12, 1774." Six children are mentioned in the will of John Bowser, Recorded in Book I, page 270, Bedford, Pa., as follows: George; Michael; Elizabeth, married to John Mauk, and Elizabeth, married to Henry Beckley; Eve married to John Arthurs, and children of his deceased daughter Modelena (Magdalena) Swoveland; also, "I give my Great Bible to my grandson John Bowser." (Miller John.) This will was probated May 20, 1809. George was the oldest son of John Bowser and Eve. A Swiss custom gives to the oldest son the right to name his oldest son after the child's grandfather. ("Descendants of Jacob Hochstetler.") Therefore George Bowser named his oldest son John, later known as "Miller" John.

1. JOHN and EVE BOWSER.

   Children:

   2. George Bowser, d. at the age of 84; m. Margaret Swartz, d. aged 85.
   3. Michael Bowser.
   4. Eve Bowser, m. John Arthurs.
   5. Elizabeth Bowser, m. John Mauk.
   6. Magdalena Bowser, m. ——— Swoveland.

2. GEORGE (2); JOHN (1). By the will of John Bowser his son George came into possession of the homestead in St. Clair Twp., Bedford Co., on condition of the payment of 670 "pounds lawful money" to the other heirs. This property was later owned by George's son "Miller" John, and deeded by the latter to Fink, as noted above.

   Children:

   7. Isaac Bowser, m. Sarah Berkheimer, daughter of Catharine (Bowser) and John Berkheimer. (See under Mathias Bowser.)
   8. Jacob Bowser, m. Catharine Imler.
   9. John Bowser, m. Margaret Zimmerman.
   10. George Bowser, Jr., b. 1791; d. 1846; m. Elizabeth Zimmerman, b. 1798; d. 1861.
   11. Mary Bowser; was killed by a fall.
   12. Catharine Bowser, b. 1808; d. Oct. 19, 1866; m. Jacob Berkheimer, b. 1806; d. July 9, 1874. (See 35 under Mathias.)
   13. Eve Bowser, d. Mar. 17, 1875, aged 79 yrs. 2 mos. and 15 days; m. Peter Amick, d. Sept. 29, 1877, aged 84 yrs. 3 mos. and 12 days.
   14. Margaret Bowser, m. Peter Berkheimer. (See 30 under Mathias.)

7. ISAAC BOWSER (3); GEORGE (2); JOHN (1). The father of Isaac Bowser, George, had a line team on the turnpike between Pittsburgh and Philadelphia. He owned a flour mill and "distillery" on Babbs Creek near St. Clairsville, Bedford Co., Pa. Isaac run the mill. Isaac and Sarah (Berkheimer) Bowser had the following children:

15. Joseph Bowser, d. about 1905.
16. Catharine W. Bowser, b. Nov. 1, 1825; d. June 25, 1898; m. Frances
17. George W. Bowser, b. Nov. 1, 1825; d. June 25, 1898; m. Frances Matilda Gillett, b. Feb. 18, 1839; d. Dec. 10, 1911.
18. Hannah Bowser, d. June 24, 1891; m. George Bollinger.
19. Henry Bowser.
20. Eve Bowser, d. 1906.
21. John Bowser, m. Mary Echert.
22. David P. Bowser, b. June 30, 1838; d. Apr. 3, 1882; m. Elizabeth Lyons, b. July 20, 1835; d. Jan. 14, 1912. (See under Mathias, 69.)
23. Margaret Bowser, m. John W. Cunningham.
24. Dr. Isaac Bowser, m. Annie M. Smith.
25. Sarah Bowser, b. 1840.
26. Solomon Bowser.
27. William Bowser, d. about 1907; m. Elizabeth Tree.

17. GEORGE (4); ISAAC (3); GEORGE (2); JOHN (1). George Bowser shortly after his marriage moved from St. Clairsville, Bedford Co., to Sunbury, Northumberland Co., Pa., where he remained the rest of his life. He was a conductor on the Pennsylvania Railroad. The writer is under great obligation to "Uncle" George for valuable information he gave us in College days long before we dreamed we would some time be writing the story of the Bowser family. The scraps of paper upon which we wrote down his interesting memories of his people in Bedford County we still have as precious mementos of many happy hours in his hospitable home. We were with him in the few last peaceful hours ere his manly, gracious spirit went to meet his Lord. He and all his family were members of the Baptist church:

Children:

28. Charles T. Bowser, b. Sept. 25, 1858; d. May 12, 1906; m. Mary Snyder, b. Apr. 28, 1863.
29. Samuel H. Bowser, b. July 16, 1860; m. Crecie Belle Nesbit, b. Sept. 3, 1862.
30. Thomas L. Bowser, b. Nov. 6, 1863; d. Aug. 5, 1901; single.
31. Sarah E. Bowser, b. July 28, 1870; m. Jesse J. Sankey, b. Dec. 18, 1869.

28. CHARLES T. and MARY (SNYDER) BOWSER. Charles T. Bowser was a successful business man, conducting a large produce and grocery store. He was a trustee in the Baptist Church.

Children:

32. May Irene Bowser, b. July 21, 1890; m. Claude C. Renn, b. Sept. 5, 1888; ch.: Claude R., b. Jan. 10, 1915; Robert K., b. Oct. 10, 1920.
33. Edna Viola Bowser, b. Dec. 18, 1891.
34. George Frank Bowser, b. Feb. 7, 1893; m. Margaret Green, b. Jan. 31, 1897; d. May, 1920.
35. G. Edward Bowser, b. Jan. 26, 1895; m. Genevive Price, b. 1900.
36. Charles Luther Bowser, b. July 8, 1897.
37. Helen Louisa Bowser, b. Aug. 22, 1900.
38. William Howard Bowser, b. Dec. 12, 1901; d. Feb. 26, 1920.

29. SAMUEL H. and GRECIE BELLE (NESBIT) BOWSER. Samuel H. Bowser has charge of the Pennsylvania Railroad station at the important junction town of Sunbury, Pa. Like his brother Charles, he serves as an officer in the Baptist Church:

Children:
- 39. Rosella Bowser, b. Dec. 17, 1882; d. Aug. 8, 1903.
- 40. George Alvin Leo Bowser, b. July 20, 1890; d. Dec. 11, 1915.
- 41. Charles Bailey Bowser, b. Sept. 8, 1892.
- 42. Myrtle Belle Bowser, b. Mar. 12, 1895; m. Charles Grove Royer, b. Jan. 27, 1897; child: Charles Huston, b. May 15, 1921.

31. SARAH E. and JESSE J. SANKEY. Mr. Sankey is a merchant, Sunbury, Pa.

Children:
- 43. Samuel Francis Sankey, b. Mar. 25, 1907.
- 44. Irma Belle Sankey, b. Sept. 13, 1910.
- 45. Marjorie Irene Sankey, b. Nov. 25, 1912.

22. DAVID (4); ISAAC (3); GEORGE (2); JOHN (1). David Bowser's widow with her two children moved to Crafton, Pa., about 1900. She died there. Both of his children live at Crafton.

Children:
- 46. Alpha L. Bowser; mail carrier.
- 47. Catharine Bowser.

24. ISAAC (4); ISAAC (3); GEORGE (2); JOHN (1). Dr. Isaac Bowser was a dentist at Woodbury, Pa.

Children:
- 48. Seward Bowser; in business in Philadelphia, Pa.
- 49. Howard Bowser.
- 50. Haller Bowser.
- 51. Carrie Bowser, m. ——— Frantz; live in Lancaster, Pa.

8. JACOB (3); GEORGE (2); JOHN (1). Jacob Bowser lived in the Blue Knob section, Blair Co., Pa., where he died about 1872. The Blue Knob is also known as the Schwitz because of its likeness to the former homeland of at least some of our Bowser family in Switzerland. Some of Jacob and Catharine (Imler) Bowser's descendants are still living in the Blue Knob region. The religious character of Jacob is disclosed in giving his sons Bible names.

Children:
- 52. Conrad Bowser, b. about 1868; lived in Juniata Twp. (Blue Knob), Blair Co., Pa.
- 53. Isaac Bowser, b. 1828; lived in Johnstown, Pa.
- 54. Aaron Bowser.
- 55. Moses Bowser, b. 1831; m. Mary Ritchie, b. 1834; d. 1897.
- 56. John Bowser, veteran of the Civil war; m. Sarah Bloom, d. about 1866; lived in Altoona, Pa.; b. 1838.
- 57. Susannah Bowser, b. 1824.
- 58. Daniel L. Bowser, b. 1833; d. at Altoona, Pa., Nov. 8, 1902; m. Mary Corl.
- 59. David Bowser, b. 1842; m. Elizabeth Feathers.
- 61. Joseph Bowser.
- 62. Gideon Bowser.
- a62. Jacob Bowser, b. 1797.
- b62. Elizabeth Bowser, b. 1835.
- c62. Catharine Bowser, b. 1797.

55. MOSES (4); JACOB (3); GEORGE (2); JOHN (1).

63. Laana Bowser, m. J. Q. Adams, Roaring Springs, Pa.
64. Rebecca E. Bowser, b. 1858; m. John Conrad, Union Twp., Bedford Co., Pa.
65. Emanuel Bowser, d. young.
66. Ida Bowser, b. 1869; m. George Berkheimer, Greenfield Twp., Bedford Co.
67. Harry Edmund Bowser, b. 1871; m. Celestia Ernest.
68. Elizabeth Bowser, b. 1860; m. George Conrad.
69. Catharine Bowser, b. 1861; m. David Martin.
70. John Calvin Bowser, b. 1865; m. Della Diehl.
a70. Mary Bowser, b. 1867; m. William George.

59. DAVID (4); JACOB (3); GEORGE (2); JOHN (1).

Children:

71. William Bowser, m. Julia Dishong.
72. John Bowser, m. Eve Imler.
73. David Sylvester Bowser, m. Jane Eller.
74. Jeremiah Bowser, m. Addie Lydicks.
75. Maud Bowser, m. Charles Boyles.
76. Aaron Bowser, m. Lucy Berkheimer.
77. Marietta Bowser.
78. Dolph Bowser.
79. Anna Bowser, m. C. A. Diehl; ch.: Mary, Samuel, Crawford, David, Vernon, Goldie, Francis, Annie, Marie, Guy, Harry, Violet.

58. DANIEL (4); JACOB (3); GEORGE (2); JOHN (1). Daniel L. Bowser was a veteran of the Civil war. He died soon after the war closed, in Altoona, Pa. He married (1) Mary Corl.

Children:

80. George B. Bowser; lives at 2116 Fourth Ave., Altoona, Pa.
81. Franklin Austin Bowser, b. Feb. 18, 1856; living near Newry, Pa.
82. David Bowser.
83. William Bowser.
84. Angeline Bowser.
85. Emma Bowser.
86. Rebecca Bowser.

Children of the second marriage:

87. Myrtle Bowser, m. Solomon Sleek.
88. Carrie Bowser, m. ——— Aungst.
89. Alberta Bowser, m. John Schniddle.
90. Millie Bowser; lives in Philadelphia.
91. Jacob Bowser, deceased.
92. Ida May Bowser, d. at Queen, Pa., July 8, 1904.

81. FRANKLIN AUGUSTUS BOWSER.

93. Della Grace Bowser, m. ——— Eicher.
94. Sarah Bertha, m. ——— Aungst.
95. Rhoda Jane Bowser, m. ——— Bowmaster.
96. Emma May Bowser, m. Harvey Berkheimer; live at Gaysport, Pa.
97. Lemon Augustus Bowser.
98. Ralph Earl Bowser.
99. Harry Franklin Bowser.
100. Merle Emory Bowser.

10. GEORGE (3); GEORGE (2); JOHN (1). George Bowser, known as Blackhawk George, was married to Elizabeth Zimmers (or Zimmerman).

Children:

101. Philip Bowser.
102. Anthony Bowser, m. Mary Grove.
103. George Bowser, m. ——— Fickes.
104. Frederick Bowser, m. ——— Fickes. George and Frederick were twins and married sisters.
105. Elizabeth Bowser, m. ——— Mauk.
106. Mary Bowser, m. Daniel Bush, Roaring Springs, Bedford Co., Pa.
107. Job Bowser.
108. Susanna Bowser.

13. EVE (3); GEORGE (2); JOHN (1). Eve Bowser, the granddaughter of John and Eve, and daughter of George and Margaret Swartz, married Peter Amick. "In 1815 Peter A. Amick came from Adams County, Pa., where he was born in 1793, and settled on the land where the borough of St. Clairsville, Bedford Co., now stands. Mr. and Mrs. Amick moved into a house which was without windows and doors. At first they hung up quilts which served in the place of doors. Shortly after settling here Mr. Amick began keeping tavern, and as his means permitted he added to his house and otherwise improved it. He was commissioned the first postmaster of the town and the office has been in the hands of the family ever since.. He kept hotel and worked at his trade (coopering) until 1877, when he died in the 87th year of his age." (Hist. Bedford and Somerset Counties.) The writer had the pleasure of a visit to this picturesque village and making pictures of Peter Amick's quaint old hotel and store. The long two-story building, which elongated as business demanded, is well preserved and is precisely the same as in the days when Mr. Amick entertained his guests and prospered there. None of his family, however, are living there. Jacob Bowser is conducting a store in the place. Benjamin S. Bowser told the writer that John Amick, son of Peter Amick, with his sister "Beckie" came out to Armstrong County in 1838 or 1839. He also stated that Joseph Bowser, son of Noah, was an uncle of John Amick. Reynolds Bowser also claimed relationship with Eve (Bowser) Amick, mother of John Amick. But we have not been able to discover even the possibility of such relationship.

Children:

109. Margaret Amick, b. 1823; d. July 9, 1880; m. (1) ——— Beam; (2) Aaron Grove.
110. George B. Amick, d. 1893; m. Mary Hinsling, b. 1825; d. 1908.
111. John H. B. Amick; m. Maria Imes.
112. Sarah Amick, d. 1867; m. Josiah Hite, Roaring Springs, Pa.
113. Jacob F. Amick, b. 1826; d. 1858; m. Mary Furney.
114. Matilda Amick; died young.
115. William B. Amick; killed in Civil war; m. Catharine Wortz.

110. GEORGE B. and MARY (HINSLING) AMICK.

Children:

116. John H. B. Amick; m. Sue Wile; dead; was a physician in Philadelphia, Pa.
117. Arthur H. Amick, m. Lillian C. Smith; in real estate business, Cumberland Md.
118. Edwin P. Amick.
119. Upton M. Amick, m. Edith McCullough; address: Philadelphia, Pa.; ch.: Earl M.
120. Ira Park Amick; druggist, Philadelphia, Pa.

121. Rev. G. W. W. Amick, b. Apr. 16, 1861; see biographies; m. (1) Florence Philips; child: Arthur Park, b. Aug. 21, 1889; m. Virgie Walters; child: Walter; m. (2) Lydia Arner; ch.: Margaret Thelma, b. Nov. 29, 1897; Howard W., b. Oct. 5, 1900, student physician, New Springfield, Ohio.
122. Georgia B. Amick, m. Charles Blackwelder.
123. Mary P. Bowser Amick, m. Dr. Alexander J. Bowser; ch.: Georgia.
124. Frank E. Amick, m. Laura Shaffer; merchant, Altoona, Pa.
125. George B. Amick, m. Mary Park Hammond; ch.: John H. B., Arthur.
126. Stanley Amick.

117. ARTHUR H. and LILLIAN C. (SMITH) AMICK.
Children:
127. Vera Ray Amick.
128. Marian Amick, m. George B. Clifton; ch.: Vera May, Anna C., Jane, Georgia.
129. Medora Amick.
130. Arthur H. Amick, Jr., m. Dorothy Street.

12. CATHARINE BOWSER and JACOB BERKHEIMER. (See 35 under Mathias.)

9. JOHN (3); GEORGE (2); JOHN (1). John Bowser, known as "Miller John," son of George and Margaret Swartz Bowser of Bedford Co., Pa., was born in 1790. "Miller John" married Margaret Zimmer, daughter of Frederick and Margaret Zimmer, of Bedford Co., Pa. She was born in 1789. Margaret Zimmer says in her will: "I, Margaret Zimmer of Bedford Twp., Bedford Co., Pa., bequeathe to Johnathan Bowser, son of John Bowser, intermarried to my daughter Margaret, $59.00, to be paid two years after my decease . . . my husband, Frederick Zimmer, deceased." Probated 1860. "Miller John" married (2) ——— Shaffer. John Bowser was a miller in Friends Cove and died there in 1860. Friends Cove is in Colerain Twp. and lies between "Evits" and Tusseys Mountain. His will was probated Dec. 22, 1860.
Children:
131. Catharine Bowser, m. Michael Holderbaum, Jr., who lived near Bedford, Pa. He was a member of the State Assembly, 1842. He died Sept. 9, 1880.
132. Johnathan Bowser, b. in Bedford Co., 1821; m. Elizabeth Earnest, b. 1823; m. (2) a Mrs. Diehl.
133. Elizabeth Bowser, m. Jacob Biddle.
134. Jacob H. Bowser, b. 1825; m. (1) Catharine Bittiger; (2) Margaret Shaffer.
135. Eve Bowser, m. William Beegle.
136. Susannah Bowser, m. ——— Miller. Mrs. Isaac Replogle, Enterprise, Pa., is their daughter.
137. Margaret Bowser, m. Charles Helsel.

131. CATHARINE (BOWSER) and MICHAEL HOLDERBAUM.
Children:
138. John Holderbaum, m. (1) ——— Yant; m. (2) ——— Diehl; address: Bedford, Pa.
139. Margaret Holderbaum; never married; lived near Bedford.
140. Elizabeth Holderbaum, m. David Ober; lived near Bedford.
141. Mary Holderbaum, m. George Weimer.
142. Susannah Holderbaum.
143. David Holderbaum, m. S. Rebecca Crisman; address: Bedford, Pa.
144. Sarah Holderbaum, m. Charles Beegle; lived near Bedford.

132. JOHNATHAN (4); JOHN (3); GEORGE (2); JOHN (1). Johnathan Bowser was a member of the Reformed Church; farmer in Colerain Twp., Freind's Cove. His real estate was valued at $40,000.00.

Children:

145. Margaret Bowser, b. 1846; m. Joseph Trostle of Greensburg, Pa.
146. Jacob Bowser, b. 1849, in Friend's Cove near Ott Town; d. 1908; m. Amanda Milburn.
147. David Bowser, b. 1851, in Bedford Co., Pa. He was in Colerain Twp. early in 1870, as also his parents and his brothers Jacob, Isaac, and Aaron, and his sister Emma. In 1919 he was living in Salem, Mass. He married Margaret Little. Ch.: William, John, David.
148. Isaac Bowser, b. in Bedford Co., Pa., 1853.
149. Aaron Bowser, b. in Bedford Co., 1859; m. Elizabeth Ridenour, b. Sept. 16, 1886; ch.: Verna, Moore, Walter, Minnie.
150. Emma Bowser, b. 1860; m. Emory Dicken; in 1919 were living in Johnstown, Pa.; child: Harper.
151. Mary Bowser, m. J. Newton Drenning; in 1919 were living in Cumberland Valley, Bedford Co., Pa., R. F. D.; ch.: Lulu, Humphry.

133. ELIZABETH (BOWSER) and JACOB BIDDLE.

Children:

152. Andrew Biddle, m. Mary Beegle, Bedford, Pa.
153. Charles Biddle, m. (1) Eva Koontz; (2) ——— Wertz, Bedford, Pa.
154. Francis Biddle, m. Jane Stucky.
155. Dr. Johnathan Biddle; m. ——— Buchannan.
156. Margaret Biddle, m. ——— Shaffer, Toledo, O.
157. William Biddle, m. ——— Wertz; lived in Ohio.

134. JACOB H. (4); JOHN (3); GEORGE (2); JOHN (1). JACOB H. BOWSER and CATHARINE (BITTINGER) BOWSER.

Children:

158. Catharine Elizabeth Bowser, b. May 15, 1849; m. Nathan Kegg, son of John and Christina (Diehl) Kegg.
159. Margaret Bowser, m. Solomon Reighard.
160. Mary Jane Bowser, m. John S. Whetstone.
161. Carrie E. Bowser, b. 1856; m. (1) Harolerode; (2) David Frank Mortimer.
162. Johnathan Bowser, m. Hilderbaugh.
163. John F. Bowser, m. Sarah E. Berkheimer.
164. Ella Bowser, m. Alexander Gates.

158. CATHARINE E. (5); JACOB H. (4); JOHN (3); GEORGE (2); JOHN (1). Catharine Elizabeth (Bowser) and Nathan Kegg were married on the 6th of January, 1868; now living at Johnstown, Pa.

Children:

165. Jennie Kegg, b. July 6, 1871; m. Robert Ferrell.
166. John Earl Kegg b. Oct. 28, 1870; m. Bessie Gross, d. July 20, 1916.
167. William Kegg, b. Aug. 26, 1873; d. Dec. 29, 1898.
168. Ella Kegg, b. May 20, 1875; m. Charles Kuckuck.
169. Samuel Frank Kegg, b. Nov. 9, 1879.
170. Edgar Nathan Kegg, b. Aug. 6, 1881; d. Nov. 15, 1885.
171. Mabel Irene Kegg, b. July 7, 1886; m. Frederick Mintmier.
172. Harry Leroy Kegg, b. Jan. 16, 1891; served in the World war; wounded in the Argonne campaign.

159. MARGARET (5); JACOB H. (4); JOHN (3); GEORGE (2); JOHN (1). Margaret Bowser and Solomon Reighard.

Children:

173. Myra Mae Reighard, b. Mar. 6, 1876; m. Martin A. Diehl.
174. Charles E. Reighard, b. Aug. 29, 1878; m. Nancy Wher.
175. Amanda Irene Reighard, b. Mar. 5, 1881; m. Martin Beegle.
176. Warren G. Reighard, b. July 1, 1883; m. Catharine Sharp.
177. Franklin Aaron Reighard, b. July 2, 1865; m. Ada Diehl.
178. Grace Ada Reighard, b. Feb. 14, 1890; m. Samuel V. Shoemaker, d. 1914.

173. MYRA MAE (REIGHARD) and MARTIN A. DIEHL; residence: Bedford, Pa., R. D. 4.

Children:

179. Margaret May Diehl; b. May 2, 1903.
180. Paul Andrew Diehl, b. Apr. 7, 1908.

174. CHARLES E. and NANCY (WHER) REIGHARD.

Child:

181. Sharron Reighard, b. Aug. 14, 1906.

175. AMANDA IRENE (REIGHARD) and MARTIN S. BEEGLE.

Children:

182. Glen Beegle, b. June 8, 1905.
183. Mildred Irene Beegle, b. June 21, 1907.

176. WARREN G. and CATHARINE (SHARP) REIGHARD.

Children:

184. Teresa K. Reighard, b. Feb. 29, 1908.
185. James W. Reighard, b. 1909.
186. Edward K. Reighard, b. 1911.
187. Margaret Mary Reighard, b. 1915.

160. MARY JANE (5) ; JACOB H. (4); JOHN (3); GEORGE (2); JOHN (1). Mary Jane (Bowser) and John S. Whetstone live in Friend's Cove, Lutzville, Pa. Mr. Whetstone is a prominent farmer and stockman.

Children:

188. Harry Whetstone, b. 1873; m. Minnie Fox; address: 618 Cherry Street, Findley, Ohio; ch.: Leola, Mildred, Edith.
189. Anna Whetstone, b. 1874; m. D. C. Ott; address: Everett, Pa.; ch.: Margaret, Grace, Clyde.
190. Frank Whetstone, b. 1876; m. Harriet England; address: Everett, Pa.; ch.: Verna, Stella, Paul, Miles.
191. Blanche Whetstone, b. 1878; m. C. M. Ott; address: Everett, Pa.; child: Alvin.
192. Prof. George Whetstone, b. 1880; address: Waynesboro, Pa.; m. Nellie Vink; ch.: John, George.
193. Margaret Whetstone, b. 1882; m. Howard Hershberger; address: Loysburg, Pa.; ch.: Ross, George, Emmert, Raymond, Kenneth.
194. Merrill Whetstone, b. 1886; m. Winifred Whipp; address: Altoona, Pa.; ch.: Donald, dead; Grace.
195. Ross Whetstone, b. 1888; m. Fern Byal; address: Lutzville, Pa.; ch.: Paul, Viola.

161. CARRIE E. (5); JACOB H. (4); JOHN (3); GEORGE (2); JOHN (1). Carrie E. Bowser m. (1) ——— Harclerode.

Children:

196. Frank Harclerode.
197. Edith Harclerode.

m. (2) David Frank Mortimore; address: Frederick St., Toledo, Ohio.

Children:

198. Ralph Mortimore, b. 1888.
199. Albert Mortimore, b. 1891.
200. Harold Mortimore, b. 1896.

163. JOHN F. (5); JACOB H. (4); JOHN (3); GEORGE (2); JOHN (1). John F. Bowser moved to Tyrone, Pa., where he engaged in business. He died there Apr. 2, 1917. He married Sarah E. Berkheimer, living at Tyrone.

Children:

201. Stella M. Bowser, m. Oscar Diehl; address: North Richard St., Bedford, Pa.
202. Mary O. Bowser, m. Earl Dickson; address: Tyrone, Pa.
203. Albert Bowser.
204. Harry F. Bowser.
205. Ruth E. Bowser.

164. ELLA (5); JACOB H. (4); JOHN (3); GEORGE (2); JOHN (1). Ella (Bowser) and Alexander Gates live at Roaring Springs, Pa.

Children: Mintie, m. Ross Croyle, Roaring Springs, Pa.; Harry, Charles, Viola, Margaret.

135. EVE (4); JOHN (3); GEORGE (2); JOHN (1);. Eve Bowser, daughter of "Miller John," m. William Beegle.

Children:

206. George Beegle m. Rebecca Diehl; address: Lutzville Pa.
207. John Beegle m. Amanda Berkheimer; address: Bedford, Pa.
208. Frank Beegle, m. Sarah Lashley; address: Everett, Pa.
209. Jackson Beegle; single.
210. Mack Beegle; single.
211. Douglas Beegle; m. Wertz.
212. Henrietta Beegle; m. John Ingard.
213. Ida Beegle.
214. Lloyd Beegle; m. ——— Grove; address: Everett, Pa.

146. JACOB (4); JOHNATHAN (3); JOHN (2); JOHN (1). Jacob and Amanda (Milburn) Bowser.

Children:

215. Frank Bowser, b. June 18, 1873; m. Mary M. Deshong.
216. Harry Bowser, b. Aug. 31, 1875; m. Emma Johnson; address: Johnstown, Pa; child: Lanna.
217. Annie E. Bowser, b. Jan. 11, 1878; m. Nicholas Manther; child: Hazel.
218. John Clarke Bowser, b. Mar. 28, 1880; m. Bertha M. Achlin, Newton, Mass.
219. Minnie Bowser, b. June 25, 1882; d. Dec. 25, 1884.
220. Ross Bowser, b. July 31, 1885; address: 143 Horner St., Johnstown, Pa.
221. Jacob Bowser, b. Feb. 23, 1887; d. Mar. 10, 1912.
222. Robert Bowser, b. Sept. 21, 1892.

215. FRANK (5); JACOB (4); JOHNATHAN (3); JOHN, JR. (2); JOHN, SR. (1). Frank Bowser is a decorator and paper hanger; in business at South Richard St., Bedford, Pa.

Children:
- 223. George E. Bowser, b. June 18, 1895.
- 224. Ralph N. Bowser, b. Sept. 28, 1878.
- 225. Sara A. Bowser, b. April 8, 1901.
- 226. Joseph R. Bowser, b. Mar. 13, 1903.
- 227. Samuel C. Bowser, b. Nov. 20, 1907.

56. JOHN (4); JACOB (3); GEORGE (2); JOHN (1). John and Sophia (Bloom) Bowser lived in Altoona, Pa.

Children:
- 228. John Bowser; moved to Iowa.
- 229. Annie Bowser; dead.
- 230. Samuel S. Bowser, b. Mar. 17, 1859; m. Mary S. O'Rear; address: 566 Fourth St., Beaver, Pa.
- 231. Margaret Bowser.
- 232. Mary Bowser; dead.

230. SAMUEL S. and MARY S. (O'REAR) BOWSER.

Children:
- 233. John Henry Bowser b. Apr. 12, 1888; a miner; in Birmingham, Ala.; m. Ida West; ch.: Bessie Lee; James Henry.
- 234. James S. Bowser, b. Sept. 3, 1889; carpenter; in Warren, Ohio; m. Lillian Coker; child: James, Jr.
- 235. William Thomas Bowser, b. Mar. 27, 1893; soldier of the World war.
- 236. Bryan B. Bowser, b. Oct. 26, 1895; a soldier of the World war; served as corporal in France.
- 237. Samuel Ira Bowser, b. Jan. 27, 1901; steelworker, Cleveland, Ohio.
- 238. Anna May Bowser, b. Sept. 27, 1886; m. ——— Tune, Birmingham, Ala.
- 239. Margaret Sophia Bowser, b. Aug. 7, 1891; m. W. F. Tucker, Muskogee, Okla.
- 240. Lola L. Bowser, b. Nov. 9, 1897; m. ——— West; residence: Birmingham, Ala.

*JAMES BOWSER, Mill Creek, Huntingdon County, Pa. James Bowser is a son of John Bowser and Elizabeth Ments, who lived in Bedford County. James married (1) Smith; (2) Shingler. His family gather each year at his home in their Bowser "Reunion." He was born 1843.

Children:

1. W. D. Bowser, b. 1863.
2. A. J. Bowser, b. 1870.
3. J. T. Bowser, b. 1872.
4. Nancy B. Bowser, b. 1873.
5. Rosetta M. Bowser, b. 1875.
6. Mary Bowser, b. 1877.
7. Speer Bowser, b. 1879; m. Mary Gregor; ch.: triplets, Martin Woodrow, David Wilson, Luther Franklin.
8. Emma B. Bowser, b. 1884.
9. C. W. Bowser, b. 1885; d. 1886.
10. Mina D. Bowser, b. 1884.
11. J. M. Bowser, b. 1887.
12. H. L. Bowser, b. 1890.

SAMUEL BOWSER. Samuel Bowser lived in Union Township, Bedford County, Pa., in 1850. He was born in 1825; married Hannah ——.

Children:

1. George W. Bowser, b. 1847; m. Martha Brooks.
2. John Bernard Bowser, b. May 12, 1849; d. April 6, 1904; ch.: Dessa Viola, b. 1870, m. Chris Mattas; Ida May, b. 1872, d. 1874; Aden Albert, b. 1874, d. 1877; George Dean, b. 1875; Anna Beretta, b. 1878, m. Otis Pincin; Charles Augustus, b. 1879, m. Edith Gray; Mary Mosouri, b. 1882, d. 1887; Grace Baird, b. 1884, m. Earl Robson; Edith M., b. 1887, m. George Baronner; Earl Lynn, b. 1892, m. Alta Ritchey. Children of Charles Augustus and Edith Gray; Charles Dale, b. 1916; Winnefred Helene, b. 1912; Mercer Gray, b. 1905; Roller King, b. 1907.
3. Albert W. Bowser.
4. Samuel P. Bowser.

---

*James Bowser, of Mill Creek family, and Samuel Bowser, Union Township, Bedford Co., Pa., connection uncertain. Inserted here for the advantage of some future historian.—[A. B. B.]

INDEX

MATHIAS BAUSSER, SR., BRANCH

DANIEL BOUSSER AND HIS DESCENDANTS

HENRY BOUSSER AND HIS DESCENDANTS

JOHN BOWSER FAMILY

JOHN AND EVE BOWSER